Communications
in Computer and Information Science   2391

Series Editors

Gang Li ⓘ, *School of Information Technology, Deakin University, Burwood, VIC,*
Australia
Joaquim Filipe ⓘ, *Polytechnic Institute of Setúbal, Setúbal, Portugal*
Zhiwei Xu, *Chinese Academy of Sciences, Beijing, China*

Rationale

The CCIS series is devoted to the publication of proceedings of computer science conferences. Its aim is to efficiently disseminate original research results in informatics in printed and electronic form. While the focus is on publication of peer-reviewed full papers presenting mature work, inclusion of reviewed short papers reporting on work in progress is welcome, too. Besides globally relevant meetings with internationally representative program committees guaranteeing a strict peer-reviewing and paper selection process, conferences run by societies or of high regional or national relevance are also considered for publication.

Topics

The topical scope of CCIS spans the entire spectrum of informatics ranging from foundational topics in the theory of computing to information and communications science and technology and a broad variety of interdisciplinary application fields.

Information for Volume Editors and Authors

Publication in CCIS is free of charge. No royalties are paid, however, we offer registered conference participants temporary free access to the online version of the conference proceedings on SpringerLink (http://link.springer.com) by means of an http referrer from the conference website and/or a number of complimentary printed copies, as specified in the official acceptance email of the event.

CCIS proceedings can be published in time for distribution at conferences or as post-proceedings, and delivered in the form of printed books and/or electronically as USBs and/or e-content licenses for accessing proceedings at SpringerLink. Furthermore, CCIS proceedings are included in the CCIS electronic book series hosted in the SpringerLink digital library at http://link.springer.com/bookseries/7899. Conferences publishing in CCIS are allowed to use Online Conference Service (OCS) for managing the whole proceedings lifecycle (from submission and reviewing to preparing for publication) free of charge.

Publication process

The language of publication is exclusively English. Authors publishing in CCIS have to sign the Springer CCIS copyright transfer form, however, they are free to use their material published in CCIS for substantially changed, more elaborate subsequent publications elsewhere. For the preparation of the camera-ready papers/files, authors have to strictly adhere to the Springer CCIS Authors' Instructions and are strongly encouraged to use the CCIS LaTeX style files or templates.

Abstracting/Indexing

CCIS is abstracted/indexed in DBLP, Google Scholar, EI-Compendex, Mathematical Reviews, SCImago, Scopus. CCIS volumes are also submitted for the inclusion in ISI Proceedings.

How to start

To start the evaluation of your proposal for inclusion in the CCIS series, please send an e-mail to ccis@springer.com.

Costin Bădică · Marjan Gušev · Adrian Iftene ·
Mirjana Ivanović · Yannis Manolopoulos ·
Stelios Xinogalos
Editors

Advances in ICT Research in the Balkans

10th Balkan Conference in Informatics, BCI 2024
Craiova, Romania, September 4-6, 2024
Proceedings

 Springer

Editors
Costin Bădică 🆔
University of Craiova
Craiova, Romania

Adrian Iftene 🆔
Alexandru Ioan Cuza University Iaşi
Iasi, Romania

Yannis Manolopoulos 🆔
University of Nicosia
Nicosia, Cyprus

Marjan Gušev 🆔
University Sts. Cyril and Methodius in Skopje
Skopje, North Macedonia

Mirjana Ivanović 🆔
University of Novi Sad
Novi Sad, Serbia

Stelios Xinogalos 🆔
University of Macedonia
Thessaloniki, Greece

ISSN 1865-0929   ISSN 1865-0937 (electronic)
Communications in Computer and Information Science
ISBN 978-3-031-84092-0   ISBN 978-3-031-84093-7 (eBook)
https://doi.org/10.1007/978-3-031-84093-7

This Springer imprint is published by the registered company Springer Nature Switzerland AG
The registered company address is: Gewerbestrasse 11, 6330 Cham, Switzerland

If disposing of this product, please recycle the paper.

Preface

This CCIS volume includes research papers presented at the 10th Balkan Conference in Informatics (BCI), which was held during September 4–6, 2024, in Craiova, Romania. It is remarkable that BCI 2024 was co-organized with the 18th International Conference on Innovations in Intelligent Systems and Applications (INISTA). This collocation helped in exchanging ideas with members of a complementary community and, thus, empowered cross-fertilization.

The first BCI event was held in Thessaloniki, Greece (2003). Since then, BCI has been held in Ohrid, North Macedonia (2005); Sofia, Bulgaria (2007); Thessaloniki, Greece (2009); Novi Sad, Serbia (2012); Thessaloniki, Greece (2013); Craiova, Romania (2015); Skopje, North Macedonia (2017), and Sofia, Bulgaria (2019). Due to the Covid pandemic, the BCI conference was cancelled after 2020, and thus, the present edition is a new start for the BCI series.

The program of BCI 2024 included keynote talks, research papers, and a PhD workshop. The main conference attracted 31 paper submissions. All the papers went through a process of rigorous single-blind reviewing by at least three reviewers. Eventually, the Program Committee selected 23 submissions as full contributions appearing in the present volume. Actually, the authors had the opportunity to submit their final camera-ready version after the end of the conference, taking into account the fruitful discussions that took place on site. Thus, one could say that there was an enhanced double review and improvement phase. The selected papers span a large spectrum of topics in the broader field of data management and were organized in groups as follows: (1) Data Mining and Machine Learning; (2) Software and Systems; (3) Languages and Text; (4) Learning Issues; (5) Distributed Systems; (6) Medical and Health Issues; (7) Web Issues and Tools; and (8) Security and Privacy.

For this BCI event we had keynote talks by experts in different fields of the broader area of informatics. In particular (in alphabetical order):

- George Bînă (oXygen XML, Romania) delivered a talk on "AI-powered XML Editing".
- Maria Ganzha (Warsaw University of Technology, Poland) delivered a talk on "Frugal AI".
- Giancarlo Fortino (University of Calabria, Italy) delivered a talk on "Integrating Machine Learning and Multi-Agent Systems for Fully Enabling Device-Edge-Cloud Continuum in Complex IoT Worlds".
- Adrian Iftene (University "Alexandru Ioan Cuza" of Iaşi, Romania) delivered a talk on "How Far Are We from Implementing Medical Projects Based on Artificial Intelligence on a Large Scale in Hospitals? Case Study on the Situation in Romania".

The invited lecturers of the special session dedicated to Ph.D. students delivered insightful and inspiring talks for the attendees (in alphabetical order):

- Donald Elmazi (University Metropolitan Tirana, Albania) delivered a talk on "Automated Machine Learning Model Selector with Improved Exploratory Data Analysis using AI".
- Mirjana Ivanović (University of Novi Sad, Serbia) delivered a talk on "Influence of Federated Learning on Contemporary Research and Applications".
- Yannis Manolopoulos (Aristotle University of Thessaloniki, Greece) delivered a talk on "Recommendation and Scientometrics".
- Vasile Manta (Technical University Gheorghe Asachi of Iaşi, Romania) delivered a talk on "Computer Vision: Classical and Quantum Computing".
- Marcin Paprzycki (Systems Research Institute, Poland) delivered a talk on "Agent-Based Model of Extended Green Cloud".
- Alexandru Popa (University of Bucharest, Romania) delivered a talk on "Techniques for Tackling Computationally Hard Problems".
- Tulay Yıldırım (Yıldız Technical University, Turkey) delivered a talk on "Privacy-Preserving Techniques and Security".

Following a successful tradition, selected best papers of BCI 2024 will be invited for special issues of the following journals: SN Computer Science (Springer), Digital (MDPI), and Computer Science & Information Systems. Therefore, the PC chairs would like to express their sincere gratitude to the Editors-in-Chief of the above journals for their approval regarding these special issues.

In addition to the academic activities, BCI 2024 also featured an excellent cultural atmosphere including special activities for discovering and enjoying local culture and traditions in the Oltenia region, South-Western Romania:

- Welcome reception at the University House "Casa Romanescu", former residence of the Mayor of Craiova "Nicolae Romanescu" and his family during 1901-1905 and 1914-1916.
- Guided visit to the "Jean Mihail" Palace in Craiova hosting the Craiova Art Museum, former residence of one of the richest boyar families in Romania.
- Conference dinner at "Casa Ghincea", built on the older site of the "Hurez" inn in Craiova.
- Sightseeing boat trip to the "Iron Gates" Danube gorges.

We would like express our gratitude to the Rector of the University of Craiova, Cezar Ionuţ Spînu, for his kind support and help with the organization and hosting of BCI 2024 at the University of Craiova, Romania. We greatly appreciate all our supporters and sponsoring organizations: Syncro Soft, Department of Computers and Information Technology of the Faculty of Automation, Computers and Electronics, Department of Statistics and Business Informatics of the Faculty of Economics and Business Administration, Department of Informatics of the Faculty of Mathematics and Natural Sciences, University of Craiova, Romania, and Doctoral School "Constantin Belea".

Finally, we would like to wholeheartedly thank all participants, authors, PC members, session chairs, volunteers, and co-organizers for their contributions in making BCI 2024 a great success. We would also like to thank the BCI Steering Committee and all sponsors.

November 2024

Costin Bădică
Marjan Gušev
Adrian Iftene
Mirjana Ivanović
Yannis Manolopoulos
Stelios Xinogalos

Organization

General Chairs

Costin Bădică   University of Craiova, Romania
Mirjana Ivanović   University of Novi Sad, Serbia
Yannis Manolopoulos   University of Nicosia, Cyprus

Program Chairs

Marjan Gušev   Ss. Cyril and Methodius University in Skopje,
                             North Macedonia
Adrian Iftene   "Alexandru Ioan Cuza" University of Iaşi,
                             Romania
Stelios Xinogalos   University of Macedonia, Greece

Local Organization Chairs

Amelia Bădică   University of Craiova, Romania
Nicolae Enescu   University of Craiova, Romania

Webmasters

Ionuţ Murareţu   University of Craiova, Romania

Steering Committee

Yannis Manolopoulos (Chair) University of Nicosia, Cyprus
Costin Bădică   University of Craiova, Romania
Betim Çiço   EPOKA University, Albania
Georgios Evangelidis   University of Macedonia, Greece
Marjan Gušev   Ss. Cyril and Methodius University in Skopje,
                             North Macedonia
Mirjana Ivanović   University of Novi Sad, Serbia

Petros Kefalas	CITY College, University of York Europe Campus, Greece
Petia Koprinkova-Hristova	IICT, Bulgarian Academy of Sciences, Bulgaria
Katerina Zdravkova	Ss. Cyril and Methodius University in Skopje, North Macedonia

Program Committee

Veneta Aleksieva	Technical University of Varna, Bulgaria
Adelina Aleksieva-Petrova	Technical University of Sofia, Bulgaria
Amelia Bădică	University of Craiova, Romania
Drazen Brdjanin	University of Banja Luka, Serbia
Mihaela Breaban	"Alexandru Ioan Cuza" University of Iași, Romania
Alexander Chatzigeorgiou	University of Macedonia, Greece
Betim Çiço	EPOKA University, Albania
Mihaela Colhon	University of Craiova, Romania
Mirel Cosulschi	University of Craiova, Romania
Christos Douligeris	University of Piraeus, Greece
Georgios Evangelidis	University of Macedonia, Greece
Vladimir Filipovic	University of Belgrade, Serbia
Delyan Genkov	Technical University of Gabrovo, Bulgaria
Christos Georgiadis	University of Macedonia, Greece
Daniela Gifu	"Alexandru Ioan Cuza" University of Iași, Romania
Dejan Gjorgjevikj	Ss. Cyril and Methodius University in Skopje, North Macedonia
George Gravvanis	Democritus University of Thrace, Greece
Ladislav Huraj	University of Ss. Cyril and Methodius in Trnava, Slovakia
Galina Ilieva	Paisii Hilendarski University of Plovdiv, Bulgaria
Valentina Ivanova	Academy Nikola Tesla, Bulgaria
Gordan Jezic	University of Zagreb, Croatia
Nikitas Karanikolas	University of West Attica, Greece
Theodore Kaskalis	University of Macedonia, Greece
Ioannis Kazanidis	International Hellenic University, Greece
Petros Kefalas	CITY College, University of York Europe Campus, Greece
Aleksandra Klasnja Milicevic	University of Novi Sad, Serbia
Georgia Koloniari	University of Macedonia, Greece
Petia Koprinkova-Hristova	IICT, Bulgarian Academy of Sciences, Bulgaria

Ivan Koychev	University of Sofia, Bulgaria
Vladimir Kurbalija	University of Novi Sad, Serbia
Milena Lazarova	Technical University of Sofia, Bulgaria
Florin Leon	"Gheorghe Asachi" Technical University of Iaşi, Romania
Ivan Lirkov	IICT, Bulgarian Academy of Sciences, Bulgaria
Ivan Lukovic	University of Belgrade, Serbia
Boris Milašinović	University of Zagreb, Croatia
Anastas Mishev	Ss. Cyril and Methodius University of Skopje, North Macedonia
Valeri Mladenov	Technical University of Sofia, Bulgaria
Mihai Mocanu	University of Craiova, Romania
Mihai Alex Moruz	"Alexandru Ioan Cuza" University of Iaşi, Romania
Iraklis Paraskakis	South-East European Research Centre, Greece
Nikolaos Polatidis	University of Brighton, UK
Horia Pop	Babeş-Bolyai University, Romania
Alexandru Popa	University of Bucharest, Romania
Elvira Popescu	University of Craiova, Romania
Paul Stefan Popescu	University of Craiova, Romania
Eftychios Protopapadakis	University of Macedonia, Greece
Boris Rachev	Technical University of Varna, Bulgaria
Milos Radovanovic	University of Novi Sad, Serbia
Ilias Sakellariou	University of Macedonia, Greece
Milos Savic	University of Novi Sad, Serbia
Zhaneta Savova	National Military University, Bulgaria
Angelo Sifaleras	University of Macedonia, Greece
Dana Simian	"Lucian Blaga" University of Sibiu, Romania
Spiros Skiadopoulos	University of the Peloponnese, Greece
Demosthenes Stamatis	International Hellenic University, Greece
Liana Stanescu	University of Craiova, Romania
Leonid Stoimenov	University of Niš, Serbia
Antoniya Tasheva	Technical University of Sofia, Bulgaria
Eleftherios Tiakas	International Hellenic University, Greece
Dimitar Trajanov	Ss. Cyril and Methodius University in Skopje, North Macedonia
Vladimir Trajkovikj	Ss. Cyril and Methodius University in Skopje, North Macedonia
Diana Trandabat	IMAGINATION PLAY S.R.L., Romania
Boris Tudjarov	Technical University of Sofia, Bulgaria
Anca Vasilescu	Transilvania University of Brasov, Romania
Goran Velinov	Ss. Cyril and Methodius University in Skopje, North Macedonia

Elior Vila   University of Elbasan, Albania
Katerina Zdravkova   Ss. Cyril and Methodius University in Skopje,
                                   North Macedonia

Local Organizing Committee

Alexandru Becheru   University of Craiova, Romania
Catalin Cerbulescu   University of Craiova, Romania
Daniela Danciulescu   University of Craiova, Romania
Eugen Ganea   University of Craiova, Romania
Sorin Ilie   University of Craiova, Romania
Elena Ruxandra Luțan   University of Craiova, Romania
Marius Marian   University of Craiova, Romania
Cristian Mihăescu   University of Craiova, Romania
Ionut Murarețu   University of Craiova, Romania
Elvira Popescu   University of Craiova, Romania
Stefan Paul Popescu   University of Craiova, Romania
Alexandra Vultureanu-Albiși   University of Craiova, Romania

Contents

Learning Issues

Distributed Systems

Medical and Health Issues

Web Issues and Tools

Security and Privacy

Data Mining and Machine Learning

Autoregressive Model for Energy Consumption Time Series

Daniel-Costin Ebâncă$^{(\boxtimes)}$ ⓘ, Claudiu-Ionuţ Popîrlanⓘ,
Irina-Valentina Tudorⓘ, and Cristina Popîrlanⓘ

University of Craiova, Craiova, Romania
danebinca@yahoo.com

Abstract. Smart homes, an important application of the Internet of Things, use the Internet to monitor and analyze data gathered from appliances within the home automation system. These intelligent appliances enable users to oversee and manage the household's energy consumption. The smart home system collects data on the appliances' energy consumption, generating time series data. Using this data and a time series approach, we employ the Autoregressive Integrated Moving Average (ARIMA) model to analyze and forecast energy consumption based on data from international datasets. Specifically, we selected datasets representing energy consumption per capita in the European Union (EU-27) and Romania, chosen for its integration within the EU-27, allowing for both global and local insights. The forecast generated by the ARIMA model aims to evaluate the energy required, optimizing smart home energy consumption. Accurate forecasting is critical for developing efficient energy management systems in smart homes, enabling dynamic adjustments to household energy use and significantly reducing overall energy consumption. This research underscores the importance of precise energy consumption predictions to enhance the sustainability and efficiency of smart home energy management.

Keywords: ARIMA model · Energy consumption · Time series

1 Introduction

Over the last years, the Internet of Things (IoT) has seen continuous growth, connecting people, activities, and devices worldwide [1]. This development has incorporated features such as big data analysis, rapid operations, easy data access, automation, and control into the IoT framework. Devices that are capable of managing and transmitting data can be integrated into the IoT network. When a home includes such smart devices and appliances (TVs, security cameras, locks, lightbulbs) that can be remotely controlled via the IoT network, it defines the concept of a smart home [2].

A smart home system enhances comfort and energy efficiency through its applications, all devices connected to the smart home system working together and sharing data to meet user preferences [3]. IoT devices utilize advanced artificial intelligence methods to perform automatic actions. The IoT is extensively applied in smart home controls to collect data on electricity usage, due to the continuous increase in household energy consumption [4]. Various factors influence this consumption, including weather conditions, house location, construction parameters or people's habits.

Energy usage is crucial for general economic growth due to its significant impact on the production process. The source of energy influences its effects on different sectors of the economy and the environment, defining an interdependent relationship between economic growth and renewable energy investment. The connection between energy consumption and energy prices is of significant importance, with the energy market undergoing minor adjustments even when prices change significantly.

Nowadays, taking into account the rising energy prices, there is a significant need to monitor and predict household energy consumption using the latest IoT features. Smart solutions that help consumers save energy are increasingly used and intensively researched [5,6]. IoT devices are continually evolving due to their growing usage, and data models are employed for forecasting energy consumption. The advancement of the Internet of Things has introduced new challenges because of the vast amount of collected data, making household energy consumption forecasting a vital method that plays a crucial role in planning for energy resource conservation [7].

In this study, smart home data are analyzed with respect to household energy consumption, focusing on the relationship between appliances' energy usage and their operation times. A time series of energy consumption is considered and analyzed using the Autoregressive Integrated Moving Average (ARIMA) model [8–11]. The study also provides an energy consumption forecast based on data collected from international datasets. This model is particularly useful for understanding and predicting future values in a time series, as it accounts for trends, seasonality, and noise in the data.

For research purposes, we selected two datasets representing energy consumption per capita in the European Union (EU-27) and in Romania. Romania was chosen because it is integrated in the EU-27 so the analysis done in the study could be regarded as being both global and local. This dual perspective is crucial for understanding regional differences within the broader context of the EU.

The forecast generated by the ARIMA model can be utilized to evaluate the energy required, thereby optimizing smart home energy consumption. Improving the accuracy of forecasts is a critical research area due to the necessity of precise consumption predictions.

The ability to predict energy demand allows for:

– Dynamic adjustment - real-time modification of appliance operation to align with energy availability and cost considerations;
– Energy savings - reducing overall energy consumption by minimizing wastage and ensuring appliances operate during off-peak hours or when renewable energy is available.

- Enhanced user comfort - maintaining optimal living conditions while minimizing energy use through intelligent scheduling and control of heating, cooling, and lighting systems.

In a smart home, energy consumption can be significantly reduced by implementing an efficient energy management system that uses these forecasts to adjust household energy use dynamically.

2 Method

The Autoregressive Integrated Moving Average (ARIMA) model has been widely used over time for predicting stochastic time series in various applications, including the electricity prices, energy consumption, daily solar energy production, daily wind speed, traffic congestion, water treatment, air pollutants or, unemployment rates and inflation [12–14]. Developed by Box and Jenkins in the 1970 s, ARIMA has become a foundational tool in time series forecasting due to its robustness and adaptability [15].

ARIMA often yields promising results across various fields, with predictions that closely align with actual values. The model assumes linear correlations in time series, which is effective for simple scenarios.

One of the key strengths of ARIMA is its capacity to handle non-stationary data, which is common in real-world time series, using the differencing process.

ARIMA is an autoregression model that is applied on linear stationary time series to forecast the value for a dependent variable. The model has three parameters:

- p : the order of the autoregression model (lag order),
- d : the level of differencing,
- q : the order of the moving average model.

The model $ARIMA(p, d, q)$ is described as follows:

- AutoRegression (AR): this model uses a dependent relation between the measured values and some observations lags;

$$Y_t = \alpha + \beta_1 Y_{t-1} + \beta_2 Y_{t-2} + \cdots + \beta_p Y_{t-p} + \epsilon_t \qquad (1)$$

where, p is the order of the AR, Y_t depends only on its own lags, Y_{t-1} is the lag of the series, β_1 is the coefficient of lag that the model estimates, α is the intercept term, also estimated by the model.
- Integrated (I): transform the time series in a stationary one by using subtraction of one value from the previous one;
- Moving Average (MA): the moving average component models the dependency between an observation and a residual error from a moving average model applied to lagged observations:

$$Y_t = \alpha + \epsilon_t + \theta_1 \epsilon_{t-1} + \theta_2 \epsilon_{t-2} + \cdots + \theta_q \epsilon_{t-q} \qquad (2)$$

where q is the order of the MA, Y_t depends only on the lagged forecast errors. $\theta_1, \ldots, \theta_q$ are the parameters of the model and the $\epsilon_t, \ldots, \epsilon_{t-q}$ are white noise error terms.

Finally, the ARIMA model can be expressed as follows:

$$Y_t = \alpha + \sum_{i=1}^{p} \beta_i Y_{t-i} + \epsilon_t - \sum_{j=1}^{q} \theta_j \epsilon_{t-j} \tag{3}$$

where Y_t is the value of the variable considered at time t, ϵ_t is the random error at time t, β_i and θ_j are the coefficients of the model [16].

The model effectiveness is further enhanced through model identification and parameter estimation processes. The Bayesian Information Criterion (BIC) and Akaike Information Criterion (AIC) values are evaluated to obtain the optimal ARIMA model for the considered dataset, after estimating the parameters p (for the AR model) and q (for the MA model) from the autocorrelation and partial autocorrelation functions plots (ACF and PACF) [17].

3 Results

The ARIMA model was employed to examine energy consumption in the EU-27 and specifically in Romania, using datasets sourced from Eurostat [18], covering the period from 2000 to 2023. For both the EU-27 and Romania, 18 years of data were used for training the model and 6 years for testing, with predictions made for a 3-year timespan. All data covers multiple years, providing longitudinal data that can capture trends, seasonal variations, and long-term changes in energy consumption.

The datasets selected for this study provide comprehensive insights into energy consumption patterns both at the regional level (EU-27) and the national level (Romania) having the following characteristics:

– EU-27 Dataset - encompasses a wide range of energy consumption data across all 27 member states of the European Union, providing a comprehensive view of average energy use per capita. It reflects diverse energy practices and infrastructure within the union offering a broad perspective on trends across diverse economic and climatic regions.
– The Romanian dataset focuses on the energy consumption patterns within Romania, offering detailed insights into the country's specific energy usage trends, challenges, practices, infrastructure and policy impacts. This allows for a comparative analysis with the broader EU-27 dataset to identify unique national trends and deviations from regional patterns.

By thoroughly understanding and leveraging these dataset characteristics, the study aims to generate precise and actionable energy consumption forecasts. This, in turn, facilitates the development of more efficient energy management systems in smart homes, contributing to both local and regional sustainability goals.

The datasets were processed using Python programming language, which was also employed to apply the ARIMA model to analyze the time series and generate the predictions.

Figures 1 and 2 represent the graphical analysis of annual energy consumption in households per capita, for the EU-27 and Romania data respectively, indicating that the ARIMA model is appropriate due to the linearity and non-stationarity of the datasets. The stationarity was verified using the Augmented Dickey-Fuller (ADF) Test [19, 20]. This statistical approach is well-suited for time series analysis and has proven effective in capturing the dynamic nature of energy consumption patterns.

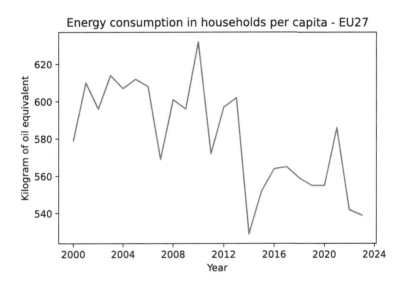

Fig. 1. Energy consumption for EU-27.

Based on the training dataset for EU-27 and Romania energy consumption, we generated the visual representation of the corresponding autocorrelation function (ACF) and partial autocorrelation function (PACF) plots (see Figs. 3 and 4).

These functions help with determining the appropriate parameters for the model. The ACF measures the correlation between the time series and its lagged values, being useful for identifying the order q of the MA component of the model. The PACF helps controlling for the values of the time series at all shorter lags and is particularly useful for identifying the order p of the AR component of ARIMA.

To construct the optimal ARIMA model, we computed the Bayesian Information Criterion (BIC) and the Akaike Information Criterion (AIC) to identify the best forecasting parameters. For EU-27, ARIMA(0, 2, 2) was the best option, with AIC=158.146 and BIC=161.236, while for Romanian dataset the computed

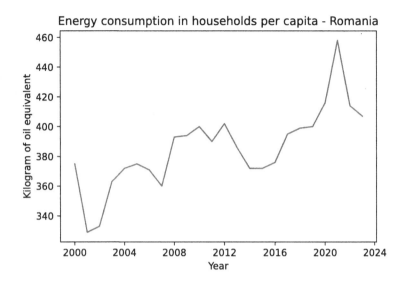

Fig. 2. Energy consumption for Romania.

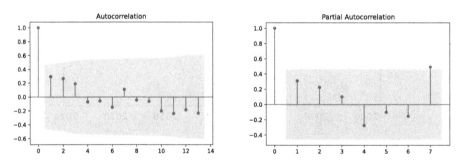

Fig. 3. Autocorrelation Function (ACF) and Partial Autocorrelation Function (PACF) for EU-27.

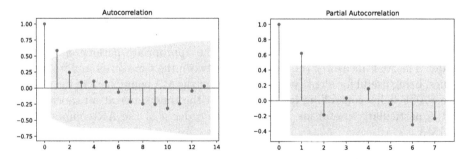

Fig. 4. Autocorrelation Function (ACF) and Partial Autocorrelation Function (PACF) for Romania.

values were ARIMA(0, 2, 1), AIC=147.271 and BIC=149.589. The accuracy values of the ARIMA model implementation are presented in Table 1.

Table 1. Residuals errors.

	EU-27	Romania
MAPE	0.0414106	0.0582632
MAE	0.2338036	0.2452534
RMSE	0.2733138	0.3269951

After fitting the model, we tested the predicted values against the actual values from the training data for the period 2018–2023, calculated the residual errors, and generated predictions for the next 3 years (2024–2026), forecasts being displayed in Figs. 5 and 6. From the visual representation and the computed data we observe that predicted values follow the actual values closely with a very small delay that is maintained for all tested values. For each residual series from the ARIMA models, we applied the Ljung-Box portmanteau test [21] with five lags to determine if the residuals were independently distributed, obtaining p-values greater than 0.05 (EU-27 p-value = 0.998, Romania p-value = 0.840), confirming the null hypothesis.

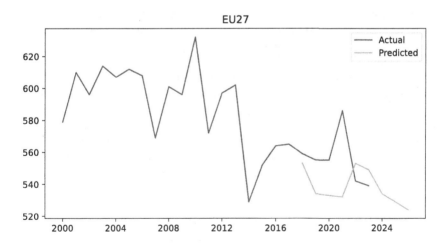

Fig. 5. Energy consumption forecast for EU-27.

From the visual representation for the EU-27 energy consumption forecast, it can be observed that the European tendency is to lower consumption to save resources. From the forecast's representation of Romania's energy consumption, it can be observed that the consumption will continue to increase. The smart

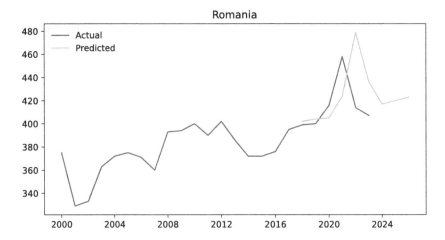

Fig. 6. Energy consumption forecast for Romania.

home concept is not yet well developed in Romania, so the energy consumption is not as optimized as in the more developed parts of the EU-27.

Romania's energy consumption is expected to grow moderately in the short term, driven by economic recovery and industrial activity. In the medium to long term, energy efficiency measures, technological advancements, and significant investments in renewable energy are likely to stabilize energy demand and increase the share of renewables in the energy mix. National and EU-27 policies will play a crucial role in shaping Romania's energy landscape, leading to a gradual reduction in fossil fuel dependency and a move towards a more sustainable energy system.

Comparing energy consumption predictions in Romania and the EU-27 reveals both common goals and unique challenges. While Romania is on a path towards increasing its renewable energy share and improving energy efficiency, it must overcome infrastructural and regulatory challenges to align with EU-27 standards. The EU-27's cohesive policy framework and ambitious climate targets set a robust example for Romania, highlighting the importance of collaborative efforts in achieving a sustainable and energy-efficient future.

Romania has the opportunity to leverage its natural resources, such as hydro and wind power, to expand its renewable energy capacity, while EU-27 funding and technical assistance can support Romania in achieving its energy transition goals. The EU-27 can capitalize on technological innovations, cross-border energy cooperation, and digitalization to enhance energy efficiency and renewable energy integration.

4   Conclusion

The results indicate that the ARIMA model demonstrates a strong capability for forecasting household energy consumption. However, it is well-known that overall household energy consumption is influenced by various factors, such as energy-using behaviors and climatic conditions. In the proposed model, the impact of these factors was not considered, so future work could involve analyzing their influence on the dataset to enhance the model's accuracy.

Forecasting energy consumption in advance is crucial for achieving energy conservation. It provides valuable data support for policymakers and energy managers, enabling them to formulate effective strategies that promote environmental protection and sustainable energy use.

Implementing an efficient energy management system in smart homes relies heavily on the accuracy of consumption forecasts. In smart homes, energy consumption can be significantly reduced by integrating these forecasts into the household's energy management system. This integration not only improves energy efficiency but also contributes to sustainability by lowering the household's carbon footprint.

By anticipating energy needs, stakeholders can better manage resources, reduce waste, and contribute to broader efforts in combating climate change.

One of the main challenges for Romania is modernizing its energy infrastructure, which requires substantial investments. Additionally, the government should address regulatory and market barriers that hinder the integration of renewable energy sources. The EU-27 faces challenges in harmonizing energy policies across diverse member states, ensuring energy security and managing the intermittent nature of renewable energy sources.

Considering that energy consumption in Romania is on the rise while the European average consumption is expected to decline, other countries have developed policies aimed at reducing energy consumption in light of limited energy resources. These policies include implementing energy efficiency measures, promoting the use of renewable energy sources, and encouraging behavioral changes among consumers to lower their energy use. Additionally, governments have introduced stricter regulations on industrial energy use, incentivized energy-saving technologies, and invested in research and development for sustainable energy solutions. These efforts are crucial in addressing the challenges posed by finite energy resources and ensuring a sustainable energy future for the region.

The study demonstrates the potential of using the ARIMA model to analyze and forecast household energy consumption in smart homes. By leveraging data from both the EU-27 and Romania, the research provides a dual perspective that enhances the understanding of regional and global energy consumption patterns. The findings highlight the importance of accurate forecasting in optimizing smart home energy use, ultimately contributing to more efficient and sustainable energy management practices.

Although ARIMA is a powerful tool for time series analysis, it is important to consider other methods or models, especially for complex datasets due to limitations that could significantly impact the model's performance, such as: long-term forecasting (ARIMA models can struggle with long-term forecasting because they rely heavily on recent past values. As the forecast horizon extends, the uncertainty and error tend to increase.), assumes constant variance

(ARIMA assumes that the variance of the time series remains constant over time - homoscedasticity. Time series with changing variance - heteroscedasticity - can lead to inaccurate forecasts.), data preprocessing (The preprocessing can be complex and time-consuming.), sensitivity to outliers (ARIMA models can be sensitive to outliers, which can skew the results and lead to poor forecasting performance. Robustness to outliers requires additional preprocessing steps.).

To further enhance the accuracy and robustness of our forecasts, we intend to explore additional models and methodologies in forthcoming work [22–25]. Future research should focus on comparing the performance of these alternative models with the ARIMA model in the context of smart home energy consumption forecasting. Additionally, integrating external factors such as weather conditions, electricity prices, and user behavior patterns could further improve the accuracy of predictions. Implementing hybrid models that combine the strengths of different forecasting techniques may also yield better results. Lastly, real-time data collection and continuous model updating should be explored to ensure the forecasts remain relevant and reliable over time.

By exploring and incorporating these advanced models, future studies can enhance the precision and utility of energy consumption forecasts, ultimately contributing to more efficient and sustainable energy management in smart homes.

References

1. Goudarzi, S., Anisi, M., Soleymani, S., Ayob, M., Zeadally, S.: An IoT-based prediction technique for efficient energy consumption in buildings. IEEE Trans. Green Commun. Network. **5**(4), 2076–2088 (2021)
2. Gellert, A., Fiore, U., Florea, A., Chis, R., Palmieri, F.: Forecasting electricity consumption and production in smart homes through statistical methods. Sustain. Cities Society **76** (2022)
3. Gopikrishna, P.B., Jiju, M.: Power consumption analysis and prediction of a smart home using ARIMA model. SSRN (2021)
4. Kalimoldayev, M., Drozdenko, A., Koplyk, I., Marinich, T., Abdildayeva, A., Zhukabayeva, T.: Analysis of modern approaches for the prediction of electric energy consumption. Open Eng. **10**(1), 350–361 (2020)
5. Fattah, J., Ezzine, L., Aman, Z., El Moussami, H., Lachhab, A.: Forecasting of demand using ARIMA model. Int. J. Eng. Business Manage. **10** (2018). https://doi.org/10.1177/1847979018808673
6. Elsaraiti, M.,Ali, G., Musbah, H., Merabet, A., Little, T.: Time series analysis of electricity consumption forecasting using ARIMA model. In: Proceedings of the IEEE Green Technologies Conference (GreenTech), pp. 259–262 (2021)
7. Cheng, Y.L., Lim, M.H., Hui, K.H.: Impact of internet of things paradigm towards energy consumption prediction: a systematic literature review. Sustain. Urban Areas **78**, 103624 (2022)
8. Introduction to Time Series and Forecasting. STS, Springer, New York (2002). https://doi.org/10.1007/0-387-21657-X_11
9. Wang, X., Meng, M.: A hybrid neural network and ARIMA model for energy consumption forecasting. J. Comput. **7**(5) (2012)

10. Song, H., Chen, Y., Zhou, N., Chen, G.: Electricity consumption forecasting for smart grid using the multi-factor back-propagation neural network. Proc. SPIE - Sensors Syst. Space Appl. XII **11017**, 1101700 (2019)
11. Chujai, P., Kerdprasop, N., Kerdprasop, K.: Time series analysis of household electric consumption with ARIMA and ARMA models. Proc. Int. Multi Conf. Eng. Comput. Sci. (IMECS) **1**, 295–300 (2013)
12. Wang, Y., Shen, Z., Jiang, Y.: Comparison of ARIMA and GM(1,1) models for prediction of hepatitis B in China. PLoS ONE **13**(9), e0201987 (2018)
13. Atique, S., Noureen, S., Roy, V., Subburaj, V., Bayne, S., Macfie, J.: Forecasting of total daily solar energy generation using ARIMA: A case study. In: Proceedings of the 9th IEEE Annual Computing and Communication Workshop and Conference (CCWC), pages 114–119 (2019)
14. Alsamamra, H.R., Salah, S., Shoqeir, J.H.: Performance analysis of ARIMA Model for wind speed forecasting in Jerusalem, Palestine. Energy Explor. Exploit. **42**(5), (2024)
15. Stellwagen, E., Tashman, L.: ARIMA: The Models of Box and Jenkins. Foresight: The Int. J. Appl. Forecast. **30** (2013)
16. Ariyo, A.A., Adewumi, A.O., Ayo, C.K.: Stock price prediction using the ARIMA Model. In: Proceedings of the 16th International Conference on Computer Modelling and Simulation (UKSim-AMSS), pp. 106–112 (2014)
17. Vrieze, S.I.: Model selection and psychological theory: a discussion of the differences between the Akaike information criterion (AIC) and the Bayesian information criterion (BIC). Psychol. Methods **17**(2), 228–243 (2012)
18. Eurostat 2023. Final energy consumption in households per capita. https://ec.europa.eu/eurostat/web/main/home. Accessed Oct 10 2024
19. Cheung, Y.W., Lai, K.: Lag order and critical values of the augmented Dickey-Fuller test. J. Bus. Econom. Stat. **13**(3), 277–280 (1995)
20. Dickey, D.A., Fuller, W.A.: Distribution of the estimators for autoregressive time series with a unit root. J. Am. Stat. Assoc. **74**(366), 427–431 (1979)
21. Ljung, G.M.: Diagnostic testing of univariate time series models. Biometrika **73**(3), 725–730 (1986)
22. Wang, J.Q., Du, Y., Wang, J.: LSTM based long-term energy consumption prediction with periodicity. Energy **197**, 117197 (2020)
23. Hora, S.K., Poongodan, R., De Prado, R.P., Wozniak, M., Divakarachari, P.B.: Long short-term memory network-based metaheuristic for effective electric energy consumption prediction. Appl. Sci. **11**(23), 11263 (2021)
24. Qiao, Q., Yunusa-Kaltungo, A., Edwards, R.E.: Feature selection strategy for machine learning methods in building energy consumption prediction. Energy Rep. **8**, 13621–13654 (2022)
25. Nie, P., Roccotelli, M., Fanti, M.P., Ming, Z., Li, Z.: Prediction of home energy consumption based on gradient boosting regression tree. Energy Rep. **7**, 1246–1255 (2021)

Enhancing Credit Card Fraud Detection Using Knowledge Graphs and Centralities

George Konstantinos Dimou$^{(\boxtimes)}$ and Georgia Koloniari

University of Macedonia, Thessaloniki, Greece
{dai18069,gkoloniari}@uom.edu.gr

Abstract. Detecting fraudulent activity in credit card transactions poses a serious challenge for financial institutions, which requires robust techniques that can accurately pinpoint fraudulent occurrences while minimizing false positives. In this study, we introduce an innovative strategy to enhance Credit Card Fraud Detection (CCFD) by utilizing Knowledge Graphs and Centrality measures. We propose creating a Knowledge Graph (KG) representing the credit card transaction network so as to capture connections and correlations between the transactions, and analyzing the KG to evaluate centrality measures that capture the importance of nodes and relationships within the graph. These centrality measures are utilized to enhance the input features that are used to train Machine Learning classifiers for fraud detection. Our experiments show that using the enhanced features significantly improved classification performance, providing better identification of fraudulent transactions, especially through the combination of HITS and degree centrality.

Keywords: Credit Card Fraud Detection · Knowledge Graphs · Centralities · Machine Learning · Supervised Learning

1 Introduction

Fraud has its origins in ancient times and is defined as deliberate deception for one's own benefit. Since then financial fraud has increased dramatically in modern society, as evident by a 70% increase in fraud cases in the United States and a startling $56 billion loss. *Fraud Detection (FD)* refers to the process of identification and prevention of fraudulent activities and *Credit Card Fraud Detection (CCFD)*, being a subcategory of FD, targets specifically unauthorized or illegal actions done with credit cards. With recorded losses of $32.3 billions, a 13.8% increase from the previous year [1], CCFD emerges as a significant priority.

The complex domain of CCFD makes a distinction between card-present and non-present fraud. While card-present fraud has decreased thanks to technological advancements, a result of those, the surge in online transactions, has made its counterpart, card-non-present fraud, increase exponentially. For that reason, the continuous evolution in CCFD mechanisms is imperative to effectively counter emerging threats.

© The Author(s), under exclusive license to Springer Nature Switzerland AG 2025
C. Bădică et al. (Eds.): BCI 2024, CCIS 2391, pp. 14–29, 2025.
https://doi.org/10.1007/978-3-031-84093-7_2

To address fraud due to its complexity requires a multi-dimensional approach encompassing both prevention and detection techniques. Preventive measures depend mainly on fraudster errors, while detection provides means to address fraudulent activities in their emergence before substantial losses occur. Europay, MasterCard, Visa (EMV) chips, which are secure microprocessor chips embedded in payment cards that use encryption, are the most common type of proactive measures utilized for fraud prevention, yet fraudsters exploit gaps in the system. In contrast, fraud detection operates in real-time and analyzes transaction patterns to quickly identify and hinder suspicious activities.

Fraud detection uses a variety of data-driven approaches, which can be broadly categorized as Artificial Intelligence (AI) based or statistical data analysis techniques. While statistical analysis relies on models and algorithms to identify patterns, AI-based techniques utilize Machine Learning (ML) and data mining for real-time analysis. A variety of effective FD systems are built on this dynamic interplay between statistical and AI-driven methodologies [7,10].

However, though conventional methods for detecting fraud have advanced significantly, they still have drawbacks. The historical disregard for transaction correlation by traditional AI-based methods presents a key obstacle. Most previous studies approached individual transactions as separate entities, which is not compatible with real-world scenarios.

To counteract this limitation, in this paper, we propose exploiting *Knowledge Graphs (KG)*, which is a structure designed to carefully model relationships. Each transaction, no matter how distinct, gets deeply ingrained in a network, allowing hidden relationships and patterns to come to light that otherwise become lost when using tabular transactional data. Modeling our data into a KG, provides us with ways to leverage additional information from the transactional data by mining appropriate network features, and in particular, network *Centrality* measures for the enhancement of CCFD. Centrality measures offer different ways to quantify the importance of nodes in the network, focusing on different definitions or aspects of importance. These measures can indicate the different roles that nodes play in a network, and we argue that they can provide enhanced features that complement the commonly used classification features used by most ML pipelines so as to improve fraud detection.

The objectives of our work include the creation of a comprehensive KG and the exploration of various centrality measures to improve the accuracy of CCFD algorithms. We exploit a graph database for the implementation of the KG that enables us to deploy its efficient graph analysis procedures instead of computing centrality measures using a generic in-memory implementation that can be considerably more expensive time and memory wise.

The main contributions of our work are summarized as follows:

– We propose modeling the transactional data as a comprehensive KG, by including contextual data so as to capture hidden connections.
– We efficiently compute various centrality measures using a graph database for implementing the KG.

- We explore the effectiveness of the centrality measures in CCFD by integrating them as additional features in ML models.
- We compare the enhanced features against typical ML features to demonstrate how they improve precision and recall for CCFD.

The rest of the paper is structured as follows. Section 2 presents related literature, while Sect. 3, details our approach, which involves the construction of the KG and the use of centralities derived from it. Section 4 presents our experimental setup and results. Finally, Sect. 5 concludes the paper.

2   Related Work

AI and ML have recently become critical in CCFD due to their adaptability, reduced manual intervention and cost-effectiveness. Existing literature demonstrates that even simple ML algorithms outperform traditional rule-based approaches [6,8].

Dornadula et al. [5] introduced an innovative approach which involves clustering and the sliding-window technique to enhance the performance of FD through a series of preprocessing steps. Issues with the Synthetic Minority Over-sampling Technique (SMOTE) used to address class imbalance, led the authors to explore alternative strategies, including incorporating a performance metric for binary classification and utilizing one-class classifiers on each user group. Varmedja et al. [17] attempted to address class imbalance and feature selection with a feature selector tool, SMOTE, and scaling. Dhankhad et al. [4] utilized ensemble techniques with the addition of under-sampling. Their experiments demonstrated a clear superiority of a stacked model when compared to traditional ML algorithms. Rahman et al. [14] conducted research on the stock market and accounting research database of China, employing CUSBoost and RUSBoost. Those two non-conventional classifier variants use their respective resampling techniques (clustering-based under-sampling and random under-sampling) to further enhance their accuracy, which outperformed AdaBoost and XGBoost.

Even though, resampling techniques are an effective measure against class imbalance, they increase computational cost exponentially, especially on larger datasets, and usually introduce unnecessary bias. Consequently, our proposed method opts not to utilize them for our research. Hussein et al. [15] proposed a novel approach which involves a stacked model integrating Fuzzy Rough Nearest Neighbor (FRNN) and Sequential Minimal Optimization (SMO). FRNN combines fuzzy and rough set theory for classification in imbalanced datasets. This is achieved by identifying k-nearest neighbors, assigning membership values based on their similarity and calculating fuzzy classification. SMO optimizes Support Vector Machines (SVM) by breaking the quadratic programming problem into smaller, more manageable steps to ensure stable solutions. The combination of FRNN and SMO provides predictions which act as second-level data input to a logistic meta-classifier for the final prediction in a stacked model. However, their proposed pipeline introduces exponential overhead which makes it nearly impossible to be utilized in larger datasets, as their experiments showcase using less than 1000 rows of data.

Knowledge graph as a term originates as early as the 1980 s [16] but has not received much attention before 2007 with DBpedia and Google's introduction in 2012. Despite their benefits, few works in FD employ KGs. Zhang et al. [19] use an Auto Insurance Knowledge Graph (AIKG) to address transaction correlation, for which they designed an ontology based on ML feature selection, evaluated by domain experts. By using geographical information and string similarity, they managed to improve Gang Fraud detection, a phenomenon occurring when associations between reporters and garages are identified, with Knowledge Graph Embeddings (KGEs). Finally, they evaluated using XGBoost, SVM and Neural Networks (NN) and managed to achieve an increase in single fraud case detection. Wen et al. [18] constructed a KG which focused on managers and their respective relationships with associated firms. Four centrality measures were employed, namely Degree, Betweenness, Closeness and Eigenvector centrality each providing unique information about companies. For their experiments they used SVM, K-NN, Decision Tree (DT) and Random Forest (RF) trained on Chinese A-share market data spanning from 2011 to 2017, while utilizing Principal Component Analysis (PCA) and SMOTE for the preprocessing. However, they did not exploit combinations of centralities, which resulted in potential contextual information loss.

3   Methodology

Significant amount of research has already been conducted on the application of traditional ML approaches in CCFD. This includes a variety of ML approaches, from supervised learning using publicly available datasets to unsupervised real-time CCFD. This study focuses primarily on supervised ML, particularly classification tasks. That is, we model CCFD as a binary classification problem. A classifier is trained based on a training set of known transactions labeled as fraudulent or not fraudulent, and given a new transaction it determines whether the transaction is fraudulent or not. Any ML classification algorithm can be used for the task, and our goal is to improve their results by exploiting additional transactional features that are not usually used in this context.

In particular, we propose using the transactional data to construct a comprehensive KG, and exploit it to derive additional features based on different centrality measures. Figure 1 visually delineates the step-by-step procedure of our data analysis pipeline, from initial data collection to final result analysis. Input transactional data are prepossessed, and then traditional features are selected, as used in most ML classification pipelines. However, the cleaned data are also modeled as a KG and through graph analysis, different centrality measures are evaluated. These features are used in addition to the traditional features to train any ML classifier so as to improve its performance.

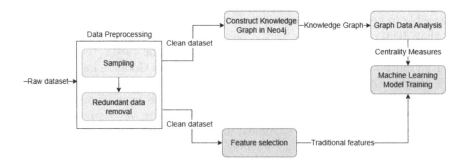

Fig. 1. Step-by-Step Data Analysis procedure

3.1   Data Modeling

As previously stated, current state-of-the-art ML approaches focus mainly on individual entities when detecting fraudulent transactions. They usually analyze each transaction separately, without considering potential relationships that financial transactions may have. For example, for a user with a historically large number of fraudulent transactions, the model would evaluate a new transaction made by them in the same manner as it would for someone with only legitimate activities. For this reason, KGs may be used thanks to their innate ability of treating transactions as interconnected entities, rather than isolated ones.

Creating a KG comes down to effectively representing information extracted from a data source, such as a relational database. Choosing the appropriate entities and relationships is imperative. These features would be indicative of different dimensions required to build the KG, which include temporal dimensions, transaction details and user information. KGs by definition require the presence of multiple entities, thus a strategy to generate those is needed.

Each feature in the dataset typically represents a different aspect of a transaction and must correctly be categorized into entities. Besides *Transaction* entities, temporal features can show when transactions occur and can be modeled as separate *Time* entities, while other features might describe the specifics and details of the transactions as corresponding properties. Finally, user-related features, such as the originator and the recipient of a transaction, are essential for defining *User* entities within a KG.

Clearly defined and logical naming conventions are necessary to establish relationships between these entities. For example, a relationship indicating initiation (MADE_A) can be used to link a user who starts a transaction to the transaction entity. Similarly, a user receiving the transaction can be linked to the transaction indicating receipt (WITH_). Moreover, the transaction can be associated with a specific point in time to capture its temporal aspect (AT).

Features closely related to account balances, before and after the transaction occurred for the two users involved, or other user-specific characteristics must be carefully considered. Since a user may participate in multiple transactions, directly attributing such features to user entities could lead to redundancy.

Alternatively, those features can be attributed to relationships between users and transactions. This not only removes unnecessary duplication but also allows the usage of weighted centrality measures by maintaining consistent relationship attributes across entities.

In Fig. 2, we visualize a possible structure, illustrating the cohesive representation of transactions and their associated entities within the KG.

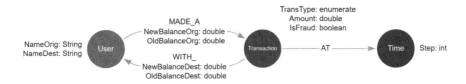

Fig. 2. Visualization of the KG structure

3.2 Centralities

For a KG's meaningful implementation into a ML model's pipeline it needs to be used in tandem with either centrality measures or Knowledge Graph embeddings. Centralities are the core aspect of our work, which focuses on analyzing several centrality measures and using them as extra input features to the ML algorithms. The usage of centralities allow us to capture different meanings associated with each different node importance within our graph. Below we provide a comprehensive explanation of the different centralities, for a graph $G := (V, E)$, where V is the set of vertices and E the set of edges in G.

The *Degree centrality* measure quantifies the number of connections a node has in the KG. Nodes with high degree centrality are considered influential as they have numerous connections with other nodes, indicating a strong presence and interaction within the network. The Degree Centrality of a node $v \in V$ is defined in Eq. 1.

$$C_D(v) = \deg(v), \tag{1}$$

where $\deg(v)$ is the degree of node v.

If the graph is directed, degree centrality can differentiate between in-degree and out-degree centrality measuring incoming and outgoing connections, respectively.

Eigenvector Centrality considers not only a node's direct connections but also the importance of those connections. Nodes connected to other highly influential nodes have higher eigenvector centrality scores, reflecting their potential impact and importance within the KG. Eigenvector centrality is defined in Eq. 2.

$$EC(v) = \frac{1}{\lambda} \sum_{u \in N(v)} A(u, v) \cdot EC(u) \tag{2}$$

where:

- $A = (u, v)$ is the adjacency matrix representing the connection between node u and node v,
- λ is the dominant eigenvalue of the adjacency matrix, and
- $N(v)$ is the neighborhood of node v, i.e., the nodes connected directly to v.

PageRank [3] and *ArticleRank* [11] can both be classified as variations of eigenvector centrality. PageRank is widely known for its application in ranking web pages based on their importance. It assigns a score to each node in the network, considering both the number and quality of incoming links. Nodes with a higher number of incoming links from important nodes receive a higher PageRank score. ArticleRank operates quite similarly with the concept of voting among articles, where articles that are cited by influential articles are considered more important. The mathematical representations for PageRank and ArticleRank are given in Eq. 3 and Eq. 4 respectively.

$$PR(u) = \frac{1-d}{|V|} + d \sum_{v \in N_{in}(u)} \frac{PR(v)}{out\_deg(v)} \tag{3}$$

$$AR_i(u) = (1-d) + d \sum_{w \in N_{in}(v)} \frac{AR_{i-1}(w)}{|N_{out}(w)| + \overline{out\_deg}} \tag{4}$$

where:

- d is the damping factor, typically set to 0.85.
- $N_{in}(u)$ is the set of incoming neighbors to u, and $N_{out}(u)$ denotes outgoing neighbors of node u,
- $out\_deg(u)$ is the out-degree of node u, representing the number of its outgoing links, and
- $\overline{out\_deg}$ is the average out-degree.

Hyperlink-Induced Topic Search (*HITS*) [9] is another centrality commonly used in network analysis. However it has some clear differences with PageRank. The primary distinction between the two comes from their focus on different aspects of network structure. While PageRank emphasizes on the importance of nodes as a whole, HITS aims to pinpoint specific nodes which act as hubs or authorities. Nodes with high authority centrality are deemed authoritative sources of information, while nodes with high hub centrality are considered as excellent providers of relevant links to authoritative sources. This way, HITS provides a thorough examination of specialized roles within the network. In Eq. 5 and Eq. 6, we show how Hubs and Authority scores are calculated.

$$h_v = \sum_{u \in N_{out}(v)} a_u \cdot w(v, u) \tag{5}$$

$$a_v = \sum_{u \in N_{in}(v)} h_u \cdot w(u, v) \tag{6}$$

where:

- h_v is the hub score of node v,
- a_v is the authority score of node v, and
- $w(v, u)$ represents the weight of the link between node v and node u.

4 Experimental Evaluation

In this section, we evaluate the performance of the proposed approach. We, first, detail our dataset and the preprocessing methodologies deployed. We, then, outline our experimental setup and the performance evaluation metrics utilized. Building upon our established baseline, we then proceed to compare and analyze the outcomes achieved through our proposed methods, showcasing the effectiveness of our approach.

4.1 Dataset

Due to the lack of publicly available real-world datasets because of privacy concerns that have been gaining increasing importance in the recent years, businesses emphasize protecting consumer privacy through innovative approaches, such as the development of specialized synthetic datasets for training ML algorithms. Compliant with the European General Data Protection Regulation (GDPR) and the US California Consumer Privacy Act (CCPA), synthetic data undergoes a synthesis process that eliminates correspondence to individuals and lacks identifiers to personal information like names or numbers. Consequently, fully synthetic datasets can be openly used and shared, unrestricted by the privacy regulations applicable to real-world datasets. Thus, in our research, we have employed the Synth Financial Dataset for Fraud Detection [12], crafted by the PaySim mobile money simulator [13].

The development of PaySim, a mobile money simulator, has significantly advanced the generation of synthetic data, which closely emulates real-world mobile money transactions. Paysim is built using real transactions from a mobile service company located in an African country, with transaction types determined by probability statistics extracted from the original dataset. Using agent-based simulation, the simulator features client agents randomly executing one of five transaction types. Adaptive, changeable behaviours contribute to realism; for example, clients-agents who have reached their daily limit cannot withdraw more money for the rest of the day. This novel technique gives PaySim the ability to mimic human-like behaviour resulting in transactions that closely resemble real-world scenarios and are flexible to new limitations as needed.

The dataset structure comprises of 11 attributes, detailed in [12]. Specifically, the *Step* attribute indicates the progression of time in the simulation, with each step representing an hour over a simulated period of 30 days. The *Type* attribute categorizes transaction types, such as CASH-IN, CASH-OUT, DEBIT, PAYMENT, and TRANSFER which represent different financial activities. *Amount*, as the name suggests, signifies the monetary value of each transaction in the local currency. *NameOrig* and *NameDest* each identify the originator and recipient of the transaction respectively. *OldbalanceOrg* and *NewbalanceOrg* indicate the initial and updated balances of the originator before and after the transaction, while *OldbalanceDest* and *NewbalanceDest* represent the same for the recipient. The *isFraud* attribute flags transactions as fraudulent (1) or legitimate (0), while *isFlaggedFraud* identifies potentially fraudulent transactions based on predefined criteria. For clarity, a sample row and brief descriptions are presented in Table 1.

Table 1. The 11 Original Headers in the Synth Dataset

Header	Description	Values	Sample
Step	Representation of time in the real world	[1 - 744]	1
Type	Type of transaction	Enumerated	PAYMENT
Amount	Transaction amount in local currency	Double	7817.71
NameOrig	Customer initiating the transaction	String	C90045638
oldbalanceOrg	Originator's old balance	Double	53860
newbalanceOrg	Originator's new balance	Double	46042.29
nameDest	Customer recipient to the transaction	String	M573487274
oldbalanceDest	Recipient's old balance	Double	0
newbalanceDest	Recipient's new balance	Double	0
isFraud	Indicates if the transaction is fraud	[0, 1]	0
isFlaggedFraud	Flags transfers over 200,000 as illegal	[0, 1]	0

4.2   Preprocessing

We have down-scaled the dataset to 25% of its original size, totaling 1,048,576 rows of transactions for efficiency. Among these, only 1,142 instances are positive fraud cases, representing a mere 0.108% of the downsized data.

To deal with this substantial class imbalance we observed, the dataset was thoroughly examined. Remarkably, within the initial million of transactions, only the CASH-OUT and TRANSFER types included instances of fraudulence. Consequently, redundant categories (CASH-IN, DEBIT, and PAYMENT) were removed, preserving the original count of fraudulent transactions, while reducing the dataset by nearly half.

The *isFlaggedFraud* feature, which consistently yielded 0 as values, was removed to simplify the dataset. Unlike conventional practices involving class resampling techniques, this study opted for a dataset of 460,395 instances and 10 features without resampling.

4.3   Experimental Setup

Our experiments were conducted on a system running Windows 10 with 16GB of RAM and an AMD Ryzen 5 processor. Python 3.10 was used alongside with necessary libraries such as scikit-learn and Neo4j[1]. The code to implement the suggested approach is available on GitHub[2].

For our experiments we leverage KGs, with Neo4j as our preferred platform for our implementation. Neo4j is a leading non-relational graph database, known for its extensive set of features and utilities designed for graph management and analysis. Neo4j simplifies graph generation with a rich set of built-in functions. Its usage promises to dramatically reduce the difficulties encountered in graph management and analysis tasks. One of those sets of functions are encapsulated in the Graph Data Science library (GDS), which as the name suggest offers a plethora of algorithms, such as the before-mentioned centralities, to be used for our experiments.

4.4   Evaluation Measures

To assess performance, we use three widely used and robust metrics for our problem; *Precision, Recall* and *F1-Score.*

The fundamental goal of CCFD is to reduce the number of undiscovered fraudulent transactions, with a focus on identifying such occurrences accurately. Within this approach, recall, defined as the fraction of correctly identified fraudulent transactions over all the fraudulent transactions, emerges as a critical evaluation parameter, evaluating the model's ability to capture genuine positive instances (fraudulent transactions) while reducing false negatives (unidentified fraud cases). On the other hand, precision, defined as the fraction of correctly identified fraudulent transactions over all the transactions flagged as fraudulent, gains relevance by attempting to reduce false positives (legitimate transactions labeled as fraudulent). Under these circumstances, algorithms with centralities which maximize recall are favored, even at the expense of a reduction of other metrics used. It is worth noting, that we refrained from using the Accuracy metric due to our imbalance dataset, which could lead to misleading evaluations.

For the evaluation, we use 5-fold cross-validation; a widely adopted technique which involves splitting the training dataset into subsets for training and prediction on distinct test sets. However, its inherent randomness can cause problems especially in the case of imbalanced class distribution such as exhibited by our dataset. For that reason, we employed *stratified sampling*, which ensures equal representation of different subgroups within the sample, including the minority class of fraudulent transactions. Finally, we utilized *grid search* to fine-tune our hyperparameters for each individual ML algorithm we used for our experiments.

4.5   Traditional Machine Learning

Using seven widely used algorithms, which all have substantial history in CCFD research, namely, K-Nearest Neighbors, Logistic Regression, SVMs, Naïve Bayes, Decision Tree, Random Forest, and XGBoost this study aims to build upon

---

[1] Neo4j.
[2] KG-Fraud-Detection.

existing knowledge. The hyperparameters used for each of these algorithms are presented in Table 2.

Table 2. Hyperparameters

Predictor	Hyperparameters	Range
K-NN	Number of neighbors (n)	4, 5, 6
	Weights	Uniform, Distance
Logistic Regression	Regularization parameter (C)	1e-6, 1e-5, ..., 1e-4
	Maximum iterations	500, 1000, 1500
SVM	Kernel	linear, polynomial
	C	1, 2
Naïve Bayes	Variance smoothing	1e-9, 1e-8, 1e-7
	Priors	[0.4, 0.6], [0.3, 0.7], None
Decision Tree	Criterion	Gini, Entropy
	Max leaf nodes	4, 5, 6
Random Forest	Number of estimators	50, 100, 150
	Criterion	Gini, Entropy
XGBoost	Number of estimators	50, 100, 150

In Table 3, we present the results of our ML algorithms using only the original preprocessed dataset as input features; All columns with the exception of *isFlaggedFraud*. Those results serve as a benchmark for assessing the performance of our upgraded with centrality models. Comparing the results of our enhanced models with our benchmark allows us to determine the influence of the centrality features on improving the selected metrics and the overall effectiveness of CCFD.

Table 3. Baseline Performance

Algorithm	Precision	Recall	F1-Score
K-NN	0.83	0.436	0.572
LR	0.798	0.382	0.516
SVM	0.806	0.42	0.552
NB	0.044	0.322	0.074
DT	0.85	0.46	0.594
RF	0.98	0.778	0.87
XGB	**0.984**	**0.826**	**0.898**

4.6   Results

To assess the effectiveness of the centrality measures, we conducted a series of experiments adding combinations of up to two centrality measures to the standard dataset input features for each evaluated classifier.

The addition of all centralities, improved classification performance with respect to our benchmark. Table 4 shows some indicative results when adding two centralities using the best classifier XGBoost. These results show that overall performance is improved, with recall showing the higher increase, while precision is at worst the same.

Table 4. Results with two centralities using XGBoost

Algorithm	Precision	Recall	F1-Score
Eigenvector (weighted) & Degree	0.984	0.836	0.904
PageRank (weighted) & Degree (weighted)	0.986	0.84	0.908
ArticleRank (unweighted) & Degree (weighted)	0.984	0.838	0.906
HITS & Eigenvector (unweighted)	0.99	0.838	0.908

Table 5. Eigenvector and Degree centrality

Algorithm	Precision	Recall	F1-Score
K-NN	0.986	0.516	0.674
LR	0.938	0.542	0.68
SVM	0.948	0.618	0.75
NB	0.096	0.258	0.14
DT	0.894	0.724	0.802
RF	0.984	0.788	0.876
XGB	**0.988**	**0.842**	**0.91**

Let us now discuss each centrality in detail. Degree centrality, even though a basic measure, is proven to be quite effective in this context. Moreover, we can further enrich its ability by considering relationship orientation as our graph is a directed one. Focusing on incoming transactions (in-degree) is proven more meaningful as it could indicate potential fraud, and is therefore used as the degree centrality in the rest of our experiments and analysis. We can also enhance it by using weights which especially for larger fraudulent transactions provide us with a performance increase up to 3%, as shown between Tables 4, 5 and 6, where orientation and weights are taken into consideration on our proposed methods.

Table 6. Hits and Degree Centrality

Algorithm	Precision	Recall	F1-Score
K-NN	0.986	0.516	0.674
LR	0.94	0.538	0.68
SVM	0.952	0.622	0.75
NB	0.096	0.258	0.14
DT	1	0.46	0.628
RF	0.99	0.78	0.872
XGB	0.99	**0.856**	**0.92**

On the other hand, Eigenvector's plethora of available configurations such as tolerance, personalized and weighted centrality, had little to no impact and for that reason the unweighted version proved superior.

PageRank and ArticleRank left much to be desired when compared to other centralities. Despite configurable parameters such as the damping factor, none improved our metrics significantly.

Finally, HITS provides a thorough examination of specialized roles within the network. As a result, HITS has demonstrated greater performance than other metrics, a steady increase of around 1% in precision and more than 3% in recall, particularly when combined with Degree which resulted in the best outcome amongst all the different centralities evaluated.

Next, we focus on the model with the best overall performance, and the one with the best recall that we consider the most important measure in this context.

Eigenvector with Degree. Among all the combinations tested, Eigenvector with Degree Centrality stood out, showing promising results in all evaluation criteria. This combination provided exceptional performance across all evaluation metrics, reaching up to 15% increase in precision and about 8% in recall in certain algorithms from our baseline. The results showcased, superior average performance. However, as stated in Sect. 4.4, our primary focus is maximizing recall, even if it means sacrificing precision and F1-score. For that reason, we prioritize the improvement of recall.

Hits with Degree. Among the combinations explored, the integration of Hits and Degree centrality emerged as a standout contender. This amalgamation showcased commendable performance, akin to the Eigenvector and Degree pairing, yet boasted marginal enhancements in the recall measure, particularly discernible in the case of the XGBoost algorithm where 3% increase was achieved. In the realm of CCFD, such an increase could potentially save more than 1 billion dollars in the US alone [2].

Finally, we conclude our study with a thorough comparison of the top-performing algorithms in each scenario showcased in Table 7 and visualized in Fig. 3. Through an analysis of key performance metrics, we observe slight but meaningful improvements across precision, recall, and F1-score. Specifically, there is a marginal increase of 0.6% in precision, 3% in recall, and almost 3% in F1-score.

Table 7. Comparison between top performing algorithms

Algorithm	Precision	Recall	F1-Score
XGB (Baseline)	0.984	0.826	0.898
XGB (Eigen. + Degree)	0.988	0.842	0.91
XGB (Hits + Degree)	**0.99**	**0.856**	**0.92**

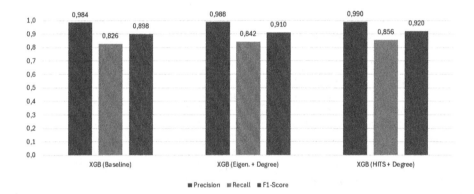

Fig. 3. Top performing algorithms w.r.t. precision, recall and F1-score

5 Conclusion

In this paper, we present a novel Knowledge Graph based framework designed specifically to improve financial fraud detection by utilizing the relationships among entities within the schema. We first identify the entities and relationships present within our data and utilize them to create a KG. We later use the KG to calculate centrality measures for the transaction entities, which contribute as extra input features to our ML algorithms. We drew a comparison between a baseline, the ML algorithms trained on the initial dataset, and the enhanced with centralities dataset. Our experiments show that, all algorithms used benefit from the usage of all centralities across all metrics in various degrees. The results also illustrate how the XGBoost model outperforms other classifiers, especially in terms of recall, which is crucial in fraud detection and highlight the potential of KGs as a valuable resource for detecting financial fraud.

However, our method has some limitations, with most important being its reliance on synthetic data. Also, our framework in to exploit the efficiency provided by a database, explores only centralities that are available in Neo4j. Future research could address these limitations by exploring the use of real-world data, broader centrality measures, and custom ensemble architectures to further improve classification performance.

References

1. Nilson report: Card fraud losses worldwide (2022). https://nilsonreport.com/articles/card-fraud-losses-worldwide/
2. Best, R.d.: Card fraud - credit cards and debit cards combined - worldwide 2014-2022 (2024). https://www.statista.com/statistics/1394119/global-card-fraud-losses/
3. Brin, S., Page, L.: The anatomy of a large-scale hypertextual web search engine. Comput. Netw. ISDN Syst. **30**(1), 107–117 (1998)
4. Dhankhad, S., Mohammed, E., Far, B.: Supervised machine learning algorithms for credit card fraudulent transaction detection: A comparative study. In: Proceedings of the IEEE International Conference on Information Reuse & Integration (IRI), pp. 122–125 (2018)
5. Dornadula, V.N., Geetha, S.: Credit card fraud detection using machine learning algorithms. In: Proceedings of the 2nd International Conference on Recent Trends in Advanced Computing (ICRTAC), pp. 631–641 (2019)
6. Gupta, P.: Leveraging machine learning and artificial intelligence for fraud prevention. Int. J. Comput. Sci. Eng. **10**(5), 47–52 (2023)
7. Ikhsan, W., Ednoer, E., Kridantika, W., Firmansyah, A.: Fraud detection automation through data analytics and artificial intelligence. Jurnal Aplikasi Ekonomi Akuntansi dan Bisnis (RISET) **4**(2), 103–119 (2022)
8. Kamuangu, P.: A review on financial fraud detection using AI and machine learning. J. Econom., Finan. Account. Stud. **6**(1), 67–77 (2024)
9. Kleinberg, J.M.: Hubs, authorities, and communities. ACM Comput. Surv. **31**(4es), 5–es (1999)
10. Kumar, V., Bhardwaj, V., Anbarasu, V.: Credit card fraud detector for lower ranged transactions using AI algorithms. In: Proceedings of the 5th International Conference on Information Management and Machine Intelligence (ICIMMI) (2023)
11. Li, J., Willett, P.: Articlerank: a pagerank-based alternative to numbers of citations for analysing citation networks. ASLIB Proc. **61**(6), 605–618 (2009)
12. Lopez-Rojas, E.: Synthetic financial datasets for fraud detection (2017). https://www.kaggle.com/datasets/ealaxi/paysim1
13. Lopez-Rojas, E.A., Elmir, A., Axelsson, S.: Paysim: A financial mobile money simulator for fraud detection. In: Proceedings of the 28th European Modeling and Simulation Symposium (EMSS) (2016)
14. Rahman, M.J., Zhu, H.: Predicting accounting fraud using imbalanced ensemble learning classifiers - evidence from China. Account. Finan. **63**(3), 3455–3486 (2023)
15. Saleh Hussein, A., Salah Khairy, R., Mohamed Najeeb, S.M., Alrikabi, H.T.: Credit card fraud detection using fuzzy rough nearest neighbor and sequential minimal optimization with logistic regression. Int. J. Interact. Mobile Technol. **15**(5), 24–42 (2021)

16. Schneider, E.: Course modularization applied: The interface system and its implications for sequence control and data analysis. Tech. rep., ERIC (1973). https://eric.ed.gov/?id=ED088424
17. Varmedja, D., Karanovic, M., Sladojevic, S., Arsenovic, M., Anderla, A.: Credit card fraud detection - machine learning methods. In: Proceedings of the 18th International Symposium on INFOTEH-JAHORINA (INFOTEH), pp. 1–5 (2019)
18. Wen, S., Li, J., Zhu, X., Liu, M.: Analysis of financial fraud based on manager knowledge graph. In: Proceedings of the 8th International Conference on Information Technology and Quantitative Management (ITQM), pp. 773–779 (2022)
19. Zhang, L., Wu, T., Chen, X., Lu, B., Na, C., Qi, G.: Auto insurance knowledge graph construction and its application to fraud detection. In: Proceedings of the 10th International Joint Conference on Knowledge Graphs (IJCKG), pp. 64–70 (2022)

Unveiling the Potential of Explainable Artificial Intelligence in Predictive Modeling, Exploring Food Security and Nutrition in Madagascar

Rosa Elysabeth Ralinirina$^{(\boxtimes)}$ (ID), Jean Christian Ralaivao (ID),
Niaiko Michaël Ralaivao (ID), Alain Josué Ratovondrahona (ID), and Thomas Mahatody (ID)

University of Fianarantsoa, Fianarantsoa, Madagascar
`ralinirinarosa7@gmail.com`

Abstract. This study leverages machine learning (ML) and explainable artificial intelligence (XAI) to predict complex phenomena, specifically focusing on forecasting food security and nutritional status in Madagascar up to 2030. By combining Support Vector Machines (SVM) with SHapley Additive exPlanations (SHAP), we aim to provide both accurate predictions and transparent, interpretable insights into the decision-making process . The predictive targets include food insecurity, underweight, chronic malnutrition, and acute malnutrition, addressing critical issues related to public health and nutrition. The robustness of SVM in handling high-dimensional data, coupled with SHAP's capability to explain individual predictions, ensures that our model not only delivers reliable forecasts but also offers clarity on the importance of each feature. The methodology involves collecting diverse datasets from reputable sources, performing exploratory data analysis, and implementing SVM for predictive modeling. SHAP is then utilized to enhance model interpretability by providing detailed explanations of feature contributions. Our contributions include methodological advancements in integrating XAI with ML, development of transparent predictive models for decision-makers, and practical applications to real-world challenges in Madagascar. This research aims to support the Sustainable Development Goals by offering actionable insights for improving food security and nutrition, while also advancing global understanding of complex predictive phenomena.

Keywords: Data Science · Explainable Artificial Intelligence · Food Security and Nutrition · Machine Learning · Predictive Modeling · Sustainable Development Goals

1 Introduction

Food security and nutrition are critical components of global health and well-being, directly influencing the quality of life and development of populations. Madagascar, like many developing countries, faces significant challenges in ensuring adequate food security and addressing malnutrition among its inhabitants. Predicting and understanding these issues is vital for creating effective interventions and policies that can mitigate adverse effects and promote sustainable development.

Technological advances and the wealth of available data have enabled significant progress and promising transformative models [1, 2]. The increasing availability of data and advancements in machine learning present new opportunities to analyze and predict complex phenomena related to food security and nutrition. However, while ML models can offer high predictive accuracy, they often operate as "black boxes", making it difficult for stakeholders to understand the rationale behind their predictions. This lack of transparency can hinder the adoption and trust of these models in critical decision-making processes.

Explainable Artificial Intelligence aims to bridge this gap by providing tools and techniques that make the predictions of ML models more interpretable and understandable to humans. By integrating XAI with predictive modeling, we can not only achieve high accuracy in forecasts but also offer clear explanations of the factors driving these predictions.

In this study, we employ SVM combined with SHAP to predict food security and nutritional status in Madagascar up to 2030. SVM is chosen for its robustness in handling high-dimensional data and its effectiveness in classification tasks. SHAP is utilized to enhance model interpretability, providing detailed insights into the contributions of individual features to the model's predictions.

We begin by collecting and preprocessing relevant datasets from reputable sources, followed by an exploratory data analysis to identify key patterns and relationships. The SVM model is then trained to forecast various indicators of food security and nutrition, including food insecurity, underweight, chronic malnutrition, and acute malnutrition. SHAP values are computed to explain the model's predictions, highlighting the most influential features and their impact.

Our research contributes to the field of data science by demonstrating the integration of XAI with ML to address real-world challenges. The transparent predictive models developed in this study aim to support decision-makers in Madagascar and other regions facing similar issues. By providing actionable insights, we strive to enhance the effectiveness of interventions and policies aimed at improving food security and nutrition, ultimately supporting the Sustainable Development Goals.

2   State of the Art

2.1   State of the Art on the General Framework of the Fields Studied

Despite advances in technology, challenges persist in ensuring transparency of prediction models, reducing algorithmic bias, and addressing security concerns related to autonomous systems. The lack of confidence in the prediction results remains crucial. Researchers are actively exploring sustainable and ethical approaches to responsible technology adoption, highlighting the importance of this study for understanding both the theoretical foundations and current advances in predicting the phenomena [3–6].

In machine learning, a subset of AI, efforts aim to replicate human-like intelligent capabilities in machines [7, 8]. Machine learning is increasingly popular in industry, leverages a data-driven approach, with roots tracing back to Alan Turing's era. Mitchell's definition underscores that a computer program learns from experience concerning a task class, improving its ability to predict phenomena through experience [9]. It provides an innovative approach to automate predictive modeling by facilitating data extraction and code generation.

The state of the art in ML and XAI in predictive modeling is characterized by a growing emphasis on transparency and interpretability. XAI is increasingly recognized as essential for building trust and ensuring the effective deployment of AI systems in critical domains [10]. In predictive modeling, XAI techniques are being applied across various fields, healthcare [11], and agriculture [12], to provide insights into the decision-making processes of complex models.

Interestingly, while XAI enhances model transparency and user trust, it also faces challenges such as balancing interpretability with performance [13]. There is a noted discrepancy in the explanations provided by different XAI methods when applied to the same underlying models, highlighting the need for more robust and consistent approaches. Additionally, the application of XAI in less traditional areas, such as the study of ancient architecture and art [14], demonstrates its versatility and potential for interdisciplinary research.

In summary, the integration of XAI into predictive modeling is crucial for advancing AI applications in sensitive and impactful areas. The current literature underscores the importance of developing interpretable models that maintain high performance while being transparent in their predictions. Future research directions include the design of intrinsically interpretable neural network architectures and the exploration of XAI's potential in novel domains [15].

2.2   State of the Art and Related Works

Probabilistic Approach. The state of the art in probabilistic approaches to predictive modeling encompasses a variety of techniques and applications across different domains. Probabilistic models are integral to predictive analytics, as they account for uncertainty and variability in predictions. Marzieh Mokarram employed Markov models to predict crop yields in 2040 [16]. Markov models, fundamental in predictive modeling, find relevance in domains with significant state transitions, like weather forecasting. The Markov chain, expressing state changes over time, uses a transfer matrix based on the current state, previous states, and neighbors.

The Cellular Automata-Markov Chain (CA-MC) method combines cellular automata and Markov chains, offering a dynamic and probabilistic modeling approach. Model validation ensures the accuracy of land cover predictions [17]. Another study applied a stochastic modeling method to develop a predictive framework for scenario analyses and risk assessment [18].

Statistical Approach. The state of the art in statistical approaches to predictive modeling encompasses a broad spectrum of techniques integral to the development of predictive models in various domains. These approaches include traditional statistical modeling, machine learning algorithms, and data mining techniques, which are applied across fields such as healthcare research, business intelligence, and public health [19, 20]. The integration of these techniques with Big Data analytics has highlighted the need for standardization and transparency while presenting both opportunities and challenges [19].

Interestingly, despite the advancements in complex models and machine learning methods, there is recognition that the incorporation of domain expertise and interpretability remains crucial. This is evident in the development of visual analytics systems that support the predictive analytics pipeline, allowing for more human-centric approaches and enabling users to incorporate expert knowledge into the prediction process [20]. Statistical modeling, a fundamental approach, relies on key concepts like probability distribution and hypothesis testing. Models, from simple linear to sophisticated generalized linear models, describe relationships between variables and estimate parameters based on empirical data [21].

Approach Based on Artificial Intelligence. AI has transformed predictive modeling, presenting advanced tools for deriving insights from complex data [22]. A recent study introduced a machine learning framework predicting food security in low-resource communities [23]. Another study highlighted the importance of interpretability in healthcare machine learning models [24].

By understanding the differences and applications of probabilistic, statistical, and AI-based approaches, researchers can select the most appropriate methods for their specific predictive modeling needs. Probabilistic models excel in accounting for uncertainty and variability, statistical models provide robust frameworks for parameter estimation and hypothesis testing, and AI models offer advanced tools for handling complex datasets and uncovering deep patterns.

3 Methodology and Implementation

The methodology employed in this research encompasses a comprehensive approach aimed at predicting the occurrence of malnutrition in both individual regions and across the entirety of Madagascar. The predictive models are developed using machine learning techniques in conjunction with explainable artificial intelligence methods. The primary objective is to forecast the incidence of food insecurity, underweight, chronic malnutrition, and acute malnutrition over a specified timeframe extending until 2030.

3.1 Collection of Data

To initiate the predictive modeling process, diverse and reliable datasets are collected from reputable sources covering various domains relevant to the study, such as population health, nutrition, and socio-economic indicators. These datasets, primarily sourced from government surveys, include:

- Multiple Indicator Cluster Surveys (MICS)
- General Population and Housing Census (RGPH)
- Demographic and Health Survey in Madagascar (EDSM)

Data from international and national institutions, including the FAO[1], the ONN[2], and the INSTAT[3], are utilized to ensure a comprehensive dataset.

---

[1] Food and Agriculture Organization.
[2] National Office of Nutrition.
[3] National Institute of Statistics.

These datasets are meticulously curated to ensure data integrity and reliability. This involves checking for missing values, outliers, and inconsistencies, and performing necessary data cleaning and preprocessing steps. The curated datasets are then used to build and train the predictive models.

Due to the diverse sources of our data, feature names are presented in French. We plan to continue developing this tool to allow users to make informed decisions based on its outputs. Additionally, we did not use all available data but performed a selection to demonstrate the feasibility and functionality of the idea.

For further exploration, the datasets are available at [25].

3.2 Exploratory Data Analysis

The exploratory data analysis (EDA) is a crucial step in understanding the dataset, addressing data quality issues, and formulating an initial approach for predictive modeling. This phase helps in identifying patterns, relationships, and anomalies in the data, which are essential for building accurate predictive models.

The Table 1 provides a summary of the findings from the exploratory data analysis.

Table 1. Results of the exploratory data analysis

SHAPE ANALYSIS	BACKGROUND ANALYSIS
• Target variable: Situation_Overweight, Situation_Undernutrition, Situation_Acute_Malnutrition • Rows and columns: (298, 88) • Variable types: qualitative: • 4, quantitative: 82, date: 2 • Missing values analysis: many NaN (5% of variables > 90% NaN) – 2 data groups: 78% - 89% • (exportation, importation, • production, cyclone), 68% to 70% (health, population, education) • Elimination of unnecessary • columns	• Target Visualization: – Underweight Situation: 54% Alert, 25% Precarious, 21% Critical – Chronic Malnutrition Situation: 34% Alert, 20% Precarious, 45% Critical, 1% Acceptable – Acute Malnutrition Situation: 15% Alert, 63% Precarious, 6% Critical, 16% Acceptable • Meaning of Variables: – Continuous variables are skewed – Quantitative variables: Some graphs are difficult to interpret, – indicating unprocessed data – Qualitative variables have many categories

Each aspect is designed to offer insights into different facets of the dataset and guide subsequent data processing steps:

- **Target variables** include the primary outcomes of interest, such as overweight, undernutrition, and acute malnutrition, which are critical for the predictive models.
- **Rows and columns** indicate the dataset's size, with 298 observations and 88 features, including various types of data.

- **Variable types** reveal the diversity in data types, which include qualitative (categorical), quantitative (numerical), and date-related variables, each requiring different handling techniques.
- **Missing values analysis** identifies significant issues with missing data, particularly in certain variables related to exportation and health. This analysis informs the strategies needed to address these gaps, such as imputation or removal of incomplete data.
- **Elimination of unnecessary columns** highlights the process of refining the dataset by removing columns that do not contribute to the analysis, which improves the model's performance and interpretability.
- **Target visualization** presents the distribution of malnutrition situations across the dataset, showing the percentage of regions categorized as Alert, Precarious, Critical, and Acceptable. This visualization helps in understanding the severity and spread of malnutrition issues.
- **Meaning of variables** discusses the characteristics of the data, such as the skewness in continuous variables, challenges in interpreting some quantitative graphs, and the complexity of qualitative variables due to their numerous categories. These insights guide the data preprocessing and feature engineering steps needed to prepare the dataset for effective modeling.

By thoroughly analyzing these aspects, the EDA phase lays the groundwork for building precise and reliable predictive models, ensuring that the data is high-quality and well-prepared for further analysis.

3.3 Preprocessing

Preprocessing is a critical phase in preparing data for machine learning models. It addresses various issues that may arise during data collection and ensures that the data is of high quality and suitable for analysis. The preprocessing steps are essential for handling errors such as incomplete information, missing values, inaccuracies, and noise, which can significantly impact model performance.

The preprocessing strategy involves several key steps:

- **Data cleaning:** This step involves identifying and correcting errors or inconsistencies in the data. Missing values are imputed or removed, and inaccuracies are corrected to ensure data integrity.
- **Normalization:** To bring all features to a common scale, normalization is applied. This step is crucial for models that rely on distance metrics or gradient-based optimization, as it ensures that no single feature disproportionately influences the results.
- **Encoding categorical variables:** Categorical variables, which represent qualitative data, need to be converted into numerical formats. Techniques such as one-hot encoding or label encoding are used to make these variables compatible with machine learning algorithms.
- **Dimensionality reduction:** This process reduces the number of features in the dataset while preserving essential information. Techniques like Principal Component Analysis (PCA) or feature selection methods help in simplifying the model and reducing computational complexity.

- **Outlier management:** Outliers, which are extreme values that differ significantly from other observations, can distort the results of predictive models. Identifying and handling outliers ensures that they do not unduly influence the model's performance.
- **New feature creation:** Creating new features through transformations or combinations of existing features can enhance the model's predictive power. This step involves deriving new insights from the data to improve model accuracy.
- **Validation:** Finally, validating the preprocessing steps ensures that the data remains consistent and reliable throughout the process. This includes checking that the data transformations have been applied correctly and that the final dataset is suitable for modeling.

Through these preprocessing steps, the dataset is effectively refined, setting the stage for more accurate and reliable machine learning models.

3.4 Modeling

The predictive models are trained using supervised learning techniques, where historical data on malnutrition indicators and associated factors serve as input features, and the observed malnutrition outcomes act as target variables. SVM are employed as the primary ML algorithm due to their robustness in handling high-dimensional data and their ability to generalize well to unseen data. To enhance the interpretability of the models, the SHAP technique is integrated, providing insights into the contribution of each feature to the model's predictions.

Support Vector Machines. SVMs are powerful models for classification and regression. They aim to find the optimal hyperplane that separates different classes in the feature space, providing flexibility and accuracy.

The given formula represents the decision function of a Support Vector Machine classifier in the context of binary classification.

$$h(x) = \sum_{k=1}^{p} \alpha_k^* l_k (x.x_k) + w_0 \tag{1}$$

- $h(x)$: This is the decision function or hypothesis function. It takes an input vector x and produces an output used to determine the class to which x belongs.
- $\sum_{k=1}^{p} \alpha_k^* l_k (x.x_k)$: This part of the decision function depends on the support vectors (x_k). Each term $\alpha_k^* l_k (x.x_k)$ represents the contribution of a support vector to the final decision.
- α_k^*: These are the Lagrange coefficients associated with the support vectors. They are determined during SVM model training and play a crucial role in defining the decision boundary.
- l_k: These are the class labels associated with the support vectors, indicating the class to which each support vector belongs (+1 or -1 in binary classification).
- x_k: These are the support vectors, which are the most important training examples for the SVM model.
- w_0: This is a bias term that helps adjust the position of the decision boundary. It contributes to shifting the decision function.

Integration of SHAP for Model Explainability. To enhance the interpretability of our models, we integrate the SHAP library. SHAP assigns importance values to each feature, providing detailed explanations on the contribution of each variable to the model's prediction. This integration aims to increase the transparency and interpretability of our models, meeting the growing requirements for explainable artificial intelligence.

The main idea of SHAP is based on the Shapley value, derived from the cooperative game theory approach. SHAP interprets the model's predicted value as the sum of values attributed to each input feature.

$$\phi_J(val) = \sum_{S \subseteq \{x_1,...,x_P\} w \setminus \{x_J\}} \frac{|S|!(p - |S| - 1)!}{p!} (val(S \cup \{x_j\}) - val(S)) \quad (2)$$

- S is the subset of features used in the model,
- x is a vector of feature values for the instances to be explained,
- p is the number of features,
- $\frac{|S|!(p-|S|-1)!}{p!}$ is the weight of subset S,
- $val(S)$ is the prediction of subset S.

Model Architecture. The model architecture outlines a systematic approach from data acquisition to decision-making. It integrates various components, each contributing to the overall process of predictive modeling and analysis.

Figure 1 depicts the architecture of the model, illustrating the flow of data through the system.

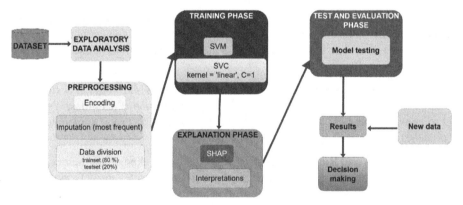

Fig. 1. Architecture of the Model. This diagram showcases the sequential stages involved in the model's operation. It begins with data collection, followed by EDA and preprocessing, feature selection, model training and explanation phase. The final stages include model evaluation and deployment. Each stage is connected, illustrating how data moves through the system and is transformed into actionable insights. This structured approach ensures a comprehensive and robust framework for predictive analytics and decision-making.

SVM is a powerful and widely used machine learning algorithm for classification and regression tasks. It is particularly effective when dealing with complex, high-dimensional data. The linear kernel, combined with a regularization parameter $C = 1$, ensures that the

SVM model finds the best linear decision boundary to separate the classes while minimizing the misclassification of data points. This helps in achieving a balance between maximizing the margin and minimizing the training errors. The linear kernel in SVM makes it suitable for problems where the data can be separated by a straight line or hyperplane. Additionally, the regularization parameter $C = 1$ in SVM controls the trade-off between the misclassification of training examples and the simplicity of the decision boundary. By setting $C = 1$, we are indicating that we want a relatively balanced trade-off between allowing misclassifications (by accepting some margin violations) and having a simpler decision boundary. This means that the SVM model with a linear kernel and $C = 1$ will prioritize finding a decision boundary that separates the classes accurately while still allowing some flexibility for misclassifications.

The Permutation Feature Importance (PFI) method in SHAP is a powerful technique for understanding the importance of different features in a model. It works by randomly shuffling the values of each feature and observing the effect on the model's performance. By comparing the original feature importance to the shuffled feature importance, we can determine which features have the greatest impact on the model's predictions. PFI is particularly useful for understanding non-linear relationships and interactions between features.

3.5 Implementation

Model Building with SVM. We implemented our predictive model using SVM, a powerful algorithm for classification and regression tasks.

Model Interpretation with SHAP. To interpret the predictions made by our SVM model, we utilized SHAP, a technique for explaining the output of machine learning models.

For the detailed code implementation and model interpretation, please refer to our GitHub repository [26].

Comparison with other Machine Learning Approaches. While SVM has been chosen as the primary algorithm for its robustness and generalization capabilities, it's essential to consider other ML algorithms for predictive modeling tasks. Some alternative approaches include:

- **Decision Trees and Random Forests**: These methods are known for their simplicity and ability to handle non-linear relationships. They can offer insights into feature importance but might lack the generalization ability of SVM.
- **Gradient Boosting Machines (GBM)**: GBM algorithms like XGBoost and Light-GBM often achieve high predictive accuracy and can handle complex datasets efficiently. However, they may not provide as much interpretability as SVM.

4 Experiments and Results

This section covers the experimentation and evaluation of the model:

4.1 Results

The case study delves into the application of AI and XAI in predicting phenomena across various scenarios, ranging from normal to critical situations. Our model demonstrates its effectiveness by maintaining stability in routine circumstances while excelling in identifying and addressing critical emergencies accurately. The incorporation of SHAP further enhances the model's reliability by providing detailed explanations for its decisions, thereby instilling confidence in diverse contexts and real-world scenarios.

To facilitate exploration of our predictive model, we have deployed it as an interactive tool on Streamlit. Users can access the tool through the Streamlit application by visiting [27].

Within the tool, users can select specific regions, such as "Androy", and choose the year for prediction, enabling them to explore the model's predictions and explanations effectively.

4.2 Assessment

The confusion matrix in Fig. 2 exposes the model's performance for each class, revealing insights and areas for improvement.

```
SVM
[[18  8  0]
 [11 61  0]
 [ 2 18  2]]
              precision    recall  f1-score   support

           2       0.58      0.69      0.63        26
           3       0.70      0.85      0.77        72
           4       1.00      0.09      0.17        22

    accuracy                           0.68       120
   macro avg       0.76      0.54      0.52       120
weighted avg       0.73      0.68      0.63       120
```

Fig. 2. Model Performance. Class 4 (critical case) shows 100% precision but low recall (9%), emphasizing the balance needed between precision and recall based on problem priorities. Class 3 (alert case) demonstrates promising results with high precision (70%) and recall (85%), yet attention is needed for false positives (11). Class 2 (precarious case) displays intermediate performance with 58% precision, 69% recall, indicating room for improvement, especially in reducing false positives (8). Overall precision is 68%, indicating quality across the test set, but class-specific analysis pinpoints areas for enhancement.

Examining the learning curve in Fig. 3 alongside highlights the model's evolving ability to generalize effectively without overfitting to training data.

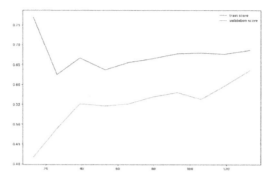

Fig. 3. Learning curve of the developed model (Color figure online)

4.3 Validation

After training and validating our models, it's evident that SVM outperforms the decision tree in predicting food and nutritional security.

This superiority is evident in various indicators, such as the confusion matrix, classification report, and precision, recall, and F1-score metrics for each class. SVM excels in distinguishing between different nutritional situations, providing high precision and recall, especially for alarming situations (class 3).

In contrast, the decision tree exhibits relatively lower performance, potentially struggling to capture the complexity of relationships between variables. Figure 4 illustrates the learning curve comparison between SVM and the decision tree, highlighting SVM's effectiveness in handling the intricacies of nutritional prediction in this context.

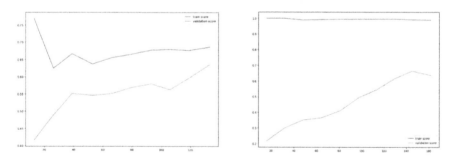

Fig. 4. Comparison of SVM and decision tree learning curves (Color figure online)

4.4 Interpretation of the SHAP Heatmap

The SHAP heatmap in the Fig. 5 provides insight into the impact of each feature on the model's predictions. Each cell in the heatmap represents the SHAP value for a specific feature and prediction, indicating how much that feature influences the prediction. Positive SHAP values (red shades) indicate a positive impact on the prediction, while negative SHAP values (blue shades) indicate a negative impact.

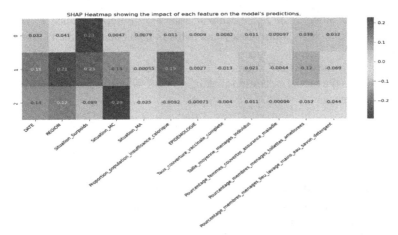

Fig. 5. SHAP Heatmap. Color intensity: The intensity of red and blue colors indicates the magnitude of the feature's impact. Darker reds signify a stronger positive influence, while darker blues signify a stronger negative influence. Patterns: Certain features consistently show either positive or negative impacts across predictions, revealing their overall influence trends. (Color figure online)

Key features analysis:

- DATE ("Date"):
- SHAP values range from -0.18 to 0.032.
- The date has a relatively minor impact on predictions, with minimal variation.
- REGION ("Region"):
- SHAP values range from -0.041 to 0.21.
- The region shows a notable influence on predictions, especially with a high impact of 0.21 in prediction 1.
- Situation_Surpoids ("Overweight"):
- SHAP values range from -0.23 to 0.23.
- Overweight status significantly affects predictions, with both positive and negative impacts.
- Situation_MC ("Chronic Malnutrition"):
- SHAP values range from -0.29 to 0.021.
- Chronic malnutrition has a generally negative impact on predictions.
- situation_MA ("Acute Malnutrition"):
- SHAP values range from -0.0092 to 0.011.
- Acute malnutrition's influence is minimal and mostly neutral.
- EPIDEMOLOGIE ("Epidemiology"):
- SHAP values range from -0.00055 to 0.19.
- This feature has a significant positive impact on some predictions.
- Other features in the heatmap exhibit generally low SHAP values, indicating a minor influence on the model's predictions.

The SHAP heatmap illustrates the varying importance of different features on the model's predictions. Features like "Overweight" and "Epidemiology" have significant impacts, whereas others like "Acute Malnutrition" have minimal influence. This analysis enhances the model's transparency and helps in understanding the factors driving predictions.

By analyzing these SHAP values and their corresponding colors, we gain valuable insights into the model's decision-making process, which is crucial for explainable artificial intelligence.

5   Conclusion

In conclusion, in the current dynamic context, understanding and making informed decisions are vital challenges. This article explores predicting phenomena through machine learning and explainable artificial intelligence, emphasizing recent technological advances. Machine learning offers unprecedented accuracy, transforming decision-making across domains. The primary objective is to explore opportunities in predictive modeling based on machine learning and explainable artificial intelligence.

Crucial issues, like optimizing data usage and model fine-tuning, are addressed through a rigorous methodology from institution introduction to results analysis.

Simulations showcase model relevance, validated by the added value of explainable artificial intelligence and machine learning. Limitations in result generalization and data availability are acknowledged, urging continued exploration with new data sources and refined models for broader applications.

Future prospects in advanced research are promising, urging researchers to delve into model clarity and real-time data management. A relevant dimension is extending this vision to spatial data analysis, exploring innovative methods to capture complex geographic relationships. This in-depth spatial analysis could enhance model accuracy, providing informed solutions to global challenges.

Acknowledgment. We extend our sincere gratitude to Mr. Ratsimisetra Andry Tsirofo Rabemanantsoa, Data Manager at the National Office of Nutrition (ONN) in Madagascar, for his invaluable expertise and guidance throughout the research process. His deep understanding of the thematic area greatly enriched our study and contributed significantly to its success.

References

1. Aworka, R., et al.: Agricultural decision system based on advanced machine learning models for yield prediction: case of East African countries. Smart Agric. Technol. **2**, 100048 (2022)
2. Bitew, F.H., Sparks, C.S., Nyarko, S.H.: Machine learning algorithms for predicting undernutrition among under-five children in Ethiopia. Public Health Nutr. **25**(2), 269–280 (2022)
3. Saranya, A., Subhashini, R.: A systematic review of explainable artificial intelligence models and applications: Recent developments and future trends. Decis. Anal. J. **7**, 100230 (2023)
4. Barredo Arrieta, A. et al.: Explainable artificial intelligence (XAI): concepts, taxonomies, opportunities and challenges toward responsible AI. Inf. Fusion **58**, 82–115 (2020)
5. Islam, M.R., Ahmed, M.U., Barua, S., Begum, S.: A systematic review of explainable artificial intelligence in terms of different application domains and tasks. Appl. Sci. **12**(3), 1353 (2022)

6. Phillips, P.J., et al.: Four principles of explainable artificial intelligence. National Institute of Standards and Technology, Gaithersburg, MD, NIST IR 8312 (2021)
7. Martinho, V.J.P.D. et al.: Machine learning and food security: insights for agricultural spatial planning in the context of agriculture 4.0. Appl. Sci. **12**(22), 11828 (2022)
8. Ratovondrahona, A.J., Rakotozanany, H.M., Mahatody, T., Manantsoa, V.: Human like programming using SPADE BDI agents and the GPT-3-based transformer. In: Proceedings of the 9th International Conference on Human Interaction and Emerging Technologies (IHIET-AI 2023), AHFE International (2023)
9. Meenal, R., et al.: Machine learning based smart weather prediction. Indonesian J. Electr. Eng. Comput. Sci. **28**(1), 508 (2022)
10. Naik, H., et al.: Explainable AI (XAI): Core ideas, techniques, and solutions. ACM Comp. Surv. **55**(9), 194 (2023)
11. Yang, C.C.: Explainable artificial intelligence for predictive modeling in healthcare. J. Healthcare Inf. Res. **6**, 228–239 (2022)
12. Ryo, M.: Explainable artificial intelligence and interpretable machine learning for agricultural data analysis. Artif. Intell. Agric. **6**, 257–265 (2022)
13. Kumar, P., Mishra, N., Sewada, R., Jangid, A.: Explainable Artificial Intelligence (XAI). J. Nonlinear Anal. Optim. 13 (2023)
14. Jiang, X., Liu, L., Harun, S.N.: Explainable artificial intelligence for ancient architecture and lacquer art. Buildings **13**(5), 1213 (2023)
15. Frej, J., Käser, T., Swamy, V.: The future of human-centric eXplainable Artificial Intelligence (XAI) is not post-hoc explanations. arXiv:2307.00364 (2023)
16. Mokarram, M., Pham, T.M.: CA-Markov model application to predict crop yield using re-mote sensing indices. Ecol. Ind. **139**, 108952 (2022)
17. Virtriana, R., et al.: Development of spatial model for food security prediction using remote sensing data in West Java, Indonesia. ISPRS Int. J. Geo Inf. **11**(5), 284 (2022)
18. Wang, D., Andree, B.P.J., Chamorro, A.F., Girouard Spencer, P.: Stochastic modeling of food insecurity. The World Bank, Policy Research Working Paper 9413 (2020)
19. Tangirala, S.: Predictive modeling in health care data analytics: a sustainable supervised learning technique. In: Big Data Analytics and Intelligence: A Perspective for Health Care, pp.263–280 (2020)
20. Lu, Y., Garcia, R., Hansen, B., Gleicher, M., Maciejewski, R.: The state-of-the-art in predictive visual analytics. Comput. Graph. Forum **36**(3), 539–562 (2017)
21. Andree, B.P.J., Chamorro, A., Kraay, A., Spencer, P., Wang, D.: Predicting food crises. The World Bank, Policy Research Working Paper 9412 (2020)
22. van den Bulk, L., et al.: Automatic classification of literature in systematic reviews on food safety using machine learning. Curr. Res. Food Sci. **5**, 84–95 (2022)
23. Gholami, S., et al.: Food security analysis and forecasting: a machine learning case study in southern Malawi. Data Policy **4**, e33 (2022)
24. Stiglic, G., et al.: Interpretability of machine learning-based prediction models in healthcare. WIREs Data Min. Knowl. Discovery **10**(5), e1379 (2020)
25. Data Madagascar - Datasets covering various domains relevant. https://www.kaggle.com/datasets/rosaelysabeth/data-madagascar
26. RosaElysabeth/modeleprediction. https://github.com/RosaElysabeth/modeleprediction
27. Streamlit. https://predictivemodelingmadagascar.streamlit.app/

Software and Systems

Comparison of Methodological Approaches: CRISP-DM vs OSEMN Methodology Using Linear Regression and Statistical Analysis

Ketjona Shameti$^{(\boxtimes)}$ and Betim Cico

Epoka University, Tirana, Albania
{kshameti19,bcico}@epoka.edu.al

Abstract. AI has contributed in changing many industries, providing new and inventive solutions to complicated challenges. Nevertheless, efficient application of AI projects needs a structured and combined technique to be updated with the latest advances in the sector. There are two methodologies, CRISP-DM and OSEMN, which are used to explain the data science project life cycle on a high level. The six-phase method framework known as the Cross Industry Standard Process for Data Mining (CRISP-DM) accurately depicts the data science life cycle. On the other hand, the overall workflow performed by data scientists is categorized under the OSEMN (Obtain, Scrub, Explore, Model, iNterpret) methodology. In our study, we examine both CRISP-DM and OSEMN frameworks, and we perform a comparative analysis. We have conducted an empirical study where the experiment was organized into three case studies, each provided insightful results whether which methodology has better model fit and which has a more accurate prediction rate. The case studies suggested that CRISP-DM offers a better performance and accurate approach. All things considered, this research advances our knowledge of best methods for the selection and use of data mining methodologies, providing practitioners and researchers with direction on which strategy is best suited for their data analysis assignments.

Keywords: CRISP-DM · OSEMN · framework · data mining · deep learning · machine learning · data science · natural language processing · Exploratory Data Analysis

1 Introduction

Artificial Intelligence (AI) has transformed a number of industries, providing creative answers to challenging issues. Nevertheless, an integrated and methodical strategy is necessary for the effective execution of AI initiatives [1]. There are particular difficulties in the creation, administration, and layout of AI platforms [2]. To develop solutions that address complicated issues in an unbiased

C. Bădică et al. (Eds.): BCI 2024, CCIS 2391, pp. 47–60, 2025.
https://doi.org/10.1007/978-3-031-84093-7_4

and moral manner, engineers frequently require assistance. Making ensuring the AI framework is accessible and comprehensible is crucial. This, considering the opaque nature of many AI systems, presents a substantial hurdle [3].

To comprehend the development and advancement of AI, it is imperative to con-duct a comparative examination of old and new AI design techniques [4]. Conventional approaches, like CRISP-DM, have been in use for many years, show proficiency in initiatives involving data mining and machine learning. But with AI technology developing so quickly, new strategies, as OSEMN, are developing that are more suited to the demands of the present [5].

While well-established and efficacious across multiple sectors, CRISP-DM, on the other hand we have OSEMN, a more modern technique provides a versatile and adaptive strategy, particularly beneficial for tasks involving substantial amounts of information and demand sophisticated machine learning methods [5]. So, in this paper we are going to compare both the methodologies by implementing them both, with the same datasets, same logic, to be able to distinguish which framework has better model fit and is more accurate.

The other sections of this paper are organized as follows: a brief state-of-art synopsis in Sect. 2. Section 3 writes the hypothesis and arises research questions to determine if the hypothesis is correct or not. Section 4 explains the methodology used to conduct the study. Section 5 discusses the experimental set up, explains how both frameworks are being implemented. Section 6 discusses the experiment and how it is organized in three case studies, each case assisting in answering the research questions. Section 7 provides discussions about the results. Section 8 you may find conclusion of our work and determines gaps for future work.

2   Literature Review

CRISP-DM (Cross Industry Standard Process for Data Mining) project is offering a thorough process model for completing data mining projects. It also needs a set of various abilities and understanding [1]. Data mining is in requirement of a normative strategy that will be in assistance of translating issues related to business into data mining assignments, propose effective data alterations and data mining methods, and offer means or assessing the efficiency of outcomes and recording the work [2]. According to Rüdiger Wirth and Jochen Hipp [1] in a reaction modeling program undertaking, they implemented and evaluated the CRISP-DM approach. The project's ultimate objective was to define a procedure that can be effectively and dependably reproduced by many individuals and modified for various contexts [6]. The initial endeavors were carried out by seasoned data mining professionals; subsequent projects will be handled by individuals with less computational expertise and minimal opportunity to try out various strategies [1]. It turns out that the CRISP-DM technique, with its differentiation between general and specialized process models, offers the flexibility and structure required to meet the requirements of both groups. The general CRISP-DM procedure paradigm is helpful for documentation, planning, and communication both inside and outside the project team. Even seasoned individuals can benefit from the general check-lists [7]. The overall procedure model offers a great starting point for creating a customized process model that outlines the actions to be done in detail and offers helpful guidance for each stage [1]. It turned out that the standard procedure framework was helpful for planning and documentation, as they had anticipated.

Kajal Kumari, Mahima Bhardwaj and Swati Sharma [3] have examined the framework that they use to gauge the precision of both languages' chirps is the information analysis system. The fact that this project is new is what matters most. They can argue that sentiment analysis is only a small portion of it, but first they must define sentiment study and categorization [9]. Sentiment classification is therefore a technique to examine the private information contained in the chirps or data and then retrieve the viewpoint [3]. Chirps examine how data is extracted from people's feelings and judgments about various objects. Fernando Martınez-Plumed, Lidia Contreras-Ochando, Cesar Ferri, Jose Hernandez-Orallo, Meelis Kull, Nicolas Lachiche, Maria Jose Ramırez-Quintana and Peter Flach [2] have examined whether CRISP-DM is still appropriate for use in data science initiatives and under what conditions. They contend that the procedure model approach is still generally valid in the event that the undertaking is goal-directed and procedure-driven. However, as data science endeavors get more preliminary, a more adaptable architecture is required because there are more possible project paths [2]. They offer some suggestions for the general structure of such a trajectory-based framework and how data science projects (goal-directed, preliminary, or data administration) can be categorized using it.

Kristina Dineva and Tatiana Atanasova [4] have discussed methods for gathering, organizing, analyzing, analyzing, modeling, and understanding IoT data are a significant problem and a significant obstacle for many researchers. The launch of the OSEMN, a standardized model of work, regulates the problem-solving procedure [4]. A consistent procedure is required for beekeeping, a sub sector of the agricultural sector, to use data from sensors housed in beehives. Important information about the behavior of individual bee colonies is obtained after appropriate data processing, which aids in the identification of connections between the various occurrences and the factors that trigger them [8]. This article's goal is to explain the OSEMN model and how beekeeping uses it.

In our work we have directed our focus on a direct comparison of the CRISP-DM and OSEMN data mining methods utilizing real-world application. Our goal is to ascertain whether strategy performs better in terms of efficiency, accuracy, and prediction by carefully analyzing both.

3   Hypothesis and Research Questions

We have raised some hypothesis and research questions that our study aims to answer at the end of the paper.

H0: The CRISP-DM framework has better model fit than OSEMN framework.

- RQ1: Has the CRISP-DM methodology performed better when considering the metrics of Coefficient of Determination (R^2) and Mean Squared Error (MSE)?

H1: The CRISP-DM methodology has a more accurate prediction rate than OSEMN methodology.

- RQ2: What does the graph representation for both indicate when comparing the prediction accuracy?
- RQ3: What does the metrics suggest us when comparing both methodologies regarding the prediction rate?

4   Methodology

In this part of our research, we have conducted an empirical research. We have presented the datasets used in our implementation, the python libraries that assisted our study, the exploratory data analysis assisting us in discovering the relationship among variables in datasets used. We have utilized Linear Regression as the predictive model in both the frameworks.

4.1   Datasets

We will show the characteristics for all the datasets used in this study. The first dataset used is Iris Dataset. In 1936, British statistician and biologist Ronald Fisher published a paper titled "The use of multiple measurements in taxonomic problems", which established the dataset [5]. The four characteristics (sepal and petal length and breadth) of fifty specimens from three different iris species (Iris setosa, Iris virginica, and Iris versicolor) are included in the Iris Dataset. To categorize the species, a linear discriminant model was constructed using these metrics. Yet, because there just two clearly distinct groups in the data set, using it for cluster analysis is not very frequent. Because of this, the data set serves as a useful illustration of the distinctions between supervised and unsupervised methods for data mining. We have provided below a short explanation about the Life Expectancy dataset.

While many studies on aspects influencing life expectancy, considering death rates, income layout, and demographic characteristics, have been conducted in past times. It was discovered that the relationship between the index of human advancement and immunizations was not previously considered. The content of this dataset are the columns: Country, Continent, Year, Status, Life Expectancy, Adult mortality, infant deaths, alcohol, percentage expenditure, hepatitis-B, measles, BMI, under five deaths, polio, HIV/AIDS, total expenditure, diphtheria, GDP, population, thinness, income composition of incomes, schooling. Each row has information for every column, there are 156 countries that contain the information expressed in the table. This dataset contains information from year 2000 till 2015.

In this other part of methodology, we have presented cases where Exploratory Data Analysis has assisted in our study.

4.2   Exploratory Data Analysis

Exploratory data analysis (EDA) is a method of characterizing the information using statistical and graphical tools to highlight significant features for additional examination. This entails examining the dataset from several perspectives and providing a description and summary of its contents without assuming anything. Before tackling statistical modeling or machine learning, EDA is an essential procedure to perform to make sure the information is indeed what it seems to be and that there are no evident errors. Many popular EDA libraries are available for Python, such as NumPy, Matplotlib, Seaborn, Plotly, and pandas. There are four types of EDA: Univariate Non-graphical; Multi-variate Non-graphical; Univariate graphical; Multivariate graphical. The most basic type of data analysis is called univariate non-graphical because it just uses a single factor to get information.

In our implementation we have outputted some statistics regarding the iris dataset. The spread and primary tendency of the numerical parameters in the dataset are briefly summarized by these statistics. We have as well the standard deviation to determine how numbers are distributed or dispersed around the mean. Then, the minimum value for every category is shown as well, the maximum value in cm for every characteristic is shown in the Table 1.

Table 1. The statistical information for Iris dataset

	sepal length (cm)	sepal width (cm)	petal length (cm)	petal width (cm)
count	150.000	150.000	150.000	150.000
mean	5.843	3.057	3.758	1.199
std	0.828	0.436	1.765	0.762
min	4.300	2.000	1.000	0.100
25 %	5.100	2.800	1.600	0.300
50 %	5.800	3.000	4.350	1.300
75 %	6.400	3.300	5.100	1.800
max	7.900	4.400	6.900	2.500

The multivariate non-graphical: This EDA method is typically employed in statistical or cross-tabulation contexts to illustrate the relationship among multiple variables. As shown in Fig. 1, We use the hist() function to see how different number factors are distributed throughout the Iris dataset. Univariate graphical: Although non-graphical approaches are unbiased and numerical, they are unable to provide an accurate representation of the facts; Because they necessitate a certain amount of subjective analysis, pictorial approaches are consequently more frequently used.

We have analyzed Linear Regression as a statistical method assisting us in determining what methodology has better model fit and accurate prediction rate.

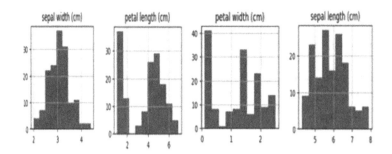

Fig. 1. Predicted vs Actual Sepal Width Values of OSEMN methodology.

4.3   Linear Regression

Determining the linear connection among a goal and one or more variables is done using linear regression. Basic and complex linear regression are the two varieties. When determining the association among two continuous variables, simple linear regression is helpful. There are two types of variables: independent or forecast and dependent or response. Statistical relationships are sought after rather than predictable ones. When two distinct factors can be precisely defined by one another, a relationship is said to be predictable. Finding the line which most matches the information is the main concept.

$$Y(pred) = b_0 + b_1 * x \tag{1}$$

Regarding a single predictor model:

- Investigating b_1: The association between x (predictor) and y (target) is positive if $b_1 > 0$. In other words, a rise in x will raise y. The association between x (predictor) and y (target) is negative if $b_1 < 0$. Thus, a rise in x will result in a fall in y.
- Examining b_0: The forecast using just b_0 will be worthless if the model does not contain $x = 0$. As an illustration, we are using a dataset that links weight y and height x. Assuming that height is zero $(x = 0)$, the formula will have merely a value of b_0, which is nonsensical because weight and height cannot possibly be zero in real life.

5   Experimental Set Up

5.1   OSEMN Framework

Obtain: This stage focuses on loading the datasets used in this experiment, provide descriptions for each and merging datasets such as Country Region Dataset with Life Expectancy dataset, to provide more information.

Scrub: This part is concerned in cleaning the data and preparing it for the next steps required in the experiment. It handles the missing values, by deleting the rows where are invalid data or no data at all. We have conducted data transformation as well in cases where the variable was changed from one name to another so as not to lose the information, and both were used for different purposes. Data preprocessing was done using the line str.replace(), to replace text that is not relevant.

Explore: This part is focused on exploring data, firstly printing descriptive statistics for each numerical value in the datasets. Then, we have used a lot of plots to show how data is distributed. Box plots and histograms are mainly used. At the end of this stage, we have conducted statistical analysis for both Iris and Life Expectancy dataset. We calculated the correlation matrix, Pearson correlation and t-tests in both datasets.

Model: With respect to the modeling part, we implemented linear regression using stats.linregress() to predict certain variables using one or multiple variables from both datasets. These relationships were shown using Seaborn's lmplot(). We also applied ANOVA to compare one variable among all the others.

Interpret: In this stage of the framework, a model evaluation is performed using values coming from the linear regression model. Also, the statistical analysis and tests, visualization of relationships among variables in the datasets, were insightful in answering the research questions.

5.2   CRISP-DM Framework

Business Understanding: In this phase the main objective is determined. In our case, the main reason is to understand data in both datasets and provide thoroughly a study in terms of efficiency, accuracy, and prediction.

Data Understanding: This stage collects data and understand the relationship among them. We loaded the datasets, cleaned them form unnecessary data, when needed we merged datasets and provided descriptive information for each.

Data Preparation: We handled the values that were missing by dropping them. We converted the data into a stacked structure. We specified data types to guarantee uniformity. Then we choose relevant variables for the model of life expectancy dataset ((features = ['GDP','Schooling','Alcohol','Life_expectancy'])).

Modeling: In this stage of the framework, we implemented a linear regression model to predict a certain variable of the dataset using relationships among features. We assessed the performance of the model utilizing the values of MSE and R^2. Then, different statistical analysis such as Pearson correlation and ANOVA were carried out to examine the relationships and variations in the datasets.

Evaluation: In this part we used the evaluation metrics to determine the accuracy and prediction rate of the model. The analysis and the visualizations were insightful in determining the conclusions.

Deployment: This part focuses on giving suggestions based on findings for possible implementation or additional research. Also, to discuss about possible next steps for investigating more datasets or improving models.

6   Experiment and Results

We have organized this part into three case studies. The first case study performs some statistical tests, data analysis on the datasets utilized in the methodologies. We have also analyzed the correlation matrix to identify the relationship among the variables. The second and third case study consist on answering the research questions raised in the hypothesis. The second case study uses the Iris dataset, while the third uses Life Expectancy dataset.

6.1   First Case Study

We analyzed the correlation matrix for both frameworks, for the same dataset: Life Expectancy dataset.

A correlation matrix can be used to reduce a substantial quantity of information, recognize patterns, and make decision relating to it. The matrix is a chart where each cell has a correlation coefficient, with 1 denoting a strong association, 0 a neutral relationship, and -1 a weak relationship between the variables. We need to check the correlations among variables in the dataset, since a high number of correlations in linear regression indicates that the results will not be trustworthy. The values generated were the same.

We can distinguish some high values of correlations in this matrix. Life expectancy variable and Income composition of resources have a correlation coefficient of 0.733, that shows that nations with longer life expectancy typically have more revenue distributed among their resources. We can clearly observe from the matrix the values that have high correlations due to stronger colors of red and blue, and we can imply that there are very few high values of correlation, resulting in reliable out-comes of the linear regression.

We have displayed the Pearson correlation among variables GDP and Life Expectancy in the CRISP-DM and OSEMN framework. The outcome values for both are: $r=0.46$ and p-value=3.55e-129. Value $r=0.46$ warrants a moderate positive progression of the GDP with the life expectancy. As the GDP rises, the life expectancy also rises and vice versa implying that there is a positive relationship between GDP and life expectancy of a given country. This is an insignificantly small p-value and according to statistical practice, a small p-value further substantiates the rejection of the null hypothesis. The r and p-values for both frameworks are the same. This implies that the statistical evidence arrived at is consistent whichever model is used to analyze them. It amplifies the reliability and confirms that the relationship between the variables is not affected by any specific method of computation used in the study between the GDP and life expectancy.

6.2   Second Case Study

In this second case study, we have utilized the Iris dataset. We will initially examine the model part of CRISP-DM methodology. We have presented the procedure of how to train as well as test a linear regression model with the aim of making a prediction of sepal width from the other variables included in the iris data set.

MSE measures the average of the squared differences between the prediction and the actual values, on the other hand R^2 measures how efficiently the values of the target variable can be predicted using the values of independent variables. As we can observe from the output, the MSE value is relatively small and extremely close to 0. This means that the sum of the squares of the individual differences in sepal width predictions and the actual sepal widths for the different types of species is almost zero.

MSE: 0.00, R^2: 1.0

This implies that the model's forecast is very accurate in relation to the actual values thus making it suitable to be used in estimating values based on given model. The predicted values are very close to the real ones. As we can observe the value of R^2 is 1, meaning a perfect model fit. When a model's fit to the data is perfect, as shown by a value of 1.0, all variance in the target variable is explained by the model.

As we can observe from the graph in Fig. 2, the predicted and actual values lie in the same line, indicating that the model have predicted accurately the values. This analysis is followed by a residual analysis, which indicates that the linear regression model that has been built based on the CRISP-DM methodology is indeed very accurate and the model fits the data so well.

We have examined the part of modeling at the OSEMN methodology as well. We have applied the linear regression and used in the prediction of sepal width given that the species is Virginica species and assesses the validity of the model based on the MSE and the R^2 scores. The outcomes from the pseudo code are MSE and R^2, as well as the scatter plot where we can observe the relationship between the actual values and predicted ones.

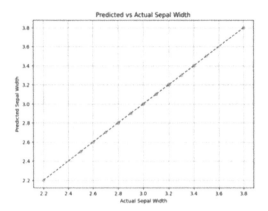

Fig. 2. Predicted vs Actual Sepal Width Values of CRISP-DM methodology.

MSE: 0.144, R^2: −0.005

An MSE value of 0.144 approximately represents the average of the squared differences between the predicted and the actual values. R^2 is the statistical measure showing the degree of variance of the target variable accounted for by the independent variables. If the value of R^2 is negative that means that the given model is not better than the horizontal line. Value is −0.005 approximately, hence the model may not be the best model for the data.

As observed from Fig. 3, it is very clear the disproportionality among actual and predicted values. Actual values are very different from those predicted indicating not only a low prediction rate, but also a low model fit and not accurate predicted values.

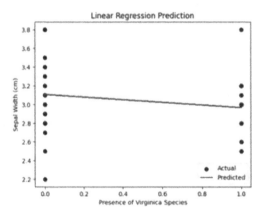

Fig. 3. Predicted vs Actual Sepal Width Values of OSEMN methodology.

When comparing values generated from both methodologies, we can suggest the following observations: For the CRISP-DM, the MSE value of the model was nearly 0, which reflected the model's nearly perfect accuracy, while for the OSEMN, the value of MSE was around 0. 144, which is substantially higher than one, meaning a greater prediction error.

This means that the model developed using CRISP-DM methodology is much more accurate in predicting sepal's width than the model developed using the OSEMN methodology. Whereas the R^2 value for the OSEMN approach was roughly -0.005, suggesting a very poor fit of the model, the R^2 result for the CRISP-DM methodology was 1.0, showing an ideal fit of the model to the data.

The obtained negative R^2 value indicates that the OSEMN methodology has constructed a model that is even less accurate than the linear model with the intercept equal to one that simply oscillates around the horizontal line, not managing to unveil connections between the features array and the target variable.

6.3   Third Case Study

In this third case study we have utilized the Life Expectancy dataset. We will initially examine the model part of CRISP-DM methodology. We have presented the procedure of how to train as well as test a linear regression model with the aim of making a prediction of variable "Life expectancy" by utilizing other variables from the dataset: GDP, schooling, alcohol, adult mortality. MSE aims at calculating the mean of squared deviations of fitted values from the observed values of the dependent variable; it thus gives a measure of how close the predicted values are to the actual values in the sample set. Low value of MSE indicated a better accuracy.

The outcomes from the model are MSE and R^2, as well as the scatter plot where we can observe the relationship between the actual values and predicted ones.

MSE: 35.865, R^2: 0.440

An MSE value of 35.865 approximately represents the average of the squared differences between the predicted and the actual values. A lower MSE value is preferred, albeit by a small margin, as it implies a smaller difference between the model's prediction and the actual value designated during feature extraction and model training. This value shows that there are errors among the predicted values and actual ones. As we can observe from the graph in Fig. 4, we can clearly distinguish that the actual values are very close to the predicted line.

Few values are far from the predicted line, but this can be associated to exceptions in the relationship between variables, since some variables van have non-linear relationship with one another.

We will examine the model part of OSEMN methodology. We have presented the procedure of how to train as well as test a linear regression model with the aim of making a prediction of variable "Life expectancy" by utilizing other variables from the dataset: GDP, schooling, alcohol, adult mortality.

A MSE value of 0.144 approximately represents the average of the squared differences between the predicted and the actual values. R^2 is the statistical

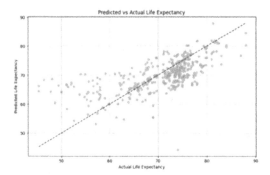

Fig. 4. Predicted vs Actual Life Expectancy Values of CRISP-DM methodology.

measure showing the degree of variance of the target variable accounted for by the independent variables. If the value of R^2 is negative that means that the given model is not better than the horizontal line. Value is -0.005 approximately, hence the model may not be the best model for the data. The outcomes from the model are MSE and R^2, as well as the scatter plot where we can observe the relationship between the actual values and predicted ones.

MSE: 0.144, R^2: -0.005

As we can observe from the graph in Fig. 5, we can distinguish that the predicted values of life expectancy variable are very different from the actual ones. There are very few values predicted correctly or that have a near distance from one another. This suggests that the accuracy of the predicted values is low and that it has a low model fit.

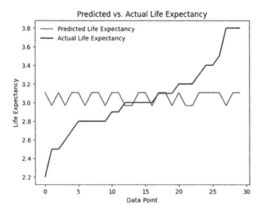

Fig. 5. Predicted vs Actual Life Expectancy Values of OSEMN methodology.

When comparing values generated from both methodologies, we can suggest the following observations: The model that was created using OSEMN methodology shown lower MSE, which means better performance and higher accuracy in the life expectancy prediction in comparison with the model created using CRISP-DM methodology. In comparison to the model created using the OSEMN approach, the model created using the CRISP-DM technique has a higher R^2 value, indicating a better overall fit to the data. From the graph, we can suggest that the actual values were very close to the predicted values line in the CRISP-DM methodology model, while the actual values were not close to the predicted values line in the OSEMN methodology, indicating that the model of CRISP-DM has in overall a better model fit.

7 Discussion

We have answered our research question by considering the results from the experiment part of our paper. To answer the research questions, we can consider the MSE and R^2 values from the second and third case study. In the second case study, for the CRISP-DM, the MSE value of the model was nearly 0, which reflected the model's nearly perfect accuracy, while for the OSEMN, the value of MSE was around 0. 144, which is substantially higher than one, meaning a greater prediction error. This means that the model developed using CRISP-DM methodology is much more accurate in predicting sepal's width than the model developed using the OSEMN methodology. Whereas the R^2 value for the OSEMN approach was roughly -0.005, suggesting a very poor fit of the model, the R^2 result for the CRISP-DM methodology was 1.0, showing an ideal fit of the model to the data.

While in the third case study, the finding changes slightly. The model that was created using OSEMN methodology shown lower MSE, which means better performance and higher accuracy in the life expectancy prediction in comparison with the model created using CRISP-DM methodology. In comparison to the model created using the OSEMN approach, the model created using the CRISP-DM technique has a higher R^2 value, indicating a better overall fit to the data.

The results of this study support the H0 Hypothesis demonstrating that the CRISP-DM framework has better model fit than OSEMN framework. To answer the second research question observing the graph, we can suggest that the actual values were very close to the predicted values line in the CRISP-DM methodology model, while the actual values were not close to the predicted values line in the OSEMN methodology, indicating that the model of CRISP-DM has in overall a better model fit. The third question is answered by the MSE values in both methodologies. Those values indicate that in one case study CRISP-DM has very high accuracy rate regarding prediction, with an extreme small value of errors. In the second case study, OSEMN methodology has higher accuracy, but the difference is not very big. Considering the answers of second and third research questions, the results support the H1 Hypothesis demonstrating that the CRISP-DM methodology has a more accurate prediction rate than OSEMN methodology.

8   Conclusion

We have examined the appropriate studies based on the following criteria in an effort to address the research issues listed in the introduction section: the metrics used in determining the model performance; the initial steps performed in the dataset to prepare and handle errors in the data provided. While equity and confidentiality were always challenging with data mining, the trajectory model does not yet clearly address all of the legal and ethical concerns surrounding data science.

In the experiment conducted, we have observed that in OSEMN methodology, MSE and R^2 values in both Iris dataset and Life Expectancy dataset remain the same, while in CRISP-DM methodology, MSE and R^2 values are different when using Iris Dataset and different when using Life Expectancy Dataset. This consistency might mean that OSEMN methodology is more general, as modeling techniques and measures used for evaluating their performance are consistently applied to all the datasets. On the other hand, the variation that exists in CRISP-DM for methodology could be considered methodical and intentional and where modeling tactics are adjusted to the characteristic of a particular dataset to produce the best result in one scenario or another. Future research aims to achieve transparency at every level of the procedure, making it simple to identify problems and quickly return to a particular stage when necessary for both frameworks.

References

1. Wirth, R., Hipp, J.: CRISP-DM: Towards a standard process model for data mining. In: Proceedings of the 4th International Conference and Exhibition on the Practical Application of Knowledge Discovery and Data Mining, pp. 29–40 (2000)
2. Martinez-Plumed, F., et al.: CRISP-DM twenty years later: from data mining processes to data science trajectories. IEEE Trans. Knowl. Data Eng. **33**(8), 3048–3061 (2016)
3. Kumari, K., Bhardwaj, M., Sharma, S.: OSEMN approach for real time data analysis. Int. J. Eng. Manage. Res. **10**(2), 107–110 (2016)
4. Dineva, K., Atanasova, T.: OSEMN process for working over data acquired by IoT devices mounted in beehives. Curr. Trends Natural Sci. **7**(13), 47–53 (2018)
5. Boudreau, P.: Applying Artificial Intelligence to Project Management. Independently Published (2019)
6. Mariscal, G., Marban, O., Fernandez, C.: A survey of data mining and knowledge discovery process models and methodologies. Knowl. Eng. Rev. **25**(2), 137–166 (2010)
7. Edelstein, H. A.: Introduction to Data Mining and Knowledge Discovery. Two Crows Corporation (1999)
8. Pang, B., Lee, L.: Opinion mining and sentiment analysis. Found. Trends Inform. Revival **2**(1–2), 1–135 (2008)
9. Cao, L.: Data science: a comprehensive overview. ACM Comput. Surv. **50**(3), 1–42 (2017)

Processing Range-Sum Queries Within Triangular Shapes

Mirel Cosulschi$^{(\boxtimes)}$, Mihai Gabroveanu, and Florin Slabu

University of Craiova, Craiova, Romania
{mirelc,mihaiug}@central.ucv.ro, florin.slabu@inf.ucv.ro

Abstract. Prefix sums represent a technique for precomputing partial sums to enable efficient range-sum queries. The concept is encountered under various names across disciplines: for example, summed-area tables in computer graphics, integral images in computer vision, and cumulative distribution functions in probability theory. This paper extends the use of prefix sums to triangular areas, proposing three algorithms tailored for isosceles right triangles with legs parallel to the coordinate axes. The first algorithm uses a straightforward summation of triangle rows, the second employs a recursive subdivision algorithm, while the third leverages elementary geometry principles.

Keywords: prefix sums · triangular shape · recursive subdivision

1 Introduction

Let's consider a monoid $(S, \oplus, e)$ where S is a set of values, $\oplus$ is a binary associative operator defined on S, and $e \in S$ is the identity for $\oplus$, and a n-dimensional array A with dimensions $d_1 \times d_2 \times \ldots \times d_n$ [19].

Definition 1. *The **prefix-sum** array P is an array with n-dimensions $d_1 \times d_2 \times \ldots \times d_n$, where each element $P_{i_1 i_2 \ldots i_n}$ can be determined as:*

$$P_{i_1 i_2 \ldots i_n} = \bigoplus_{j_1=0}^{i_1} \bigoplus_{j_2=0}^{i_2} \cdots \bigoplus_{j_n=0}^{i_n} A_{j_1 j_2 \ldots j_n}. \tag{1}$$

Prefix-sum implies *the sum* of the elements located inside a hyper-rectangle within the original array. The bottom-left corner of the hyper-rectangle is always the origin, while the upper-right corner is defined by the current element's indices in the prefix-sum array.

Definition 2. *A **range-sum query** for the elements within a hyper-rectangular region defined by its corners $(i_1^1, i_2^1, \ldots, i_n^1)$ and $(i_1^2, i_2^2, \ldots, i_n^2)$ is:*

$$\bigoplus_{j_1=i_1^1}^{i_1^2} \bigoplus_{j_2=i_2^1}^{i_2^2} \cdots \bigoplus_{j_n=i_n^1}^{i_n^2} A_{j_1 j_2 \ldots j_n}. \tag{2}$$

In other words, range-sum queries involve applying the $\oplus$ operator to the values of elements within a specified hyper-rectangular subarray of an n-dimensional array. Usually in practice, the concepts of prefix sums and range-sum queries are used for arrays of dimensions less than 3. The concept of prefix sums can be encountered with different names across many disciplines such as *summed area tables* in computer graphics, *prefix sums* in database systems, *integral images* in computer vision, and *cumulative distribution functions* (CDFs) in probability theory. Despite the varied terminology, the underlying principle remains the same: precomputing partial sums to facilitate quick and efficient calculations over specific ranges. Range-sum queries involve summing the values of cells within rectangular areas.

As examples of usage, we can mention their application in computer vision for efficiently computing features for object recognition [1–3,13,18], in computer graphics for various rendering and image processing tasks [7,16], in Online Analytical Processing (OLAP) for answering aggregate range queries [8,10,15], and in data mining for effectively identifying maximum rectangular subarrays [17].

In this paper, our research focuses on summing values from triangular areas, specifically range-sum queries that aggregate cell values within triangular shapes. The results obtained can be of interest in fields such as computational geometry, mathematical algorithms, and specific applications like graphics or physics simulations. These topics are often explored in the context of geometric computations, mesh processing, and algorithms used in image processing, where triangular domains play an important role.

We present three algorithms for summing the values of elements located within a triangular shape. The triangular shape used by the algorithms is described by an isosceles right triangle with its legs parallel to the coordinate axes. The first algorithm, named 'SumofRows', employs a straightforward approach of summing the elements of each row within the triangle and has a time complexity of $O(n)$. The second one, called 'Recursive Subdivision', is based on an idea similar to the rectangular decomposition described by Bowman et al. [4]. This algorithm has a time complexity of $O(n)$, as can be demonstrated using *the master theorem* [9]. The third method, based on ideas from elementary geometry, results in an algorithm with $O(1)$ time complexity.

2   Previous Work

The concept of a *summed-area table* was first introduced by Franklin C. Crow in 1984 [6]. Crow described this technique as a method for quickly calculating the sum of values within a rectangular area of a grid. It was aimed at improving the efficiency of operations in computer graphics, specifically for tasks such as texture mapping and antialiasing.

In the field of computer vision, J.P. Lewis further popularized the concept in 1995 [12]. He extended the use of the summed-area table to image processing, where it facilitated rapid computation of image features. The term *integral image* became widely recognized due to its implementation in the Viola-Jones object detection framework established in 2001 [18]. This framework used the *integral image* to efficiently compute Haar-like features, enabling real-time object detection. Integral images are also used in real-time image processing and filtering applications [11].

Prefix sums are particularly useful in Online Analytical Processing (OLAP) for data cubes that are sparse, where a significant portion of the data points are null. In the paper [14], the authors explore a novel method for analyzing interactome data (a complex network of interactions between molecules within a cell) efficiently using sparse prefix sums within the field of bioinformatics.

3   Description of the Approaches

3.1   The Problem Formulation

Let's consider a matrix A, $A \in \mathcal{M}_{n \times n}(\mathbb{Z})$.

Definition 3. *We will denote by $\triangle_{l,c,k}$ an isosceles right triangle having the vertex of the right angle at the coordinate point (l, c) and the legs of length $|k|$ parallel to the coordinate axes.*

If $k > 0$, the surface of an isosceles right triangle $\triangle_{l,c,k}$ having the vertex of the right angle at the coordinate point (l, c) and the legs of length k parallel to the coordinate axes, can be defined such as

$$
\begin{array}{llllll}
a_{l,c} & a_{l,c+1} & \cdots & a_{l,c+k-3} & a_{l,c+k-2} & a_{l,c+k-1} \\
a_{l+1,c} & a_{l+1,c+1} & \cdots & a_{l+1,c+k-3} & a_{l+1,c+k-2} & \\
a_{l+2,c} & a_{l+2,c+1} & \cdots & a_{l+2,c+k-3} & & \\
\vdots & & & & & \\
a_{l+k-1,c} & & & & &
\end{array}
$$

while if $k < 0$, the area of an isosceles right triangle $\triangle_{l,c,k}$ can be defined in the following way:

$$
\begin{array}{cccccc}
 & & & & & a_{l-|k|+1,c} \\
 & & & & a_{l-|k|+2,c-1} & a_{l+|k|+2,c} \\
 & & & a_{l-|k|+3,c-2} & a_{l-|k|+3,c-1} & a_{l+|k|+3,c} \\
 & & & \vdots & \vdots & \vdots \\
 & a_{l-1,c-|k|+2} & \cdots & a_{l-1,c-2} & a_{l-1,c-1} & a_{l-1,c} \\
a_{l,c-|k|+1} & a_{l,c-|k|+2} & \cdots & a_{l,c-2} & a_{l,c-1} & a_{l,c}
\end{array}
$$

The problem: For a matrix A $(A \in \mathcal{M}_{n \times n}(\mathbb{Z}))$, we want to efficiently calculate the sum of the values of the elements situated in the area of the isosceles right triangle $\triangle_{l,c,k}$, the triangle having the vertex of the right angle at the coordinate point (l, c) and the legs of length $|k|$ parallel to the coordinate axes:

$$
\sum_{\triangle_{l,c,k}} \overset{notation}{=} \sum_{\forall (i,j) \in \triangle_{l,c,k}} a_{i,j}. \tag{3}
$$

3.2 Iterative Variant

For this calculation method we will need prefix sum for each line of matrix A: let's denote by $sr_{i,k}$ the sum of the first k elements from the i-th row. Thus we will have:

$$sr_{i,k} = \sum_{j=1}^{k} a_{i,j} = a_{i,1} + a_{i,2} + \ldots + a_{i,k}. \tag{4}$$

For the triangular area $\triangle_{l,c,k}$, we will calculate the sum of the elements located inside of that triangular area as a sum of lines:

a) *The case for $k \geq 0$:*

    1: $sum_{\triangle_{l,c,k}} \leftarrow 0$
    2: **for** $i \leftarrow 0, k-1$ **do**
    3:     $sum_{\triangle_{l,c,k}} \leftarrow sum_{\triangle_{l,c,k}} + sr_{l+i,c+k-1-i} - sr_{l+i,c-1}$
    4: **end for**

b) *The case for $k < 0$:*

    1: $k \leftarrow -k$
    2: $sum_{\triangle_{l,c,k}} \leftarrow 0$
    3: **for** $i \leftarrow 0, k-1$ **do**
    4:     $sum_{\triangle_{l,c,k}} \leftarrow sum_{\triangle_{l,c,k}} + sr_{l-k+1+i,c} - sr_{l-k+1+i,c-1-i}$
    5: **end for**

Algorithm 1 illustrates the first method that can be used for computing the value of $\sum_{\triangle_{l,c,k}}$.

Algorithm 1. Algorithm SumOfRows

  1: **function** GETSUMTRIANGULARAREAV1(l, c, k, SR)
  2:     $sum_{\triangle_{l,c,k}} \leftarrow 0$
  3:     **if** $(k \geq 0)$ **then**
  4:         **for** $i \leftarrow 0, k-1$ **do**
  5:             $sum_{\triangle_{l,c,k}} \leftarrow sum_{\triangle_{l,c,k}} + sr_{l+i,c+k-1-i} - sr_{l+i,c-1}$
  6:         **end for**
  7:     **else**
  8:         $k \leftarrow -k$
  9:         **for** $i \leftarrow 0, k-1$ **do**
10:            $sum_{\triangle_{l,c,k}} \leftarrow sum_{\triangle_{l,c,k}} + sr_{l-k+1+i,c} - sr_{l-k+1+i,c-1-i}$
11:         **end for**
12:     **end if**
13:     **return** $sum_{\triangle_{l,c,k}}$
14: **end function**

In the preparation phase, the computation of the elements of SR matrix has a time complexity of $\mathcal{O}(n^2)$, while the time complexity of the GetSumTriangular-AreaV1 function (see Algorithm 1) is $\mathcal{O}(n)$.

3.3   Recursive Subdivision Scheme

Let's denote by $P_{l,c}$ the prefix sum of the cell with coordinates (l,c). $P_{l,c}$ is defined as:

$$P_{l,c} = \sum_{i=1}^{l}\sum_{j=1}^{c} a_{i,j} \tag{5}$$

e.g. the sum of all cells in the range with lower corner $(1,1)$ (or i.e. the origin of the data space $(0,0)$), and upper corner (l,c).

For the triangular area $\triangle_{l,c,k}$, the sum of the elements located inside that triangular area will be computed as follows: the isosceles right triangle associated with $\triangle_{l,c,k}$ will be decomposed into a square SQ and two smaller isosceles right triangles IRT_1 and IRT_2, so that the result is the sum of the elements located inside the square area SQ plus the sum of the elements located inside the isosceles right triangles areas IRT_1 and IRT_2:

$$\sum_{\forall(i,j)\in\triangle_{l,c,k}} a_{i,j} = \sum_{\forall(i,j)\in\square SQ} a_{i,j} + \sum_{\forall(i,j)\in\triangle IRT_1} a_{i,j} + \sum_{\forall(i,j)\in\triangle IRT_2} a_{i,j} \tag{6}$$

From now on, we will simplify the notation:

$$\sum_{\forall(i,j)\in FIG} a_{i,j} \overset{notation}{=} \sum\nolimits_{FIG}. \tag{7}$$

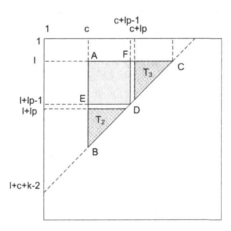

Fig. 1. The triangle $\triangle ABC$ breaks down into a square and two smaller isosceles right triangles.

We identify the following situations:

a) *The case for* $k \geq 0$: An isosceles right triangle ($\triangle ABC$) will be decomposed into a square ($\square AFDE$) and two smaller isosceles right triangles (triangles denoted by T_2 and T_3, as seen in Fig. 1).

The sum of the elements inside the triangular area of $\triangle ABC$ ($\triangle_{l,c,k}$) will be computed as the sum of the elements located inside the square $\square AFDE$ (the square having the upper-left corner $A(l,c)$ and the lower-left corner $D(l + lp - 1, c + cp - 1)$) plus the sum of the of the elements located inside the isosceles right triangles T_2 and T_3, where lp is the length of of one side of square $\square AFDE$:

$$\sum\nolimits_{\triangle_{l,c,k}} = \sum\nolimits_{\square AFDE} + \sum\nolimits_{\triangle_{l+lp,c,k-lp}} + \sum\nolimits_{\triangle_{l,c+lp,k-lp}}. \tag{8}$$

The recursive character of Eq. 8 can be observed.

The square AFDE ($\square AFDE$) is the square with the maximum side inscribed in the triangular area $\triangle_{l,c,k}$ ($\triangle ABC$) and having the upper left corner at the point $A(l,c)$. The length of one side of the square AFDE can be determined such as:

$$lp = ||AF|| = k/2 + (k \mod 2). \tag{9}$$

The sum of the elements located in the area of the square with top left point at $A(l,c)$ and bottom right at $D(l + lp - 1, c + lp - 1)$ (the AFDE square in Fig. 2) is calculated as follows:

$$\sum\nolimits_{\square AFDE} = P_{l+lp-1,c+lp-1} - P_{l+lp-1,c-1} - P_{l-1,c+lp-1} + P_{l-1,c-1}. \tag{10}$$

The sum of the elements located in the area of the square defined by its upper-left corner $A(l,c)$ and by its bottom-right corner $D(l + lp - 1, c + lp - 1)$ is obtained from the sum of the elements located in the area of the rectangle defined by its upper-left corner $M(1,1)$ and by its bottom-right corner $D(l + lp - 1, c + lp - 1)$, from which is subtracted the sum of the elements located in the area of the rectangle defined by its upper-left corner $M(1,1)$ and by its bottom-right corner $E_1(l + lp - 1, c - 1)$ and the sum of the elements located in the area of the rectangle defined by its upper-left corner $M(1,1)$ and by its bottom-right corner $F_1(l - 1, c + lp - 1)$, to which is added the sum of the elements located in the area of the rectangle defined by its upper-left corner $M(1,1)$ and by its bottom-right corner $A_1(l - 1, c - 1)$.

b) *The case for $k < 0$:* The sum of the elements inside the triangular area $\triangle_{l,c,k}$ can be computed as follows:

$$\sum\nolimits_{\triangle_{l,c,k}} = \sum\nolimits_{\square SQ} + \sum\nolimits_{\triangle_{l,c-lp,lp-|k|}} + \sum\nolimits_{\triangle_{l-lp,c,lp-|k|}}. \tag{11}$$

It is identified the square SQ with the maximum side inscribed in the triangular area $\triangle_{l,c,k}$ and having its bottom-right corner at the point (l,c). The length of one side of the maximum inscribed square SQ is:

$$lp = |k|/2 + (|k| \mod 2) \tag{12}$$

The sum of the elements located inside the square SQ defined by its upper-left corner $(l - lp + 1, c - lp + 1)$ and by its bottom-right corner (l,c) can be computed as follows:

$$\sum\nolimits_{\square SQ} = P_{l,c} - P_{l,c-lp} - P_{l-lp,c} + P_{l-lp,c-lp}. \tag{13}$$

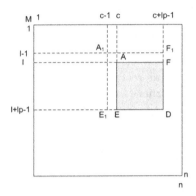

Fig. 2. How can be computed the sum of the elements located in the area of the square $AFDE$ using the sums of the elements located inside the area of the rectangles defined by the points $M(1,1)$ - $D(l+lp-1,c+lp-1)$, $M(1,1)$ - $E_1(l+lp-1,c-1)$, $M(1,1)$ - $F_1(l-1,c+lp-1)$ and $M(1,1)$ - $A_1(l-1,c-1)$.

Algorithm 2. Algorithm Recursive Subdivision

1: **function** GETSUMTRIANGULARAREARECURSIVE(l, c, k, P)
2:   **if** $((k = 1) \vee (k = -1))$ **then**
3:     **return** $(P_{l,c} - P_{l,c-1} - P_{l-1,c} + P_{l-1,c-1})$
4:   **end if**
5:   **if** $(k > 0)$ **then**
6:     $lp \leftarrow k/2 + (k \bmod 2)$
7:     $result \leftarrow P_{l+lp-1,c+lp-1} - P_{l+lp-1,c-1} - P_{l-1,c+lp-1} + P_{l-1,c-1}$
8:     $result \leftarrow result + GetSumTriangularAreaRecursive(l + lp, c, k - lp, P)$
            $+ GetSumTriangularAreaRecursive(l, c + lp, k - lp, P))$
9:   **else**
10:     $k \leftarrow -k$
11:     $lp \leftarrow k/2 + (k \bmod 2)$
12:     $result \leftarrow P_{l,c} - P_{l,c-lp} - P_{l-lp,c} + P_{l-lp,c-lp}$
13:     $result \leftarrow result + GetSumTriangularAreaRecursive(l, c - lp, lp - k, P)$
            $+ GetSumTriangularAreaRecursive(l - lp, c, lp - k, P))$
14:   **end if**
15:   **return** $result$
16: **end function**

If we gather together Eqs. 8 and 11 from the two cases above, we obtain Algorithm 2. The complexity of the recursive algorithm for determining the sum of the elements located inside the triangular area $\triangle_{l,c,k}$ (see Algorithm 2) is $\mathcal{O}(n)$ [5]. The strategy from this variant is similar to the rectangular decomposition from the paper of Bowman et al. [4].

3.4   A Geometrically Inspired Method

For the method described in this section, we will use the following matrices:

1. $P_{l,c}$ - the prefix sum of the cell with coordinates (l,c) (the sum of the elements located inside the area of the rectangle defined by its upper-left corner $(1,1)$ and by its bottom-right corner (l,c)).
2. $tl_{i,k}$ - the sum of the elements located inside the triangle $\triangle ABC$ defined by $A(i,1)$, $B(i,k)$ and $C(i+k-1,1)$.
3. $tr_{i,k}$ - the sum of the elements located inside the triangle $\triangle ABC$ defined by $A(i,n)$, $B(i-k+1,n)$ and $C(i,n-k+1)$.
4. $tu_{j,k}$ - the sum of the elements located inside the triangle $\triangle ABC$ defined by $A(1,j)$, $B(1,j+k-1)$ and $C(k,j)$.
5. $td_{j,k}$ - the sum of the elements located inside the triangle $\triangle ABC$ defined by $A(n,j)$, $B(n-k+1,j)$ and $C(n,j-k+1)$.

Each of the matrices Tl, Tr, Tu and Td represents one half of a square matrix. The total required memory space is $\sim 3 * n^2$ elements. If we precompute the values of the elements of the matrices P, Tl, Tr, Tu and Td then we will be able to efficiently determine the value of:

$$\sum_{\triangle_{l,c,k}} \overset{notation}{\equiv} \sum_{\forall(i,j)\in\triangle_{l,c,k}} a_{i,j}.$$

The elements of the matrix P can be computed such as:

$$P_{i,j} = P_{i,j-1} + P_{i-1,j} + a_{i,j} - P_{i-1,j-1}. \tag{14}$$

The elements of the Tl matrix can be determined using the following relation:

$$tl_{i-k+1,k} = tl_{i-k+2,k-1} + (P_{i-k+1,k} - P_{i-k,k}). \tag{15}$$

The values of the Tl array can be computed using the following fragment of algorithm:

```
1: for i ← n, 1 STEP − 1 do
2:     tl_{i,1} ← P_{i,1} − P_{i−1,1}
3:     for k ← 2, i do
4:         tl_{i−k+1,k} ← tl_{i−k+2,k−1} + (P_{i−k+1,k} − P_{i−k,k})
5:     end for
6: end for
```

The elements of the Tu matrix can be determined using the following formula:

$$tu_{j-k+1,k} = tu_{j-k+2,k-1} + (P_{k,j-k+1} - P_{k,j-k}) \tag{16}$$

The values of the Tu array can be computed with the following fragment of algorithm:

```
1: for j ← n, 1 STEP − 1 do
2:     tu_{j,1} ← P_{1,j} − P_{1,j−1}
3:     for k ← 2, j do
4:         tu_{j−k+1,k} ← tu_{j−k+2,k−1} + (P_{k,j−k+1} − P_{k,j−k})
5:     end for
6: end for
```

The elements of the matrix Tr can be computed using the formula:

$$tr_{i+k-1,k} = tr_{i+k-2,k-1} + ((P_{i+k-1,n} - P_{i+k-2,n}) - (P_{i+k-1,n-k} - P_{i+k-2,n-k})) \tag{17}$$

The values of the Tr array can be computed with the following fragment of algorithm:

```
1: for i ← 1, n do
2:     tr_{i,1} ← P_{i,n} − P_{i,n−1} − P_{i−1,n} + P_{i−1,n−1}
3:     for k ← 2, n − i + 1 do
4:         line1 ← P_{i+k−1,n} − P_{i+k−2,n}
5:         line2 ← P_{i+k−1,n−k} − P_{i+k−2,n−k}
6:         tr_{i+k−1,k} ← tr_{i+k−2,k−1} + (line1 − line2)
7:     end for
8: end for
```

The elements of the Td matrix can be determined using the following formula:

$$td_{j+k-1,k} = td_{j+k-2,k-1} + ((P_{n,j+k-1} - P_{n,j+k-2}) \\ - (P_{n-k,j+k-1} - P_{n-k,j+k-2})); \tag{18}$$

The values of the Td array can be computed with the following fragment of algorithm:

```
1: for j ← 1, n do
2:     td_{j,1} ← P_{n,j} − P_{n−1,j} − P_{n,j−1} + P_{n−1,j−1}
3:     for k ← 2, n − j + 1 do
4:         column1 ← P_{n,j+k−1} − P_{n,j+k−2}
5:         column2 ← P_{n−k,j+k−1} − P_{n−k,j+k−2}
6:         td_{j+k−1,k} ← td_{j+k−2,k−1} + (column1 − column2)
7:     end for
8: end for
```

For the triangular area $\triangle_{l,c,k}$, the sum of the elements inside that triangular area, $\sum_{\triangle_{l,c,k}}$, will be computed as follows:

a) *The cases for $k > 0$:*

   (1) *Case 1* corresponds to the situation where $l + c + k - 1 \leq n + 1$, i.e. all vertices of the triangle EFG ($\triangle EFG$) are situated above the secondary diagonal (as seen in Fig. 3(a)). The triangle EFG is an isosceles right triangle where E(1,c) is the vertex of the right angle and the legs EF and

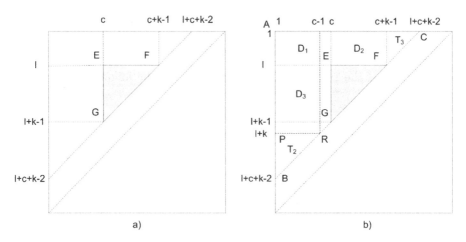

Fig. 3. Case 1: All vertices of a triangle lie above the secondary diagonal: a) configuration with a brief overview, b) detailed view of the same setup.

EG are parallel to the coordinate axes.

In this situation, we will proceed as follows: from the sum of the elements located inside of the triangular area ABC ($\triangle ABC$), determined by the vertices having the coordinates $A(1,1)$, $B(l + c + k - 2, 1)$ and $C(1, l + c + k - 2)$), we will subtract the sum of the elements located inside of the rectangular areas D_1, D_2, D_3 and the sum of the elements

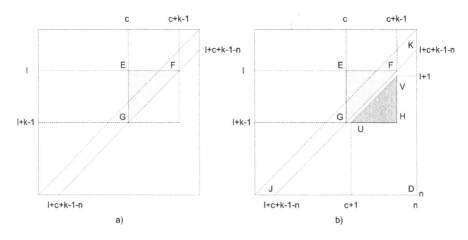

Fig. 4. Case 2: two vertices, F and G, that determine the hypotenuse of the triangle (which is parallel to the secondary diagonal), are positioned below the secondary diagonal: a) configuration with a brief overview, b) detailed view of the same configuration.

situated inside of the triangular areas T_2 and T_3 (see Fig. 3(b)).

$$\sum_{\triangle EFG} = \sum_{\triangle ABC} - \left(\sum_{\square D_1} + \sum_{\square D_2} + \sum_{\square D_3}\right)$$
$$- \left(\sum_{\triangle T_2} + \sum_{\triangle T_3}\right). \tag{19}$$

The sum of the elements located inside of the triangular area ABC ($\triangle ABC$) corresponds to the value of the element $tl_{1,l+c+k-2}$ (the sum of the elements located inside the triangular area described by the points of coordinates $(1,1)$, $(1, l+c+k-2)$ and $(l+c+k-2, 1)$).

$$\sum_{\triangle ABC} = tl_{1,l+c+k-2}. \tag{20}$$

The sum of the elements located inside the rectangular areas D_1, D_2, D_3 is calculated as follows: the sum of the elements located inside the rectangular area defined by its upper-left corner $(1,1)$ and also by its bottom-right corner $(l-1, c+k-1)$ plus the sum of the elements located inside the rectangular area defined by its upper-left corner $(1,1)$ and by its bottom-right corner $(l+k-1, c-1)$ from which is subtracted the sum of the elements located inside the rectangular area defined by its upper-left corner $(1,1)$ and also by its bottom-right corner $(l-1, c-1)$.

$$\sum_{\square D_1} + \sum_{\square D_2} + \sum_{\square D_3} = P_{l-1,c+k-1} + P_{l+k-1,c-1} - P_{l-1,c-1}. \tag{21}$$

The triangular area T_2 is determined by the triangle PRB ($\triangle PRB$) (the vertices of the triangle have coordinates $P(l+k, 1)$, $R(l+k, c-1)$ and $B(l+c+k-2, 1)$). The sum of the elements located inside this triangular area corresponds to the value of the element $tl_{l+k,c-1}$.

$$\sum_{\triangle T_2} = \sum_{\triangle PRB} = tl_{l+k,c-1}. \tag{22}$$

Similarly, the sum of the elements situated inside the triangular area T_3 corresponds to the value of the element $tu_{c+k,l-1}$.

$$\sum_{\triangle T_3} = tu_{c+k,l-1}. \tag{23}$$

By replacing Eqs. 20, 21, 22 and 23, into 19, we obtain:

$$\sum_{\triangle EFG} = tl_{1,l+c+k-2} - (P_{l-1,c+k-1} + P_{l+k-1,c-1} - P_{l-1,c-1})$$
$$- tl_{l+k,c-1} - tu_{c+k,l-1}. \tag{24}$$

(2) *Case* 2 corresponds to the situation where $l+c+k-1 > n+1$, i.e. that is the two vertices, F and G, that determine the hypotenuse of the triangle (which is parallel to the secondary diagonal), are positioned below the secondary diagonal (as seen in Fig. 4(a)).

To compute the sum of the elements from the triangular area EFG ($\triangle EFG$), we will proceed as follows: from the sum of the elements located inside the square area EFHG ($\square EFGH$) defined by its upper-left corner $E(l, c)$ and by its bottom-right corner $H(l + k - 1, c + k - 1)$ subtract the sum of the elements located inside the triangular area HVU ($\triangle HVU$) (see Fig. 4(b)).

$$\sum_{\triangle EFG} = \sum_{\square EFHG} - \sum_{\triangle HVU}. \tag{25}$$

The sum of the elements situated inside the square area EFHG ($\square EFHG$) can be determined as follows:

$$\sum_{\square EFHG} = P_{l+k-1,c+k-1} - P_{l-1,c+k-1} - P_{l+k-1,c-1} + P_{l-1,c-1}. \tag{26}$$

The sum of the elements located inside of the triangular area HVU ($\triangle HVU$) will be computed with the formulas obtained for *Case* 3 (the three vertices that determine the isosceles right triangle HVU have the coordinates $H(l + k - 1, c + k - 1)$, $V(l + 1, c + k - 1)$ and $U(l + k - 1, c + 1)$). In conclusion, the code that deals with the two mentioned situations (Case 1 and Case 2) is depicted in Algorithm 3.

Algorithm 3. The cases for $k > 0$

1: **function** GETSUMTRIANGULARAREAV3(l, c, k, n, P)
2:    **if** $(k > 0)$ **then**
3:       **if** $(l + c + k - 1 \leq n + 1)$ **then**   ▷ above secondary diagonal
4:          $result \leftarrow Tl_{1,l+c+k-2} - (P_{l-1,c+k-1} + P_{l+k-1,c-1} - P_{l-1,c-1})$
5:          **if** $(l + k \leq n)$ **then**
6:             $result \leftarrow result - Tl_{l+k,c-1}$
7:          **end if**
8:          **if** $(c + k \leq n)$ **then**
9:             $result \leftarrow result - Tu_{c+k,l-1}$
10:          **end if**
11:       **else**   ▷ below secondary diagonal
12:          $result \leftarrow GetSumTriangularAreaV3(l + k - 1, c + k - 1, -(k - 1), n)$
13:          $result \leftarrow P_{l+k-1,c+k-1} - P_{l-1,c+k-1} - P_{l+k-1,c-1} + P_{l-1,c-1} - result$
14:       **end if**
15:    **else**
16:       $\ldots$
17:    **end if**
18:    **return** $result$
19: **end function**

---

b) *The cases for $k < 0$:*

(3) *The 3rd case* corresponds to the situation where $l + c - k + 1 > n + 1$, i.e. all three vertices of the isosceles right triangle EFG ($\triangle EFG$) lie below the secondary diagonal (see Fig. 5).

(4) *The 4th case* corresponds to the situation where $l + c - k + 1 \le n + 1$ i.e. the two vertices, F and G, that determine the hypotenuse of the triangle, parallel to the secondary diagonal, are positioned above the secondary diagonal (see Fig. 6).

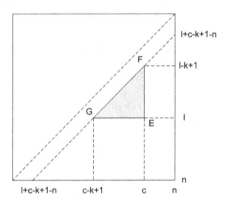

Fig. 5. Case 3: all three vertices of the isosceles right triangle EFG ($\triangle EFG$) lie below the secondary diagonal.

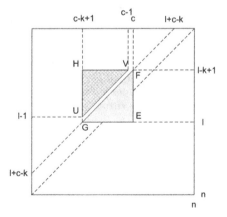

Fig. 6. Case 4: Two vertices, F and G, that determine the hypotenuse of the triangle are positioned above the secondary diagonal.

We can gather now all the formulas obtained for all four cases, and design Algorithm 4. The complexity of Algorithm 4 for determining the sum of the elements located inside the triangular area $\triangle_{l,c,k}$ is $\mathcal{O}(1)$.

Algorithm 4. Algorithm get sum of elements in triangular area - third version

---

1: **function** GETSUMRECTANGULARAREA(l, c, n)
2:    **if** $(l < 1) \vee (l > n) \vee (c < 1) \vee (c > n)$ **then**
3:        **return** 0
4:    **else**
5:        **return** $(P_{n,n} - P_{l-1,n} - P_{n,c-1} + P_{l-1,c-1})$
6:    **end if**
7: **end function**
8: **function** GETSUMTRIANGULARAREAV3(l, c, k, n)
9:    **if** $(k > 0)$ **then**
10:        **if** $(l + c + k - 1 \leq n + 1)$ **then**   ▷ above secondary diagonal
11:            $result \leftarrow P_{l-1,c+k-1} + P_{l+k-1,c-1} - P_{l-1,c-1}$
12:            $result \leftarrow Tl_{1,l+c+k-2} - result$
13:            **if** $(l + k \leq n)$ **then**
14:                $result \leftarrow result - Tl_{l+k,c-1}$
15:            **end if**
16:            **if** $(c + k \leq n)$ **then**
17:                $result \leftarrow result - Tu_{c+k,l-1}$
18:            **end if**
19:        **else**   ▷ below secondary diagonal
20:            $result \leftarrow GetSumTriangularAreaV3(l + k - 1, c + k - 1, -(k - 1), n)$
21:            $result \leftarrow P_{l+k-1,c+k-1} - P_{l-1,c+k-1} - P_{l+k-1,c-1} + P_{l-1,c-1} - result$
22:        **end if**
23:    **else**
24:        $k \leftarrow -k$
25:        **if** $(l + c - k + 1 \leq n + 1)$ **then**   ▷ above secondary diagonal
26:            $result \leftarrow GetSumTriangularAreaV3(l - k + 1, c - k + 1, k - 1, n)$
27:            $result \leftarrow P_{l,c} - P_{l-k,c} - P_{l,c-k} + P_{l-k,c-k} - result$
28:        **else**   ▷ below secondary diagonal
            $result \leftarrow \quad GetSumRectangularArea(l - k + 1, c + 1, n)$
29:                    $+ \ GetSumRectangularArea(l + 1, c - k + 1, n)$
                    $- \ GetSumRectangularArea(l + 1, c + 1, n)$
30:            $result \leftarrow Tr_{n,2*n-l-c+k} - result$
31:            **if** $(l - k > 0)$ **then**
32:                $result \leftarrow result - Tr_{l-k,n-c}$
33:            **end if**
34:            **if** $(c - k > 0)$ **then**
35:                $result \leftarrow result - Td_{c-k,n-l}$
36:            **end if**
37:        **end if**
38:    **end if**
39:    **return** $result$
40: **end function**

---

4   Conclusion

In this paper, we introduced three algorithms designed to sum values from triangular areas, specifically addressing range-sum queries that aggregate cell values within triangular shapes with specific properties: isosceles right triangles with legs parallel to the coordinate axes.

The last algorithm described has $O(1)$ time complexity and $O(n^2)$ space complexity, where n represents one dimension of the rectangular grid. It is noteworthy that the $O(1)$ time complexity of this algorithm is optimal. This is an improvement over previous methods, which typically required $O(n)$ time for similar queries. By reducing the time complexity to $O(1)$, we obtain an efficient solution for real-time applications, albeit at the cost of increased space complexity. This trade-off between time and space complexity highlights a common axiom in the optimization of computational resources.

Acknowledgment. The work of M. Cosulschi and M. Gabroveanu have been supported by a grant of the Romanian Ministry of Research, Innovation and Digitalization (MCID), project number 22 - Nonlinear Differential Systems in Applied Sciences, within PNRR-III-C9-2022-I8.

References

1. An, S., Peursum, P., Liu, W., Venkatesh, S.: Efficient algorithms for subwindow search in object detection and localization. In: Proceedings of the IEEE Conference on Computer Vision and Pattern Recognition (CVPR), pp. 264–271 (2009)
2. Bay, H., Ess, A., Tuytelaars, T., Van Gool, L.: Speeded-up robust features (SURF). Comput. Vis. Image Underst. **110**(3), 346–359 (2008)
3. Bodnár, P., Nyúl, L.G.: Improved QR code localization using boosted cascade of weak classifiers. Acta Cybernet. **22**(1), 21–33 (2015)
4. Bowman, J.C., Ghoggali, Z.: The partial fast fourier transform. J. Sci. Comput. **76**(3), 1578–1593 (2018)
5. Cormen, T.H., Leiserson, C.E., Rivest, R.L., Stein, C.: Introduction to Algorithms, 4th edn., The MIT Press (2022)
6. Crow, F.: Summed-area tables for texture mapping. Comput. Graph. **18**(3), 207–212 (1984)
7. Facciolo, G., Limare, N., Meinhardt-Llopis, E.: Integral images for block matching. Image Process. Line **4**, 344–369 (2014)
8. Geffner, S., Agrawal, D., El Abbadi, A., Smith, T.: Relative prefix sums: an efficient approach for querying dynamic OLAP data cubes. In: Proceedings of the 15th International Conference on Data Engineering (ICDE), pp. 328–335 (1999)
9. Goodrich, M.T., Tamassia, R.: Algorithm Design: Foundation, Analysis, and Internet Examples. Wiley (2002)
10. Ho, C., Agrawal, R., Megiddo, N., Srikant, R.: Range queries in OLAP data cubes. In: Proceedings of the ACM International Conference on Management of Data (SIGMOD), pp. 73–88 (1997)
11. Hensley, J., Scheuermann, T., Coombe, G., Singh, M., Lastra, A.: Fast summed-area table generation and its applications. Comput. Graph. Forum **24**(3), 547–555 (2005)

12. Lewis, J.P.: Fast template matching. Vis. Interface **95**, 120–123 (1995)
13. Nguyen, T.-T., Nguyen, T.T.: A real time license plate detection system based on boosting learning algorithm. In: Proceedings of the 5th International Congress on Image and Signal Processing (CISP), pp. 819–823 (2012)
14. Schmidt, M.R., Barcons-Simon, A., Rabuffo, C., Siegel, T.N.: Smoother: on-the-fly processing of interactome data using prefix sums. Nucleic Acids Res. **52**, e23 (2024)
15. Shekelyan, M., Dignös, A., Gamper, J.: Sparse prefix sums: constant-time range sum queries over sparse multidimensional data cubes. Inf. Syst. **82**, 136–147 (2019)
16. Szeliski, R.: Summed area table (integral image). In: Computer vision: algorithms and applications, pp. 106–107. Texts in Computer Science, Springer (2010). https://doi.org/10.1007/978-3-030-34372-9
17. Takaoka, T.: Efficient algorithms for the maximum subarray problem by distance matrix multiplication. In: Proceedings of Computing: the Australasian Theory Symposium (CATS), pp. 191–200 (2002)
18. Viola, P., Jones, M.: Rapid object detection using a boosted cascade of simple features, In: Proceedings of the IEEE Conference on Computer Vision and Pattern Recognition (CVPR), pp. 511–518 (2001)
19. Xu, H., Fraser, S., Leiserson, C. E.: Multidimensional Included and Excluded Sums. In: Proceedings of the SIAM Conference on Applied and Computational Discrete Algorithms (ACDA), pp. 182–192 (2021)

Microservice-Based Distributed Application for Unifying Social Networks

Theodor Stanica, Mirel Cosulschi$^{(\boxtimes)}$, Marian Cristian Mihaescu, and Florin Slabu

University of Craiova, Craiova, Romania
stanica.theodor.q3z@student.ucv.ro, mirelc@central.ucv.ro,
cristian.mihaescu@edu.ucv.ro, florin.slabu@inf.ucv.ro

Abstract. This paper presents a microservices-based distributed application designed to unify accounts management from various social networks. This application improves performance, functionality and user experience, marking a significant advance in online social networking technology. Built on a microservices architecture, the application includes noteworthy features such as a GPT 3.5-based campaign assistant designed to help users create engaging content, machine learning modules for sentiment analysis, and text summarization for posts displayed on the dashboard.

Keywords: Microservices architecture · social media · text summarization

1 Introduction

This paper describes an application to ease the burden on users who manage multiple social media accounts simultaneously. It aims to simplify and optimize managing social media accounts by providing an intuitive interface and advanced tools for interacting with different social media platforms. Another aspect pursued is the desire to significantly improve content planning and creation, sentiment analysis and text summarization, thus contributing to the effectiveness of online marketing and communication strategies.

One of the main goals is to simplify managing social media accounts by eliminating the need for users to access and switch between multiple applications or websites. This platform allows users to connect and manage multiple Twitter and Facebook accounts and benefit from a unified and intuitive interface to access and interact with their content.

The application also aims to improve user experience by providing advanced functionality. These include an integrated scheduler that allows users to schedule and organize posts in advance, facilitating strategic and effective content management. By integrating a campaign assistant supervised by GPT 3.5, users are supported in creating new and attractive content tailored to their needs and preferences.

C. Bădică et al. (Eds.): BCI 2024, CCIS 2391, pp. 77–88, 2025.
https://doi.org/10.1007/978-3-031-84093-7_6

Consequently, the application aims to provide a comprehensive and efficient solution for managing social media accounts, integrating advanced functionalities and simplifying the administration process. The application represents an evolution in online social networking technology, helping to optimize marketing and communication activities in the digital environment.

2   Sentiment Analysis

Sentiment analysis is critical for understanding and interpreting user-generated content's emotions, perspectives, and attitudes. Its purpose is to extract useful information from text data, enabling businesses and organizations to gauge audience sentiment, customer satisfaction, and brand perception. By analyzing the sentiment behind social media posts, customer reviews, or online discussions, businesses can make data-driven decisions, improve customer experiences, and adapt their marketing strategies.

This field has evolved significantly over the last few years, with various approaches being developed to improve the accuracy and efficiency of sentiment classification. These range from deep learning approaches (Convolutional Neural Networks - CNNs, Recurrent Neural Networks - RNNs, Bidirectional LSTMs - BiLSTMs) to transformer-based approaches (Bidirectional Encoder Representations from Transformers - BERT [2,4], Generative Pre-trained Transformer - GPT, RoBERTa, DistilBERT), to mention the latest trends [1,8].

2.1   Model and Data Set

The application used a sentiment analysis machine learning model called LSTM. This model is the basis for understanding and classifying the sentiment represented in text data. During the implementation process, we made changes and improvements to the reference model to adjust and better fit the application requirements and increase its performance.

Long Short-Term Memory (LSTM) networks, a form of Recurrent Neural Network (RNN), were introduced by Hochreiter and Schmidhuber to address the limitations of traditional RNNs in handling long-term dependencies [7]. Then, researchers used LSTM networks to classify the sentiment of text based on the context provided by sequences of words. The ability of LSTMs to remember the previous words in the sequence helped to understand the sentiment of the entire sentence or document [18].

The model used in our application excels at capturing the sequential relationships prevalent in text input data. By examining contextual information and connections between words, LSTM can identify patterns and extract relevant features contributing to sentiment classification.

The Sentiment140 dataset [11] was used to train the sentiment analysis machine learning model. This dataset contains 1.6 million tweets extracted via the Twitter API[1]. Each tweet in the dataset was manually labelled with a polarity label, indicating whether the sentiment is negative, neutral, or positive, [5].

---

[1] https://developer.twitter.com/en/products/twitter-api.

Several essential actions were performed during the data processing phase of the sentiment analysis model to prepare the text data for analysis. Procedures involved include stemming/lemmatization and deletion of hyperlinks and references.

2.2 Training the Model

During the training phase, the dataset was split into two sets: 80% for training the model and 20% for testing its performance. This method allows the model to learn from a large amount of data while independently assessing its accuracy on unseen text samples.

The model can capture and understand the contextual relationships between words in the text by leveraging the performance of LSTM, which allows it to make accurate predictions about sentiment.

The stopword removal step was excepted from the data processing procedure to improve model performance. By keeping stop words in the text, the model can consider the presence of negations and other important linguistic cues, leading to more accurate sentiment predictions. This change aims to capture nuanced differences in sentiment that removing stop words may obscure. After this modification, the model's performance increased from 78% to 82%, i.e. by 4%.

3 Text Summarization

Text summarization focuses on creating concise and coherent summaries of longer texts and is essential for managing and understanding large volumes of text data. The task of text summarization can be approached in two ways: extractive summarization and abstractive summarization [10,13].

For text summarization, the Pegasus-Xsum model from Google was chosen. Pegasus (Pre-training with Extracted Gap-sentences for Abstractive Summarization) is an abstractive summarization model developed by Google Research [12,20].

XSum is a dataset for summarization tasks that contains 227, 000 BBC news articles paired with single-sentence summaries. Pegasus-XSum is a version of the Pegasus model, explicitly built for abstract text summarization tasks, trained on a vast news corpus - the XSum (Extreme Summarization) dataset, that generates concise, single-sentence summaries from BBC news articles. Pegasus-XSum uses the Transformer architecture designed explicitly for sequence-to-sequence tasks like text summarization.

The pre-trained Pegasus-Xsum model was obtained from HuggingFace's model registry[2]. This model has extensive proficiency and understanding in generating succinct and helpful summaries from text input. Using a pre-trained model saves time and computational resources that would otherwise have been required to build a model from scratch.

The text summarization microservice can create accurate and coherent summaries for various text documents.

---

[2] https://huggingface.co/google/pegasus-xsum.

3.1   GPT 3.x

GPT-3 (Generative Pre-trained Transformer) [15,19] is a third-generation autoregressive language model that uses deep learning to produce human-like text. Or, more simply, it is a computational system designed to generate sequences of words, codes, or other data from an input source called a prompt. It is used, for example, in machine translation to predict sequences of words statistically. The language model is trained on an unlabeled dataset consisting of texts. Substantial advances in GPT-3 have catapulted autoregressive language models to new horizons. Using deep learning, the model can create writing that closely mimics human language.

4   Application Description

The application aims to provide users with an advanced and centralized platform to manage multiple social media accounts from one place efficiently. This approach is intended to significantly improve how users interact and manage their accounts on different social media platforms.

The social media management application is a modern software-as-a-service (SaaS) [3] solution designed to simplify and improve the management of personal Twitter and Facebook accounts. The application links and manages social media user profiles from a centralized platform, providing a simplified experience for posting messages and setting up message streams with specific search criteria.

The implementation contains a complete set of capabilities designed to facilitate individual users' administration of social media accounts. Compatible with Twitter and Facebook accounts, offering an intuitive system for posting messages through a scheduler and integrating machine learning models, the application enables users to engage their audience effectively, streamline their marketing strategy content and achieve their social media goals. It offers a powerful solution for improving users' social media presence and generating meaningful interactions on Twitter and Facebook, whether engaging with followers, measuring engagement or optimizing content.

4.1   Application Architecture

Microservices-based architecture [14] is used to build the application. Microservices are distributed and loosely coupled architectural structures that ensure that changes made by one team do not disrupt the entire program.

A microservices-based architecture differs from typical monolithic techniques in breaking a program into its main functionalities [16]. Each feature is known as a service and can be designed and implemented individually, allowing each service to function independently. Because it provides flexibility and scalability, this modular approach is suitable for an application that aims to improve its range of services offered and increase the number of users.

One of the most critical considerations when implementing microservices is the range of technologies and platforms involved in development. Centralized-based administration approaches are not appropriate in these circumstances. Microservices design emphasizes decentralized data management compared to monolithic systems that rely on a single database. Each service in a microservices-based application typically has its database.

Docker containers[3] and Kubernetes orchestration[4] are used to develop and deploy microservices within the platform. This strategy ensures scalability, adaptability, and efficient management of platform components.

Docker containers are essential for packaging microservices. Each microservice is contained in its container, resulting in an isolated, lightweight environment with all the necessary dependencies and parameters. This containerization enables easy portability and uniform deployment across environments, allowing microservices to be deployed across various infrastructure configurations.

Kubernetes is used to orchestrate and manage the deployment of microservices. Kubernetes simplifies the deployment, scaling, and management of containerized applications. It lays the foundation for running and managing numerous containers on a server cluster, ensuring high availability and fault tolerance.

Kubernetes configuration YAML files are used to deploy microservices. These files specify the desired state of the microservices, detailing aspects such as the number of replicas, resource allocation, networking, and service discovery. By using these parameters, Kubernetes effectively manages microservices' deployment, scaling, and load balancing.

4.2 APIs Refactorization

The platform's APIs, the result of several iterations of refactoring, have been significantly improved to increase maintainability, scalability, and code structure. The main goal was to establish a layered architecture and introduce a clear separation of duties, thereby increasing the modularity and ease of the source code testing process.

Segregation of tasks for taking requests, processing data and connecting to databases was pursued.

The application presents a layered architecture [17], following the separation on several levels, each with its own set of responsibilities and functionalities:

- *The routes/controllers layer* processes incoming requests and serves as the entry point to the API. Its primary task is to evaluate request parameters, authenticate users as appropriate, and forward requests to the relevant service level.
- *The service layer* connects the routes/controllers with the databases. It includes the application's business logic and is responsible for processing the data from the routes, implementing the business rules and organizing the interactions between the different components.

---

[3] https://www.docker.com/resources/what-container/.
[4] https://kubernetes.io/docs/concepts/overview/.

- *Repository layer*: data access and persistence logic is included in this layer. Its responsibility is communicating with the database or other external data sources, getting and storing data, and providing an interface for services to perform CRUD (create, read, update, delete) actions.

Data Transfer Objects (DTOs) were created to ensure data integrity and layer decoupling. DTOs are used to pass data in a standardized manner between layers. They specify the structure of the transmitted data, making validation and transformation possible. DTOs contribute to the coherence of layers by acting as a contract between them[5].

Separating the software into different layers makes it more modular and easier to test. Each layer can be evaluated individually, allowing detection and isolation of potential problems. In addition, the layered design contributes to the foundation for scalability. As the system expands, new features and capabilities can be introduced into the appropriate layer without affecting the overall source.

4.3   Scalability, Monitoring and Resource Management Features

The project infrastructure was designed to increase scalability, monitoring capabilities and resource management. Horizontal pod autoscaling (HPA), resource allocation for Kubernetes objects in YAML configuration files, connection monitoring with Grafana and Prometheus, and using express-prom-bundle to export data to Prometheus are among the significant infrastructure improvements implemented in this platform.

1. Horizontal pod autoscaling (HPA): except for the machine learning service, HPA has been implemented to maximize resource utilization and ensure responsiveness during periods of high demand. HPA automatically changes the number of operational pods based on parameters such as CPU utilization or request traffic. This ability to scale dynamically allows the project to cope with changing workloads while maintaining a smooth user experience.
2. Resource assignment in YAML configuration files: to precisely manage resource allocation for Kubernetes objects, resource assignment has been introduced in YAML configuration files. The project optimizes resource usage and eliminates resource contention between different components. This allows for improved resource allocation, application performance and stability.
3. Grafana and Prometheus Monitoring: Grafana and Prometheus, two sophisticated monitoring technologies [9], have been added to the infrastructure to enable extensive insight into system health and performance. Prometheus[6] captures and saves time series data, while Grafana[7] visualizes critical metrics and performance indicators. This interface provides real-time monitoring, trend analysis, and troubleshooting, allowing the development team to anticipate and manage future difficulties [6].

---

[5] https://martinfowler.com/eaaCatalog/dataTransferObject.html.

[6] https://prometheus.io/docs/introduction/overview/.

[7] https://grafana.com/.

4. Express-prom-bundle[8]: The express-prom-bundle middleware has been made available to export essential data from the project's Express-based services to Prometheus. This middleware automatically collects and exposes metrics to Prometheus for monitoring and analysis, such as the number of requests, response times, and error rates. This connection facilitates the collection of vital performance data and provides additional insights and improvements.

A Secrets[9] YAML file was also generated as part of infrastructure management to help load environment variables smoothly into the Kubernetes cluster. This file enables secure and efficient management of sensitive information such as API keys, database credentials, and other configuration settings.

5   Machine Learning Modules

The application includes a machine learning microservice that has changed content generation and analysis capabilities. This application functionality has three main features: sentiment analysis, text summarization using Google's PEGASUS transformer model and a virtual assistant powered by GPT 3.5. These functionalities give users additional options for optimizing their content strategy and obtaining valuable information.

1. Sentiment analysis is a machine learning microservice that enables users to identify the emotional tone and sentiment behind textual information. With the help of algorithms, the microservice can automatically evaluate the content and classify it as positive or negative. This tool gives clients a complete view of how their target audience views their content, allowing them to make data-driven decisions and optimize their content.
2. The microservice uses Google's PEGASUS state-of-the-art transformer paradigm for text summarization. This advanced technique can generate concise and easy-to-understand summaries of extensive textual content. By harnessing the power of machine learning, users can quickly get a brief and informative overview of articles or any other textual content. This feature allows users to absorb the material more efficiently and extract crucial information, saving time and effort while viewing the content.
3. The microservice contains a virtual assistant based on the GPT 3.5-turbo model that drives content creation to a high level of productivity. Users can give instructions to the virtual assistant, and it will respond with coherent and context-appropriate material. This feature allows users to overcome writer's block, boost creativity and speed up the content creation process.

6   Client Interface

The client application's user interface is built to provide a pleasant and attractive user experience. It combines cutting-edge technology and design concepts to

---

[8] https://www.npmjs.com/package/express-prom-bundle.
[9] https://kubernetes.io/docs/concepts/configuration/secret/.

increase performance, scalability and maintainability. The client application was developed entirely in Typescript[10]. The main dashboard of the application can be seen in Fig. 1.

Fig. 1. The main dashboard

The use of Material UI (MUI) components[11] provided a modern interface that led to a smoother user experience.

Typescript's simple and predictable interfaces allowed for more efficient communication and better code readability. Users can expect a sleek, responsive user interface, good functionality, and seamless experience.

6.1   Client Architecture

The client application is built with various modern technologies and adopts a solid architectural approach, resulting in a stable and efficient user experience.

The front-end development of the client application is mainly done with React[12], which allows the building of reusable components.

To develop a visually appealing and responsive design, the client's application uses Material UI (MUI), a UI component framework composed of a multitude of predefined components and themes to provide consistency and usability across multiple screens and devices. This technology selection simplifies the development process while improving the overall user interface.

---

[10] https://www.typescriptlang.org/.
[11] https://mui.com/material-ui/.
[12] https://react.dev/.

Redux[13] is used in the application to manage the global application state and promote a smooth data flow between components.

The client application uses the Redux Toolkit (RTK), tools and abstractions to facilitate Redux development. RTK Query[14] handles data retrieval and storage, eliminating the hassle of manually interacting with the API. This guarantees that data is fetched and synchronized between the client application and the server as quickly as possible.

Apart from RTK Query, Slices[15] is used by the client application to perform authentication-related operations. Slices define how authentication keys and their associated state are saved and managed within the application[16].

7   The Social Microservice

Social Microservices are essential for seamless application integration and interaction with major social media sites like Twitter and Facebook. They link the application and social networks, allowing secure and fast access to user accounts.

The Social Microservice, in addition to bridging social networks, connects with the OpenAI API[17] to provide sophisticated content creation tools. Although the OpenAI API is not used for text summarization or sentiment analysis in this context, it powers the virtual assistant feature that improves the user experience during content generation. The Social Microservice powered by OpenAI provides intelligent ideas, content suggestions and other valuable tools to help users generate engaging and effective social media posts.

Users can use the virtual assistant to sketch out content ideas, and the AI-powered model will create recommendations and finalize the material in a natural language format. This feature saves users time and effort by providing quick content inspiration and helps develop compelling social media posts.

The Assistant service communicates between the platform and the OpenAI API. Setting up and using the service is seamless. An OpenAI API access key (`OPENAI_API_KEY`) is necessary for service configuration. To use `GPT3.5-turbo`, we need to call a built-in method with parameters that specify the model as "gpt-3.5-turbo-0301" and the query (see Fig. 2).

---

[13] https://redux.js.org/.

[14] https://redux-toolkit.js.org/rtk-query/overview.

[15] https://www.slices-ri.eu/.

[16] https://learn.microsoft.com/en-us/previous-versions/windows/desktop/dd565670(v=vs.85).

[17] https://openai.com/index/openai-api/.

```
7    @Service()
8    export class AssistantService {
9      private _chatGPT: OpenAIApi;
10
11     constructor() {
12       const configuration = new Configuration({
13         apiKey: process.env.OPENAI_API_KEY!,
14       });
15       this._chatGPT = new OpenAIApi(configuration);
16     }
17
18     async ask(message: string) {
19       const result = await this._chatGPT.createChatCompletion({
20         model: 'gpt-3.5-turbo-0301',
21         messages: [{ role: 'user', content: message }],
22       });
23       return {
24         message: result.data.choices[0].message?.content,
25       };
26     }
27
28     async suggestPosts(data: BuildPlannerMessageDto) {
29       const message = buildAssistantPostPlannerMessage(data);
30       const result = await this.ask(message);
31
```

Fig. 2. A code snippet from the virtual assistant implementation.

8   ML Microservice

The ML microservice is an application component that uses machine learning to provide sentiment analysis and text summarization capabilities. By including such models, this microservice improves text processing and analysis, gaining important insights and greater productivity.

The sentiment analysis model provided with the ML microservice automatically interprets sentiment in text data. Using natural language processing techniques, the model can identify text as positive or negative, enabling sentiment-based analysis and decision-making. This capability is handy for evaluating customer feedback, monitoring social media sentiment, and determining general sentiment on specific topics.

In addition to sentiment analysis, the ML microservice provides a text summarization model. This strategy aims to reduce large texts into concise summaries while retaining vital information and main themes. By creating shortened versions of textual materials, the text summarization model increases the efficiency of information consumption, making it more straightforward to understand the substance of long texts and quickly extract essential information.

9   Conclusions and Future Work

The work presented in this paper simplifies the process of managing social media accounts by eliminating the need for users to access and switch between multiple applications or websites. Through this platform, users can connect and manage various social media accounts, benefiting from a unified and intuitive interface to access and interact with their content.

Users can get insights into audience sentiment, quickly summarize massive amounts of textual material, and use an intelligent virtual assistant to generate new ideas. This powerful combination allows users to fine-tune their content strategy, increase engagement, and develop engaging and compelling content relevant to their target audience.

In the future, we intend to replace the LSTM model with a hybrid model that can combine the strengths of various approaches so that the application achieves better performance and robustness in sentiment classification tasks. Additionally, we will implement the BART model for text summarization alongside the existing PEGASUS-XSum to obtain better performance.

References

1. Birjali, M., Kasri, M., Beni Hssane, A.: A comprehensive survey on sentiment analysis: approaches, challenges and trends. Knowl. Based Syst. **226**(05), 107–134 (2021)
2. Devlin, J., Chang, M.-W., Lee, K., Toutanova, K.: BERT: pre-training of deep bidirectional transformers for language understanding, In: Proceedings of the Conference of the North American Chapter of the Association for Computational Linguistics: Human Language Technologies (NAACL-HLT), Volume 1, pp. 4171-4186, 2019
3. Fox, A., Patterson, D.: Engineering Software as a Service: An Agile Approach Using Cloud Computing, 2nd edn. Pogo Press (2020)
4. Gao, Z., Feng, A., Song, X., Wu, X.: Target-dependent sentiment classification with BERT. IEEE Access **7**, 154290–154299 (2019)
5. Go, A., Bhayani, R., Huang, L.: Twitter sentiment classification using distant supervision. In: Processing, pp. 1–6 (2009)
6. Ödegaard, T.: The (mostly) complete history of grafana UX (2019). https://grafana.com/blog/2019/09/03/the-mostly-complete-history-of-grafana-ux/
7. Hochreiter, S., Schmidhuber, J.: Long short-term memory. Neural Comput. **9**(8), 1735–1780 (1997)
8. Jamshidi, S., Mohammadi, M., et al.: Effective text classification using BERT. MTM LSTM, and DT, Data Knowl. Eng. **151**, 102306 (2024)
9. Jones, A.: Open source monitoring stack: prometheus and Grafana, Bizety (2019). https://www.bizety.com/2019/01/25/open-source-monitoring-stack-prometheus-and-grafana/
10. El-Kassas, W.S., Salama, C.R., Rafea, A.A., Mohamed, H.K.: Automatic text summarization: a comprehensive survey. Expert Syst. Appl. **165**, 113679 (2021)
11. Kazanov, M.: Sentiment140 dataset with 1.6 million tweets (2017). https://www.kaggle.com/datasets/kazanova/sentiment140

12. Liu, P., Zhao, Y.: PEGASUS: a state-of-the-art model for abstractive text summarization (2020). https://research.google/blog/pegasus-a-state-of-the-art-model-for-abstractive-text-summarization/
13. Nenkova, A., McKeown, K.: A survey of text summarization techniques. In: Aggarwal C., Zhai C. (eds) Mining Text Data, pp. 43–76. Springer, Boston (2012). https://doi.org/10.1007/978-1-4614-3223-4_3
14. Newman, S.: Building Microservices: Designing Fine-Grained Systems, 2nd edn. O'Reilly Media (2021)
15. OpenAI's Guide to GPT Models. https://platform.openai.com/docs/guides/gpt
16. Richardson, C.: Microservices Patterns: With Examples in Java, Manning (2018)
17. Richards, M.: Software Architecture Patterns, 2nd edn. O'Reilly Media (2022)
18. Tai, K.S., Socher, R., Manning, C. D.: Improved semantic representations from tree-structured long short-term memory networks, in Proceedings of the 53rd Annual Meeting of the Association for Computational Linguistics and the 7th International Joint Conference on Natural Language Processing (Vol 1: Long Papers), pp. 1556–1566 (2015)
19. Yenduri, G., et al.: GPT (Generative pre-trained transformer)- A comprehensive review on enabling technologies, potential applications, emerging challenges, and future directions. IEEE Access **12**, 54608–54649 (2024)
20. Zhang, J., Zhao, Y., Saleh, M., Liu, P.: PEGASUS: Pre-training with extracted gap-sentences for abstractive summarization. In: Proceedings of the 37th International Conference on Machine Learning (ICML), pp. 11328–11339 (2020)

Languages and Text

Towards an Ontology for Describing the Contextualization of Written Cultural Heritage in the Light of Semiotics

Dimitra Sarakatsianou(✉) ⓘ and Georgia Koloniari ⓘ

Applied Informatics Department, University of Macedonia, Thessaloniki, Greece
{dsarakatsianou,gkoloniari}@uom.edu.gr

Abstract. Semiotics of culture is a valuable consideration, as it illuminates indiscernible aspects associated with social practices and processes of signification. Against this background, the goal of this paper is to delineate the *cultural and social (contextual) dimensions* of written cultural heritage from a semiotic point of view. Hence, an ontology defining a light vocabulary of *high-level concepts* is developed to describe these contextual dimensions. The proposed ontology, called *Onto-Semiotics DCT (Describing the Contextualization of Text)*, is essentially a general theoretical conceptual model based on the semantic idea that a text penetrates into a communication circuit. This perspective makes a clear distinction between *intra-textual* and *extra-textual semiotic context*, as well as *cultural micro-situation* and *social macro-situation*. However, in this paper, we focus on the description of the situations that refer to the social and cultural dimensions of a text. Thus, context-aware information representation is applied. This description is crucial for the correct analysis and interpretation of texts, as according to a prevailing semiotic position, texts are influenced by the environment that produces them. As a result, knowing and recording their context reinforces text semantics, through the methodological transition from logo-centrism to culture-centrism, and even further to socio-centrism.

Keywords: Context · Cultural Situation · Knowledge Representation · Ontology Modeling · Semiotics · Social Situation · Written Cultural Heritage

1 Introduction

A computational ontology aims at documenting a domain of discourse since it is a strict delimited conceptual representation, which maps out the concepts and relationships that capture a domain of knowledge [14]. As this artifact describes possible worlds through a set of terms and relations that convey some meaning, it sets the basis for creating computational cognition [13] usable by machines. In addition, going one step further, it supports reasoning for drawing conclusions [11, 30]. The recognition of the importance of these systems is expressed through many and varied studies we encounter in recent literature. For example, a related study [25] emphasizes the importance of formal ontologies over traditional knowledge organization systems, notably in the field

© The Author(s), under exclusive license to Springer Nature Switzerland AG 2025
C. Bădică et al. (Eds.): BCI 2024, CCIS 2391, pp. 91–104, 2025.
https://doi.org/10.1007/978-3-031-84093-7_7

of cultural heritage, in view of the fact that these Semantic Web technologies enhance common understanding and interoperability. Indeed, one of the current research trends in both computer science and other fields is the study of ontologies, and this interest is expressed in practice by their use in a wide scale of applications and in numerous fields; one such field is that of cultural heritage [3, 26–28].

In this setting, a widespread approach is the utilization of ontology-based annotations [8, 9]. This feature is singularly beneficial if one wants to use the vocabulary of an ontology and annotate cultural objects such as historical documents. In general, it can be said that ontologies are helpful tools for understanding and describing the world, which can help scientists in several ways. Thus, the vocabulary of an ontology or a conceptual model may, among other things, be used to clarify descriptions of cultural resources or materials—in our case, for *written texts* (henceforth, *texts*) of cultural heritage—to facilitate access to them, as well as information retrieval from them. At a second level, the retrieved information can be further exploited to interpret such cultural texts.

Let us not forget that culture is both a system of significance and a *system of cultural values* [19]. Thus, from a semiotic point of view, all cultural products are treated as *texts* [20], that is, as carriers of significance, which can be studied through suitable analysis tools. In other words, a *semiotic text* can be anything that is a vehicle of meaning such as works of art, music, cultural practices and values, written texts, audio-visual texts, and so on.

Based on the above, an attempt is made here to model the basic elements that can semantically enrich the cultural and social contextual dimensions of texts, following a semiotic perspective. Semiotics is the study of signs and their signification, and it focuses on how meaning is created and communicated. In this light, the cultural and social contextual dimensions of texts include the extra-textual environment of a text that contributes to its interpretation, as a text, according to a prevailing semiotic view, is born in a specific cultural and social environment that directly or indirectly influences its meaning.

In other words, cultural and social situations, that is the extra-textual environment of a text (as it is also called) point to the idea that a text does not exist separately but is closely connected to the culture and society in which it is born. Therefore, these elements help to decode the meaning of a text through the reconstruction of its production setting. In this way, for instance, a basic problem related to the information gap that exists between the author and the (contemporary) reader of a text is bridged. In practice, this means that, as long as texts are annotated with metadata that describe the conditions of creation of a text (that is, the factors related to the socio-economic, political-institutional, and ideological situation of the time they were produced), researchers of humanities and social sciences are equipped with a valuable range of information that enhances the task of understanding and interpreting the texts they study. This is a significant advantage not only for researchers but also for intelligent machines that have the ability to reason and infer.

As a consequence, it is worth emphasizing the *cultural and social situations* of a text, because non-textual dimensions are rarely examined systematically, and are only sporadically incorporated into ontologies. On the other hand, the textual dimensions of a text, which in semiotics are called *semiotic context* (also known by the narrower term, linguistic context), are long-known and utilized in many ontologies. However, the cultural and social situations are becoming more and more interesting, as they include many factors. Thus, if we want machines to become even smarter, that is, to perform good reasoning, it is important to incorporate the factors of these situations into their knowledge base.

To this end, we propose a general-conceptual model, expressed as an ontology that describes the contextual dimensions of a text (with an emphasis on cultural and social situations). Protégé[1], an open-source ontology editor that supports the OWL 2 Web Ontology Language [29, 32], was used for ontological modeling. Currently, the proposed ontology provides a light vocabulary for expressing the terms describing the contextualization of texts. This means that the ontology defines basic descriptive terms, without providing an exhaustive set of terms, so that it can be extended according to the intended application. The design of this model is based on a semiotic perspective on the concept of contextualization [19] (or in simple terms, *context*), which presupposes the penetration of the text within a communication circuit. This vocabulary can be used to annotate cultural texts, greatly enhancing, as already mentioned, the work of researchers and intelligent machines, substantially facilitating the tasks of access, information retrieval and even interpretation of texts.

To the best of our knowledge, this is the first attempt at defining a formal mod of the factors of contextualization of texts based on a semiotic perspective. Various ontologies have been proposed or developed that are related to the description of cultural heritage resources [1, 24]. Several of them incorporate elements related to the contextualization of these resources. For example, in an ontology that models elements of historical research documents, there is an entity for the description of historical events [1] (that is, in semiotic terms, it describes parts of a historical situation). Also, in another ontology that models cultural heritage resources, some entities describe the time dimension of an event (e.g., historical periods, date), which concerns its temporal conceptual dimension [24]. The general sense that such works emit is that they model specific aspects of contextualization that meet the needs of some application context. Therefore all such works provide a partial description of the contextualization of cultural heritage resources and not a complete description as our proposed model attempts. By incorporating all related information, our ontology can be considered as general-purpose, thus, improving its usability. Furthermore, its extensible properties make its specialization possible when needed, while ensuring interoperability.

The rest of the paper is structured as follows. Section 2 includes a brief introduction to the field of semiotics, with an emphasis on the semiotics of cultural products, as well as the theory of the contextualization of text in light of semiotics. Section 3 presents the proposed ontological model, and finally, Sect. 4 offers conclusions.

---

[1] https://protege.stanford.edu

2 Semiotics, Culture, and Text

2.1 The Semiotics of Cultural Products

Ideas, behaviors, practices, material constructs, written texts, discourses, and many other human creations are well-known products of culture. The semiotic approach to culture is related to a logic that sees the dependence of one (material or mental) thing on a particular culture or its distance from another. In different terms, cultural semiotics emphasizes social practices and *activities of signification* [20]. For example, to satisfy the social practice of road traffic, in a specific society and/or culture, the red color of the traffic lights is chosen to indicate the word 'stop'. This fact, that a material element of society (red color) has been used as a symbol to satisfy the need of a social practice, is an act of signification. Of course, the red color in another culture can symbolize something completely different.

Therefore, it becomes obvious that the conceptual description of any cultural construction is sterile if it does not include information connected to the factors that have somehow influenced the formation of this construction. Such factors may be linguistic, cultural, social, geographical, communicative, etc. Indeed, one key challenge in the representation of knowledge is to model both its linguistic and socio-cultural contextualization [4, 5], a challenge with a two-fold meaning, as modeling the contextual dimensions of an ontology helps, on the one hand, in further describing, understanding, analyzing, and interpreting a knowledge domain, and on the other hand, in the processes of merging and aligning the knowledge contained in one ontology with the knowledge of other ontologies.

This general semiotic idea can become the guide based on which we can organize the classification of the terms of an ontology that describes the contextualization of the cultural and social dimensions of a text. We must not forget that cultural products, in our case cultural texts, in addition to their cultural dimension also have a social one. The cultural dimension includes semiotic context and semiotic situation, as well as other cultural factors, for example, ideology. The social dimension involves external factors, specifically, history (which in turn involves two factors, society and material culture), geography, and the producer of a text. All the above are data, which include the main external dimensions of a text (Fig. 1), and should be taken into account in the formation of the proposed ontology.

Within this background, one primary concern is to clearly define these dimensions and their individual elements, so as to achieve their modeling. In turn, this modeling will open new paths for context-aware information representation. But, to define this model, one must first discuss in more detail how semiotics understands the contextualization of texts. This discussion takes place in the next section.

2.2 Text Contextualization in the Light of Semiotics

It is a fact that the concept of contextualization—commonly known as context—has been used in different scientific fields (e.g., linguistics, sociolinguistics, semiotics, computer science, and literature), and therefore has acquired different meanings. For example, the context of a text, in its narrow sense, refers to words that are in close syntactic relation (in semiotic terms, syntagmatic relation), i.e., it is the linguistic context. On the other hand, contextualization 'as an umbrella term, it refers to several possible dimensions outside a text which could contribute to its interpretation' (p. 67) [31]. In the second case, we are talking about the external environment of a text (in semiotic terms, situation). In fact, this environment is 'especially important where a cultural and situational gap exists between writer and reader' (p. 68) [31].

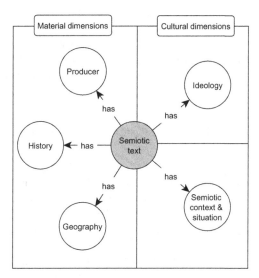

Fig. 1. Main external dimensions of a text.

This means that external factors (e.g., historical, cultural, social, and geographical in nature) are recognized as components of the meaning of a text. These factors can help to reconstruct the production situation of a text and thus to decode its wider meaning. By extension, these external data are useful because they help the analyst acquire a piece of knowledge about the wider framework concerning the era in which the author of a text has acted. Consequently, these shape the cognitive background that the researcher should have to be able to understand the studied text synchronically, that is, in the context of the era of its writing. All the more, these data are exceptionally important in a knowledge base that will be used for reasoning, as this socio-cultural background can become the guidepost for reasoning.

Let us, however, give an example to make the above more clear. In Orthodox canonical texts—which are considered cultural texts with legal and theological Christian content—we find various words or phrases that have a specific meaning, which one can understand if one is aware of the wider social and cultural context of its era. For instance, in Apostolic Canon 62 [2] the word *Greek* has a very narrow sense, but also more generally throughout the body of Orthodox Canons. The sense implied in these texts refers to the concept of a *heathen*. Here, we observe that this sense acquires a second denotative meaning that has a religious dimension, and not a national one, because the apostolic age when this Canon was formulated is characterized by socio-religious turmoil. Therefore, the recording of the general setting of the era fills the cognitive gap between the modern-day reader and the author's era, but mainly achieves a direct association of the word with the specific meaning that has a religious dimension.

At this point, it is particularly important to see how semiotics understands the concept of contextualization. In typology by Lagopoulos and Boklund-Lagopoulou, there are four different contextualization environments of a text as shown in Table 1. As mentioned by Lagopoulos and Boklund-Lagopoulou [19], there is a difference between *context* and *situation* (or circumstance). While context is the textual environment of a text, which can be either *intra-textual* (L1) or *extra-textual* (L2), situation concerns two circumstances that can be exploited by semiotics, the *cultural micro-situation* (L3) and the *social macro-situation* (L4). This division is made taking into account that the text has been inserted into a communication circuit.

Table 1. Typology of environments of a text.

Code	Environment	Description
L1	(Intra-textual) context	Direct semiotic contexts (other texts) within the text e.g., linguistic co-text, prologue, figures, tables, footnotes, etc. This belongs to the textual level of analysis.
L2	Extra-textual context	Indirect semiotic contexts (other texts) that are found outside the text in other external functional textual sets, e.g., volumes of the same work, thematic collections, etc. This belongs to the inter-textual level of analysis.
L3	Cultural micro-situation	Cultural factors that have been articulated in the text and affect its formation, e.g. worldviews, ideology, values, etc. This is an extra-textual environment but still a semiotic one.
L4	Social macro-situation	External factors such as history, society, material culture, geography, and text producer, which influence, to some extent, the formation of a text. This is an extra-textual environment but a (material) social one.

In other terms, the *intra-textual semiotic environment* is understood as the narrow or wide semiotic context, which constitutes the intra-semiotic reality of the text under consideration (henceforth, study text). The intra-semiotic reality is the sum of all the signs (L1)—elements that carry meaning—that exist within the semantic world (or semantics) of a text. While the *extra-textual semiotic reality* is the sum of all the data (L2, L3, and L4), which do not exist within the semantic world of a text. These data, nevertheless, becomes non-inherent signs of text, when incorporated into a semiotic analysis. It should be noted that to semiotics, the relevant texts that are outside the study text (L2), are also marginally considered intra-textual data.

Also, the factors of social macro-situation (L4) are an integral part of the study text because they carry a sub-meaning associated with it. Semiotics borrows these data from other scientific fields and uses them carefully in the interpretation of texts. This means that these external data do not come from a semiotic analysis, however, they become elements that can be articulated with it, and are evaluated and utilized properly. For example, it could be said that the extra-textual environment of the collection of laws concerns the data related to the conditions under which the laws were written. Such data can be captured by finding answers to some crucial questions: (i) What kind of society and culture were these laws written for? (ii) Which state authority passed these laws? (iii) What were the social or other issues (e.g., economic) that led to the formation of these laws?

In different terms, we would say that the *semiotic context and semiotics situation* are the object of study of *textual semiotics* and *socio-semiotics*. The social *macro-situation* is the object of study of *social semiotics* [16–19], which is an approach that accepts that semiotic systems (i.e. belief systems, such as worldviews, ideologies, and value systems) are articulated with the material extra-semiotic world. To put it simply, in our material world, the things we create are reflections of our beliefs. However, at the same time, our beliefs are shaped by the social environment we live in. This encloses an endless process of flow and the passing down of ideas from one generation to the next. Nevertheless, it is worth emphasizing that social semiotics is a relatively recent semiotic direction, which is supported by the so-called *Thessaloniki School of Semiotics*.

Thus, methodologically, a transition takes place from traditional (linguistic and inherent semiotic) analysis toward the analysis of the ideologies of society, and even further to the analysis of the extra-textual factors. This implies that a methodological transition from the *logo-centric* approach to the *culture-centric* one, and then to the *socio-centric* approach is achieved. Talking in practical terms, this methodological transition is nothing more than the transition to different levels of reading a text (Fig. 2), gradually passing from the meaning of the words derived from their linguistic context (logo-centric approach), to the ideology and axiology of the text which stems from the immaterial processes of culture (culture-centric approach), up to the social reading (understanding) of the text which is derived from the (material) social processes (e.g. the political conditions of a given era) implemented within the society (socio-centric approach).

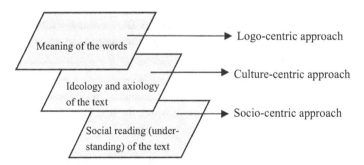

Fig. 2. Schematic illustration of the different reading levels of a text.

3   The Proposed Ontological Model

Now, we can use the previous ideas to model the contextualization of a text. The key to the design of this model rests on the semiotic notion that texts are inextricably linked to external factors of cultural and social situations, which infiltrate semantically into them. The proposed theoretical conceptual model focuses on the representation of the basic elements of the cultural and social dimensions of written cultural heritage. It should be noted that the delimitation of these elements is general and not exhaustive, given that the proposed ontology includes high-level concepts. The further specialization of these concepts is a future task that requires interdisciplinary collaboration between researchers dealing with cultural heritage texts to identify their respective descriptive needs.

Figure 3 depicts a conceptual graph of the basic elements of contextualization and their relationships, which is implemented in the OWL 2 Web Ontology Language using the Protégé tool. The formality and generality of the proposed ontology are limited to the development of a taxonomy of general concepts that define this contextualization. This means that the proposed ontology is a *lightweight ontology* [10], that is, it consists only of the taxonomy of concepts that forms the backbone of ontological modeling. This ontology, called Onto-Semiotics DCT (Describing the Contextualization of Text), is publicly accessible[2] so that it is readily available to the wider community.

The Onto-Semiotics DCT ontology was created by a team of two knowledge engineers, one of whom is also an expert in the domain of semiotics. As already mentioned, this ontological model is inspired by the typology of Lagopoulos and Boklund-Lagopoulou [19]. Although the possibility of reusing some existing similar ontology was studied, ultimately, at this stage, it was important to accurately capture the concepts of the field of cultural semiotics and that is why we defined a new ontology that in the future we will link with other related ontologies. For example, the CIDOC-CRM ontology [7], which is an ontology for the description of cultural heritage resources can be exploited in the future as an extension of the ontology, as it contains concepts of a lower level of generality than the proposed ontology. In the same context, the LACRIMALit Ontology [23], which is an extension of some CIDOC-CRM classes (mainly for the description of historical events), can also be used.

The basic requirements that the Onto-Semiotics DCT ontology satisfies are determined based on competency questions (CQs), a commonly used practice in the field of ontology engineering [21, 22]. These CQs are:

– CQ1: Who produced the text?
– CQ2: What elements of contextualization have been recorded for a text?
– CQ3: What is the geographical situation in which the text was created?
– CQ4: In what historical situation was the text created?
– CQ5: In what social situation was the text created?
– CQ6: What elements of material culture influenced the creation of the text?
– CQ7: What is the semiotic situation of the text?
– CQ8: What is the semiotic context of the text? (With which other texts is it connected?)

---

[2] https://orthocclproject.sde.uom.gr/other-relevant-ontologies/

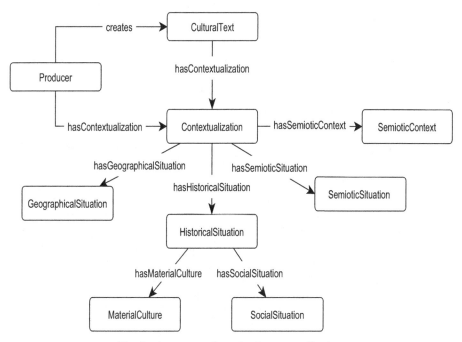

Fig. 3. A conceptual graph of contextualization.

As a consequence, the basic backbone of the concepts taxonomy of the Onto-Semiotics DCT ontology consists of: (i) three main classes: Contextualization, Producer, CulturalText, (ii) four subclasses of the class Contextualiza-tion: GeographicalSituation, HistoricalSituation, SemioticSi-tuation, SemioticContext, and (iii) two subclasses of the class Historical-Situation: SosialSituation and MaterialCulture.

Table 2 presents the definitions of the main classes and sub-classes of the contextu-alization of a text. Figure 4 shows the taxonomy of the basic terms of contextualization, with emphasis on the delimitation of the terms concerning its cultural and social situa-tion—for the reasons we have explained in the foregoing. Generally, a taxonomy shows that the subclasses are subsumed by their superclasses. Subsumption relations can also be used in object properties so that automatic reasoning can be performed. For instance, Fig. 5 illustrates the subsumption relations for the hasContextualization object property.

Table 2. Definition of the main classes and sub-classes.

Classes and sub-classes	Definition
Main classes	
Producer	An entity that makes a cultural text.
CulturalText	A fully meaningful text.
Contextualization	The different contexts and situations of a cultural text i.e., the many possible dimensions inside and outside a text that could contribute to its understanding and interpretation.
Sub-classes of contextualization	
GeographicalSituation	The geographical circumstance of the production of a text that concerns the geographical context in which this text was born.
HistoricalSituation	The historical circumstance of the production of a text that concerns all kinds of elements of the time of the text. For example, historical events that took place locally or globally, when the text was born.
SemioticContext	The intra-textual and extra-textual semiotic environment of a text that refers to other texts that frame it.
SemioticSituation	The cultural context of the production of a text that concerns the cultural elements in which the text was born, e.g. its ideology, axiology, and language.
Sub-classes of HistoricalSituation	
MaterialCulture	The tangible items, places, and resources that individuals utilize to express their culture and lifestyle. These can include items such as tools, artifacts, buildings, clothing, art, etc.
SocialSituation	The social circumstance of the production of a text that concerns all kinds of social (functional) systems (i.e., socio-economic, political and institutional systems) that existed when the text was born.

A crucial task, before making the ontology available to stakeholders, is to conduct its evaluation [12, 15] to attain the measurement of its quality. This evaluation was done in three ways: (1) through two domain experts of semiotics, who were asked about the taxonomic correctness and completeness of the terms of the ontology; as part of this check, the experts identified some errors in the taxonomy of concepts, which were corrected, (2) through two Protégé built-in logic reasoners, HermiT and ELK, to verify the logical consistency of the ontology, i.e. to identify the subsumption relationships between classes and other semantics of elements of the ontology, and (3) through the SPARQL query tool available in Protégé, which was used to ensure that the ontology can efficiently answer various CQs [6]. For this last check, first some individuals were introduced to the ontology, and then indicative questions were issued from the list of CQs confirming the correctness of the answers.

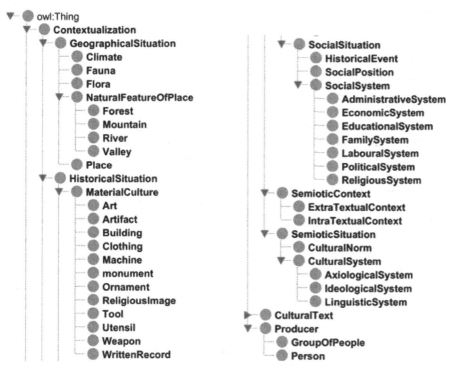

Fig. 4. Subclass hierarchy.

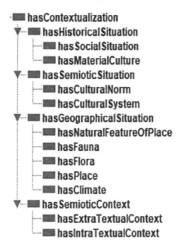

Fig. 5. Object property hierarchy.

4 Conclusions

In this paper, we tried to delineate, in the light of semiotics, the basic contextual information for the description of a cultural heritage text. Our model outlines the primary components that could potentially be involved in describing cultural texts, to achieve context-aware information representation. In other words, in this first phase of work, a core vocabulary—in broader terms, a metadata schema—covering the key elements of socio-cultural contextualization of the texts is defined, although, for reasons of completeness, other elements were also recorded. This vocabulary is useful for annotating cultural texts, interpreting a text in the light of its socio-cultural setting, supporting information retrieval, and generally aiding cultural heritage experts.

The present work is still in its infancy, as it can be further developed. For example, it is useful to add lower-level concepts to the Onto-Semiotics DCT ontology that will specify specialized concepts for describing the contextualization of written cultural heritage under the light of semiotics, covering a larger descriptive range of metadata, while still offering interoperability between different applications. However, it is important to mention that the Onto-Semiotics DCT ontology as such is a generic ontology that could be used both in different contexts and for different purposes, fulfilling a variety of informational needs. Also, in the near future, we intend to address open research challenges, such as how a particular culture characterized by specific cultural and social dimensions could be captured in an ontological form. As we all now know, culture is a living organism that evolves over time (namely diachronic) but to be studied it should be mapped synchronically (namely in a specific temporal context).

Acknowledgments. This work is part of a project that has received funding from University Of Macedonia Research Fund under the Basic Research 2023 funding programme.

Appreciations. We would also like to thank Mr. Alexandros Lagopoulos (Corresponding Member of the Academy of Athens and Professor Emeritus of the Aristotle University of Thessaloniki) and Mrs. Karin Boklund-Lagopoulou (Professor Emerita of the Aristotle University of Thessaloniki) who participated in the evaluation of the ontology.

Disclosure of Interests. The authors have no competing interests to declare that are relevant to the content of this article.

References

1. Adorni, G., Maratea, M., Pandolfo, L., Pulina, L.: An ontology for historical research documents. In: Proceedings of the 9th International Conference on Web Reasoning & Rule Systems (RR), pp. 11–18 (2015)
2. Agapius the Monk: Nicodemus the Hagiorite: The Rudder (Pedalion): Of the metaphorical ship of the one holy Catholic and Apostolic Church of the Orthodox Christians or all the sacred and divine canons of the holy and renowned Apostles, of the holy Councils, ecu-menical as well as regional, and of individual fathers. Orthodox Christian Educational So-ciety, Chicago (1957)

3. Alberti, V., Cocco, C., Consoli, S., Montalto, V., Panella, F.: Ontology engineering to model the European cultural heritage: the case of cultural gems. In: Proceedings of the 8th International Congress on Information & Communication Technology (ICICT), pp. 1–10 (2023)
4. Basile, V., Caselli, T., Radicioni, D.P.: Meaning in context: ontologically and linguistically motivated representations of objects and events. Appl. Ontol. **14**(4), 335–341 (2019)
5. Bateman, J.A., Pomarlan, M., Kazhoyan, G.: Embodied contextualization: towards a multistratal ontological treatment. Appl. Ontol. **14**(4), 379–413 (2019)
6. Bezerra, C., Freitas, F., Santana, F.: Evaluating ontologies with competency questions. In: Proceedimgs of the IEEE/WIC/ACM International Joint Conferences on Web Intelligence (WI) & Intelligent Agent Technologies (IAT), pp. 284–285 (2013)
7. Doerr, M.: The CIDOC CRM, an ontological approach to schema heterogeneity. In: Semantic Interoperability and Integration, Dagstuhl Seminar Proceedings, vol. 4391 (2005)
8. Garozzo, R., Murabito, F., Santagati, C., Pino, C., Spampinato, C.: CulTO: an ontology-based annotation tool for data curation in cultural heritage. ISPRS Int. Arch. Photogrammetry Remote Sens. Spat. Inf. **42**, 267–274 (2017)
9. Gašević, D., Jovanović, J., Devedžić, V.: Ontology-based annotation of learning object content. Interact. Learn. Environ. **15**(1), 1–26 (2007)
10. Giunchiglia, F., Zaihrayeu, I.: Lightweight ontologies. Encyclopedia of Database Systems. Springer, Boston (2007)
11. Gómez-Pérez, A., Fernández-López, M., Corcho, O.: Ontological Engineering: With examples from the areas of knowledge management, e-commerce and the Semantic Web. Springer, London, New York (2004)
12. Vrandečić, D.: Ontology evaluation. In: Staab, S., Studer, R. (eds.) Handbook on Ontologies. IHIS, pp. 293–313. Springer, Heidelberg (2009). https://doi.org/10.1007/978-3-540-92673-3_13
13. Hausser, R.: Computational Cognition. Springer, Cham (2023)
14. Kishore, R., Sharman, R.: Computational ontologies and information systems I: foundations. Commun. Assoc. Inf. Syst. **14**, 158–183 (2004)
15. Kumar, S., Baliyan, N.: Quality evaluation of ontologies. In: Semantic Web-Based Systems: Quality Assessment Models. Springer, Singapore, pp. 19–50 (2018)
16. Lagopoulos, A.: A global model of communication. Semiotica **131**(1–2), 45–78 (2000)
17. Lagopoulos, A.: The social semiotics of space: Metaphor, ideology, and political economy. Semiotica **173**, 169–213 (2009)
18. Lagopoulos, A., Boklund-Lagopoulou, K.: Social semiotics: towards a sociologically grounded semiotics. In: Semiotics and its Masters. Walter de Gruyter, pp. 121–145 (2017)
19. Lagopoulos, A., Boklund-Lagopoulou, K.: Theory and methodology of semiotics: the tradition of ferdinand de saussure. De Gruyter Mouton, Berlin, Boston (2021)
20. Lorusso, A.M.: Cultural Semiotics. Palgrave Macmillan, New York (2015)
21. Monfardini, G.K.Q., Salamon, J.S., Barcellos, M.P.: Use of competency questions in ontology engineering: a survey. In: Proceedings of the 42nd International Conference on Conceptual Modeling (ER), pp. 45–64 (2023)
22. Nejković, V., Petrović, N.: Ontology development approach adopting analogy and competency questions. In: Proceedings of the 13th International Conference on Information Society & Technology (ICIST), pp. 288–297 (2024)
23. Papadopoulou, M., Roche, C., Tamiolaki, E.M.: The LACRIMALit ontology of crisis: An event-centric model for digital history. Information **13**(8), 398 (2022)
24. Pattuelli, M.C.: Modeling a domain ontology for cultural heritage resources: a user-centered approach. J. Am. Soc. Inf. Sci. Technol. **62**(2), 314–342 (2011)
25. Ranjgar, B., Sadeghi-Niaraki, A., Shakeri, M., Rahimi, F., Choi, S.M.: Cultural heritage information retrieval: past, present, and future trends. IEEE Access. **12**, 42992–43026 (2024)

26. Savard, I., Mizoguchi, R.: Ontology of culture: a procedural approach for cultural adaptation in ITSs. In: Proceedings of the 24th International Conference on Computers in Educa-tion, pp. 64–69 (2016)
27. Sevilla, J., Samper, J.J., Fernández, M., León, A.: Ontology and software tools for the formal-ization of the visualisation of cultural heritage knowledge graphs. Heritage **6**(6), 4722–4736 (2023)
28. Silva, A.L., Terra, A.L.: Cultural heritage on the semantic web: the Europeana data model. IFLA J. **50**(1), 93–107 (2024)
29. Smith, M., Welty, C., McGuinness, D. (eds.): OWL Web Ontology Language Guide (2004)
30. Taniar, D., Rahayu, J.W.: Web Semantics and Ontology. Idea Group Publishing, Hershey, PA (2006)
31. de Villiers, P.G.R.: The interpretation of a text in the light of its socio-cultural setting. Neotestamentica. **18**, 66–79 (1984)
32. W3C OWL Working Group (eds.): OWL 2 Web Ontology Language Document Over-view, 2nd edition (2012)

Affective Analysis of Literature Books - Detective Novels and Short Stories of Agatha Christie

Elena-Ruxandra Luţan$^{(\boxtimes)}$ and Costin Bădică

Department of Computers and Information Technology, University of Craiova,
200585 Craiova, Romania
elena.ruxandra.lutan@gmail.com, costin.badica@edu.ucv.ro

Abstract. In this contribution, we propose a method for analyzing the similarities between books considering the emotions present in their content and in online reviews, focusing on a very specific category of literature books - the novels and short stories written by Agatha Christie. The method was experimentally validated using our own reviews dataset that we collected from *Goodreads* and *Amazon* websites using our customized web scrapers. We created an experimental setup to process the book content and the book reviews towards emotion extraction and create an affective categorization of books. Lastly we discuss our research findings regarding the identified similarities between emotions conveyed by the author's writing and those revealed in book reviews.

Keywords: Emotions Analysis · Books Similarity

1 Introduction

Natural Language Processing (NLP) algorithms can help analyze and understand texts by comparing text context and language against training data. A particular interest is represented by the analysis of long texts, such as books, academic papers, technical manuals, articles [19]. Some popular use cases of NLP algorithms in context of books are: entity extraction [13], fanfiction analysis - relationship between fanfiction and original story [11, 18] or even solving of mystery puzzles [6].

In this paper, we present a method for creating an affective categorization of literature books considering emotions from social media reviews and from actual book content.

We are interested in identifying the emotions expressed in a specific category of literature books - the detective novels and short stories written by Agatha Christie. Agatha Christie is known for employing serious plots with many suspects to stir the imagination and emotions of readers [14]. We consider that the research we propose is quite fascinating because we want to identify if there is any correlation or similarity between emotions present in author's writing and book

C. Bădică et al. (Eds.): BCI 2024, CCIS 2391, pp. 105–117, 2025.
https://doi.org/10.1007/978-3-031-84093-7_8

reviews from two social media sources to reveal the benefits of using different emotions sources for finding books similarities and provide books recommendations.

We recognize two sources for emotions which characterize a book: emotions in the content of the book and emotions in the associated book reviews. The emotions from the book content reflect the style of the book, and they can be used to make content-based associations between books, while the emotions identified in the reviews show how readers perceived the book, and they can be used for finding similarities between users, thus enabling the use of collaborative methods for providing books recommendations.

In our contribution, we present a model for extracting the book content emotions using BookNLP [8] and Emolex [9]. The same Emolex emotion model is used to extract the emotions from online reviews.

We consider two sets of reviews, that we collected using our customized web scrapers from *Goodreads* and *Amazon* websites. On one hand, we use reviews from *Goodreads* website, which is a book-oriented social network where book passionate can review their readings, and on the other hand we have reviews from *Amazon*, where the reviews are related to book experience as a result of purchasing rather than related to the passion of book reading. We consider this different review sources would give interesting insights of users emotional preferences in rather different contexts.

Following, we discuss the similarities identified for the three sets of emotions: Book Content Emotions, Book Goodreads Emotions and Book Amazon Emotions.

The paper is structured as follows. In Sect. 2, we present related works. Section 3 describes our proposed model: the pipelines used for extracting the emotions from book content and book reviews. In Sect. 4, we provide an overview of the experimental datasets, the data preprocessing for calculating the similarities and then we discuss the experimental results. The last section presents our conclusions.

2   Related Works

BookNLP is a NLP pipeline suitable for analysing book content or large text documents [8]. It receives as input a text, tokenizes the text into sentences and words and identifies different textual characteristics (part-of-speech tags, entity recognition, pronominal coreference resolution, supersense tags, event tags). In particular, supersense tagging provides coarse semantic information by matching words with 41 lexical semantic categories from WordNet spanning nouns and verbs [3], including reference to feelings - emotions. We leverage on the BookNLP benefits of supersense tagging to develop our experimental analysis.

Several emotions models and approaches for detecting emotions from text can be identified [10]. Gunes and Pantic [5] recognize three major approaches used in psychology research: categorical approach, dimensional approach and appraisal based approach. The categorical approach is based on basic emotions, which refers to a small number of universally recognized emotions. Dimensional approach considers that emotional states are rather bound to each other than independent, and shall be represented in a multi-dimensional space. Appraisal-based approach can be seen as an extension of dimensional approach, and it refers to the fact that different emotions can arise from the same event.

Plutchick's model of emotions [16] is a categorical model based on 8 fundamental emotions, which can be expressed in opposite pairs: Surprise - Anticipation, Joy - Sadness, Anger - Fear, Truest - Disgust. Ekman [4] initially proposed a seven basic emotions model (fear, anger, joy, sad, contempt, disgust, and surprise), but changed it to six basic emotions model (fear, anger, joy, sadness, disgust, and surprise).

Zinck and Newen [20] reduce the classification proposed by Ekman [4] to only 4 types of basic emotions (fear, anger, joy, sadness), while Ortony et al. [12] propose a much wider representation of emotions, by adding 16 emotions to the basic 6 Ekman emotions. Semeraro et al. [17] make an analysis of how to visualize the emotional patterns of human-produced texts. For illustration, they use Plutchik emotions present in different datasets: Amazon products reviews, movie synopses from IMDB, tweets regarding certain subject. For extracting the emotions, NRCLex [9] Python library is used, which consists in a lexicon for word-emotion associations.

Jurado and Rodriguez [7] provide an approach for automatically generating target language independent lexicons, which can be used for affective analysis. The authors start from a set of emotional English words and their associated Ekman emotions. They expand the emotional words set with synonyms from lexical database WordNet and use context sentences to validate their lexicons for German and Spanish language.

Zadeh et al. [18] analyze the content of fanfiction and original story for a set of 5 most popular original series. They start from the idea that fanfiction helps to understand what people like or dislike about the original story, and how they would prefer the story to be. They analyse different content aspects of the texts: emotional arcs (emotions throughout each section of the story) and characters graph, and discuss their relationship with the genres and popularity of the book. For identifying the characters clusters, the authors use BookNLP pipeline.

Nguyen et al. [11] extract high-level features from fanfictions, such as sentiments and main character details, and use NLP to predict the popularity of a story by examining the features that contribute to a fanfiction popularity. Choudhury [2] presents an example for analysing author's witting style using NLP. For this, the author uses two books, "The Hound of the Baskervilles" by Sir Arthur Conan Doyle and "The Murder on the Links" by Agatha Christie, and analyzes their content with respect to part of speech elements (verbs, nouns, sentences) to provide insights about characters such as actions or descriptions.

3   System Design

We propose an experimental system for computing similarities between books based on the emotions present in their content and social media reviews gathered from *Goodreads* and *Amazon*. We use the generic term *book* to refer a literary work, regardless if it belongs to the novels or short stories category.

For extracting the emotions we used *NRC Word-Emotion Association Lexicon (Emolex)* [9], which provides sentimental and emotional categorization for 14182 English words. Emotional categorization is done using Plutchik model [15], which includes 8 fundamental emotions expressed as opposite pairs: surprise - anticipation, joy - sadness, anger - fear, trust - disgust. Each English word considered in *Emolex* is represented as an 8-dimensional vector, where each dimension represents the presence of an emotion from Plutchik model.

A book b_i can be represented as follows:

1. as vector of emotions extracted from Book Content
2. as vector of emotions extracted from *Goodreads* Reviews
3. as vector of emotions extracted from *Amazon* Reviews

In what follows, the books representations will be named Book Content Emotions, Book Goodreads Emotions and Book Amazon Emotions. Each representation r_i of book b_i is an 8-dimensional vector:

$$r_i = [em_1, em_2, em_3, em_4, em_5, em_6, em_7.em_8]$$

where each element em_j corresponds to the number of occurrences of emotion j inside the analyzed text (book content or set of reviews for the respective book). We are interested to identify how similar are these book vector representations.

The first step is to compute the three emotional book representations. The processing pipelines are shown in Figs. 1 and 2.

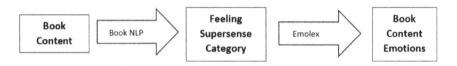

Fig. 1. Pipeline for computing Book Content Emotions.

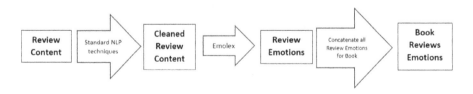

Fig. 2. Pipeline for computing the Book Goodreads Emotions and Book Amazon Emotions.

The Book Content is extracted from *Internet Archive* website [1], which is an online library offering cultural artifacts in digital form. We have collected the

Book Content and stored it in separate files for each book, so that it can be easily accessed using the processing pipeline (see Fig. 1).

The Book Content is analysed using BookNLP pipeline and the supersense tags are identified and stored in a tabular file. The file contains information of the word, its supersense category and its position inside the Book Content. 41 lexical semantic categories from WordNet spanning nouns and verbs are considered.

We are interested only in words belonging to one category - the supersense category *feeling* (tagged by BookNLP as *noun.feeling*), which includes various words expressing emotions. The words belonging to the *feeling* category are processed using *Emolex* to extract the associated emotions and to add them them to the Book Content Emotions.

For defining the Book Reviews Emotions (see Fig. 2), we use reviews from two different profile websites, that we collected with our own customized web scrapers based on *Selenium* and *Beautiful Soup* Python libraries.

For processing the book reviews and extracting their emotions, we use the pipeline illustrated in Fig. 2. We only considered the reviews written in English language for our analysis.

The first step is to use standard NLP techniques to clean the Review Content: lowercasing, tokenization, punctuation removal, stop words removal, stemming. Then we use *Emolex* to identify the emotions present in the review. After processing all the reviews, the emotions identified for each book are concatenated to define Book Goodreads Emotions, respectively Book Amazon Emotions.

4   Experiments and Discussions

4.1   Dataset Overview

Our dataset includes the detective novels and short stories written by Agatha Christie (66 novels and 153 short stories).

Goodreads website does not offer a genre classification of books. Instead, the books are classified into clusters named shelves, which are socially defined when users are tagging the shelf. Often, these shelf tags match literature defined genres or sub-genres, but they can also reveal other characteristics of the book.

Figure 3 shows the shelves distribution for all the books included in our dataset, split by their category: novel or short story. All novels available in the dataset were assigned to the shelves Mystery, Fiction, Crime (see Fig. 3a), while all short stories were assigned to the shelves Short Stories and Mystery (see Fig. 3b). Other popular shelves are Mystery Thriller, Classics, Detective, Thriller, Murder Mystery, which are expected considering the literary works chosen for our analysis. The tag Audio book is quite popular, although this does not refer to a literary genre or sub-genre, or to other characteristics of the book e.g. temporal (Halloween, Christmas, 20th Century, Historical Fiction), location (Egypt), content description (Suspense, Paranormal).

We collected book reviews from *Goodreads* and *Amazon* websites using our customized web scraper. For both websites, we accessed the book reviews section,

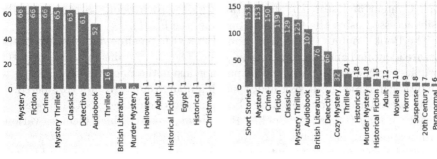

(a) Novels Shelves Distribution   (b) Short Stories Shelves Distribution

Fig. 3. Books Shelves Distribution.

and we collected the reviews available on the first 10 pages of reviews, ordered by popularity.

On *Goodreads* website, when opening the reviews section, the first set of 60 reviews are displayed. In addition to these, we collected the next 10 pages of reviews (30 reviews per page), finally resulting a set of 23514 reviews for novels and 9436 reviews for short stories (see Table 1). On average, there are 356 reviews per novel (between 329 and 360), and only 61 reviews per short story (between 7 and 360).

Table 1. Experimental Dataset Statistics

Statistic	Novels		Short Stories	
	Goodreads	Amazon	Goodreads	Amazon
# *Books*	66		153	
# Collected Reviews	23514	6582	9436	2819
Collected Reviews # per *Book*	[329, 360]	[89, 100]	[7, 360]	[1, 100]
Average # Reviews # per *Book*	356	99	61	18
# English Reviews	15549	6450	7788	2713
English Reviews # per *Book*	[165, 295]	[86, 100]	[6, 277]	[1, 100]
Average # English Reviews # per *Book*	235	97	60	17

On *Amazon* website, the reviews are clustered as 10 reviews per page. Using the default reviews order (based by popularity), only first 10 reviews pages can be collected - this is a known *Amazon* limitation, which results in a maximum of 100 reviews that can be collected per each book. In our dataset, there are 6582 reviews for novels and 2819 reviews for short stories. On average, there are 99 reviews per novel (between 89 and 100) and 18 reviews per short story (between 1 and 100).

In general, the reason for the lower review numbers for short stories is due to the fact that short stories are usually published as collections, and therefore users might review the whole set of stories instead of each story separately. In our case, we considered each story as an individual, and we collected only the reviews available on that specific short story web page.

We were only interested in English reviews in our analysis. As a result, we analyzed 15549 *Goodreads* reviews and 6450 *Amazon* reviews of novels, and respectively 7788 *Goodreads* reviews and 2713 *Amazon* reviews of short stories.

We observed that a higher number of reviews were written in English language in *Amazon* compared to *Goodreads*: for novels, 97% for *Amazon* compared to 66% for *Goodreads* and for short stories, 96% for *Amazon* compared to 82% for *Goodreads*.

The average number of words per novel in our dataset is 62658 words. The minimum number of words was found for novel "The Body in the Library" (49094 words) and the maximum number of words was found for novel "Death on the Nile" (76949 words). The average number of words per short story is 5808. The maximum number of words was found to be 23234 for short story "Dead Man's Mirror" and the minimum number of words was found to be 1920 for short story "A Fairy in the Flat". These values are summarized in Table 2.

Table 2. Experimental Dataset Statistics of Book Content

Statistic	Novels	Short Stories
MAX # words	76949	23234
MIN # words	49094	1920
AVG # words	62658	5808

4.2 Data Preprocessing

The books dataset is represented as a tabular file. The three vectors of emotions are stored as separate columns for each book in the dataset. To ensure that the vectors have a consistent scale, we normalized them using *min-max* normalization. Each element of the vectors becomes:

$$x'_i = \frac{x_i - x_{min}}{x_{max} - x_{min}}$$

where x_{min} and x_{max} are the minimum, respectively maximum of all x_i values in the dataset for each respective emotion representation.

Next, we compute the similarity matrices containing the similarities for each pair of books. Two similarity matrices were computed, corresponding to the two similarity measures used: Cosine Similarity and Jaccard Similarity.

Let n be the number of books in the dataset. The similarity matrices have size $n \times n$. Each element M_{ij} stores the similarity between two books emotions vector representations r_i and r_j. The obtained similarity matrices are symmetric on the main diagonal, while the elements of main diagonal are equal to 1 (similarity between book r_i and itself is 1).

The similarities are computed as follows:

– for Cosine similarity measure:

$$M_{ij} = \frac{r_i \cdot r_j}{||r_i|| \cdot ||r_j||} = \frac{\sum_{k=1}^{8} r_{ik} r_{jk}}{\sqrt{(\sum_{k=1}^{8} r_{ik}^2)(\sum_{k=1}^{8} r_{jk}^2)}}$$

– for Jaccard similarity measure:

$$M_{ij} = \frac{\sum_{k \in [1,8]} \min(r_{ik}, r_{jk})}{\sum_{k \in [1,8]} \max(r_{ik}, r_{jk})}$$

4.3   Experimental Results

We are interested to identify the similarities between books considering their emotional representations. The similarities are computed for each pair of books. In total, we have 2145 pairs of novels and 11628 pairs of short stories.

Table 3 shows the distribution of novels similarities per sub-intervals of length 0.1 of interval [0, 1]. First, observe that most vectors are quite similar, as all similarities identified are > 0.5. The emotions extracted from novels reviews prove to be almost identical for both *Goodreads* and *Amazon* reviews.

Table 3. Distribution of Similarities Emotions identified for Novels per sub-intervals of length 0.1

Sim. interval	Cosine Similarity			Jaccard Similarity		
	Content	Goodreads	Amazon	Content	Goodreads	Amazon
0.0	0	0	0	0	0	0
(0.0. 0.1)	0	0	0	0	0	0
[0.1, 0.2)	0	0	0	0	0	0
[0.2, 0.3)	0	0	0	0	0	0
[0.3, 0.4)	0	0	0	0	0	0
[0.4, 0.5)	0	0	0	0	0	0
[0.5, 0.6)	4	0	0	4	0	0
[0.6, 0.7)	55	0	0	20	0	0
[0.7, 0.8)	176	0	0	165	0	6
[0.8, 0.9)	640	2	15	1956	2145	2139
[0.9, 1.0)	1283	2143	2130	0	0	0

In case of Cosine similarity measure, most novel pairs resemble $> 90\%$ emotional wise: 2143 of 2145 for *Goodreads* emotions and 2130 for *Amazon* emotions. On the other hand, the emotions extracted from the content show a higher range of similarities (more specifically between 0.5705 and 0.9952). Most of them, 1283, are in interval $[0.9, 1)$, while 640 are in interval $[0.8, 0.9)$ and only 235 are less than 0.8 (between 0.5 and 0.8).

Alike similarities distribution is observed also when using Jaccard Similarity, with the difference that in this case the reviews emotions similarities are a little lower (a known mathematical result), in internal $[0.8, 0.9)$. The content emotions show close resemblance, 1956 similarities are in interval $[0.8, 0.9)$ and 189 are lower than 0.8 (between 0.5 and 0.8).

Table 4. Distribution of Similarities Emotions identified for Short Stories per subintervals of length 0.1

Sim. interval	Cosine Similarity			Jaccard Similarity		
	Content	Goodreads	Amazon	Content	Goodreads	Amazon
0.0	11	0	3878	537	1	383
(0.0. 0.1)	6	0	0	0	0	0
[0.1, 0.2)	49	0	1	359	0	11
[0.2, 0.3)	139	0	4	300	0	11
[0.3, 0.4)	267	0	4	377	1	24
[0.4, 0.5)	513	0	17	640	0	18
[0.5, 0.6)	1034	0	68	1184	3	102
[0.6, 0.7)	1896	4	172	2593	13	325
[0.7, 0.8)	2920	112	649	4512	165	1299
[0.8, 0.9)	3428	1692	1480	1126	11445	9455
[0.9, 1.0)	1365	9820	5355	0	0	0

When it comes to similarities of emotions identified for short stories, we observe that the number of less similar pairs increases (see Table 4). Considering the content is smaller compared to novels, there are less emotional words in the content, but at the same time, these emotional words create a more specific emotional categorization. When using Cosine Similarity measure, 1365 pairs have similarity in interval $[0.9, 1)$, highest similarity being 0.9903. 3428 are in interval $[0.8, 0.9)$, 2920 in $[0.7, 0.8)$, 1896 in $[0.6, 0.7)$ and 1034 in $[0.5, 0.6)$, while 985 pairs have similarity < 0.5, 11 of them having similarity 0. Analogous, when using Jaccard Similarity, most pairs of short stories prove to be rather similar, highest similarity being 0.8571. 1126 have similarity in interval $[0.8, 0.9)$, 4512 in interval $[0.7, 0.8)$, 2593 in interval $[0.6, 0.7)$, 1184 in interval $[0.5, 0.6)$, 2213 with similarity in interval $[0, 0.5)$, 537 of them having similarity 0. In this case, we observe higher number of 0 similarity (4.6% of the short stories pairs).

Looking at the similarities for reviews emotions, note there is a quite discrepancy between emotions similarity in *Goodreads* reviews and *Amazon* reviews. For *Goodreads*, most short stories are fairly similar - 9820 are between [0.9, 1), highest similarity actually being 0.9999 when using Cosine Similarity, and 11445 are between [0.8, 0.9) when using Jaccard Similarity. Following, 1692 pairs have similarity in interval [0.8, 0.9), and only 116 have similarity < 0.8 (between 0.6 and 0.8) for Cosine Similarity, respectively 183 < 0.8 for Jaccard Similarity.

For *Amazon* reviews, we observe high number of short stories pairs with 0 similarity: 3878 for Cosine Similarity and 383 for Jaccard Similarity. This is a limitation, caused by the fact that 28 out of 153 considered short stories do not have any *Amazon* reviews, as these short stories were not found as individual items on the website. Following, majority of the similarities have high values, for Cosine Similarity 5355 have values in interval [0.9, 1), 1480 in interval [0.8, 0.9) and only 915 in interval [0.1, 0.8), while for Jaccard Similarity 9455 are in interval [0.8, 0.9), 1299 in interval [0.7, 0.8) and 491 in interval [0.1, 0.7).

Table 5 summarizes the actual minimum and maximum similarities identified for pair of novels or short stories, considering the three emotional representations. The novels show a higher emotions similarity compared to the short stories. On one hand, for content emotions, this is related to the fact that the novels content is significantly larger than the novels content (in our case > 10 times bigger), which means there are more words with potential to reflect emotions. On the other hand, we can consider that for short stories, although the number of identified emotions is smaller, they better reflect the emotions which can be triggered by the content.

Table 5. Similarity Min - Max of Emotions identified for Novels (N.) and Short Stories (SS.)

Sim. interval	Cosine Similarity			Jaccard Similarity		
	Content	Goodreads	Amazon	Content	Goodreads	Amazon
N. Min similarity	0.5705	0.8720	0.8676	0.5000	0.8571	0.7500
N. Max similarity	0.9952	0.9992	0.9995	0.8571	0.8571	0.8571
SS. Min similarity	0.0000	0.6819	0.0000	0.0000	0.0000	0.0000
SS. Max similarity	0.9903	0.9999	0.9999	0.8571	0.8571	0.8750

Following, for reviews emotions, we observed that novels have in general more reviews than short stories, which results in a larger variety of emotional words. This difference comes from the fact that short stories are usually included in forms of collections, and readers tend to write reviews for the entire collection, rather than for each short story individually.

5   Conclusions

In this contribution, we proposed an experimental system which computes similarities between books based on emotions extracted from the actual book content and from online reviews.

We focused on a very specific set of books - the detective novels and short stories written by Agatha Christie. Our aim is to investigate how similar are the emotions raised by books which share similar background, i.e. belong to the same genre, are written by the same author, partly share the same characters.

For experiments, we used two reviews datasets collected using our customized web scrapers from *Goodreads* and *Amazon* websites. The *Goodreads* reviews dataset was significantly larger than *Amazon*, which is justified by the fact that *Goodreads* is a social network dedicated to books, where readers regularly share their reading experience, while *Amazon* is an online retailer, where people review books rather as a result to purchase.

We considered that a book is represented by three types of emotions: Content Emotions, *Goodreads* emotions and *Amazon* emotions.

The Content Emotions are extracted from the actual content of the book, using Book NLP pipeline for identifying the words expressing emotions. The emotional words are processed using Emolex to define their emotional categorization. The Reviews Emotions undergo to a series of standard NLP techniques (lowercasing, tokenization, punctuation removal, stop words removal, stemming) and then are processed using Emolex.

Our analysis shows that the novels share a stronger similarity between each other compared to the short stories. When it comes to Content Emotions, this higher similarity of emotional words is justified by the fact that novels contain more words compared to short stories, which gives the potential of more words to express emotions. On the other hand, comparing the collected number of reviews per book between novels and short stories, the novels show in average considerable more number of reviews, which result in a more stable emotional words distribution.

Comparing the emotions sources, the Content Emotions prove to be the most diverse, followed by *Amazon* reviews and lastly *Goodreads* reviews.

The similarities identified on the reviews can be used in favour of users to decide their next reading, considering the emotions emanating from the book based on peers feedback. This information can also be used in case of Collaborative Filtering Recommender Systems to consider that users are similar if they share the similar emotions with regard to the same book.

As future work, we would like to further investigate the field of books similarities, by (1) expanding the books dataset with books belonging to the same genre - detective crime fiction; (2) analysing similarities between other key factors of books such as characters personality type, characters occupations, crime victims, investigations development.

References

1. Internet archive website (2024). https://archive.org/. Accessed 4 July 2024
2. Choudhury, K.: Natural language processing (NLP) with NLTK and spaCy - Sir Arthur Conan Doyle and Agatha Christie's writing style analysis (2020). https://towardsdatascience.com/natural-language-processing-nlp-with-nltk-and-spacy-sir-arthur-conan-doyle-and-agatha-christies-d3ba967bd666. Accessed 4 July 2024
3. Ciaramita, M., Altun, Y.: Broad-coverage sense disambiguation and information extraction with a supersense sequence tagger. In: Proceedings of the Conference on Empirical Methods in Natural Language Processing (EMNLP), pp. 594–602 (2006)
4. Ekman, P.: An argument for basic emotions. Cognit. Emotion **6**, 169–200 (1992)
5. Gunes, H., Pantic, M.: Automatic, dimensional and continuous emotion recognition. Int. J. Synthetic Emotions **1**, 68–99 (2010)
6. Hughes-Castleberry, K.: AI can't solve this famous murder mystery puzzle (2023). https://www.scientificamerican.com/article/ai-cant-solve-this-famous-murder-mystery-puzzle1/. Accessed 4 July 2024
7. Jurado, F., Rodriguez, P.: An experience in automatically building lexicons for affective computing in multiple target languages. Comput. Sci. Inf. Syst. **16**, 273–287 (2019)
8. Mattingly, W.: Introduction to BookNLP (2022). https://booknlp.pythonhumanities.com/intro.html. Accessed 4 July 2024
9. Mohammad, S.M., Turney, P.D.: Crowdsourcing a word-emotion association lexicon. Comput. Intell. **29**, 436–465 (2013)
10. Murthy, A.R., Kumar, K.M.A.: A review of different approaches for detecting emotion from text. In: Proceedings of the Annual International Conference on Data Science, Machine Learning & Blockchain Technology (AICDMB), p. 012009 (2021)
11. Nguyen, D., Zigmond, S., Glassco, S., Tran,B., Giabbanelli, P.J.: Big data meets storytelling: using machine learning to predict popular fanfiction. Soc. Netw. Anal. Min. **14**(58) (2024). https://doi.org/10.1007/s13278-024-01224-x
12. Ortony, A., Clore, G.L., Collins, A.: The Cognitive Structure of Emotions. Cambridge University Press (1990)
13. Parulian, N.N., et al.: Tuning out the noise: benchmarking entity extraction for digitized native American literature. Proc. Assoc. Inf. Sci. Technol. **60**, 681–685 (2023)
14. Pathinathan, T., Dison, E.M., Ponnivalavan, K.: Semantic ordering relation-applied to Agatha Christie crime thrillers. Int. J. Comput. Algorithm **3**, 1006–1015 (2014)
15. Plutchik, R.: A general psychoevolutionary theory of emotion. In: Theories of Emotion, pp. 3–33 (1980)
16. Plutchik, R.: The nature of emotions: Human emotions have deep evolutionary roots, a fact that may explain their complexity and provide tools for clinical practice. Am. Sci. **89**, 344–350 (2001)
17. Semeraro, A., Vilella, S., Ruffo, G.: PyPlutchik: visualising and comparing emotion-annotated corpora. PLOS ONE **16**, e0256503 (2021)
18. Sourati Hassan Zadeh, Z., Sabri, N., Chamani, H., Bahrak, B.: Quantitative analysis of fanfictions' popularity. Soc. Netw. Anal. Min., **12**(42) (2022). https://doi.org/10.1007/s13278-021-00854-9

19. Tsirmpas, D., Gkionis, I., Papadopoulos, G.T., Mademlis, I.: Neural natural language processing for long texts: a survey on classification and summarization. Eng. Appl. Artif. Intell. **133**, 108231 (2024)
20. Zinck, A., Newen, A.: Classifying emotion: a developmental account. Synthese **161**, 1–25 (2008)

Preventing Academic Dishonesty Originating from Large Language Models

Katerina Zdravkova$^{(\boxtimes)}$ ⓘ and Bojan Ilijoski ⓘ

Ss. Cyril and Methodius University in Skopje, Skopje, North Macedonia
{katerina.zdravkova,bojan.ilijoski}@finki.ukim.mk

Abstract. After the creation of ChatGPT, many students were tempted to appropriate AI-generated texts and present them as own original contribution. Therefore, professors all around the world are skeptical of integrating large language models into their courses because they fear that they will additionally increase academic dishonesty. After the professors of the Computer Ethics course, whose goal is, among other things, to raise the ethical standards of students and increase their academic integrity, noted massive cheating in academic writing at the end of 2022, they prepared a strategy for the realization and delivery of assignments that explicitly shows where and how used large language models. Students applied this approach for producing two group essay assignments during the winter semester of this academic year. This paper explains the approach in detail and, based on the experience with a group of over 150 students, evaluates its impact on essay writing, stimulating the responsible use of technology and improving the quality of delivered assignments. Based on extensive observations of the use of artificial intelligence in writing and personal impressions of students, this paper offers recommendations on how various applications of large language models can be used to improve student outcomes without encouraging academic dishonesty.

Keywords: AI-generated text · Contract cheating · Plagiarism

1 Introduction

For years, academic dishonesty has been one of the greatest challenges of education. It was first publicly discussed back in 1930, when Time magazine announced that many students from Yale University cheated during their exams [1]. Although this problem seems to be of recent date, it seems the roots go back to ancient times, for example in China, where noticed cheating was punishable by death not only for the dishonest student, but also for the proctors who tolerated it [2].

Academic dishonesty seriously bothers professors, who consider the fight against it to be a roller coaster ride, especially when trying to crack down on plagiarism [3]. Unfortunately, students are prone to various types of cheating, which reach epic proportions according to Kate Maupin [4]. She discovered that as many as 80% of bright students sometimes cheated without ever being caught [4].

What motivates students to resort to academic dishonesty? Sometimes it's laziness [5], at times poor organization of time [6], from time to time a bad habit acquired in childhood [7], often the result of relying on the help of parents or tutors [4], and often a lack of self-confidence to successfully complete the exams or assignments independently [5, 8]. Foreign doctoral students at the State University of New York at Buffalo, in addition to their limited English language skills, cited a lack of professional writing experience and misunderstandings between themselves and their advisors [9].

Although the motives for student cheating have not changed dramatically during the COVID-19 pandemic, many educators feel that it has culminated during online exams [10, 11] and remote assignment preparation [12, 13]. Unfortunately, the situation worsened with the appearance of large language models (LLMs), especially the popular ChatGPT [14, 15]. The pandemic and the LLMs had an extremely negative impact on the Computer Ethics course, which, in addition to making students aware of the key ethical challenges of new technologies and ways to prevent them, also wants to encourage students' honest academic behavior and raise their general ethical standards.

To reduce the temptation of passing the exams by cheating, we have adapted the activities that are evaluated so that the effect of academic misconduct is kept to a minimum or if they can occur, their detection is easy and convincing. The examinations are organized under strictly controlled conditions. During the exam periods, access to the test systems is allowed only from the IP addresses of the faculty laboratories where all computer resources are disabled except for those that are part of the exam. For this purpose, we use a firewall system, developed by our faculty, which not only prevents external access to the Moodle system used for the exams, but also prevents students from using external connections and web sites that are not allowed during that exam. Students leave all their smart devices, including watches, outside the work area; assignments and open questions change every exam term, so collecting exam combinations is not of much help; the time slots for taking the exam are short, which requires concentrated work; proctors constantly circulate around the laboratory. According to the atmosphere prevailing at all the exams, especially this year, we tend to believe that the results during the exam at Computer Ethics course reflect their own knowledge and skills.

However, the problem of preparing writing assignments remains a great challenge that we try to detect and prevent in every way. To detect dishonesty during essay writing, we use different methods. They are mainly focused on spotting the following unconscious or conscious mistakes:

- Verbatim copy, which is discovered by searching for suspicious sentences whose writing style does not resemble computer science students directly on the web,
- Cross-lingual plagiarism, which is detected by translating the suspicious sentences using Google Translate and searching them on the web,
- Forgotten or wrong referencing, which is visually noticed, and
- Contract cheating (or ghostwriting), which is detected by suspicious metadata in the original document or unexpected writing style and confirmed by discussing the essay about which the student is unable to answer the questions extracted from the essay.

To easily spot these four mistakes, we have created several applications for most frauds related to essay writing, but apart from the successful detection of similar essays and especially student journals, which are another student obligation, careful reading of short essays is sometimes more effective than them. Once unethical behavior is noticed, students are privately warned about the offense committed in the hope that they will not repeat it. By comparing their first and second projects, we concluded that the amount of plagiarism remained similar and even increased, despite the warning during the assessment of the first. On the other hand, contract cheating was significantly reduced in the second project.

Everything seemed usual until the end of 2022, when the amount of plagiarism and questionable essays, as a result of contract cheating suddenly increased significantly. As usual, the authors of essays that may have been written by someone else were invited to publicly present and discuss the topic they submitted. It turned out that only one student was familiar with the content of the essay, two had a rough idea of what it was about, and the other nine had no idea about the topic, let alone the content. When asked who helped them with the essay, they had only one answer: ChatGPT.

Among other things, our students had an impression that they had not done anything illegal, given that ChatGPT is publicly available to everyone. Therefore, as part of the usual impression survey about the course realization that we conduct every year, we also asked the following questions:

- Do they check the relevance of AI-generated information prior to copying them into their essays?
- Did they carefully read the text they signed as their own contribution, despite having taken it dominantly from some LLM??
- Did they check the AI-generated essays for plagiarism [16]?

Out of 114 students who responded to the survey, 87 were curious to check the relevance of the answer they received, and 50 students read it and corrected it. Only a minority of 24 students checked whether someone had already published identical or similar text. Their high tolerance towards plagiarism was the reason to find a way as soon as possible to prevent them from stealing other people's intellectual property, and to find a remedy for this pressing problem, without banning them from using the LLM.

Aware that LLMs must be integrated into education, but only in a very fair way, we devised three strategies that were practically implemented this academic year. They proved to be quite effective not only for the prevention, but also for better detection of plagiarism and contract cheating. The paper explains what we did, what effects the proposed approach had on academic integrity and how the students reacted to it.

In the second section of the paper, an overview of the experiences regarding academic dishonesty when writing texts prior and after the integration of LLMs. The third section introduces our original approach and shows the distribution of detected dishonesty without and with generative AI. The fourth section presents the results of a survey among students. Based on these observations, within the conclusion, a discussion of the impressions about the effectiveness of the offered approach is given together with an assessment of what we have done and recommendations on how to improve it.

2 A Review of Academic Dishonesty During Essay Writing with and Without LLMs

Academic writing is a great skill that is acquired through carefully designed instructions and long-term practice, often on the principle of trial and error. The writing process itself is usually realized in four phases: prewriting, organizing, writing and polishing, of which the first two are part of essay planning [17]. Students pretend that they know how to do it, but after the first unsuccessful attempts, they realize that they don't have enough confidence in their writing ability, that they don't have enough time to do it well, and that they don't know how to use scientific sources [18].

To overcome these frustrations, students resort to cheating. The first problem we faced and which we have been unable to overcome for years is the so-called cross-lingual plagiarism, i.e. translating a text written by someone in another language and downloading it as if it were one's own. Unlike the students from the University of Lleida, who in the vast majority understand that this is a type of plagiarism, we still cannot convince our students that the translator is not the author or co-author of the written work [19]. Another frequent problem is verbatim copying, which some insightful students mask by quoting, instead of paraphrasing the copied text in their own words, extracting key elements of the original text [20]. The smallest of these plagiarisms is wrong referencing, which is sometimes manifested by forgetting to cite the sources used, forgetting to cite them, and sometimes also by wrongly presenting them, which does not allow you to access them [21]. In addition to plagiarism, students often resort to the so-called ghostwriting or contract cheating, i.e. hiring someone else to do the task for them for appropriate compensation [22]. What has been noticed not only by us, but also by others, for example Dixon and George [23], is the existence of crowdsourcing platforms through which students can exchange their coursework [13].

Although LLMs can contribute to time savings, greater self-efficacy, and relief from perceived stress [24], they raise serious concerns about academic integrity and AI-assisted cheating. Cotton et al. [25] estimate that academic dishonesty will increase and the possibility of its detection will decrease. They suggest a remedy that professors can use to prevent the use of plagiarism, including prior training on what plagiarism is, prompting draft papers, plagiarism checking, and automatic monitoring. We explicitly applied some of these strategies even before the emergence of LLM, and the quizzes enable the display of draft versions generated by artificial intelligence. While plagiarism can be reduced by responsible behavior that includes proper citation and attribution of the contributions of the LLM used [26] which is directly embedded in our quizzes, the problem of incorrect answers given by the LLM remains a serious problem [27]. What is even more worrying is that comparing the quality of the answers given by the students and the answers generated by ChatGPT, a slight difference was noted [28].

The academic community became seriously concerned about the quality of education after the emergence of LLMs, aware that by banning them, they would turn a blind eye to the cheating that students would secretly commit. In the extension of the work, we explain our contribution in overcoming the problem.

3   Integration of LLMs for Academic Essay Writing

All courses and all exams of our faculty are managed via learning management system Moodle. While planning how to integrate LLMs for essay writing, we found that embedded Moodle quizzes are quite suitable not only for delivering and grading student essays, but also for supporting the writing process, which is still unknown to most students. After an initial survey and several interviews with students who had already successfully completed the course in previous years [29], and conversations with current students, we decided to define three mutually independent quizzes:

- A quiz intended for those students who prefer to write an essay independently. They should apply traditional writing methods without the help of any LLMs. In the continuation of the work, they are annotated as No LLM.
- The quiz is intended for students who are already "hooked" on large language models and expect that it will be sufficient for them to create their own essay. They should choose the LLM that suits them best and prepare their essay based on LLMs' answers. They are annotated as Only LLM.
- A quiz intended for students who intend to combine traditional and AI-guided writing. They partially integrate LLMs to help with essay writing. Their mode is annotated as Hybrid.

Each of the three quizzes starts with two ungraded items 1 and 2 (Fig. 1.). They contain the information of the broad project topic, as well as the specific theme the students are supposed to elaborate. They all end with 3 graded items that are reserved for the essay introduction (starting from item 12 in the No LLM mode, item 13 in the Only LLM mode and item 16 in the Hybrid mode), the elaboration of the topic and the conclusions with critical attitude. The final item presents the list of references and it is ungraded. The colors in the quiz navigation represent the approximate grade for each item, green means A or B, yellow: C, D, and red: E and F.

Fig. 1. Preview of the quizzes for No LLM (left), Only LLM (central) and Hybrid mode (right).

The quizzes dedicated to Only LLM and hybrid mode have an additional ungraded question 3, where students enter the name of the LLM they predominantly used.

Students who have chosen the non-LLM mode must define three research questions based on which they have prepared an essay (items 3, 6 and 9). After each research question, they should list at least three references they consulted to answer the questions (items 4, 7, and 10) and the key content they used for their essay (items 5, 8, and 11). Since research questions, found sources and their most significant content are interconnected, the entire block is jointly evaluated at the beginning of the block.

Those students who preferred the Only LLM mode have a very similar task: to define the questions posed to the preferred LLM (items 4, 7 and 10), to copy the LLM-generated answer (items 5, 8 and 11) and to list those relevant references that prove the relevance of generated facts (items 6, 9 and 12). Again, each of the three interconnected blocks is jointly evaluated.

The Hybrid mode is more complex, because it combines two research questions and their two following parts (blocks starting with the items 4 and 7), together with two questions posed to the preferred LLM (blocks starting with the items 10 and 13). The evaluation of the four interconnected blocks with 3 questions is again joined.

Each graded item has its own importance in the final grade. Academic dishonesty due to various forms of plagiarism is part of the grades for the introduction, elaboration and conclusion of the essay, while contract cheating is part of the metadata by which the points obtained from the quiz are scaled. This made it much easier for us to assess the type and amount of accidental or intentional cheating. The comparison of the proportion of academic dishonesty, together with the distribution of different cheating methods are presented in the following subsections.

3.1 Evaluating Academic Dishonesty of AI-Facilitated Essay Writing

Thanks to quizzes in which students had to attach retrieved sources and AI-generated answers based on which they wrote their own essay, verbatim copying and multilingual plagiarism were easier to spot, resulting in a fairly high percentage of observed academic dishonesty. All the quizzes were evaluated by one teacher to guarantee uniform evaluation criterion. The evaluation included active checking of research questions and searching for LLM-generated answers that students asked them in several attempts, aware that, for example, ChatGPT gives different answers to the same questions to different users.

Academic Dishonesty During the First Project

Figure 2 presents the distribution of the five components of cheating according to the method of preparation chosen by the students. It is interesting that the greatest academic dishonesty was recorded among those students who relied entirely on the LLM, but it originated from the forgotten referencing (Fig. 2). However, during informal discussions, some students confirmed that they used Quillbot, which is a paraphrasing tool, when creating their essays. Paraphrasing tools effectively mask plagiarism and the accuracy of its detection is significantly reduced [30]. We don't know whether these students used any paraphrasing tool to conceal the plagiarism, but it seems quite likely, especially since they were the only ones whose work was fully complemented by the LLM, and no verbatim copying, literal translation, or even contract cheating was noticed.

Cross-lingual plagiarism was detected among 10.29% of the students who submitted their essays using the hybrid mode and 15.38% of the students who independently prepared them. It seems that cross-lingual plagiarism among those students who used the hybrid mode is less prevalent when they rely on the LLMs, but the proof of the hypothesis needs a slightly deeper linguistic analysis, which we would not like to go into at this time.

What we can confidently conclude is that improper citation increases in direct proportion to the degree of reliance on LLM. It was a deficiency of only 8.97% of the students who prepared the essays traditionally, 22.06% who preferred the hybrid mode, and 40% of those who produced their text on LLMs only. This problem stems directly from the LLM applications, because they do not explicitly reveal the sources they consulted to generate the answer. It seems that some students were not aware of that. What made a

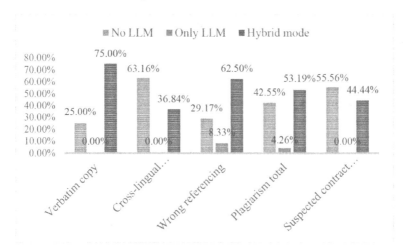

Fig. 2. Distribution of academic dishonesty during the first project

big impression on us was that two students asked ChatGPT on the basis of which references it generated the answer. ChatGPT answered them, we quote: "I don't have direct access to my training data or know where it came from, but I was trained on a mixture of licensed data, data created by human trainers, and publicly available data. My training also involved large-scale datasets obtained from a variety of sources, including books, websites, and other texts, to develop a wide-ranging understanding of human language. The training process involves running computations on thousands of GPUs over weeks or months, but exact details and timescales are proprietary to OpenAI". As expected, both were satisfied with the answer and submitted it within the quiz, without searching the web for references proving the relevance of the AI-generated answer themselves.

Suspicion of contract cheating was the least common problem, observed in 5.88% of students who used the hybrid mode and 6.41% of those who wrote the text themselves. On the other hand, it is our impression that the LLM itself is a mill of essays, so in the future we are planning how to overcome this problem, first of all by organizing frequent live discussions that will become part of the evaluation.

The amount of academic dishonesty in the first project exceeded even our most pessimistic expectations. We estimate that it was around 25%, since some students made several frauds in their essay at the same time. It is twice as much as the last pre-pandemic year, when communication with students was face-to-face, and we were able to directly influence the improvement of the situation.

We are not aware if this was the result of excessive reliance on technology or perhaps the way of presenting the research, the parts of the references that were the basis of students' assignments and the strategy of delivering the essay in parts made it easier for us to notice verbatim translations and cross-lingual plagiarism.

Whatever the reason, the alarm was now on full blast. We learned our lesson and decided to change something to introduce order and discipline, and respect for the defined rules of conduct. The first activity was that immediately after the publication of the results, in which each student can also see the detailed comments related to the content and mistakes in the essay, we hold a dedicated lecture on what were the problems associated with completing the quizzes. We explained again what academic dishonesty is and how it should be overcome. Moreover, we published the key elements of that lecture on the course website, trying to make them as short and unambiguous as possible. When asked if everything was clear, the students agreed. This encouraged us to continue with the same strategy in the second project, optimistically hoping that dishonesty will be significantly reduced. Unfortunately, the optimism turned out to be premature.

Academic Dishonesty during the Second Project

Before assessing student cheating during the second project, we did a little analysis on the shift from one model to another. As many as 50 students did not realize either of those two projects. The same number of students remained consistent with traditional writing. 28 students who used the hybrid method and only two who relied only on the LLM continued to use the same method of creating assignments. 31 students, of which 13 wrote the essay by hand, and 18 were directed to the hybrid way of working, did not submit the second project. It is interesting that the transition from the hybrid to the traditional way of working and vice versa was relatively large and was applied by 16 students in the first way and 14 students in the opposite direction. Of the students who became active only in the second project, 8 students opted for traditional writing, and four each for a hybrid or full LLM approach. Almost 60 students changed the way they prepared the assignment, which might influence the academic dishonesty shown, especially as a result of contract cheating. This hypothesis will be discussed at the end of this section.

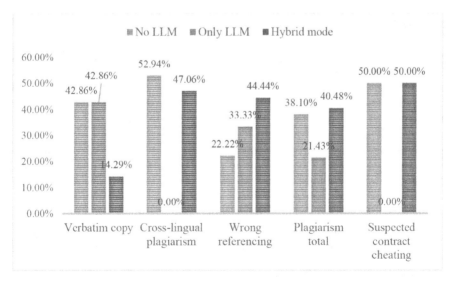

Fig. 3. Distribution of academic dishonesty during the second project

Unlike the first project, when the students who relied on the LLM only had problems only with wrong referencing, in the second, they also had a verbatim copy of the AI-generated answers in their essays (Fig. 3.). Even now, none of them were suspected of using the services of essay mills. But LLMs are essentially such mills, right?

In general, students who used the hybrid mode improved their behavior, except in the case of suspicious ghostwriting. Students who wrote the assignment independently copied texts that someone else published on the web and were as suspicious that someone did the assignment for them as their colleagues who left their research to large language models. Obviously, LLM had almost no effect on cheating.

We were curious to find out what caused the increased cheating during the second project. A detailed check made us quite satisfied, because we discovered that as many as 10 out of a total of 16 students who did not do the first task had a problem with one type of cheating. What is interesting is that with three out of four students who decided to rely completely on the LLM, we did not encounter any, and even seven out of a total of eight who decided on traditional writing made at least one violation.

Solving the challenge of unfair use of LLM together with paraphrasing tools will require a lot of effort, although the eye of an experienced teacher can easily detect a writing style that is significantly different from the way students express themselves during public discussions. In such cases, as before, we will "accidentally" forget to evaluate the student, trying to find out at the consultation whether the student wrote the assignment independently or not. If the student knows exactly what is written in the text, the result has been achieved, because new knowledge has been acquired, regardless of the methodology of its acquisition.

4 Students' Feedback Towards the Proposed Approach

Two case studies where we tried to integrate LLMs have been completed. The final results are partially pessimistic, especially because the professors researched for a long time to combine different didactic strategies and their creativity, and the students made a lot of effort to understand what was expected of them. The survey was answered by 60 students.

The first questions were related to their age and the years of experience with writing essays. The average age of all students is 22.87 years, and their impression is that they started writing essays at an average age of 15.61, i.e. in the middle of high school. It is interesting that two students stated that this was their first writing experience, and as many as 18 students only started writing at the university. Although English is not their native language, 18 students stated that they predominantly use it for writing texts. 49.35% of surveyed students completely or partially relied on LLM when creating their first project, and 53.33% stated that they already had experience with it. We were aware of this from the experience of other colleagues in whose courses LLMs are also used not only for writing texts, but also for coding, debugging and code optimization.

The next five block of questions were related to familiarity, preference, comfort, productivity and overall satisfaction with the three proposed approaches: No LLM, Only LLM and Hybrid mode. The ratings were based on a 5-point Likert scale (1 = strongly disagree, 5 = strongly agree). Figure 4 jointly presents the results.

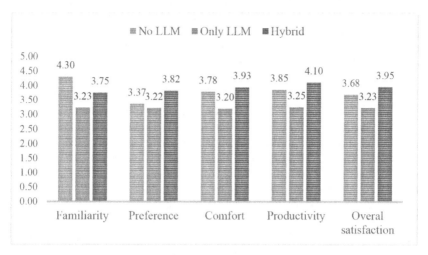

Fig. 4. Students' opinion related to three proposed approaches

The students' answers to all questions were above average. The relatively low evaluation of the completely LLM-based approach coincides with the small number of students who applied it during the realization of two projects. Although they have the most experience with traditional writing, when it comes to comfort, productivity and overall satisfaction, students gave a slight advantage to the hybrid approach. This is essentially what they announced to us when we discussed the realization of the first project. Therefore, at the end, we asked them which approach they would prefer, with the possibility of choosing two answers. The hybrid mode was the first choice for exactly half of the students (Fig. 5.). It was chosen as a complementary approach together with the remaining two, or in total by a majority of 70% of all students. Full reliance on LLMs was the first choice of only 6.67%, and even in a combination with the remaining two approaches, it reached only 13.33%. Despite frequent implementation of the traditional writing, after finishing the projects, 21.67% decided to carry on with it.

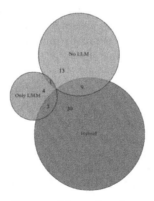

Fig. 5. Venn diagram of the preferred preparation mode

4.1 Students' Comments About the Approach and Academic Dishonesty

In both projects, students preferred traditional writing (on average, 52.23%) over writing with partially or fully LLM-based (on average, 47.77%). According to their statements, what motivated them to do so?

Students who preferred to research and write the essay themselves are incredulous about the relevance of the answers. They gave the following statements: "I noticed it does produce incorrect answers/text to some things", "Fantastic, but it still feels that it is not a human who wrote, even it does not always generate what asked, sometimes it adds irrelevant things", "I still feel that I need to double check a lot of stuff, because the bot will never say 'I don't know' and will rather say some random stuff. It's very good at understanding my questions though". Against these claims, two students had a completely opposite impression and stated: "I was positively surprised as I did not expect it to be that accurate" and "It was disturbing to see how accurate its writing was. If a human would've written it, it would've taken a longer time and the grammar would've been worse". Expanding LLM training sets with verified facts will have a favorable effect on increasing their relevance, but for manual verification of these massive pools of knowledge, long-term expertise is crucial.

Another objection is the quality of the response generated. The statements: "It's mediocre at best. One of my friends summed it the best, "It's like a student that at best can get a D. Sometimes it is just plain wrong", and "The model is not trusted to be correct at all circumstances, it can be used as an alternative to 20 min of reading Wikipedia articles when one is first trying to understand a new term. But for anything more than that, it is simply not capable. It does not possess the ability to create things that are truly new, and the work that it produces many times are prevent be wrong. And learning is about thinking and processing information, usage of ChatGPT is directly the opposite of this". If the quality of LLMs is equated with the quality of machine translation, it is certain that the answers generated by LLMs will soon improve significantly.

In addition, several students reacted to the lack of explicit referencing: "I used Chat-GPT to get inspiration but when I asked about getting specific articles with references it never gave me an actual reference and since then I have not used it", "It's great, but it has too short a context memory and can't print long enough texts. I am absolutely sure that this is a problem that will be solved soon. It lacks references, which Bing does better", and "It gives back useful information in a valid form and proper grammar. Of course, it also gives some Information that are not really important and sometimes things, which are not completely correct. I think the quality of the answers is not consistent. Users should never just copy or use as a reference. It's like a 24h-teaching service you never can totally rely on". The problem of referencing can be overcome with wise questions posed to the LLM. However, at least for now, the key is to convince students to find information on their own that confirms the relevance of the answers.

Moreover, one student had concerns related to privacy: "If you ask me, I will not be 100% confident in writing essays and texts. We may inadvertently commit a breach of privacy". It was a great pleasure to read this assertion, especially because people often disclose personal information unaware of who is reading it and what consequences it will cause.

Students who are supporters of LLMs for writing essays stated that they are a great inspiration ("It's great for getting inspiration of how to express the information when writing"), help in research ("I like the way ChatGPT gives and writes the information in a more clear way so it can be easy to understand"), the possibility to quickly get to the initial information ("Instead of wasting time searching Google for answers ChatGPT can save a lot of time and give more specific answers"), but also the possibility to improve the quality of writing ("I believe it's great to produce a clear text and to reformulate an idea one can have. Mostly when English (or other languages) are not our native language"), and even grammar and spelling ("For example writing a text then send it into the ChatGPT and let it correct your spelling to see if the AI can improve your text"). We fully agree with them, believing that they will honestly use the LLM only for those goals, and not for the scams that we saw were their main motivation.

Three students mentioned plagiarism as a potential problem of LLMs. These are their views: "While it is very good if you are stuck trying to understand a question in an assignment, it can easily be misused for plagiarism", "There are obvious possibilities of plagiarism, however I believe that when properly used it can serve as a teacher to help prepare for exams and answer whatever questions you may have. Questions that might be poorly explained in course literature or hard to find", and "This is something that you can work with or against. If you work against it I think that you will be wasting a lot of time since a lot of people will still use it and it might be hard to track. If you work with it you give us an additional tool in our lives and education which we can use. But we need to use this technology the right way and you need to teach us that. No plagiarism, use it as someone to exchange ideas with". Their attitude towards plagiarism gives hope that the awareness of other students will soon increase and that plagiarism and academic dishonesty will decrease significantly over time.

5 Conclusions and Recommendation for Future Integration of LLMs for Essay Writing

What have we learned from the application of the novel approach in which LLMs are transparently integrated in the creation of essays? Firstly, the obligation of stating the research questions, and/or the questions directed to the LLM contributes to the process of writing academic essays, which for some students was the first such experience. The following impression is that checking the relevance of the AI-generated answer contributes to critical thinking, which for the majority of computer science students is incomparably more difficult than computer programming. Presenting the extracted key parts from the used references on the basis of which the students created their own essay is also extremely important because it enables them to distinguish the important from the unimportant. For students who did their assignments honestly, these steps enabled them to improve the quality of their work. For both professors in the course, these key pieces made detecting plagiarism easier than ever, while also providing irrefutable evidence that the offense was inadvertently committed.

Regardless of all attempts to influence the reduction of academic dishonesty after the first project, we have the impression that some students did not care how they passed the course. They were ready to stay in their comfort zone and haven't done anything to honestly accomplish the task with minimal effort. Moreover, most students who were on the borderline between two grades did not take advantage of the opportunity to rework the assignment in which minor flaws were discovered or to create a new assignment that would enable them to get a higher grade. This is an additional argument to our impression that the goal of most students is to get a passing grade with minimal effort, without the ambition to get the most out of themselves and excel. Fortunately, there were such students who were impeccable and confirmed to us that our effort was worthwhile.

The amount of academic dishonesty was much higher than expected, which made us very excited. We are sure that the passing of the exam went in the best order, because we diligently monitored the students and noticed that during the passing each student was concentrating only on the own exam, and in the laboratories not a single sound could be heard except typing on the keyboard. We compared essay preparation cheating with the average value of plagiarism and contract cheating in the previous 5 years and concluded that plagiarism increased from 15.70% to an incredible 30.24%, and contract cheating from 4.00% to 7.90%.

Although at first glance it seems that this is the result of large language models integration, our intimate impression is that we were not quibblers when we looked for dishonesty, but that the new transparent approach enabled us to see in a better light where students are deceiving us.

To change these alarming results for the better, it is necessary to find a way to teach students what a responsible student must not do and to convince them that the rules for fair essay preparation are consistently followed not only in our course, but also in the future.

We have enough time to devise a feasible strategy. The first thing that comes to our mind now is to introduce an entry exam, the successful passing of which will be a prerequisite for the extension of the obligations on the course, immediately after the dedicated lecture against academic dishonesty. We will allow students who did not qualify for group projects to try again. We expect that increasing awareness of academic cheating and verifying that the familiarity has been achieved will contribute to its reduction. Time will tell if we were right.

References

1. Gallagher, J.A.: Academic integrity and personality. Doctoral dissertation, California State University, Sacramento (2010)
2. Bushway, A., Nash, W.R.: School cheating behavior. Rev. Educ. Res. **47**(4), 623–632 (1977)
3. Wang, X.: Like riding a roller coaster: university teachers' emotional experiences dealing with student plagiarism. Int. J. Environ. Res. Public Health **20**(4), 3276 (2023)
4. Maupin, K.: Cheating, Dishonesty, and Manipulation: Why Bright Kids Do It. SCB Distributors (2014)
5. Cardina, Y., Kristiani, K.B.S.: Qualitative survey of academic dishonesty on higher education: identify the factors and solutions. J. Positive Sch. Psychol. **6**(3), 8705–8719 (2022)
6. Henning, M.A., Ram, S., Malpas, P., Sisley, R., Thompson, A., Hawken, S.J.: Reasons for academic honesty and dishonesty with solutions: a study of pharmacy and medical students in New Zealand. J. Med. Ethics **40**(10), 702–709 (2014)

7. Jensen, L.A., Arnett, J.J., Feldman, S.S., Cauffman, E.: It's wrong, but everybody does it: academic dishonesty among high school and college students. Contemp. Educ. Psychol. **27**(2), 209–228 (2002)
8. Bélanger, C.H., Leonard, V.M., LeBrasseur, R.: Moral reasoning, academic dishonesty, and business students. Int. J. High. Educ. **1**(1), 72–89 (2012)
9. Huang, J.C.: Publishing and learning writing for publication in english: perspectives of NNES PhD students in science. J. Engl. Acad. Purp. **9**(1), 33–44 (2010)
10. Gamage, K.A., Silva, E.K.D., Gunawardhana, N.: Online delivery and assessment during COVID-19: safeguarding academic integrity. Educ. Sci. **10**(11), 301 (2020)
11. Elsalem, L., Al-Azzam, N., Jum'ah, A.A., Obeidat, N.: Remote e-exams during Covid-19 pandemic: a cross-sectional study of students' preferences and academic dishonesty in faculties of medical sciences. Ann. Med. Surg. **62**, 326–333 (2021)
12. Bylieva, D., Lobatyuk, V., Tolpygin, S., Rubtsova, A.: Academic dishonesty prevention in e-learning university system. In: Proceedings of the World Conference on Information Systems and Technologies (WorldCIST), pp. 225–234 (2020)
13. Zdravkova, K.: Evolution of academic dishonesty in computer science courses. In: Proceedings of the 9th International Conference on Higher Education Advances (HEAd), pp. 421–428 (2023)
14. Perkins, M.: Academic integrity considerations of AI large language models in the post-pandemic era: ChatGPT and beyond. J. Univ. Teach. Learn. Pract. **20**(2), 07 (2023)
15. Kasneci, E., et al.: ChatGPT for good? On opportunities and challenges of large language models for education. Learn. Individ. Differ. **103**, 102274 (2023)
16. Zdravkova, K, Dalipi, F., Ahlgren, F.: Integration of large language models into higher education: a perspective from learners. In: Proceedings of the International Symposium on Computers in Education (SIIE), pp. 1–6 (2023)
17. Oshima, A., Hogue, A.: Introduction to Academic Writing, 3rd edn. Pearson/Longman (2007)
18. Holmes, B., Waterbury, T., Baltrinic, E., Davis, A.: Angst about academic writing: graduate students at the brink. Contemp. Issues Educ. Res. **11**(2), 67–72 (2018)
19. Olivia-Dumitrina, N., Casanovas, M., Capdevila, Y.: Academic writing and the internet: cyber-plagiarism amongst university students. J. New Approaches Educ. Res. **8**(2), 112–125 (2019)
20. Childers, D., Bruton, S.: Should it be considered plagiarism? student perceptions of complex citation issues. J. Acad. Ethics **14**, 1–17 (2016)
21. Neville, C.: The complete guide to referencing and avoiding plagiarism. 2nd edn. McGraw-Hill (2010)
22. Morris, E.J.: Academic integrity matters: five considerations for addressing contract cheating. Int. J. Educ. Integr. **14**(1), 15 (2018)
23. Dixon, Z., George, K.: Monitoring uncharted communities of crowdsourced plagiarism. J. Acad. Ethics **19**, 291–301 (2021)
24. Bin-Nashwan, S.A., Sadallah, M., Bouteraa, M.: Use of ChatGPT in academia: academic integrity hangs in the balance. Technol. Soc. **75**, 102370 (2023)
25. Cotton, D.R., Cotton, P.A., Shipway, J.R.: Chatting and cheating: ensuring academic integrity in the era of ChatGPT. Innovations Educ. Teach. Int. **61**(2), 228–239 (2023)
26. Jarrah, A.M., Wardat, Y., Fidalgo, P.: Using ChatGPT in academic writing is (not) a form of plagiarism: what does the literature say. Online J. Commun. Media Technol. **13**(4), e202346 (2023)
27. Currie, G.M.: Academic integrity and artificial intelligence: is ChatGPT hype, hero or heresy? Semin. Nucl. Med. **53**(5), 719–730 (2023)
28. Busch, P.A., Hausvik, G.I.: Too good to be true? an empirical study of ChatGPT capabilities for academic writing and implications for academic misconduct. In: Proceedings of the 29th Americas Conference on Information Systems (AMCIS) (2023)

29. Zdravkova, K, Dalipi, F., Ahlgren, F. Ilijoski. B., Olsson, T.: Unveiling the impact of large language models on student learning: a comprehensive case study. In: Proceedings of the IEEE Global Engineering Education Conference (EDUCON), pp. 1–8 (2024)
30. Rogerson, A.M., McCarthy, G.: Using internet based paraphrasing tools: original work, patchwriting or facilitated plagiarism? Int. J. Educ. Integr. **13**, 1–15 (2017)

Learning Issues

A Gamified Approach for Monitoring Student Attendance and Fostering Learner Engagement: AttendanceManager Platform

Ana-Maria Marinescu and Elvira Popescu[(⊠)]

Computers and Information Technology Department, University of Craiova, Craiova, Romania
marinescu.ana.g7s@student.ucv.ro, elvira.popescu@edu.ucv.ro

Abstract. Because of the academic freedom they are offered, many students choose to skip a certain number of classes, which increases the absenteeism rate and affects the quality of their learning outcome and training. The goal of this paper is to propose a tool for monitoring students' attendance and fostering their engagement and motivation for educational activities. The platform, called AttendanceManager, has three main components. The first part is a mechanism that facilitates and improves the registration of student attendance. The second component is based on gamification; taking into account the positive effects highlighted by research on this technique, the system incorporates a wide variety of badges designed to increase the engagement rate of both parties, students and teachers. The last part of the system is the analytics dashboard; teachers can visualize various student data in suggestive graphical formats and track the effects of using the platform during the semester or over the years.

Keywords: Attendance tracking · Learner engagement · Gamification · Badges · Analytics dashboard · Learning support tool

1 Introduction

Engaging students in academic activities and keeping their interest during the instructional process pose great challenges to the teachers. Of the many approaches proposed over the years to mitigate declining class attendance, we will focus on monitoring student presence and offering rewards. Attendance tracking is usually a time-consuming process, so teachers ignore it or use traditional methods such as handing out a paper list during the lecture so that students can write down their names, or calling out learner names from a catalogue. Some institutions of higher education make class attendance compulsory, to identify and improve poor student attendance and to combat low performance that may result from absenteeism [19].

An alternative for increasing attendance rates is represented by the integration of gamification into the educational process. In recent years, gamification has already been applied in other areas, such as promoting greener energy consumption or taking care of one's health [5]. Game elements are fun and motivating and their use in non-game environments can lead to a positive behavioral outcome [5]. As far as education is concerned, there is a large body of literature showing the positive effects of gamification [7–10, 17]. For example, the study presented in [1] investigates the impact of gamification on student motivation. PeerWise system is used, which is a badge-based achievement system built as an innovative approach that requires student participation in constructing and evaluating a set of multiple-choice questions [2]. At the end of the experimental period, the results show that students who had access to badges reported a measurable effect on their participation and motivation and appreciated the presence of gamification elements in the system [1]. Another positive aspect was described in [11]: one of the powers of gamification elements is to transform a boring task or project into a more attractive and challenging one, improving student engagement and participation, and leading to increased attendance and completion of challenging activities. In addition, introverted students who have difficulty expressing themselves in a classroom environment are more determined to participate in those types of unusual but attractive activities [11].

However, choosing the right elements that will gamify the environment is not always easy since each element has a different learning outcome. According to [15], the most used gamification elements include rewards, leaderboards, badges, and challenges, that create an effective learning environment which fosters student motivation and positively impacts their desire to participate in class activities [4]. The presence of rewards creates competition between players, which increases student interaction and engagement in learning. Leaderboards promote competition and motivate the students to maintain positions when they are on top or to chase the ones on top. Badges make the students more active while studying and display status and achievements, while challenges increase the dynamic of the task and make it more interesting [15].

In this context, our goal is to propose a platform for gamifying the attendance monitoring process, aiming to leverage the positive effects of gamification on student motivation and engagement. Thus, we designed and implemented the AttendanceManager tool, which enhances attendance tracking with a variety of badges. In addition, it provides teachers with an analytics dashboard that summarizes students' activity and offers various statistics and insights. The rest of the paper is structured as follows: the next section presents similar platforms for attendance monitoring. Section 3 describes the main components of the AttendanceManager tool, outlining their mechanisms and rationale, while Sect. 4 illustrates the functionalities of the platform. The paper ends with some conclusions and future research directions.

2 Related Work

Automating the attendance tracking process inspired researchers to come up with ideas that combine web, desktop, or mobile applications with technologies like Bluetooth, NFC (Near Field Communication), RFID (Radio Frequency Identification), and IoT (Internet of Things) to speed up the process. For instance, paper [6] proposes a monitoring and managing attendance system which combines an Arduino microcontroller and RFID readers that communicate via GSM and Wi-Fi to automatically analyze data and prepare detailed reports about the attendance of students. Another example is the IoT-based attendance management system presented in [16]. The proposed application uses biometric recognition to mark the students' attendance by capturing an image of them through a camera placed in the classroom. The students are matched from images using the computer vision face detection algorithms with the students enrolled in a database. When the process is complete, all the collected data are available for users to be manipulated and visualized via a web interface [16].

An alternative approach for attendance management was proposed in [12], consisting in a web-based system that uses QRs (Quick Response). The teacher reads the QR code to register the lecture based on a predefined schedule set up by the administrator. Then the system automatically inserts all students with an 'Absent' state. Using the devices placed in each classroom which are connected to a camera, students read their code to change the status to 'Present'. Then, with the help of the web application, teachers can visualize the student attendance, compute percentages of absences and presences, and generate monthly reports [12].

Visualizing the absenteeism rate through dashboards is an idea implemented also in [18]. According to the university rules described in the paper, if students want to take the final exam, they need to have at least 80% of the class attendance throughout the semester. For that, the system incorporates a dashboard mechanism that allows instructors to visualize the trending of data over time to detect any irregularities and to drill down a summary of the student's activity [18].

There are also a few systems that combine attendance tracking methods with gamification elements, obtaining measurable results on students' motivation and participation. An example is the system presented in [14], which consists of an Android application responsible for identifying the students via Bluetooth when they are in its proximity and recording their presence. There is also a desktop application for managing the database and processing attendance data, which uses an Arduino that acts as a bridge between the mobile and desktop applications. Gamification techniques used are high-score lists, points, and badges, which are shown to make students attend classes and actively engage in learning activities [14]. Similar positive results were obtained in [13], which introduced a cloud-based platform with web and mobile clients that would improve student attendance in tertiary education. The gamification-based system allows lecturers to configure gamification campaigns and students to participate in them. During two academic periods of using the system in real settings, the results revealed a beneficial impact on student attendance and behavioral changes [13].

Starting from these findings, our goal is to propose a simple solution for tracking student attendance that does not require any costly hardware components. Thus, we developed a web-based platform, called AttendanceManager, which integrates gamification elements in the attendance monitoring process. To provide additional support for the instructor, the system also includes a comprehensive analytics dashboard, with various suggestive visualizations. More details regarding the underlying mechanisms and rationale are presented in the following section.

3 AttendanceManager Prototype

3.1 Attendance Recording Mechanisms

Helping teachers spend less time tracking attendance is a key functionality that AttendanceManager implements by means of three different methods: manual checking, uploading an Excel file, and using attendance codes.

The first approach is based on a simple interface in which the teachers can manually mark each student's presence and the bonus points obtained. The second method allows the teachers to upload an Excel file with all attending students, like the ones automatically generated by Google Classroom; this ensures that all kinds of attendances (physical and online) are easily recorded in the same place. The third method is based on generating an attendance code (valid for a certain class), which is shared by the teacher and used by the students to confirm their presence.

3.2 Gamification Elements

AttendanceManager relies on two gamification elements to enhance student engagement: bonus points and badges. The bonus points can be earned by active involvement in class activity (e.g., answering teacher's questions, solving a task, contributing to a challenge etc.). The badges are mostly related to attendance, aiming to boost students' presence in class. As a novel element, teachers can also earn badges based on the attendance rate in their classes, which introduces an additional motivational layer. Table 1 provides an overview of the badges that can be earned by students and teachers for a particular course.

As can be seen, most of the badges target student attendance (B1-B8), which is the first step for learners to acquire knowledge about the course topic and also start earning bonus points. In particular, B1 and B5 badges encourage students to attend the first and last class, in which the teacher usually provides important details about the exam and the course content. Based on the fact that students are more involved when given incentives for performing learning tasks [15], there are also badges that reward the accumulation of bonus points (B9 and B10). In addition, the predefined badges in Table 1 can be extended by the teacher with new ones that require earning more attendances or bonus points. On the other hand, the teacher badges (B11-B18) aim to motivate instructors to track and increase student attendance, by proposing more challenging activities and teaching in a more dynamic and interactive way.

3.3 Teacher Dashboard

Teachers have the option to get an overview of all earned badges per course by means of an analytics dashboard. In addition, various charts are included, which offer useful insights into the attendance and active involvement of the students in the learning activities. Three main categories of graphical visualizations are provided:

A. Charts that offer an overview of students' engagement during a semester
B. Charts that focus on a single selected course

Table 1. List of badges provided by AttendanceManager

User role	Badge name	Description
Student	Met your teacher	Attend the first class in a semester (B1)
	Half-master of theory	Attend half of the lectures (B2)
	Half-master of laboratory	Attend half of the laboratories (B3)
	Half-master of seminar	Attend half of the seminars (B4)
	First goodbye!	Attend the last class in a semester (B5)
	Master of theory	Attend all lectures (B6)
	Master of laboratory	Attend all laboratories (B7)
	Master of seminar	Attend all seminars (B8)
	First bonus	Obtain the first bonus point (B9)
	Smart owl	Obtain the highest number of bonus points in the group (B10)
Teacher	First code generated	Generate the first attendance code for a course (B11)
	First code used	Students used the first attendance code (B12)
	Full class	All students present in a class (B13)
	Good teacher	At least half of the students attend one class (B14)
	Best teacher	At least half of the students achieved half attendance in a class (B15)
	Goodbye lecture	At least half of the students attended the last lecture (B16)
	Goodbye laboratory	At least half of the students attended the last laboratory (B17)
	Goodbye seminar	At least half of the students attended the last seminar (B18)

C. Charts that offer insights into the student's involvement in all courses taught by the current teacher.

Some examples of charts from each category are included in Table 2. Thus, teachers can monitor each individual student's involvement, but also get an overview of the whole class and even make comparisons between different courses and different instances of the same course in various years.

From a technical point of view, AttendanceManager system is a RESTful application that consists of two parts: server and client. The server side is developed using ASP.NET Core API 7.0 and C# 11; it follows the clean architecture pattern, being organized in several layers that keep a clear separation of concerns between components and make the code more robust and maintainable. All the data is stored in an SQL Server database and is managed using Entity Framework Core integrated into one of the layers. The

Table 2. Examples of charts provided by AttendanceManager

Category	Chart name	Description
A	*Student interest*	Students' interest in a course computed based on the weighted average of attendances and bonus points recorded during the semester
	Daily attendance frequency	Percentage of attendees per day for each activity type
	Total attendance per student	Number of attendances for each student (for each activity type)
B	*Total attendance per class*	Number of presences per class for a selected course
	Attendance percentage per class	Percentage of presences per class for a selected course
	Total bonus points per class	Sum of bonus points per class for a selected course
C	*Total attendance per course*	Number of presences for each course
	Attendance percentage per course	Percentage of presences for each course
	Total bonus points per course	Sum of bonus points accumulated for each course

client side is a SPA (Single-Page Application) developed using Vue.js 2, a Javascript framework aimed at building fast, responsive, and rich interfaces.

4   Illustrating AttendanceManager Functionalities

The platform has three user roles: administrator, teacher and student. In what follows, we describe the main features provided by AttendanceManager from the point of view of each role.

The **administrator** has the following functionalities:

- *User management:* adding / editing / deleting users (students and teachers); user data can also be imported from an Excel file.
- *Study program management:* adding / editing / deleting study programs and specializations.

The **teacher** is provided with three main functionalities in AttendanceManager:

- *Course management*
- *Class management*
- *Analytics dashboard*

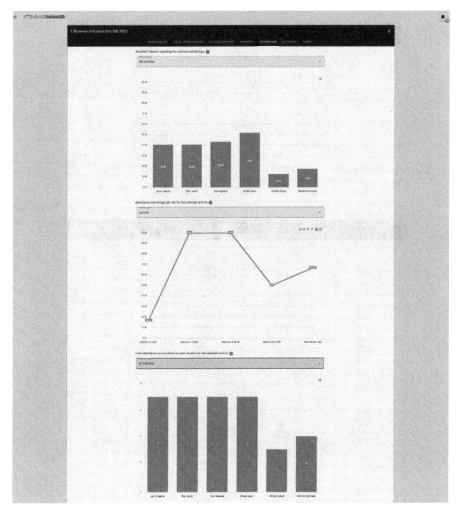

Fig. 1. AttendanceManager – Teacher dashboard (excerpt)

Thus, the teacher can add, edit or delete a course. Next, for each course, the instructor can manage the associated classes (i.e., lectures, seminars, laboratories for each student group), by enrolling students to class, setting the number of activities per semester and the weights for each activity type. In addition, teachers can track student attendance and bonus points as described in Sect. 3.1. Finally, they can visualize data in various formats, by means of the dedicated analytics dashboards, as described in Sect. 3.3. An excerpt from the teacher dashboard is included in Fig. 1; it provides insights into the students' interest in the course, the evolution of the attendance rate during the semester, and the number of accumulated bonus points per student. Another functionality available for the teacher is badge management, which includes visualizing existing badges, defining new badges according to the particularities of the course and tracking students' badge status. This feature is illustrated in Fig. 2.

Fig. 2. AttendanceManager – Badge management module (teacher view): (top) Creating a new badge; (bottom) Visualizing badge statistics

Finally, the **student** has the following main functionalities:

- *View the list of courses* in which they are enrolled
- *Use the attendance code* to record presence in a class activity
- *Visualize all attendances, badges and bonus points* (a part of this functionality is presented in Fig. 3).

In addition to the features mentioned above, there is a notification module which aims to increase users' engagement with the system. The list of notifications provided to both teachers and students is included in Table 3.

Table 3. Examples of notifications provided by AttendanceManager

User role	Notification description	Notification type
Teacher	The teacher was added as a collaborator in a class	Information
	A badge was earned	Information
Student	The student was added as a member of a class	Information
	A badge was earned	Information
	A teacher started to record attendance for a specific activity	Warning
	A teacher created a new badge	Warning
	Mid-semester is reached and the student does not have enough attendances	Alert
	A teacher started recording attendance for the last day of the semester and the student does not have enough attendances	Alert

Fig. 3. AttendanceManager – Visualizing badges (student view)

5   Conclusion

We proposed an interactive and gamified solution to mitigate the lack of interest and engagement decline of students in academic activities. As reported in the literature [3], adding gamification elements like badges, points, rewards or leaderboards can improve the learning outcome; this can be more effective if the gamified actions are perceived as being valuable by the students, and attending classes is an example of a valuable activity that can have a positive effect on the learning process. Besides gamification, the AttendanceManager platform integrates a dashboard module that provides an overview of the students' attendance and interest rate throughout the semester. This dashboard is available for the teachers, in addition to three methods for recording attendance and the possibility to extend the predefined system badges; these have the potential to make classes more dynamic and more challenging, encouraging students' involvement.

Future developments of the platform could be focused on implementing an automatic and faster solution to record the attendances by using technologies such as fingerprint, face recognition, Bluetooth or NFC. Another direction is to extend the gamification strategy with more attractive badges, or other elements like leaderboards or challenges. In addition, we plan to test AttendanceManager in real world settings, with students from the University of Craiova, Romania, to assess the usefulness and effectiveness of the platform.

References

1. Denny, P.: The effect of virtual achievements on student engagement. In: Proceedings of the SIGCHI Conference on Human Factors in Computing Systems (CHI), pp. 763–772 (2013)
2. Denny, P., Luxton-Reilly, A., Hamer, J.: The PeerWise system of student contributed assessment questions. In: Proceedings of the 10th Conference on Australasian Computing Education (ACE), vol. 78, pp. 69–74 (2008)
3. Denny, P., McDonald, F., Empson, R., Kelly, P., Petersen, A.: Empirical support for a causal relationship between gamification and learning outcomes. In: Proceedings of the CHI Conference on Human Factors in Computing Systems, pp. 1–13 (2018)
4. Dicheva, D., Dichev, C., Agre, G., Angelova, G.: Gamification in education: a systematic mapping study. Educ. Technol. Soc. **18**(3), 75–88 (2015)
5. Hamari, J.: Do badges increase user activity? a field experiment on the effects of gamification. Comput. Hum. Behav. **71**, 469–478 (2017)
6. Kovelan, P., Thisenthira, N., Kartheeswaran, T.: Automated attendance monitoring system using IoT. In: Proceedings of the International Conference on Advancements in Computing (ICAC), pp. 376–379 (2019)
7. Majuri, J., Koivisto, J., Hamari, J.: Gamification of education and learning: a review of empirical literature. In: Proceedings of the 2nd International GamiFIN Conference (GamiFIN), pp. 11–19 (2018)
8. Manzano León, A., et al.: Between level up and game over: a systematic literature review of gamification in education. Sustainability **13**(4), 2247 (2021)
9. Nastase, M.M., Popescu, E.: Towards integrating learnersourcing, microlearning and gamification in Moodle. In: Proceedings of the 19th International Conference on Augmented Intelligence and Intelligent Tutoring Systems (ITS), pp. 352–363 (2023)
10. Nastase, M.M., Popescu, E.: Kahoot! as a tool to maintain students' attention and increase retention rates: an experience report with computer science students. In: Proceedings of the 20th International Conference on Augmented Intelligence and Intelligent Tutoring Systems (ITS), pp. 80–87 (2024)
11. Ngandu, M.R., Risinamhodzi, D., Dzvapatsva, G.P., Matobobo, C.: Capturing student interest in software engineering through gamification: a systematic literature review. Discov. Educ. **2**(1), 47 (2023)
12. Nuhi, A., Memeti, A., Imeri, F., Cico, B.: Smart attendance system using QR code. In: Proceedings of the 9th Mediterranean Conference on Embedded Computing (MECO), pp. 1–4 (2020)

13. Paspallis, N., Andreou, P., Bullo, A.: Design and evaluation of a gamification-based information system for improving student attendance. In: Proceedings of the 27th International Conference on Information Systems Development (ISD) (2018)
14. Pinter, R., Čisar, S. M.: "B here" class attendance tracking system with gamification. In: Proceedings of the 10th IEEE International Conference on Cognitive Infocommunications (CogInfoCom), pp. 271–276 (2019)
15. Hishamuddin, M., et al.: Gamification elements and their impacts on teaching and learning a review. Int. J. Multimedia Appl. **10**(6), 37–46 (2018)
16. Raza, H.W.: IoT-based automatic attendance management system using middleware. Preprints, 2022050185 (2022)
17. Smarandache, A., Popescu, E.: Designing a collaborative learning platform based on learner sourcing and gamification. Interact. Des. Architect. J. (2024)
18. Yahya, H., Anwar, R.M.: Monitoring student attendance using dashboard. Int. J. Asian Soc. Sci. **3**(9), 1906–1912 (2013)
19. Zhi, T.J., Ibrahim, Z., Aris, H.: Effective and efficient attendance tracking system using secret code. In: Proceedings of the 6th International Conference on Information Technology and Multimedia (ICIM), pp. 108–112 (2014)

Personalized Online Learning Based on IoT (Systematic Mapping Study)

Edlir Spaho$^{(\boxtimes)}$ and Betim Çiço

Epoka University, Tirana, Vore 1032, Albania
{espaho,bcico}@epoka.edu.al

Abstract. The Internet of Things (IoT) has a wide application in different domains. One domain in which IoT has considerable impact is in Education. In this context, IoT plays an important role in obtaining information about the environment and actors in which the educational processes take place. This paper is a systematic study of literature to identify how IoT is integrated in Education to enhance personalization of online learning processes. We have conducted a thorough mapping study on the different techniques and methods used to integrate IoT in Education with particular focus on Personalized Online Learning (POL). From our mapping study, we screened 3000 research and academic articles and identified approximately 60 papers have done some implementation as experimental and solution research regarding IoT. From preliminary results, we determined that the use of IoT in Education to implement POL is in its infancy state. This study illustrates the possible gaps in implementing IoT in POL and suggests future work opportunities for researchers, educators, and practitioners.

Keywords: Personalized Online Learning · Internet of Things · Systematic Mapping Study

1 Introduction

The Internet of Things (IoT) is becoming more pervasive and it is currently used in several domains such as healthcare, transportation, manufacturing, agriculture, commerce and energy. IoT has also been implemented successfully in the education domain where it has not only changed the traditional learning and teaching practices, but has brought changes to the infrastructure and teaching methodology of educational institutions. Simply put, integration of IoT in education is shifting the structure of educational systems. Use of IoT in education spans the e-learning ecosystem, provides new research opportunities, boosts engagement in learning and e-learning processes and increases creativity and collaboration through its hyper-connectivity properties [1]. IoT is being integrated into education domain to provide onsite or online personalized learning experience through implementation of smart classrooms equipped with sensors, cameras, beacons, wearables and other devices that collect data on student behavior

C. Bădică et al. (Eds.): BCI 2024, CCIS 2391, pp. 146–163, 2025.
https://doi.org/10.1007/978-3-031-84093-7_11

learning preferences, and performance to adjust the pace or difficulty of lessons based on a student's learning style or performance [2].

The main contributions of this mapping study are as follows:

- Scoping of the research area of using IoT into POL and identifying the recommended IoT tools;
- Assessing the current utilization of IoT for personalizing online learning as evidenced in Educational Data Mining research and scientific publications;
- Evaluating implementation of IoT for personalizing online learning in different educational levels;
- Identifying research gaps in the use of IoT for personalizing online learning to provide guidance for future studies.

The structure of the study is outlined below: Sect. 2 presents the research background; Sect. 3 describes the systematic mapping approach implemented for paper selection; Sect. 4 provides the analysis of the results addressed by the research questions (RQs); and Sect. 5 concludes the study and outlines potential research areas. After this study based on literature review, we are trying to present background of our research.

2   Research Background

POL is an educational methodology that uses electronic and distance learning, computer algorithms and artificial intelligence to adapt online learning materials and activities based on each learner model [3]. We define IoT in Education as a new technology that can be used to increase POL by extracting physical environment properties and allow the learner to interact with existing POL frameworks. This study considers the possible methods, technologies, processes and set of practices used in integrating IoT properties, technologies, protocols and frameworks into adaptive online learning systems. Additionally, the study examined systematic reviews in IoT in education and future trends of IoT in education literature with a special focus on POL systems.

2.1   Existing Systematic Reviews of IoT in Education to Personalize Online Learning

Use of IoT in the Education domain with a special focus on POL is in its early stages. Sneesl et al. (2022) conducted a systematic review concerning the theoretical framework of the adoption of IoT technology related to smart campus adoption [4]. Laksmi et al. (2022) carried out a systematic review with a focus on the IoT platform's usage in educational processes especially in teaching and learning processes [5]. A state-of-the-art review on integrating Industrial Revolution 4.0 and IoT in academia to identify the factors that affect the level of motivation toward the integration of these technologies was performed by Butt et.al. [6] (2020). Asad et al. (2022) executed a review study on sophisticated insights regarding the impact of IoT-based smart laboratories on students' academic performance in higher education in terms of conceptual and practical implementations [7]. Chen et al. (2021) carried out a comprehensive review to understand the past, present, and future academic structure, major research topics and contributors in smart learning research [8].

2.2   Use of IoT in Education to Personalize Online Learning

The use of IoT, cloud computing, and learning analytics tools can enable personalized learning by providing a data-driven approach where learners can become co-creators of knowledge, leading to interactive, customized curricula that are scalable, recordable, and replicable, replacing rigid one-size-fits-all instructions with data-driven decision-making. It is assumed that IoT has tremendous potential in education, particularly with the implementation of the "hypersituation" concept, which amplifies the information generated by multiple sources in real-time, thereby providing contextualized learning framework supported by the surrounding environment [9]. IoT can also be used in education domain to create more significant learning spaces by engaging physical objects in learners environment with digitally association with a particular learning subject [10].

The use of wearable devices like smartwatches, fitness trackers, and biometric sensors has notably increased in educational contexts. Many schools and universities now utilize these wearables to gather data on students' behavior, physiological responses, and health metrics. This information facilitates personalized learning experiences by adjusting lessons when students lose focus, tailoring the intensity of physical activities, or offering recommendations on healthy eating habits [11]. In addition, the student behavioral and learning preferences data collected by IoT devices with utilization of learning analytics can provide insights to create personalized learning plans for each student [12].

IoT is also used in collaborative learning to collaborate on a project or share resources [13] or in Virtual and Augmented Reality to create immersive and personalized learning experiences [14] or in Intelligent Tutoring Systems to provide real-time feedback and personalized instruction to students [15]. IoT in Education has proved to be effective in improving teaching and learning activities in analyzing the impact of physical environmental properties such as temperature, noise pollution and CO_2 level on students' attention [16], and in observing students' reactions to lectures with the use of sensing and monitoring technologies which provide real-time feedback [17].

To make online learning more personalized there are a number of different adaptive learning platforms that use data analytics and machine learning algorithms [18]. These algorithms use collected data through IoT devices which identify areas where students are struggling and provide additional support or resources as needed. For example, an adaptive learning platform may implement sensing devices to capture the effect on learners during their interaction with learning material and adjust the content or pace of the lesson accordingly [19]. Of note, Zhao et al. (2022) combine IoT and electroencephalography device to monitor student's brain activities to assess students' levels of engagement to provide better POL experience [20].

Integration of IoT and data mining in e-learning brings challenges and opportunities to educational institutions and students [21]. Some of the challenges identified by Alfoudari et al. (2021) in their study were lack of engagement, interactivity and personalization of external factors, learning attitudes and teaching methods [22]; whereas some of the challenges addressed by Ennouamani and Mahani (2017) were finding the most influential characteristics of e-learners and proper integration of adaptive learning platforms modules [18]. Also identified were common challenges of security and privacy, in addition the size and heterogeneity of data that need to be handled were identified by Arishi and Mavaluru (2018), where Ghallabi et al. (2020) identified challenges of sensors high costs, IoT devices battery life, wireless coverage, adaption of m-learning and augmented reality, meanwhile Kassab et al. (2020) identified scalability, and humanization [21,23]. Considering this background in the use of IoT and POL, this paper will address this study's methodology of research.

3   Research Methodology

3.1   Motivation for Conducting the Systematic Literature Mapping

The objective of this study is to identify to what extent and how IoT is implemented into existing POL models. Its original focus is on the intersection between IoT and POL. From the researcher perspective, we partially explore this intersection by looking at how IoT is implemented in POL. To achieve a complete overview of the area, we comprehensively review IoT in Education papers that address POL methods, techniques and frameworks identified in Sect. 2.2.

There are different reviews and mapping studies about POL or IoT as described in Sect. 2.1. Chweya and Ibrahim (2021) investigated implementation of IoT in learning institutes and concluded there was a lack of studies in respect to models and methodologies used to implement IoT in Education [25]. In their systematic literature review Kassab et al. (2020), stated that there were few, if any, consolidated and coherent reviews in implementing IoT in education [23].

In addition, within the last decade, there has been no systematic map addressing common ways of implementing IoT in POL. Our mapping study allows researchers and stakeholders to make informed decisions regarding implementation of IoT in online learning, by taking into consideration present and future challenges and requirements.

3.2   Systematic Mapping Study

There are different systematic mapping study guidelines that can be implemented to conduct the systematic mapping; however, other researchers have consolidated the best practices suggested by those proposed guidelines. According to Petersen et al. (2015) a systematic mapping study can provide a clearer structure for understanding the types of research reports and results that have been published by categorizing papers. The process begins by formulating research questions (RQs). The next steps involve screening the papers based on their title, abstract, and keyword metadata to answer the RQs.

The primary goal of a systematic mapping study is to identify the gaps in the research area being investigated. The systematic mapping process we have used in this study is represented in Fig. 1 [24].

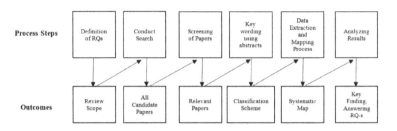

Fig. 1. The systematic mapping process [24].

Definition of Research Questions
RQ: How can IoT be integrated within existing POL systems?

- RQ1: What are potential techniques used to integrate IoT in existing POL systems?
- RQ2: What are the POL models that may be added or enhanced by using IoT?
- RQ3: What are the POL system components/parameters that may be added or enhanced by using IoT?
- RQ4: What are the tools/methods used to measure POL components or parameters?
- RQ5: What are the POL algorithms that may be added or enhanced by using IoT?
- RQ6: What are the IoT tools that may be used in POL?

Conducting the Search.
Identifying the search string of publications was the first step in conducting a systematic research process. To identify keywords and formulate search string from research questions we followed PICO (Population, Intervention, Comparison and Outcomes) criteria developed by Petersen et al. (2015) [24]. These criteria are defined in Table 1.

To explore how IoT is integrated in POL systems in primary studies we formulated a search string that reveals combination of IoT and POL systems. There are three main concepts of the search string "Internet of Things", "Personalized" and "Online Learning" derived from research questions. Our basic string

Table 1. PICO of the study

Dimension	Description
Population	Primary studies which integrate IoT in POL systems (both theoretical and empirical studies).
Intervention	Techniques, models, components, algorithms, and tools used to integrate IoT in POL systems.
Comparison	Comparing different techniques, models, components, algorithms and Tools used to integrate IoT in POL systems.
Outcome	Evaluation of collected empirical studies, which integrate IoT in POL systems.

was (Internet of Things AND Personalized AND Online Learning). To extend the scope of research we conducted an investigation of literature for synonyms or interchangeably used terms of identified main concepts. To construct the full string, we used AND Boolean operator to combine main concepts and OR Boolean operator to express synonyms or interchangeably used terms of main concepts.

The constructed full search string was ("IoT" OR "Internet of Things" OR "IoE" OR "Internet of Everything" OR "Industry 4.0" OR "Web of Things" OR "WoT" OR "Machine to Machine" OR "M2M" OR "CoT" OR "Cloud of Things" OR "NoT" OR "Network of Things") AND ("Personalized" OR "Adapted" OR "Individualized" OR "Tailored" OR "Customized" OR "Context-aware" OR "Learner-centric") AND ("Online Learning" OR "Distance Learning" OR "Distance Education" OR "e-learning" OR "Elearning" OR "Electronic Learning" OR "Virtual Learning" OR "Digital Learning" OR "Computer-Supported Learning" OR "Internet-Based Learning") [18,23,25]. Various systematic literature reviews about IoT or POL used several options for electronic database selection such as ACM Digital Library, IEEE Xplore, Education Resources Information Center (ERIC), Scopus, Springer Link, Web of Science, Science Direct and DBLP bibliography. To conduct our research, we implemented the search string in ACM, IEEE Xplore, Education Resources Information Center (ERIC), Scopus and Springer Link digital libraries. To find latest trends we limited the research from January 2017 to March 2023. Detailed results of implementation of search string and results are show in Table 2.

Screening Papers.
Based on the research questions and inclusion and exclusion criteria of this mapping study the most relevant papers were identified during screening process. Based on study title, abstract and keywords we included or excluded each study found with the search string. From the database search, we identified a total of 3286 papers published during 2017–2023 time span. Most of publications were in the Springer Link digital database (see Table 2).

Table 2. Number of unique studies and search strings (Time interval: 2017–2023)

Source	Basic string	Full String	Duplicates	Library Total
IEEE Xplore	36	119	3	152
ACM Digital Library	305	165	17	453
Education Resources Information Center (ERIC)	4	761	1	764
Springer Link	127	1812	22	1917

Table 3. Criteria used for including and excluding research studies

Inclusion Criteria	Exclusion Criteria
– Included content of IoT that investigates Educational perspectives to Personalize Online Learning i.e., methods, frameworks and use cases; – Published between January 2017 and March 2023; – Written in English with full-text available; – Peer-reviewed journal literature.	– Duplicate papers from the same study in different databases; – Mention of IoT is tangential with different scopes not directly related to POL; – Publications not written in English; –Publications not directly related to our topic; – Full-text is inaccessible; – Books and gray literature.

Extracted research papers database was processed through the use of spreadsheet software. (see Table 3). Phase 1 involved the automatic removal of 380 invalid sources filtering research types not meant for citation, such as conference/workshop programs, keynotes, book covers, retracted articles, PhD theses and unpublished works. Furthermore, we automatically removed 49 duplicate papers based on their titles. Thus, 2857 references remained. In phase 2, we applied further filtering, based on the inclusion and exclusion criteria, to titles, keywords, and publication year, thus producing 1097 studies and then to abstracts as recommended by Carrera-Rivera (2022) resulting on 76 candidate studies [26]. In the final phase, we excluded 16 papers that were not entirely relevant to our systematic mapping study, resulting in 60 accepted studies. The number of included and excluded papers for each Phase is presented in Fig 2.

Keywording Using Abstracts and Classification Scheme Generation.
The goal of keywording in the context of systematic mapping studies, according to Petersen et al. (2008) is to facilitate the classification and organization of research papers [27]. This process involves identifying key terms from abstracts, which helps in creating a structured overview of a research area. This systematic approach aims to categorize the studies, making it easier to identify trends, research gaps, and the distribution of research efforts across different topics within the field.

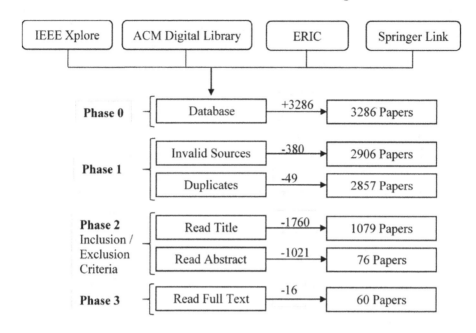

Fig. 2. Selection of primary studies [24].

To classify the papers, we followed the classification scheme generation process proposed by Petersen et al. (2008), who rated classification schemes based on the basis of a set of quality attributes [27]:

- Scheme Definition: The taxonomy/classification is created on the basis of analysis of existing literature in the field;
- Scheme Terminology: The taxonomy uses terms that are used in existing literature;
- Orthogonality: There are clear boundaries between categories which facilitates classification;
- Accepted: The community accepts and knows the classification/taxonomy.

In Fig 3 we present the classification scheme where the all facets are derived referring to the existing literature on the subject we have conducted and also by the results of our study. To build the classification scheme we conducted following steps as described in [27]:

Step 1: Reading the abstracts of the primary studies and searching for keywords relative to the context of our research, identified the main contribution area of relevant papers. When abstracts were not sufficient or not precise, introduction or conclusion sections of the paper were reviewed for a better understanding of the paper's substance. Extracted keywords are strictly related to the RQs to classify and map papers accordingly;

Step 2: Combining sets of keywords from different papers allowed for categories representative of the research area of the relevant primary studies. We pro-

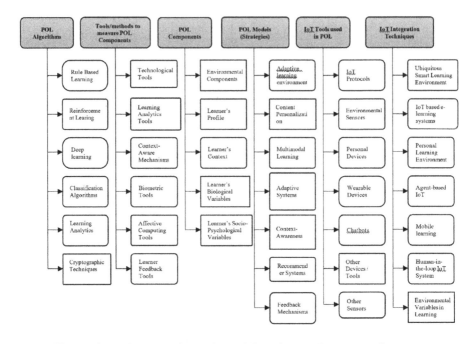

Fig. 3. Classification scheme derived from keywording using abstracts.

gressively included the papers into categories, which were, in turn, refined and updated while accommodating new data;

Step 3: Categories formed by final set of clustered keywords were classified into hierarchical levels, to develop levels of understanding about the nature and contribution of selected primary studies.

For presenting the results we followed the structure and layout of a systematic mapping study conducted by Cico et al. [28]

4   Results

As indicated above, our main research question was "How can IoT be integrated within existing POL systems?" From an initial sample of 3000 papers, 60 primary relevant studies were selected for answering RQ. To analyze the main dimensions of this specific question, six other sub-questions were included (e.g. RQ1), with the results allowing for each article to be classified into categories pertinent to specific sub-questions. The results of the systematic mapping study are presented as follows:

4.1   RQ1: What Are Potential Techniques Used to Integrate IoT in POL Systems?

RQ1 deals with techniques that can be used to integrate IoT in existing POL systems. To answer this question, we created the "IoT Integration Techniques" classification for the papers.

Table 4. Number of papers according to used IoT Integration Technique.

IoT Integration Technique	Number of Studies	Percentage
Ubiquitous Smart Learning Environment	22	37%
Personal Learning Environment	16	27%
Mobile Learning	8	13%
IoT-based Learning Systems	6	10%
Agent-based IoT	4	7%
Environmental Variables in Learning	2	3%
Human-in-the-loop IoT system	2	3%

From Table 4 we observe that 37% of the papers have as main focus the creation of Ubiquitous Smart Learning Environment, which makes sense, since the main intention of integrating IoT into POLs is the creation of Smart Learning Environments. Main techniques involved in creation of Ubiquitous Smart Learning Environments includes technologies like Smart Learning Environments [3], ubiquitous computing [12], augmented and virtual reality [14] and distributed and cloud computing [29] to create a comprehensive and immersive learning experience. The second most prevalent technique involves creation of Personal Learning Environments [2,30]. Mobile Learning techniques use mobile devices for arts-based strategies and personalized data collection [13]. Other significant methods include IoT-based e-learning systems, flipped classrooms, smart laboratories and educational tools, which leverage real-time data for adaptive learning [15,16]. Additional approaches include Agent-based IoT with robotics and educational chatbots, and IoT integration for Environmental Physical Variables, using learner's environmental data [16,31,32]. In addition, a Human-in-the-loop IoT system uses wearable devices and a reinforcement learning framework to adapt IoT applications to human variability [33].

4.2   RQ2: What Are the POL Models that May Be Added or Enhanced by Using IoT?

Table 5. Number of papers according to used POL Models or Strategies.

POL Models or Strategies	Number of Studies	Percentage
Adaptive learning environment	11	18%
Content Personalization	9	15%
Multi-modal Learning	8	13%
Adaptive Systems	7	12%
Context-Awareness	7	12%
Recommender Systems	6	10%
Feedback Mechanisms	3	5%
Collaborative Learning	2	3%
Gamification	2	3%
Not clearly specified	2	3%
Personalized Learning Plans	2	3%
Intelligent Tutoring Systems	1	2%

In the realm of educational technology, various models and strategies can be enhanced by IoT (see Table 5). Adaptive Learning Environments incorporates interactive, personalized, and interpretable systems, whereas Content Personalization adapts learning and teaching content alongside educational strategies [14,20,32]. Multi-modal Learning models utilize multiple data types for adaptation, such as engagement, emotion recognition, and academic performance [30]. Context-Aware and Adaptive Systems personalize learning paths, curriculum, and instructional methods based on learner modeling and contextual data [2,29,33].

Recommendation and Adaptive Feedback Models provide tailored educational resources and real-time feedback using biofeedback and IoT monitoring [11,13,17,34]. Collaborative Learning and Personalized Learning Plans engage students in meaningful projects and adapt learning scenarios based on emotional and cognitive feedback [3,12,13,31]. Intelligent Tutoring and Gamification offer personalized teaching and assessments through real-time data analysis and implement IoT within gamified settings [15], effectively enhancing the educational experience through dynamic and personalized approaches.

4.3   RQ3: What Are the POL System Components or Parameters that May Be Added or Enhanced by Using IoT?

POL systems are designed to cater to individual learner needs by integrating various components to build comprehensive learner profile. Different range of factors are considered to build the learner profile including prior knowledge, learning styles, preferences, personality, emotional and cognitive states, demographic information, and performance data. As shown in Table 6, around 40% of studies in this area focus on creating the learner profile to enhance personalization in learning [15,31,35]. The enhancement of POL systems also utilizes contextual and socio-psychological elements.

Table 6. Number of papers according to used POL Components.

POL Components	Number of Studies	Percentage
Learner's Profile	24	40%
Learner's Context	10	17%
Learner's Socio-Psychological Components	10	17%
Learner's Biological Components	7	12%
Not clearly specified	5	8%
Environmental Components	4	7%

Contextual elements are represented through wireless-enabled edge devices and IoT-based educational tools to generate high-level context information from physical and multi-domain contexts. Socio-psychological components further personalize the experience by analyzing learners' behavioral patterns, emotions, motivation, engagement, and cognitive load [11,30]. They also include environmental factors such as location, temperature, humidity, and light, or noise level, and time of day alongside with graphic elements like layout and background texture, which contribute to creating an optimal learning environment [16,32].

4.4 RQ4: What Are the Tools or Methods Used to Measure POL Components or Parameters?

The tools and methods used in POL leverage a variety of technological tools to tailor educational experiences to individual learner needs (see Table 7). These tools include IoT Edge Devices, which use various sensors to detail the state of physical objects and their contexts, thereby enhancing ubiquitous learning environments [35]. In addition, learning design tools, authoring systems for interactive environments, educational chatbots, and intelligent agents facilitate the mapping of learning scenarios, the delivery of personalized assistance, and the evaluation of personalization processes [12,31].

IoT frameworks and machine learning algorithms are utilized to develop intelligent, adaptive applications that process data to optimize learning outcomes [33]. Learning analytics tools and context-aware mechanisms are also integrated in measuring and enhancing POL systems. Tools like Myers-Briggs Type Indicator (MBTI) and multi-modal learning analytics use personality assessments and engagement tracking to adapt learning environments to individual

Table 7. Tools or methods used to measure POL Components.

Tools or methods to measure POL Components	Number of Studies	Percentage
Technological Tools	10	17%
Learning Analytics Tools	10	17%
Not clearly specified	10	17%
Context-Aware Mechanisms	6	10%
Biometric Tools	5	8%
Affective Computing Tools	5	8%
Learner Feedback Tools	5	8%
Assessment and Performance Metrics	3	5%
Educational Theories and Frameworks	3	5%
Engagement Metrics	2	3%
Social Learning Metrics	1	2%

psychological and behavioral patterns [30]. Context-aware mechanisms utilize GPS technology, QR codes, and context fusion models to provide real-time, location-based learning content tailored to the environmental and individual learner's context [32]. Together, these tools not only support the personalization of learning pathways and content but also enhance the overall effectiveness and responsiveness of educational systems to diverse learning needs and environments.

4.5   RQ5: What Are the POL Algorithms that May Be Added or Enhanced by Using IoT?

Different types of algorithms are used to provide POL. Classification algorithms include decision trees, Instance-Based Classifier, SVM algorithm, AdaBoost classifier, facial recognition algorithms, and the linear learner algorithm [17,29].

Deep learning algorithms include deep neural networks and graph neural networks. Reinforcement learning includes techniques like reinforcement learning and multi-armed bandit problems. Rule-based learning relies on systems using IF-THEN rules, meanwhile cryptographic techniques are represented by Zero Knowledge Proof and learning analytics incorporates machine learning algorithms and learning analytics methods [16,33,34]. Detailed results are presented in Table 8.

Table 8. Algorithms used in POL Systems

POL Algorithms	Number of Studies	Percentage
Learning Analytics (LA)	14	23%
Combination of Multiple Algorithms	13	22%
Not Clearly Specified	12	20%
Different Algorithms	6	10%
Deep Learning	5	8%
Classification Algorithms	4	7%
Rule Based Algorithms	3	5%
Cryptographic Techniques	1	2%
Genetic Algorithms	1	2%
Reinforcement Learning	1	2%

Table 9. IoT tools integrated into POL Systems.

IoT Tools	Number of Studies	Percentage
Different Devices / Tools	21	35%
Not Clearly Specified	17	28%
Personal Devices	6	10%
Wearable Devices	6	10%
Environmental Sensors	5	8%
Smart and Wearable Devices	4	7%
Communication Technologies	1	2%

4.6 RQ6: What Are the IoT Tools that May Be Used in POL??

The integration of IoT tools in POL systems utilizes a variety of protocols, devices, and sensors to enhance the learning experience, as shown in Table 9. Environmental sensors like proximity sensors, ambient light sensors, and GPS, are used to adapt the learning environment to individual needs [16]. Personal devices, including Android mobile phones, computers, and mobile cameras along with wearable devices such as smartwatches, EEG devices, and smart glasses provide continuous data on user interactions and physical conditions [13,30].

Additionally, chatbots like Textit via Telegram offer interactive support, while other tools like Raspberry Pi, smart boards, and QR codes, along with various sensors such as RFID, fingerprint scanners, NFC tags, and accelerometers contribute to a rich, responsive learning ecosystem [14,20,31].

5   Conclusions and Future Works

This research systematically explores various dimensions of IoT integration within existing POL environments, providing a comprehensive understanding of techniques, models, components, tools, and algorithms involved. Based on our research questions, IoT is most commonly used in creation of ubiquitous smart learning environments, however only few papers (7%) used IoT to integrate environmental conditions into POL systems.

From 60 selected studies, majority of them (72%) focused on solution research, where majority of them (75%) were solution proposals, framework or methods. The POL models that can benefit mostly from IoT integration are adaptive e-learning environments, content personalization and multi-modal learning to personalize learning experiences based on individual learner needs and contextual factors. However, there is a lack of using IoT to seamlessly integrate the adaption of physical and virtual learning environments.

Almost half of selected studies (40%) use learner profile to provide personalization services, however IoT is mostly used to extract the context from sociopsychological, and biological components. Technological and learning analytical tools are main tools used to integrate IoT into POL systems. Main algorithms used to analyze generated multiple heterogeneous data are learning analytics (23%) and combination of multiple algorithms (22%). IoT is commonly integrated in POL systems by using embedded sensors within wearable and mobile devices (27%), non-embedded environmental sensors (7%), Raspberry Pi (7%) and simulators (7%).

Based on study finding we conclude that there is a need for new pedagogical approaches to accommodate IoT innovations and there is a lack of longitudinal studies examining the long-term impacts of IoT-enhanced learning environments on educational outcomes. In our future study, we intend to further evaluate the use of IoT to seamlessly integrate the physical learning environments conditions in POL systems.

For citations of references, we prefer the use of square brackets and consecutive numbers. Citations using labels or the author/year convention are also acceptable. The following bibliography provides a sample reference list with entries for journal articles [6], an LNCS chapter [6], a book [6], proceedings without editors [1], and a homepage [1]. Multiple citations are grouped [1,2,6].

References

1. Ramlowat, D.D., Pattanayak, B.K.: Exploring the internet of things (IoT) in education: a review. In: Proceedings of the 5th International Conference on Information Systems Design & Intelligent Applications (INDIA), pp. 245–255, University of Mascareignes, Mauritius (2018). https://doi.org/10.1007/978-981-13-3338-5_23
2. Ciolacu, M.I., Binder, L., Svasta, P., Tache, I., Stoichescu, D.: Education 4.0-jump to innovation with IoT in higher education. In: Proceedings of the 25th IEEE International Symposium for Design & Technology in Electronic Packaging (SIITME), pp. 135–141, Cluj-Napoca, Romania (2019). https://doi.org/10.1109/SIITME47687.2019.8990763

3. Spyrou, E., Vretos, N., Pomazanskyi, A., Asteriadis, S., Leligou, H.C.: Exploiting IoT technologies for personalized learning. In: Proceedings of the IEEE Conference on Computational Intelligence & Games (CIG), pp. 1–8, Maastricht, Netherlands (2018). https://doi.org/10.1109/CIG.2018.8490454

4. Sneesl, R., Jusoh, Y.Y., Jabar, M.A., Abdullah, S.: Revising technology adoption factors for IoT-based smart campuses: a systematic review. Sustainability **14**(8), 4840 (2022). https://doi.org/10.3390/su14084840

5. Laksmi, I.C., Hatta, P., Wihidayat, E.S.: A systematic review of IoT platforms in educational processes. In: Proceedings of the 12th Annual International Conference on Industrial Engineering & Operations Management (IEOM), pp. 5265–5274, Istanbul, Turkey (2022). https://doi.org/10.46254/AN12.20221063

6. Butt, R., Siddiqui, H., Soomro, R.A., Asad, M.M.: Integration of industrial revolution 4.0 and IOTs in academia: a state-of-the-art review on the concept of Education 4.0 in Pakistan. Interact. Technol. Smart Educ. **17**(4), 337–354 (2020). https://doi.org/10.1108/ITSE-02-2020-0022

7. Asad, M.M., Naz, A., Shaikh, A., Alrizq, M., Akram, M., Alghamdi, A.: Investigating the impact of IoT-based smart laboratories on students' academic performance in higher education. Univ. Access Inf. Soc. **23**, 1135–1149 (2022). https://doi.org/10.1007/s10209-022-00944-1

8. Chen, X., Zou, D., Xie, H., Wang, F.L.: Past, present, and future of smart learning: a topic-based bibliometric analysis. Int. J. Educ. Technol. High. Educ. **18**(1), 1–29 (2021). https://doi.org/10.1186/s41239-020-00239-6

9. Moreira, F.T., Magalhães, A., Ramos, F., Vairinhos, M.: The power of the internet of things in education: an overview of current status and potential. In: Proceedings of the 2nd International Conference on Smart Learning Ecosystems & Regional Development (SLERD), pp. 51–63, University of Aveiro, Portugal (2017). https://doi.org/10.1007/978-3-319-61322-2_6

10. Gómez, J., Huete, J.F., Hoyos, O., Perez, L.., Grigori, D.: Interaction system based on Internet of Things as support for education. Procedia Comput. Sci. **21**, 132–139 (2013). https://doi.org/10.1016/j.procs.2013.09.019, https://www.sciencedirect.com/science/article/pii/S1877050913008120

11. Ciolacu, M.I., Binder, L., Popp, H.: Enabling IoT in education 4.0 with bioSensors from wearables and artificial intelligence. In: Proceedings of the 25th IEEE International Symposium for Design & Technology in Electronic Packaging (SIITME), pp. 17–24, Cluj-Napoca, Romania (2019). https://doi.org/10.1109/SIITME47687.2019.8990763

12. Mavroudi, A., Fragou, O., Goumopoulos, C.: Design concepts, principles and patterns in the curriculum of the new computing education era. Des. Learn. **11**(1), 141–153 (2019). https://doi.org/10.16993/dfl.140

13. Perry, B., Edwards, M.: Innovative arts-based learning approaches adapted for mobile learning. Open Praxis **11**(3), 303–310 (2019). https://doi.org/10.5944/openpraxis.11.3.967

14. Mahapatra, S.K., Pattanayak, B.K., Pati, B.: Flip learning: a novel IoT-based learning initiative. In: Proceedings of the International Conference on Intelligent & Cloud Computing (ICICC), vol. 2, pp. 59–67, Siksha 'O' Anusandhan, Bhubaneswar, India (2019). https://doi.org/10.1007/978-981-15-6202-0_7

15. Mylonas, G., Paganelli, F., Cuffaro, G., Nesi, I., Karantzis, D.: Using gamification and IoT-based educational tools towards energy savings: Some experiences from two schools in Italy and Greece. J. Ambient Intell. Humanized Comput. **14**, 15725–15744 (2023). https://doi.org/10.1007/s12652-020-02838-7

16. Aydin, A., Göktaş, Y.: Examining the effects of physical variables in classrooms on students' attention via the Internet of Things. Participatory Educ. Res. **10**(1), 160–177 (2023). https://doi.org/10.17275/per.23.9.10.1

17. Soui, M., Srinivasan, K., Albesher, A.: Intelligent personalized e-learning platform using machine learning algorithms. Mach. Learn. Methods Eng. Appl. Dev. **1**, 110 (2022). https://doi.org/10.2174/9879815079180122010011

18. Ennouamani, S., Mahani, Z.: An overview of adaptive e-learning systems. In: Proceedings of the 8th IEEE International Conference on Intelligent Computing & Information Systems (ICICIS), pp. 342–347, Cairo, Egypt (2017). https://doi.org/10.1109/INTELCIS.2017.8260060

19. Spyrou, E., Vretos, N., Pomazanskyi, A., Asteriadis, S., Leligou, H.C.: Exploiting IoT technologies for personalized learning. In: Proceedings of the IEEE Conference on Computational Intelligence & Games (CIG), pp. 1–8, Maastricht, Netherlands (2018). https://doi.org/10.1109/CIG.2018.8490454

20. Zhao, Z., Zhao, B., Ji, Z., Liang, Z.: On the personalized learning space in educational metaverse based on heart rate signal. Int. J. Inf. Commun. Technol. Educ. **18**(2), 1–12 (2022). https://doi.org/10.4018/ijicte.314565

21. Arishi, H.A., Mavaluru, D.: Internet of Things (IoT) technology for smart e-learning using data mining: review and challenges. J. Adv. Res. Dyn. Control Syst. **10**(13), 626–632 (2018)

22. Alfoudari, A.M., Durugbo, C.M., Aldhmour, F.M.: Understanding socio-technological challenges of smart classrooms using a systematic review. Comput. Educ. **173**, 104282 (2021). https://doi.org/10.1016/j.compedu.2021.104282

23. Kassab, M., DeFranco, J., Laplante, P.: A systematic literature review on Internet of things in education: benefits and challenges. J. Comput. Assist. Learn. **36**, 115–127 (2020). https://doi.org/10.1111/jcal.12383

24. Petersen, K., Feldt, R., Mujtaba, S., Mattsson, M.: Guidelines for conducting systematic mapping studies in software engineering: an update. Inf. Softw. Technol. **64**, 1–18 (2015). https://doi.org/10.1016/j.infsof.2015.03.007

25. Chweya, R., Ibrahim, O.: Internet of Things (IoT) implementation in learning institutions: a systematic literature review. J. Pertanika J. Sci. Technol. **29**(1), 471—517 (2021). https://doi.org/10.47836/pjst.29.1.26

26. Carrera-Rivera, A., Ochoa, W., Larrinaga, F., Lasa, G.: How-to conduct a systematic literature review: a quick guide for computer science research. MethodsX **9**, 101895 (2022). https://doi.org/10.1016/j.mex.2022.101895

27. Petersen, K., Feldt, R., Mujtaba, S., Mattsson, M.: Systematic mapping studies in software engineering. In: Proceedings of the 12th International Conference on Evaluation & Assessment in Software Engineering (EASE), pp. 68–77, Bari, Italy (2008). https://doi.org/10.14236/ewic/ease2008.8

28. Cico, O., Jaccheri, L., Nguyen-Duc, A., Zhang, H.: Exploring the intersection between software industry and software engineering education - A systematic mapping of software engineering trends. J. Syst. Softw. **172**, 110736 (2021). https://doi.org/10.1016/j.jss.2020.110736

29. Ghallabi, S., Essalmi, F., Jemni, M.: Kinshuk: Learner modeling in cloud computing. Educ. Inf. Technol. **25**, 5581–5599 (2020). https://doi.org/10.1007/s10639-020-10185-5

30. Camacho, V.L., La Guia, E.D., Olivares, T., Julia Flores, M., Orozco-Barbosa, L.: Data capture and multimodal learning analytics focused on engagement with a new wearable IoT approach. IEEE Trans. Learning Technol. **13**, 704–717 (2020). https://doi.org/10.1109/TLT.2020.2999787

31. Kumar, J.A.: Educational chatbots for project-based learning: investigating learning outcomes for a team-based design course. Int. J. Educ. Technol. High. Educ. **18**, 65 (2021). https://doi.org/10.1186/s41239-021-00302-w

32. Yau, J.Y.K., Hristova, Z.: Evaluation of an extendable context-aware Learning Java' app with personalized user profiling. Technol. Knowl. Learn. **23**, 315–330 (2018). https://doi.org/10.1007/s10758-017-9339-7

33. Elmalaki, S.: FaiR-IoT: fairness-aware human-in-the-loop reinforcement learning for harnessing human variability in personalized IoT. In: Proceedings of the International Conference on Internet-of-Things Design and Implementation (IoTDI), pp. 119-132, Charlottesville, VA (2021). https://doi.org/10.1145/3450268.3453525

34. Guo, Z., Wang, H.: A deep graph neural network-based mechanism for social recommendations. IEEE Trans. Industr. Inf. **17**(4), 2776–2783 (2021). https://doi.org/10.1109/TII.2020.2986316

35. Shapsough, S.Y., Zualkernan, I.A.: A generic IoT architecture for ubiquitous context-aware learning. IEEE Trans. Learn. Technol. **13**(3), 449–464 (2020). https://doi.org/10.1109/TLT.2020.3007708

Student Perspectives on Generative AI Use in Higher Education: The Automation and Augmentation of Learning

Liana Razmerita[1]([✉]) [ID], Sarah Emilie Mortensen[1], Zsofia Mate-Toth[1], and Jonathan P. Allen[2] [ID]

[1] Copenhagen Business School, Frederiksberg, Denmark
lra.msc@cbs.dk, zsma20ab@student.cbs.dk
[2] University of San Francisco, San Francisco, USA
jpallen@usfca.edu

Abstract. This study explores the use of generative artificial intelligence (AI) in higher education from a student perspective. Using survey and interview data from business undergraduates on their main uses of generative AI, and their perceived benefits and drawbacks, this study explores AI use for the augmentation and automation of learning. Though students report AI uses that have the potential for both the automation of existing learning tasks, and for higher level learning and creativity augmentation, the main perceived benefits are focused on automation and immediate productivity outcomes. We conclude that the interplay between using generative AI for automation, augmentation or both is a useful lens for providing valuable insights for the responsible integration of generative AI in higher education.

Keywords: AI · generative AI · ChatGPT · collaboration · higher education

1 Introduction

AI has gained momentum in education with the development of generative AI and Large Language Models (LLM). Since the adoption of AI in higher education is increasing, it is important to explore the consequences of this large-scale adoption for management learning. This paper focuses on the changing nature of academic knowledge work due to the rise of a new generation of generative artificial intelligence tools (AI) (such as ChatGPT by OpenAI, and Gemini by Google).

There are at least 10 different roles of ChatGPT use in teaching and learning, according to a UNESCO report [1]. While some previous studies have emphasized the opportunities to improve teaching strategies and education [2], there are also challenges and risks when introducing AI [3] and for traditional forms of exams and assessments [4]. The use of AI tools gives the impression that humans are in control, but they are suppressing judgment in decision-making [5, 6]. While most of the extant articles about AI in management education are conceptual in nature, few articles to date incorporate empirical data, especially from the student perspective.

C. Bădică et al. (Eds.): BCI 2024, CCIS 2391, pp. 164–174, 2025.
https://doi.org/10.1007/978-3-031-84093-7_12

AI encompasses a cluster of computing technologies, including intelligent agents, machine learning, natural language processing, and decision-making supported by algorithms [7]. AI has started to play an increasingly important role in knowledge collaboration through facilitation of human-AI interaction in different forms, including AI-based assistants (e.g., chatbots or voice-based assistants (e.g. Siri by Apple, Alexa by Amazon), algorithmic technologies and recommender systems. Digital platforms increasingly incorporate AI to support communication and knowledge collaboration [8]. AI-based assistants can be delegated different tasks, help people learn [2, 3, 9] and/or adopt new behaviors [10].

AI technologies offer new possibilities for the relationship between humans and machines to perform work tasks on digital platforms, for the effective design and governance of platforms [11].

The augmentation, delegation and collaboration between knowledge workers and AI and the changing nature of work upon the adoption of AI in the workplace are areas in need of in-depth exploration [12]. As AI becomes prevalent in learning, knowledge collaboration, decision making and the future of work, it becomes imperative to understand how collaboration with AI will impact student behavior, their agency and their learning. Furthermore, as AI-based interaction, e.g. human-chatbot conversations [13], and different forms of persuasion or content personalization will proliferate, we expect AI will play an instrumental role in the future of education. It is unclear what the long-term consequences will be for management education and learning. The use of AI in academia by students is less explored and how should business school adapt teaching, learning and exams to the AI age are subject to an ongoing debate [4].

This paper aims to investigate the multifaceted role of AI for management learning, and in shaping new forms of collaboration and the future of education, by focusing on a student perspective. We take as a point of departure knowledge collaboration combined with an automation-augmentation paradox view adopted recently in AI in management literature [14] Taking the automation-augmentation paradox as a conceptual starting point, the question is how the competing logics of automation and augmentation will be designed, implemented, and deployed in management education work:

- Human-AI augmentation is an expansion of human knowledge, where humans and machines combine their complementary strengths to improve their capabilities [14]. Augmenting intelligence involves human-machine collaboration in which machines perform what they do best (e.g., computing, doing repetitive tasks) to aid humans in doing what humans do best (e.g., abstract reasoning, creating, and making discoveries) [15, 16].
- Automation is the replacement of humans for more tedious or routine tasks. In the context of the academic work, however, which automatable learning, thinking, writing or other essential human activities should be replaced?

Particularly, the aim is to address the following research questions: How does collaboration with AI affect student academic work? And how do students in higher education use generative AI (ChatGPT) for academic work?

1.1   The Emerging Role of (Generative) AI in Knowledge Collaboration

The advent of AI has opened up opportunities for collaborative relationships to emerge between humans and machines in the performance of knowledge work [11]. Collaboration with AI in organizations can take different forms [5, 17–19]. In this context of collaboration different types of hybrid-AI configurations can emerge [20].

Knowledge collaboration involves sharing, transfer, accumulation, transformation and co-creation of knowledge [21]. Knowledge collaboration can be defined as the articulation of personal knowledge into collective wisdom which is possible via a diversity of digital platforms including enterprise social media (e.g., blogs, micro-blogs and wikis) [22], collaborative platforms (e.g. GoogleDocs, Dropbox), AI models or enterprise AI platforms (e.g. Grace[1], Starmind[2]).

Knowledge collaboration that may include different forms of collaborative processes that involves knowledge sharing, communication or contribution of ideas through collaborative work using different ICTs and more recently AI technology. However, the integration of AI into knowledge work can be difficult and may lead to different outcomes. AI tools are often characterized as "black box" and opaque. Due to their opacity, knowledge workers may rely on embedded algorithms and analytical technologies without understanding how they work [5, 17]. Knowledge collaboration is also important for learning and management education.

2   Methodology

The study draws on a mixed method approach. Both qualitative and quantitative data have been collected from students at Copenhagen Business School. In a first phase we have conducted 16 interviews with students to understand how they use generative AI (ChatGPT) for academic work, and to understand about their use, perception of benefits and challenges. The qualitative interviews have been coded for preliminary descriptive themes following an open inductive approach [23].

In a second phase we have created and distributed a survey. The questionnaire was built to measure 1) the tasks that students are using generative AI (ChatGPT) for 2) the associated benefits and drawbacks 3) the factors that impact the intention and use of Generative AI based on Unified Theory of Acceptance and Usage of Technology (UTAUT) [24]. The survey design prioritized multiple choice questions and closed-end questions to make it easy to answer and insure a higher level of response. The survey items were measured using a 5 item likert-scale ranging from strongly agree to strongly disagree. Likert-scale question design provides the respondent with a neutral answer option which is important to increase the measurement reliability [25]. We have collected 199 answers from students from various study programs during March-April 2023.

The survey data provides insights into Human-AI collaboration in relation with academic tasks, students' attitudes towards chatGPT including ethical considerations, the perceived benefits and challenges of adoption of chatbots in higher education but also

---

[1] https://2021.ai/offerings/grace-enterprise-ai-platform/.
[2] Https://www.starmind.ai.

other AI tools they use. It also includes behavioural data (e.g. performance expectancy, social influence, facilitating conditions and behavioural intention). This article will draw on preliminary data related to the knowledge collaboration tasks by combining both qualitative and quantitative data.

3 Data Analysis and Results

The final dataset used for analysis consists of 16 qualitative interviews combined with 124 complete survey responses out of 199 collected answers. The data was cleaned and prepared for data analysis by removing all incomplete responses and the responses of non-CBS students. We retained 124 complete answers out of 199 answers. About one third of students have dropped out before completing the questionnaire.

The final dataset used for analysis consists of 16 qualitative interviews combined with 124 responses. The gender distribution in the dataset is fairly even with 58% female and 41% male (1% non-binary).

Figure 1 summarizes the general information about the respondents' demographics. The gender distribution in the dataset is fairly even with 58% female and 41% male (1% non-binary).

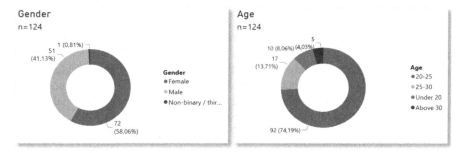

Fig. 1. Respondents' demographics information (age, gender)

Half of the respondents are bachelor's students in the Business Administration and Digital Management program, and the rest of the respondents are close to evenly distributed among other master and bachelor programs at a Business School in Scandinavia. Around 75% of the respondents being between 20 and 25 years old. 13,71% are between 25 and 30 years 10 respondents are under 20 years and 5 respondents are over 30 years.

The survey data emphasized the popularity of ChatGPT in particular version 3.5 as generative AI tool. Only 9 students had access to ChatGPT version 4. Other tools used by the students include Grammarly, Bing, Quillbot (https://quillbot.com/) and "You.com" (https://you.com/). The main themes derived from qualitative interviews have been coded for following an open inductive approach [23] with the first phase of results presented below.

Table 1. Knowledge intensive tasks associated with the usage of ChatGPT

Overview of findings from Preliminary Interviews (n=16)		
Category	*Code*	*Example*
Tasks	Summarizing academic literature	*"I use ChatGPT for summarizing academic articles, as it saves me a lot of time, especially if I am doing something where it's not as necessary to read every detail of a paper"*
	Knowledge generation (exploring different topics)	*"I have also used the tool [...] to further expand my knowledge about specific topics related to my studies"*
	Generating references	*"[...] to find references on certain knowledge that I can look into"*
	Proofreading, improving and editing text (written by myself)	*"I also sometimes use it to proofread text I have written or to give me ideas for how I can make it better"*
	Explaining & evaluating theories and concepts	*"I use it to clarify terms and concepts that I don't fully understand, and also to give me some critique of authors' academic work for example what are some drawbacks of this person's theory"*
	Idea generation (research questions, exam topics, methods)	*"I have recently used it quite a bit to give me ideas or examples of research questions and how to make my research question or methods better within a specific topic"*
	Support in the preliminary processes (survey question generations, literature reviews, pros & cons of choices etc.)	*"I actually also use it as an inspiration and creativity source on first drafts for things like survey questions"*
	Essay/Text writing (actual paragraph writing)	*"if I have some bullet points but can't figure out how to turn it into a paragraph that sounds good I ask it to turn them into a text and then give it instructions for what to focus on"*
	Problem Solving (solving academic exercises)	*"also to help me during the exercise classes, especially in programming classes"*

The coding of data resulted in 9 themes associated with knowledge-intensive tasks as represented in Table 1. An overview of the main benefits derived from the interviews are presented in Table 2. The benefits include enhanced productivity, time saving but also improved quality of writing, learning and creativity. Furthermore, students appreciate the user-friendly characteristics of the interface, personalization of responses and human-like characteristics in the human-chatbot interaction.

An overview of the main drawbacks mentioned by the students in relation with the usage of ChatGPT in higher education are integrated in nine themes in Table 3. A majority of student are using chatGPT because of timesaving: "It saves me so many hours of reading and research" and "it answers anything I ask superfast."

Enhanced productivity is also important as "…it allows me to spend my time more productively and get more things done." Students associate human like characteristics to AI as "it feels like talking to an actual person because I can ask questions in a spoken language format, and it understands it."

Among the main drawbacks mentioned are limitations of chatGPT as technology such as: inaccuracy of responses, dependency on prior knowledge, not updated in terms of access to the most recent knowledge (only trained on internet data until 2021), unreliable answers and flawed references. Students have also referred to ethical concerns and risk of plagiarism but also to loss of learning and loss of creativity.

Table 2. Perceived benefits in using ChatGPT

Overview of findings from Preliminary Interviews (n=16)		
Benefits	Time-saving	*"it saves me so many hours of reading and research"*
		"I think its quickness is a benefit - it answers anything you ask it super fast."
	Improved writing quality	*"It also makes text sound so much better and all I have to do is ask it to make something sound more academic or more professional"*
	User-friendly	*"I like that it is easy to use and to access and that it can understand my commands despite some grammar errors or when I type in a quick sentence without checking it"*
	Conversation history. (it saves previous questions/answers)	*"I like that it considers the previous part of the conversation and gives following answers in that context"*
	Enhanced Productivity	*"It really saves a lot of time for me [...] which allows me to spend my time more productively and get more things done in a short period of time which is super helpful during exams for example"*
	Improved learning processes	*"I like the fact that it can help you get started and inspire you in terms of what scholars to explore further or dive deeper into"*
		"for me I feel that it improves my learning and thought process"
	Enhanced creativity	*I actually feel that it increases my creativity because it gets me over these blocks and allows me to be more creative in a faster way."*
	Human-like characteristics. (e.g. uses spoken language format, can understand prompts despite grammar)	*"it feels like talking to an actual person because I can just ask questions in a spoken language format and it understands it"*
	Personalization of responses	*"It is incredible at delivering very specified answers and perspectives to my questions"*

Table 3. Perceived drawbacks in using chatGPT

Drawbacks	Inaccuracy in responses	*"It doesn't always give the correct information because it seems like it's designed to always try to give something that sounds correct"*
	Dependency on prior knowledge	*"It's sometimes a barrier to use the tool if you don't really know what you're looking for"*
	Risk of plagiarism	*"I am also worried about plagiarism and whether or not I have modified the information I get from there enough to not be caught."*
	Unreliable	*"it also spews out a lot of inaccurate information to satisfy your prompt, so it's not always reliable"*
	Not up to date (only trained on internet data until 2021)	*"I think that it's a shame it doesn't have access to the internet or at least up to date information, since it makes it give false information"*
	Loss of learning	*"In terms of actually learning, I'm not so sure, because when you use it you don't get any background, you just get a summary and go with that"*
	Loss of creativity	*"I wonder about how much it takes over my own ability to think critically [...] I already feel like I am loosing my creativity."*
	Ethical concerns	*"I never know to what extent it is ethical to use it for schoolwork"*
	Flawed references	*"It also doesn't give any sources which makes it difficult to use in an academic project where I need make reference lists"*

The data shows that for some students perceived an improved learning process "for me I feel like it improves my learning and thought process" while for other students it is associated with a loss of learning. For some students the use of chatGPT leads to enhanced creativity "it allows to be more creative in a faster way" while others perceived the contrary. "I wonder how much it takes over my own ability to think critically [..] I already feel like I am losing my creativity."

Tasks

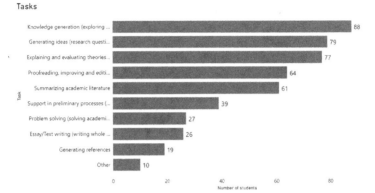

Fig. 2. An overview of the main tasks accomplished using ChatGPT

The students are using chatGPT for a multitude of educational tasks, as presented in Fig. 2: knowledge generation (ranked 1st 70% of students), generating ideas for research questions, exam topics or methods (ranked 2nd 63% of students), explaining and evaluating theories and concepts (ranked the 3rd 61% of students). Students are frequently using ChatGPT for proofreading and improving/editing their own written text (ranked 4th, 51% of students). Summarizing academic literature is ranked 5th, support in preliminary research processes for exams is ranked 6th and problem-solving tasks such as support with exercises is ranked 7th. Only 20% of students stated that they write essays or texts (ranked 8th) and only 15% of students report using ChatGPT for generating references (ranked the 9th). These tasks were selected based on the analysis of the preliminary interviews. Students were asked to check all boxes that applied to what they were using the AI tool for.

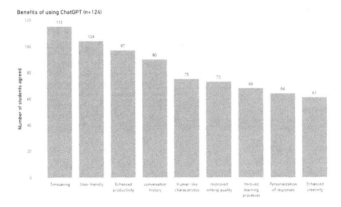

Fig. 3. Main benefits of using ChatGPT in higher education.

An overview of the most important benefits perceived by students, presented in Fig. 3, are time saving (115 students), user friendly tool (104 students), enhanced productivity (97 students), keeping the conversation history, human-like characteristics (75 students)

and improved writing quality (73 students). The least stated benefits are improved learning processes (68 students which represent more than 50%), personalization of responses (64 students) and enhanced creativity (51 students). The main drawbacks in student-AI collaboration using chatGPT, as represented in Fig. 4. The identified drawbacks are: the risk of plagiarism, inaccuracy of responses, not up to date in terms of knowledge, flawed referencing, dependency on prior knowledge, unreliable, ethical concerns, loss of creativity and loss of learning.

In relation with attitude towards ChatGPT, a majority of students (about 80%) agreed that the benefits outweigh the drawbacks. Despite these drawbacks students prefer to improve their productivity and save time. By trying to save time and improve their productivity, students may automate human knowledge processes such as learning, thinking and writing which can be detrimental for their future work skills.

The study findings emphasize that students perceive human-AI collaboration beneficial even though it may lead to "controversial" outcomes improved learning and "thought process" or loss of learning, loss of creativity or enhanced creativity. One student states that "I like the fact that it can help you get started and inspire you in terms of what scholars to explore further or dive deeper into."

The process of knowledge collaboration can be extended and augmented through engineered prompts and personalized interaction. Generative AI brings new opportunities for creating personalized learning environments which may integrate personal assistants or a "study buddy" [1]. Students acknowledge that chatGPT "is incredible at delivering very specified answers and perspectives to my questions".

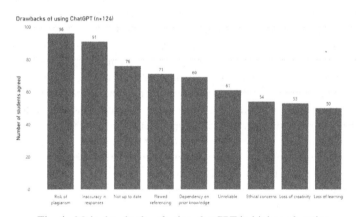

Fig. 4. Main drawbacks of using chatGPT in higher education.

The management of plagiarism risk creates an interesting definition of trustworthy AI from the student perspective. This suggests that although they experience risk of plagiarism, inaccuracy in responses and perceived to be unreliable they still collaborate with chatGPT for academic tasks.

4 Discussion and Conclusions

The transformative potential of AI in education and management learning has been widely discussed, but empirical results and theoretical development have been lacking in the literature so far. This preliminary research investigates the evolving relationship between humans and AI in performing learning and knowledge-intensive tasks, using knowledge collaboration theories and the automation-augmentation paradox. Students are collaborating with AI using ChatGPT for expanding knowledge on academic themes, summarizing concepts, theories, and generating ideas for research topics and methods.

Though students report AI uses that have the potential for higher level learning and creativity augmentation, the main perceived benefits are focused on automation and immediate productivity outcomes. Time saving, enhanced productivity and user-friendliness of the tool were identified as main benefits associated with ChatGPT, whereas the risk of plagiarism, its inaccuracy in responses and the need for prior knowledge were identified as the main drawbacks.

For the next phase of this research, we intend to use the preliminary data to explore the relationship between the automation/augmentation paradox and concepts from the student-centered learning literature (e.g., [26]). As the set of learning tasks is subject to a combination of automation and augmentation in partnership with the AI, the benefits of increased task efficiency and time-savings may come at the expense of future learning and skills. The augmentation and automation of learning take place across a complex process that is not completely controlled by either students, instructors, or other institutional actors. Tracing the interplay of augmentation and automation through the responses of multiple actors will be important for understanding how the overall learning process transforms. What changes will be necessary across the entire process for the augmentation uses of generative AI to come to the forefront?

Despite the fact that AI tools were banned for exams, the students have still adopted ChatGPT because students believe that it supports their academic performance. The results of the study findings might be influenced by the policy that was in place at CBS at the time of the study. The policies at universities regarding the use of chatGPT and similar AI tools are evolving and reflect an open debate on how to best integrate these AI tools into educational practices while upholding the academic and ethical integrity. The responsible integration of AI tools such as ChatGPT would require clear guidance for both students and faculty that ensure both academic integrity and prevent cheating.

From a student-centric perspective, teaching work faces new challenges of how to optimize learning opportunities in collaboration with AI, how to teach life-long learning skills, and how to obtain student buy-in for more active learning approaches. With this AI-human collaboration research, we hope to contribute to the literature on student-centered learning, and on the changing nature of knowledge work more generally. *We conclude that the interplay between using generative AI for automation, augmentation or both is a useful lens for understanding the future directions of AI in higher education and guiding a more responsible integration of Generative AI.*

Acknowledgments. The paper was written in the framework of the EURIDICE project, and will be used as an educational resource, for which it received partially funding from the European Union in the Digital Europe Programme.

References

1. Sabzalieva, E., Valentini, A.: ChatGPT and artificial intelligence in higher education: quick start guide. United Nations Educational, Scientific and Cultural Organization (2023). https://unesdoc.unesco.org/ark:/48223/pf0000385146
2. Ellis, A.R., Slade, E.: A new era of learning: considerations for ChatGPT as a tool to enhance statistics and data science education. J. Statist. Data Sci. Educ. **31**(2), 1–10 (2023)
3. Kasneci, E., et al.: ChatGPT for good? On opportunities and challenges of large language models for education. Learn. Individ. Differ. **103**, 102274 (2023)
4. Rudolph, J., Tan, S., Tan, S.: ChatGPT: bullshit spewer or the end of traditional assessments in higher education? J. Appl. Learn. Teach. **6**(1), 342–363 (2023)
5. Lebovitz, S., Lifshitz-Assaf, H., Levina, N.: To engage or not to engage with AI for critical judgments: how professionals deal with opacity when using AI for medical diagnosis. Organ. Sci. **33**(1), 126–148 (2022)
6. Moser, C., Den Hond, F., Lindebaum, D.: Morality in the age of artificially intelligent algorithms. Acad. Manage. Learn. Educ. **21**(1) (2022)
7. Tredinnick, L.: Artificial intelligence and professional roles. Bus. Inf. Rev. **34**(1), 37–41 (2017)
8. Maedche, A., et al.: AI-based digital assistants. Bus. Inf. Syst. Eng. **61**(4), 535–544 (2019)
9. Okonkwo, C.W., Ade-Ibijola, A.: Chatbots applications in education: a systematic review. Comput. Educ. Artific. Intell. **2**, 100033 (2021)
10. Roda, C., Angehrn, A., Nabeth, T., Razmerita, L.: Using conversational agents to support the adoption of knowledge sharing practices. Interact. Comput. **15**(1), 57–89 (2003)
11. Rai, A., Constantinides, P., Sarker, S.: Editor's comments: next-generation digital platforms: toward human-AI hybrids. Manag. Inf. Syst. Q. **43**(1), 9 (2019)
12. Fuegener, A., Grahl, J., Gupta, A., Ketter, W.: Cognitive challenges in human–artificial intelligence collaboration: investigating the path toward productive delegation. Inf. Syst. Res. **33**(2), 678–696 (2022)
13. Hill, J., Randolph Ford, W., Farreras, I.G.: Real conversations with artificial intelligence: a comparison between human-human online conversations and human-chatbot conversations. Comput. Hum. Behav. **49**, 245–250 (2015)
14. Raisch, S., Krakowski, S.: Artificial intelligence and management: the automation–augmentation paradox. Acad. Manage. Rev. **46**(1) (2021)
15. Paul, S., et al.: Intelligence augmentation: human factors in AI and future of work. AIS Trans. Hum.-Comput. Interact. **14**(3), 426–445 (2022)
16. Jain, H., Padmanabhan, B., Pavlou, P.A., Raghu, T.S.: Editorial for the special section on humans, algorithms, and augmented intelligence: The future of work, organizations, and society. Inf. Syst. Res. **32**(3), 675–687 (2021)
17. Anthony, C.: When knowledge work and analytical technologies collide: the practices and consequences of black boxing algorithmic technologies. Adm. Sci. Q. **66**(4), 1173–1212 (2021)
18. Faraj, S., Pachidi, S., Sayegh, K.: Working and organizing in the age of the learning algorithm. Inf. Organ. **28**(1), 62–70 (2018)
19. Willcocks, L.: Robo-Apocalypse cancelled? Reframing the automation and future of work debate. J. Inf. Technol. **35**(4), 286–302 (2020)
20. Ebel, P., et al.: Hybrid intelligence in business networks. Electronic Mark. **31**(2), 313–318 (2021)
21. Faraj, S., Jarvenpaa, S.L., Majchrzak, A.: Knowledge collaboration in online communities. Organ. Sci. **22**(5), 1224–1239 (2011)

22. Razmerita, L., Kirchner, K., Nabeth, T.: Social media in organizations: leveraging personal and collective knowledge processes. J. Organ. Comput. Electron. Commer. **24**(1), 74–93 (2014)

23. Myers, M.D.: Qualitative research in business and management, 3rd edn. Sage Publications (2019)

24. Venkatesh, V., Morris, M.G., Davis, G.B., Davis, F.D.: User acceptance of information technology: toward a unified view. MIS Q. Manage. Inform. Syst. **27**(3), 425–478 (2003)

25. Schutt, R.K.: Investigating the social world: The process and practice of research. In: Making Sense of the Social World: Methods of Investigation, 9th edn. Sage Publications (2019)

26. Doyle, T.: Helping students learn in a learner-centered environment: a guide to facilitating learning in higher education. Taylor & Francis (2023)

Distributed Systems

Leveraging Fitness Functions to Assess Cloud Migration Readiness of Clean Architecture

Florin Olariu[✉] and Adrian Smău

Alexandru Ioan Cuza University, Strada General Henri Mathias Berthelot Nr. 16, Iaşi 700259, România
olariu@gmail.com

Abstract. Fitness functions quantitatively assess how well a specific architecture complies with its stated architectural goals. In test-driven development, we write tests to ensure the system's features match the intended business results. But when we turn our attention to fitness function development, we take this idea one step further and create tests that measure how well the system adheres to design goals. During our research, we found that two essential routes - applying architectural rule tests and enforcing design rules - are necessary to reach our objective. These two components cooperate to guarantee that the system's architecture is solid and consistent with its intended purpose. We deliberately use a public domain project built with.NET to achieve this goal. This project best exemplifies a design philosophy emphasizing the division of concerns and the autonomous deployment of system components, known as Clean Architecture. This study aims to improve software engineering by encouraging the use of fitness functions earlier in the development lifecycle and improving strategic planning for cloud migrations. Creating a clear and established methodology for migration evaluation will enable this aspect. After reviewing the initial step, we introduced an additional public repository, which included creating 26 fitness functions to assess the Clean Architecture. This strategic integration allowed us to use Fitness Functions Driven Development to streamline the code reworking process, providing a smooth transition to a cloud environment. These utilities help to confirm that the product is ready for any cloud migration so that it may move to a new environment without losing any of its features or performance.

Keywords: Fitness Functions · .NET · Fitness Function Driven Development · Cloud Migration Readiness · Clean Architecture · Design Rules

1 Introduction

1.1 Context

A cloud computing revolution has brought a new era of operational effectiveness. The attraction of features like increased flexibility, scalability, and economy has propelled the worldwide cloud market to expand quickly. Industry statistics point to a rising dependence of firms on cloud services to take advantage of these benefits; according to recent

C. Bădică et al. (Eds.): BCI 2024, CCIS 2391, pp. 177–192, 2025.
https://doi.org/10.1007/978-3-031-84093-7_13

studies, 90% of enterprises believe that cloud technology is essential for growth [1]. In addition, the most current estimate from Gartner, Inc. Projects that end-user expenditure on public cloud services worldwide will rise by 20.4% to $678.8 billion by 2024 [2]. As a self-service, on-demand platform, cloud computing is now essential to achieving complete digital transformation and allowing businesses to innovate, carry on with operations, and manage uncertainties. Moving to such an environment, however, can be difficult, and if the migration readiness process is handled better than it should, it can result in unanticipated negative consequences. This emphasizes the need for a comprehensive assessment of migration readiness, which requires careful consideration.

1.2 Motivation

We have previously shown that architectures following the concepts of Clean Architecture are highly flexible, allowing them to be migrated across different cloud providers and models, such as Serverless computing [3], Platform as a Service (PaaS) [4], and Infrastructure as a Service (IaaS) [4–6].

Our primary objective is establishing guidelines utilizing fitness functions [7] to assess an architecture's readiness for cloud migration. Fitness functions are a solid way to confirm a system's functionality and migration readiness by quantitatively evaluating how well an architecture aligns with its stated goals:

To accomplish this, we propose to use the features of the NetArchTest [7] NuGet package to construct several generic tests. We design these tests to systematically evaluate the system across various settings, ensuring its dependability and robustness. We want to develop a complete working method that guarantees successful transfer and advances the scholarly conversation in software architecture and system migration by fusing academic rigor with practical application. This strategy emphasizes our dedication to developing the field through creative methods and intellectual participation.

2   Case Study – Verifying Readiness of a Modular Monolith Based on a Clean Architecture Pattern to Be Migrated to the Cloud

Over the last twenty years, many architectural patterns have included more features, resulting in less coupling from an infrastructure and coding perspective. Here, we showcase a handful of these patterns: They include Clean Architecture [8], Command and Query Responsibility Segregation [9], Hexagonal Architecture [10], and Onion Architecture [11].

Robert C. Martin observed that all the architectures we have seen thus far may be grouped under the broad category of Clean Architecture and that, while having some tiny, detailed variations, they are all somewhat similar. Their mutual goal is to divide concerns. To achieve this, they all divide the software into layers. Everyone has at least two levels: business rules and user and system interfaces.

The author also observed that a system created using the architectures has the following advantages: it is testable, independent of the framework, and independent of the user interface and databases. These findings in [8] lead to the suggestion of an architectural schematic for every scenario.

Figure 1 shows several concentric circles that represent various program sections. In this case, the inner circle comprises policies, and the outside circles are technologies.

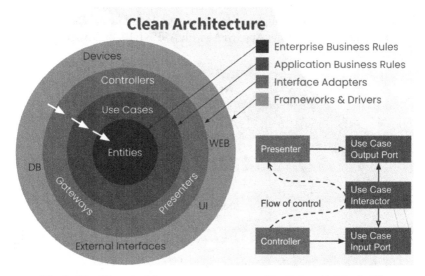

Fig. 1. The Clean Architecture pattern proposed by Robert C. Martin [8]

Robert C. Martin dubbed this rule, "Dependency rule: Source code dependencies must point only inward, toward higher-level policies" [8]. Robert C. Martin invented the Dependency Rule, which has also been emphasized by Jeffrey Palermo in Onion Architecture and Alistair Cockburn in Hexagonal Architecture. Even if following basic guidelines may seem easy, but it is essential to improve specific factors, including application testability, application maintainability, and application flexibility (changing external databases and UI implementations because some of them can become outdated).

By making use of the dependency rule coined by Robert C. Martin in [8], we will extend the examples presented in [13] and apply them to a public GitHub repository project [12]. We will employ NetArchTest [8]; this project offers a seamless API for the.Net Standard, capable of enforcing architectural guidelines during unit testing. With this project, we may write tests that impose dependencies, names, and class design standards, the foundations of.Net coding. We can incorporate these into a build pipeline and apply them to any unit test framework. Its fluid API allows us to set up clear rules that test assertions can use.

Although several static analysis tools are available to assess application structure, their primary goal is to enforce general best practices rather than conventions particular to a specific application. While it is possible to press-gang the better tools in this market into developing unique rules for a specific architecture, the goal here is to include rules in a test suite and produce a self-testing architecture.

The project draws inspiration from ArchUnit [13], a Java-based library that aims to tackle the challenges of maintaining architectural design patterns in code bases over an extended period. Convention, which depends on a meticulous and uniform code review process, is the only way to uphold several patterns. This discipline frequently deteriorates as projects expand, use cases become more intricate, and developers join and leave.

When it comes to public GitHub projects, though, this template intends to offer an easy-to-use and effective way to construct enterprise applications using ASP.NET Core and Clean Architecture. This template allows us to easily follow the Clean Architecture concepts and build a Single-Page App (SPA) with ASP.NET Core, Angular, or React.

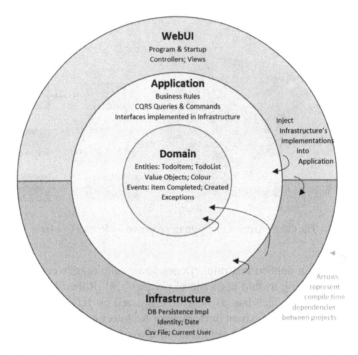

Fig. 2. Project structure for Clean Architecture proposed by Jason Taylor [12]

As depicted in Fig. 2, the project structure proposed by Jason Taylor consists of the following building blocks: the Domain layer containing enterprise or domain logic, the Application layer containing business logic that implements CQRS [9], the Infrastructure containing classes for accessing the external layers (in our case, the SQL Server database) and the Web layer containing a SPA [14] build in Angular and a Web API (RESTful API) build in.NET 8 exposing the backend features to be consumed by the Angular Application [15].

In conclusion, to test the architecture based on Dependency Rules coined by Robert C. Martin [8], we have to:

- Verify that Domain doesn't have any dependencies on Infrastructure or Application.
- Verify that the Application doesn't have any dependencies on the Infrastructure.
- Verify that the API should depend on the Application and the Infrastructure.

We will dive deep into these verifications using the NetArchTest tool in the following two subsections.

2.1 Testing the Architecture

Figure 3 illustrates the improvement of the current project's architectural framework by incorporating a new xUnit [16] project named FitnessFunctions.Tests. This addition signifies a broadening of the project's framework.

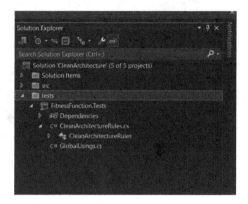

Fig. 3. Extending the structure for Clean Architecture proposed by Jason Taylor [12]

Figure 4 demonstrates that we conducted 26-unit tests to verify the following principles: the Domain should not rely on the Application or the Infrastructure, the Application should not rely on the Infrastructure, and the API, being an external layer according to Fig. 1, should depend on both the Application and the Infrastructure. We demonstrated in Fig. 4 that we can extend these tests to incorporate code quality measures. This includes measures such as a method's maximum number of parameters and ways to manage custom exceptions properly. These generic tests can be repurposed to evaluate other projects built around clean architecture. Only the terminology of namespaces requires modification.

Furthermore, we can extend the tests by testing other aspects, such as the following. If we use a Repository pattern [19], we might check that all the repository implementations can rely on the Domain project.

However, when it comes to testing the architecture, we can go beyond the testing of dependency rules, which Robert C. Martin coined in Clean Architecture [9]. In the following subsection, we will explain this approach in detail.

2.2 Enforcing Design Rules

As stated in [17], we can also use architectural testing to ensure your application adheres to design principles. These design guidelines go beyond simple project references and focus on the precise details of your class implementations.

Here are a few examples of design principles that are applicable:

- Services should be classified as internal.
- Entities and Value objects should be sealed.

Fig. 4. Proposed tests to validate the Clean Architecture.

- Controllers should not have direct dependencies on repositories.
- Command and query handlers should follow a specific naming standard.

The extent to which design principles can be enforced is extensive and ultimately depends on the choice of the number of rules you choose to apply. Now, let's get into the process of creating tests that guarantee compliance with these design principles (Fig. 5).

Fig. 5. Layer isolation and Dependency Rule enforcing

3 Fitness Functions Driven Development in Practice

3.1 Introduction to Fitness Functions Driven Development

Like Test-Driven Development (TDD), fitness-function-driven development involves creating tests to ensure a system's features align with its desired business results. Tim Sommer states that architects must consider more than technical architecture when creating evolvable software systems [18].

Each project has unique dimensions to consider. Our theoretical architectural fitness functions, derived from "glorified metrics" [18], perfectly align with their application. They offer an iterative approach to architecture, guiding the design towards desired results. Addressing functional and non-functional system requirements is essential to ensure a successful migration. According to Ben Morris [19], an evolutionary approach to design allows for objective and repeatable tests to evaluate the feasibility of technical solutions. These assessments compromise architectural design rigor and the ability to adapt quickly. Iterative experimentation with fitness functions can help guide the evolution of architecture. His belief appears that the way architectural fitness functions are applied distinguishes them from "glorified metrics" [18]. They offer an iterative approach to architecture, guiding the design towards desired results.

3.2 Case Study – Contoso University Project

3.2.1 Contoso University Project – Short Description

The Contoso University project [20] layout is divided into multiple folders, with Controllers handling the application's flow through CRUD endpoints. Models include entity classes and ViewModels, whereas Views contain Razor view files for rendering the UI. Data flow involves a user making a request to the application, which is routed to the appropriate Controller method. The Controller interacts with the DBContext to retrieve or manipulate data, which is then passed to a view model and rendered.

However, all Fitness Functions tests from the previously developed suite fail when run on the preliminary codebase. We must take appropriate steps to leverage fitness functions and refactor the project properly. ValueObjects, Event-driven architecture, and exception handling can be avoided for simpler codebases. Still, they are recommended for more complex ones due to their improved flexibility, modularity, and scalability, as demonstrated by Jason Taylor in his comprehensive template (Fig. 6).

Fig. 6. Test run on our preliminary code base

Figure 7 illustrates the first stage in Clean Architecture refactoring: initializing Layers and describing their layout. To use FFDD and gain insight into how the architecture is shifting, focus on each layer at a time and run the fitness function test suite after each code update.

Fig. 7. Initial MVC application layout and the beginning of architectural layering

3.2.2 Domain Layer

To create the new layout and adhere to Fitness Functions, identify and extract resource entities and Enums from the application's operations into the Domain Layer. The only change needed is to remove the data annotations from the Entities, which will be handled in other layers. The Domain Layer might have a structure-like Fig. 8 (left), with Entities implementing the Base Entity class, which centralizes their common ID field, as seen in Fig. 8 (right).

Fig. 8. The refactored Domain Layer and Entities declaration

Figure 9 shows that the Domain Layer has passed the fitness functions, indicating that this layer is architecturally ready for cloud migration.

Fig. 9. Passed fitness functions tests after refactoring

3.2.3   Application Layer

The Application Layer proved to be the most time-consuming component to modify due to using the CQRS paradigm. Most of the refactoring effort focused on understanding business logic and transferring it from the prior flow to a Command and Query-based one.

Each entity type has its commands and queries with handlers to provide separation of concerns, maintainability, scalability, and testability. Figure 10 shows an example of a Command and its related Handler.

Fig. 10. The refactored Application Layer

We made Handlers rely on abstractions to respect dependency injection and provide parallelism through asynchronous database operations. As we indicated when developing the fitness functions test suite, Queries should avoid returning Entities at all costs.

The refactored Application Layer employs ViewModels (VMs) to collect and display internal resources through AutoMapper [21]. The Web layer also uses View Models to present application views effectively. The fitness functions require transforming the DBContext to an interface that follows Clean Architecture principles. We left the DbSets specified within the interface and the data-saving methods to the database. This interface will be implemented at the Infrastructure layer; nevertheless, DbContext will be injected through this interface for the reasons stated in the previous section. To handle our business needs centrally, we created a custom exception. By making these adjustments, we ensured that the Application Layer adhered to Clean Architecture. This is proven by executing the adapted fitness functions associated with this Layer and passing them all. Figure 11 shows an example of a Command and Handler, and Fig. 12 displays the fitness testing results.

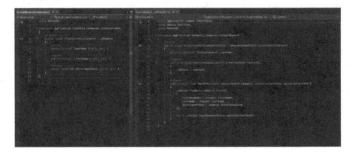

Fig. 11. The refactored Application Layer for CQRS Command and Handler

⊿ ✅ FitnessFunctions.Suite (22)	425 ms
▷ ◔ CleanArchitecture FitnessFunctions.Suite (13)	
⊿ ✅ FitnessFunctions.Suite (9)	425 ms
⊿ ✅ ApplicationLayer (4)	129 ms
✅ ApplicationLayer_ShouldNotImplementDeclaredInterfaces	52 ms
✅ CommandAndQueryHandlers_ShouldBeClearlyDefined	11 ms
✅ CommandsAndQueries_ShouldBeClearlyDefined	12 ms
✅ Handlers_ShouldHaveExpectedEffects	54 ms
▷ ✅ DomainLayer (5)	296 ms

Fig. 12. Passed fitness functions tests after refactoring

3.2.4   Infrastructure Layer

The Infrastructure Layer supports connectivity between business logic and external sources, like databases and APIs. In Fig. 13, we use EntityFrameworkCore to develop configurations mediating entities and database schematization, like Taylor's approach. The Database Context implementation is also here, ensuring we meet the Clean Architecture pattern's requirements.

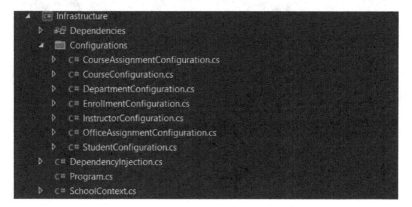

Fig. 13. The refactored Infrastructure Layer

Finally, Fig. 14 demonstrates that we have met the architectural limitations that have guided us thus far.

Fig. 14. Passed fitness functions tests after refactoring

3.2.5 Web Layer

The application's front-end components represent many Web Layer components, so the fitness functions did not significantly alter the system. We used a Controller-based method to expose the application's endpoints and concurrently handle Commands and Queries. Views were configured to use the ViewModels defined in the Application Layer. Figure 15 illustrates controller deployment.

Fig. 15. Implementation details of the Controller

Finally, Fig. 16 demonstrates the effective development of the Web Layer to adhere to the intended architectural restrictions.

Fig. 16. Passed fitness functions tests after refactoring

We incorporated fitness functions that move individual layers towards a specific architectural pattern and general-purpose functions to ensure compliant communication between levels and the project. As seen in Fig. 17, the overall application design is now compliant with our test suite.

Overall (6)	344 ms
ApplicationLayer_MethodsShouldDeclareLessThan10LocalVariables	39 ms
ApplicationLayer_ShouldNotDependOnInfrastructureOrPresentation	120 ms
DomainLayer_ShouldNotDependOnOtherLayers	37 ms
InfrastructureLayer_ShouldNotDependOnPresentation	32 ms
PresentationLayer_ShouldDependOnApplicationAndInfrastructure	41 ms
ShouldHaveDefinedCleanArchitectureLayers	75 ms
WebLayer (3)	182 ms

Fig. 17. Passed fitness functions tests after refactoring

4 Conclusions

The chapter addresses implementing and using a fitness functions test suite to examine and impact cloud migration study from an architectural perspective. The tool compares the accuracy of a project's codebase to a template, focusing on a particular system trait. It provides valuable insight into failed tests because it reveals that an area of the application does not meet the assertion's criteria. It also serves as the project's shifting mechanism, constantly adapting the application to the specified rules and directions offered by the framework. We can extend fitness functions to address non-functional criteria, offering an advantage over typical cloud migration preparedness methodologies and technologies.

Cloud migration can be approached from several perspectives and used as a development technique, as Fitness Functions Driven Development demonstrated. Furthermore, the evaluations are dynamic, adaptable to specific situations, and can continuously or frequently assess the system's state. The tool's versatility and adaptability make it an excellent choice for assessing cloud migration preparedness.

The emergence of cloud computing has introduced a new period of operational effectiveness, leading to a greater dependence on cloud services. Given that an impressive 90% of businesses consider cloud technology an essential factor in their expansion, it is necessary to emphasize the importance of conducting a thorough readiness assessment before migrating. Known for its flexibility, the Clean Architecture easily transfers between cloud providers and models. The main goal is to make recommendations using fitness functions to assess the readiness of an architecture for cloud migration.

We recommend using the NetArchTest NuGet package for.NET-based projects, and ArchUnit for Spring-based projects to achieve this. This package enables the development of universal tests to methodically examine the system in different settings, ensuring its reliability and resilience. This technique guarantees a smooth and effective transfer and advances the academic discussion in software design and system migration by combining scholarly rigor with practical implementation.

We present a case study to confirm the readiness of a modular monolith, adhering to the Clean Architecture pattern, for cloud migration. Robert C. Martin's Dependency Rule enhances essential aspects like a program's testability, maintainability, and flexibility.

To enforce the Dependency Rule in a public GitHub repository project, we employ NetArchTest, a NuGet package that offers a streamlined API for the.Net Standard. This software package guarantees adherence to architectural rules in unit testing, facilitating the creation of a self-testing architecture. Being developed using an approach ArchUnit, a Java-based library, influences this approach by maintaining architectural design patterns in code bases over an extended period not only on.NET projects but also on Spring and Java projects.

We designed the template to offer a streamlined and effective approach for building enterprise apps using ASP.NET Core and Clean Architecture. The Clean Architecture project structure consists of four layers: the Domain layer, the Application layer, the Infrastructure layer, and the Web layer.

To evaluate the design according to Dependency Rules, it is imperative to verify that the Domain is independent of both Infrastructure and Application, the Application does not have any dependencies on Infrastructure, and the API is reliant on both. Architectural testing can also ensure that design ideas are put into action. For example, it can ensure that classes are categorized, entities and value objects are protected, controllers don't directly depend on repositories are avoided, or command and query handlers are named correctly.

The number of rules utilized determines the level of implementation of these design principles. We employ a specific procedure to construct tests that verify compliance with naming standards for all queries, ensuring adherence to these design principles.

Using architectural tests and design principles, we can determine whether the product is ready for migration during the cloud migration assessment phase or needs more restructuring to achieve this goal.

Automated architecture tests are a direct and effective way to enforce the principles of software architecture and design. Automated testing is a highly advantageous investment for software engineers. Once written, these tests are an enduring validation tool for your system. Nevertheless, it is essential to remember that your testing must adapt as your system progresses. The manual enforcement of software architecture, utilizing techniques such as pair programming and continuous peer review, has inherent limitations. It is prone to errors, requires significant time, and could be more economically efficient. This is where the intrinsic worth of architecture tests becomes evident. We can quickly compose them and significantly reduce the expenses of maintaining your software architecture rules to almost zero.

Fitness functions offer a robust way of evaluating both functional and non-functional requirements of a software system, which proves essential in a cloud environment. This provides a more nuanced and rigorous evaluation of the project to be migrated since they analyze all aspects of this process.

Moreover, through Fitness Function Driven Development (FFDD), organizations can take full advantage of this technology by iteratively refining their software architecture to align with various architectural patterns and best practices and enforce design rules. For the practical part of this study, we have chosen Clean Architecture as the pattern to be adopted, creating a comprehensive fitness function test suite to evaluate and constrain the codebase to adopt our desired shape. Then, by utilizing this framework, we refactored a codebase that initially was not compliant with the Clean Architecture pattern using the FFDD technique. The positive results from the practical implementation and testing indicate that fitness functions could become a standard tool in cloud migration strategies. We evaluated the initial project, highlighted its shortcomings, and shifted its architecture. FFDD can easily be automated and integrated into the development process via CI/CD. It is versatile and flexible since it can accommodate any architectural pattern, programming language, or framework's specific behaviors and implementations.

With further development and industry collaboration, this approach has the prospect of significantly streamlining the migration process.

To summarize, this paper makes a valuable contribution to the world of cloud computing and software development by introducing a practical and creative technique for assessing migration readiness. Organizations can achieve more dependable, efficient, and successful cloud transfers by including fitness functions in their development and migration processes. Future research and development activities will improve the applicability and effectiveness of this method, opening the door for industry-wide adoption and standardization.

Acknowledgements. The authors thank the Romanian Ministry of Research, Innovation, and Digitization, within Program 1- Development of the national RD system, Subprogram 1.2 - Institutional Performance - RDI excellence funding projects, Contract no.11PFE/30.12.2021, for financial support.

References

1. Cloud Computing Deloitte. https://www2.deloitte.com/ro/en/pages/about-deloitte/articles/studiu-deloitte-din-companii-considera-ca-tehnologia-cloud-este-esentiala-pentru-dezvoltare-transformare-digitala-si-competitivitate-pe-piata.html. Accessed 25 May 2024
2. Public Cloud-Gartner. https://www.gartner.com/en/newsroom/press-releases/11-13-2023-gartner-forecasts-worldwide-public-cloud-end-user-spending-to-reach-679-billion-in-20240#:~:text=Worldwide%20end%2Duser%20spending%20on,Vice%20President%20Analyst%20at%20Gartner. Accessed 25 May 2024
3. Serverless on AWS. https://aws.amazon.com/serverless/. Accessed 07 Sep 2023
4. IaaS and PaaS. https://www.koombea.com/blog/iaas-vs-paas-vs-serverless/. Accessed 21 Apr 2024
5. Olariu, F., Alboaie, L.: Challenges in optimizing migration costs from on-premises to microsoft azure. In: Proceedings of the 27th International Conference on Knowledge Based & Intelligent Information and Engineering Systems (KES), pp. 3649–3659. Athens, Greece (2023)
6. Olariu, F.: Overcoming challenges in migrating modular monolith from on-premises to AWS cloud. In: Proceedings of the 22nd Conference on Networking in Education and Research (RoEduNet), pp. 1–6. Craiova, Romania (2023)
7. NetArchTest. https://github.com/BenMorris/NetArchTest. Accessed 25 May 2024
8. Martin, R.C.: Clean Architecture: A Craftsman's Guide to Software Structure and Design. Prentice Hall, London, England (2018)
9. Fowler, M.: CQRS. https://martinfowler.com/bliki/CQRS.html. Accessed 14 Aug 2023
10. Cockburn, A.: Hexagonal Architecture (2008). https://jeffreypalermo.com/2008/07/the-onion-architecture-part-1/. Accessed 14 Aug 2023
11. Palermo, J.: Onion Architecture. https://jeffreypalermo.com/2008/07/the-onion-architecture-part-1/. Accessed 14 Aug 2023
12. Taylor, J.: Clean Architecture - Jason Taylor. https://github.com/jasontaylordev/CleanArchitecture. Accessed 25 May 2024
13. ArchUnit. https://www.archunit.org/. Accessed 25 May 2024
14. Subotin, O.: SPA - Single Page Application. https://codefinity.com/blog/Unlocking-the-Potential-of-Single-Page-Applications?utm_source=google&utm_medium=cpc&utm_campaign=20955067105&utm_content=158811191432&utm_term=&gad_source=1&gclid=Cj0KCQjwmMayBhDuARIsAM9HM8dEyl7UEBPO780g_wMfhz8aaM_O_kN658NUbLapMWfva387vlXtFa0aAi5vEALw_wcB. Accessed 25 May 2024
15. Taylor, J.: Clean Architecture .NET - explained. https://jasontaylor.dev/clean-architecture-getting-started/. Accessed 26 May 2024
16. XUnit. https://xunit.net/. Accessed 26 May 2024
17. Jovanovici, M.: Enforcing software architecture with architecture tests. https://www.milanjovanovic.tech/blog/enforcing-software-architecture-with-architecture-tests?utm_source=newsletter&utm_medium=email&utm_campaign=tnw91. Accessed 25 May 2024
18. Sommer, T.: Using fitness functions to create evolving architectures. Using Fitness Functions to create evolving architectures. Accessed 24 Jul 2024

19. Morris, B.: Using Architectural <<Fitness Functions>> as a guide to system design. Using Architectural <<Fitness Func-tions>> as a guide to system design. Accessed 24 Jul 2024
20. Taylor, J.: Contoso University Project. https://github.com/jasontaylordev/ContosoUniversity. Accessed 24 Jul 2024
21. Automapper. https://automapper.org/. Accessed 24 Jul 2024

Resource Management in Cloud IaaS via Machine Learning Algorithms

Megi Tartari$^{(\boxtimes)}$ (iD), Genti Daci$^{(\boxtimes)}$, Elinda Kajo Meçe$^{(\boxtimes)}$, and Enida Sheme$^{(\boxtimes)}$

Department of Computer Engineering, Faculty of Information Technology, Polytechnic University of Tirana, Tiranë, Albania
{megi.tartari,gdaci,ekajo,esheme}@fti.edu.al

Abstract. Cloud computing is a prevalent technology in the IT market today, providing enterprises with the necessary infrastructure to achieve high performance levels for running their applications using the pay-as-you-go model. The lowest layer in Cloud is Infrastructure-as-a-Service (IaaS), which provides the resource pool. A primary challenge to cloud providers in IaaS is to effectively manage resources to reduce power consumption, which is a critical issue of paramount importance today, due to its substantial environmental impact stemming from the widespread use of cloud computing, while simultaneously maintaining Quality of Service. In this paper, we review the latest solutions that utilize Machine Learning (ML) algorithms for resource management. We focus on the processes of auto-scaling, Virtual Machine (VM) consolidation, and VM placement, which directly influence power consumption. We identify the benefits and innovations these solutions bring to the optimization of resource management, but also their drawbacks.

Keywords: Infrastructure-as-a-Service · resource allocation · auto-scaling · VM consolidation · VM placement · workload forecast

1 Introduction

Cloud Computing has emerged as a baseline technology today supporting the latest trends in computer science such as Artificial Intelligence, Internet of Things, and Big Data, by providing powerful infrastructure suitable for processing the large data volumes these technological trends face. The most powerful qualities that make cloud ubiquitous today are scalability, to handle the workload growth without compromising performance, and elasticity, which involves adding or reducing resources according to workload fluctuations.

Today's cloud services rely on highly scalable data centers, composed of hundreds or thousands of physical servers, which provide their resources (CPU, RAM, disk) in a virtualized form. Users access low-level infrastructure resources to run higher-level cloud services. This type of cloud infrastructure is known as Infrastructure as a Service (IaaS). IaaS Providers offer for rent various types of VMs, based on the billing method and their level of availability: a) on-demand VMs offer high availability but are paid for the usage time, b) reserved VMs offer better billing plans but require to predict how much resources we will need thus there is a risk of over provisioning or under provisioning, c) spot VMs are instances that are not currently in use and are cheaper, but do not offer high availability, so they can be interrupted at any time.

The primary objectives of cloud providers are to deliver the service performance specified in the Service Level Agreement (SLA), while simultaneously reducing costs associated with the provided resources. Therefore, cloud providers must effectively manage these conflicting objectives. Cost is directly related to resource management, through which we aim to effectively utilize resources to meet SLA conditions and also reduce power consumption. Given that services running in the multi-tenant cloud environment have dynamic resource requirements that vary over time based on user demands, one of the major challenges cloud providers face today is the efficient management of resources to achieve a good trade-off between these conflicting objectives.

Resource management is conducted through a series of processes. We will focus on the processes of auto-scaling, VM consolidation, and VM placement. Every cloud platform includes an auto-scaler module that periodically makes decisions for scaling out or in resources to adapt to workload fluctuations, with the primary goal of not degrading performance in cases of increased workload but also reducing costs in cases of decreased workload. VM consolidation periodically remaps all VMs to physical machines (PMs), mainly to address overloaded or under loaded PMs with the primary goal of keeping active a minimal number of servers; whereas VM placement is a process that periodically analyzes workload progression, and at every time step, considers new VM requests from the user and aims to find the optimal PM placement.

ML algorithms are proposed as a promising solution to the resource management problem. Workload forecasting is a crucial aspect that must be considered to optimize resource utilization, due to the fact that resource requirements fluctuate significantly over time based on user activity. Workload forecasting relies on time series models, which analyze how the trend of workload varies over time. The prediction outcomes are further utilized by the auto-scaler, VM placement and consolidation processes.

1.1 Our Contributions

- We present a review of the recent ML-proposed solutions for:

    (1) workload forecasting, specially addressing time series models.
    (2) auto-scaling frameworks.
    (3) optimizing VM placement and consolidation.

- We identify the benefits and drawbacks of these solutions.
- We identify the set of parameters that seriously impact the prediction accuracy of time series forecasting models.
- We identify the types of overhead that the scaling process generates and should be considered before decision-making.
- We emphasize the constraints, key objectives and the tradeoffs that should be analyzed to optimize the VM placement and consolidation.

1.2 Article Structure

The rest of the paper is organized as follows: In Sect. 2, we briefly describe our research methodology. In Sect. 3 we discuss time series forecasting models, critical for optimizing resource provisioning. In Sects. 4 and 5, respectively, we examine proposed ML solutions for proactive auto-scalers and for addressing the intricate multi-objective VM consolidation and placement problem. We conclude our findings in Sect. 6. In Sect. 7, we emphasize the open challenges that still need to be addressed.

2 Research Methodology

2.1 Data Sources, Search String and the Filtering Criteria

To establish the necessary background for our research topic, we utilized the following digital libraries, concentrating on conferences and journals with significant impact in the field of Computer Science that maintain a rigorous peer review process:

- ACM Digital library
- IEEE Explore
- Science Direct
- Scopus
- Springer

Our review paper concentrates on recent advancements, sourcing primarily from articles published in the last five years, and including earlier influential works notable for their innovative ideas in resource management optimization. We used the search string: ("cloud" + "Infrastructure-as-a-Service") * ("resource management" + "scheduling" + "consolidation" + "placement" + "workload forecast" + "time series"). Articles were filtered based on: 1) relevance to our research by analyzing the title, abstract, and introduction; 2) reliability, assessed through the methodology for experiments and result evaluation; 3) significance, indicated by the number of citations.

2.2 Research Questions

- What are the ML-based techniques used in cloud resource management?
- What constraints need to be predefined to minimize SLA violations?
- How can we enhance the prediction accuracy of workload forecasting models?
- Which are the overhead types generated during the auto-scaling process?
- What objectives should be optimized in VM placement and consolidation?

3 Workload Forecasting

The workload in cloud environments is highly dynamic, making the prediction of its trend over time a critical step towards the efficient use of cloud resources. In this context, we will discuss time series forecasting models, used to identify patterns, trends, and seasonality in historical resource usage data to predict future resource demands [1]. Table 1 highlights the parameters that directly impact the quality of the time series prediction model.

Table 1. List of parameters that impact prediction of Time Series Forecast Model

Parameter	Description	Considerations when defining parameter value
Dataset size	Size of the training dataset	Should be large enough to capture behavior patterns
Lag period	the number of past time periods (observations) used to predict future outcome	Using too many lags can increase the complexity of the model, potentially leading to overfitting. It is important to balance the amount of historical data used with the need for generalization in the model
Forecasting horizon	the length of the predicted sequence produced by the forecasting model	A longer horizon provides early warnings and more preparation time but increases the prediction error, while a shorter horizon may offer more accuracy but less preparation time
Time window length	the frequency of making prediction decisions	A shorter window may be good for detecting rapid changes but can lead to noisier data and more complex models, while a longer window smooths out short-term fluctuations and may miss short-term anomalies or spikes in usage

3.1 Pre-processing of Training Dataset and Anomaly Detection

The presence of noise and anomalies in the training dataset can result in distorted prediction outcomes, leading to suboptimal decision-making. In this section, we highlight studies that have addressed this issue, demonstrating its impact on enhancing the accuracy of predictions.

In their workload forecast model, Bi, Yuan, Zhang. L, and Zhang. J incorporated the Savitzky-Golay filter to eliminate outliers and noise [2]. This integration led to an enhanced forecasting accuracy, as evaluated through Mean Squared Error (MSE). The MSE, measured in original (not smoothed) data, yielded a value of 0.0166, while the MSE in the smoothed data produced a result of 0.0058.

The resource provisioning solution proposed by Nawrocki and Osypanka leverages the exchangeability martingales function to filter out anomalies and address distortions stemming from the cloud provider's underlying hardware infrastructure [3]. This function demonstrates exceptional efficiency while operating in an unsupervised manner.

Zhang, Guo, Tian, & Ma introduced a reactive solution for handling anomalies [4]. If a mismatch between actual and predicted workload was detected, Deep Reinforcement Learning (DRL) was used to reconsider the workload and make a new prediction. This correction is only made if the number of consecutive anomalies exceeds the maximum tolerance value.

Awad, Leivadeas, & Awad used Kalman filter for data preprocessing to enhance the prediction accuracy by removing noise from the data [5].

3.2 Time Series Forecast Models

ML techniques are commonly used to capture the complex, non-linear dynamics of cloud workloads and are trained based on resource or performance metrics that are regularly monitored. Chouliaras and Sotiriadis employed Convolutional Neural Networks (CNN) for forecasting future CPU usage, since it is particularly adept at recognizing patterns and intricate structures within the data, which is essential for accurate workload prediction in cloud services [6]. The workload forecasting model in single-tenant environment achieved an RMSE score of 0.0181 in the testing data; while in multi-tenant a RMSE score of 0.0627 in the testing data.

Bi, Yuan, Zhang.L, & Zhang.J built the forecasting model using Stochastic Configuration Network (SCN), a supervised ML algorithm, chosen for its advantages such as faster training time, reduced risk of overfitting, and simplified model selection process [2]. SCN introduces a stochastic component in the process of configuring network architecture and dynamically adjusts the architecture based on accuracy metrics.

In their study, Lanciano, Galli, Cucinotta, Bacciu, Passarella, experimented with Linear Regression (LR), Multi-Layer Perceptron (MLP) and Recurrent Neural Networks (RNN). RNN are suitable for handling sequential data, as they utilize cycles that retain crucial information from previous time steps, thereby enhancing prediction accuracy [7]. The prediction of future CPU usage relied solely on the current measured CPU value and an H-dimensional vector computed recurrently from the past l samples, which represented the system's state. Regarding drawbacks, it was observed that RNNs required more effort in fine-tuning, including the design of an appropriate network topology, which leads to longer forecasting times.

To avoid the drawbacks caused by neural networks, such as the challenge of designing efficient network topology, slow training rate, and the risk of getting stuck in local minima, Awad. M, Leivadeas & Awad, Moreno-Vozmediano, Montero, Huedo & Llorente, chose Support Vector Machine regression (SVR) technique, for its ability to accurately fit data that exhibits both linear and nonlinear patterns while consistently reaching a unique global solution and maintaining reasonable training time [5] [8]. SVR achieved lower prediction errors in terms of MAE, MSE, RMSE compared with basic methods.

Khan, Tian, Ilager, & Buyya [9] compared various ML regression techniques for workload prediction, including LR, Ridge Regression (RR), ARD Regression (ARDR), ElasticNet (EN), and a deep learning algorithm such as Gated Recurrent Unit (GRU). GRU performed exceptionally well, by maintaining context-specific temporal dependencies between workload features for a longer time. It achieved the lowest value of RMSE for all predicted features.

Identifying a versatile algorithm that can adapt to various workload scenarios is a challenge. Messias, Estrella, Ehlers, Santana, M. J., Santana, R. C., & Reiff-Marganiec forecasted workload using a Genetic Algorithm (GA) that combines multiple forecasting models like Naive, AR, ARMA, ARIMA, and ETS [10]. GAs are particularly effective in optimization problems due to their robustness, versatility, and adaptability, making them ideal for addressing complex issues. The individual represents the combination of five forecasting models, while the genes represent the contribution weights of each model in predicting the number of requests per second. GA allocates appropriate weights for each model, making the solution generic and adaptable to any new workload as the algorithm evolves its population through direct interaction with incoming data. According to the experimental results, GA has demonstrated that by evolving the weights for each forecasting model used, it has adapted to the dataset and always converged towards the best result.

Zhang, Guo, Tian & Ma employed ensemble learning to enhance the workload prediction accuracy [4]. Historical workload data is segregated into multiple training datasets for various LSTM models. The AdaBoost algorithm is utilized to obtain a combined prediction from the independent LSTM models, resulting in a more stable and precise prediction model for different scenarios by integrating multiple trained models. The Root Mean Squared Error (RMSE), measured in traditional LSTM, yielded a value of 0.1369, while in this approach yielded 0.0958.

4 Proactive Auto-scaling

Our research concentrates on proactive auto-scalers, distinguished for their ability to predict workload demands and adjust resources in advance to effectively manage the dynamic nature of workloads. The decision-making of the proactive auto-scaler module is based on the workload forecasting outcome, as depicted in Fig. 1.

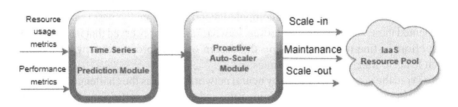

Fig. 1. Pro-Active Auto Scaler based on Time Series Prediction

Besides the primary impact of the prediction accuracy, it is imperative to consider the types of overhead introduced by the scaling process, listed in Table 2.

Another crucial factor is choosing an appropriate value of the scaling parameter, which refers to the number of scaled instances. This parameter impacts the scaler's performance in terms of how quickly resources are adjusted to meet the demands of the forecasted workload. Excessively high values can cause instability by causing the application to oscillate between high and low demand states without stabilizing at the desired medium state. Lower values result in a slower adoption to the medium state but increase the likelihood of reaching the medium demand state.

4.1 Key Issues

The key issues that the auto-scaler module should address for optimal decision-making are as follows:

Table 2. Overhead types generated during scaling

Type of overhead	Description	Additional notes
Scaling time	The time it takes to execute a scaling operation, from the moment a decision is made, to the point where the resources are fully functional and integrated into the system	On service-based application, this overhead is dependent on the type of service. For a stateful service, the scaling time for horizontal scaling is longer compared to vertical scaling, and inappropriate scaling may occur
Booting delay	The time required to start up a new instance	This delay can significantly affect the responsiveness of the cloud service, as it determines how quickly additional resources can be brought online to handle increased load
Cool down period	It is a predefined time interval during which the auto-scaler does not initiate additional scaling actions	This period allows the system to stabilize after a scaling event before making further adjustments

- *Analyzing the trade-off between QoS and cost*: The objective of the auto-scaler is to identify the minimal number of servers needed to handle the forecasted workload, aiming to reduce costs. However, this could lead to performance degradation. Therefore, for optimal decision-making, it is essential to manage the tradeoff between QoS and cost. A practical solution often employed is to set QoS as a constraint. Consequently, ML-based forecasting models must determine the number of resources to be added or removed, guided by the need to meet QoS while also aiming to minimize cost.
- *Maintaining system stability*: The scaling process significantly affects system stability. Given the dynamic nature of workloads, an effective auto-scaler should utilize workload forecasting outcome across the entire forecasting horizon to observe the trend of the workload over several consecutive time steps. This approach helps avoid hasty scaling decisions in case of short-term changes, that could lead to unnecessary scaling operations, destabilizing the system.

4.2 Proposed Solutions

Lanciano, Galli, Cucinotta, Bacciu, & Passarella to prevent system instability, proposed a threshold-based auto-scaler, which scales only if the threshold exceedance is observed for more than three consecutive predictions [7]. Monasca provides an alerting feature that notifies in case of threshold exceedance. MLP and RNN models scaled earlier by maintaining reasonable response times. Authors stress the importance of addressing the concept drift phenomenon, which can lead to the degradation of the forecasting model's accuracy due to dynamic workload behavior.

The innovation presented from Lin, Pan & Liu lies in considering the various types of VMs offered by cloud providers, which differ in terms of price and availability, highlighting on-demand and spot VMs [12]. By considering AWS-proposed spot VMs as an alternative, the study increases the complexity of the system. The authors suggest using D3QN, a reinforcement learning (RL) algorithm that combines with deep neural networks to address the uncertainty regarding prior knowledge of spot VM. The observation space includes the current workload, types and number of available spot instances, and their current price. The reward function is designed to calculate the final revenue of the Cloud Provider, taking into account the compensations for SLA violations. To address the slow training speed of RL, the researchers employed two parallel approaches: a multi-agent RL-based approach for auto-scaling spot VMs and a passive approach that quickly initiates equivalent capacity on-demand VMs to maintain service continuity when an alarm for a spot VM interruption is raised. This approach resulted in faster training speed, reduced SLA violations and improved overall revenue.

The significance of the hybrid auto-scaler proposed by Zhang, Guo, Tian & Ma, lies in evaluating the type of service (stateful or stateless) as an influencing factor in scaling time [4]. Based on workload forecast, the service type and available resources, the auto-scaler takes the appropriate decision by selecting an action that defines two criteria: vertical or horizontal scaling, and the number of resources to be scaled. The objective is the maximization of resource usage and resource balance degree, considering QoS constraints. In the case of stateful services, vertical scaling is used for short-term changes to respond promptly; while horizontal scaling is suggested to avoid performance bottleneck of resources. This approach compared to other approaches reduced the number of scaling actions and also improved the effective scaling ratios of stateless and stateful services, that are 79.25% and 69.57% respectively.

Panwar and Supriya propose a MAPE-K autonomic resource provisioning framework [13]. In the monitoring phase, sensors collect environmental data like response time, CPU and memory usage, as well as user-specific information like request arrival rate, request type, length of requests, and rejected requests. In the analysis phase, a LR model forecasts future resource needs based on request arrival rates and average VM load. The planning phase based on the prediction outcome, response time and request rejection percentage uses Bayesian learning to determine the optimal scaling plan. This approach resulted in reduced rejection percentage (SLA), response time, number of VMs used and cost.

Xu et al. proposed a resource provisioning technique for multi-service container-based application scenarios with diverse resource demands and interacting services [14]. To prevent performance degradation due to resource bottlenecks, the authors use a policy gradient RL approach that directly learns optimal actions with model parameters. This approach predicts resource usage, including CPU and network bandwidth, to identify potential bottlenecks and also forecasts performance metrics like Query Per Second (QPS) and response time, to optimize resource allocation. It maximizes system rewards by selecting control actions, resulting in improved overall system performance. This approach has the highest value of RMSE, achieving the highest accuracy compared to other algorithms.

The auto-scaler mechanism proposed by Moreno-Vozmediano, Montero, Huedo & Llorente estimates the minimum number of backend servers needed to optimize service latency, ensuring the response time meets the SLA conditions, by utilizing M/M/c queuing theory to model the system performance [8]. Authors experimented with different kernel functions, among which SVM-normalized polynomial and SVM-RBF kernel exhibited the best trade-off for the three considered metrics: number of provisioned resources, number of SLA violations, and number of unserved requests. The application of the queuing theory model has also been implemented by Messias, Estrella, Ehlers, Santana, M. J., Santana, R. C., & Reiff-Marganiec [10]. By incorporating the arrival rate prediction generated by the time series forecast model, along with the maximum response time and processing rate, the auto-scaler determines the minimum number of servers to be allocated in the next time interval. GA resulted in the lowest total number of under and over provisioned resources compared with the other basic models.

Nawrocki and Osypanka implemented control measures to prevent the degradation of QoS by setting it as constraint [3]. Their solution, the Long-Term Prediction System (LTPS), uses ML to explore the relationship between load, QoS, and resources available. This allows for resource demand forecasting to be guided by QoS constraint. They implemented four different ML algorithms: Bayesian Linear Regression (BL), Neural Network Regression (NN), Poisson Regression (P) and Decision Forest Regression (DF) known as the QoS model. After predicting resource demand, a particle swarm optimization algorithm is used to select a cost-optimal resource configuration plan, based on the current resource prices. DF outperformed the other algorithms, in terms of Relative Absolute Error (RAE) and Relative Squared Error (RSE). The experiments demonstrated significant cost reduction from 72% to 85% for IaaS.

The vertical auto-scaler developed by Chouliaras & Sotiriadis is designed for containerized services in the cloud [6]. K-Means is used to categorize the predicted CPU utilization and focuses on scaling the vCPU within Linux containers based on the predicted future workload categories and a predefined scaling parameter. They consider QPS reduction threshold to ensure QoS and consider budget constraints for auto-scaling decision. This solution in a single-tenant environment reduced cloud costs by 48% with a decrease of 6.9% in executed QPS; in multi-tenant environment the auto-scaler realized application performance recovery in terms of QPS. The same authors introduced PACE, with the main improvement on employing a reactive solution to effectively scale container memory after exceeding a predefined threshold [15].

The PETAS auto-scaler framework proposed by Ivanovic & Simic supports the optimization problems that utilize genetic algorithms, by predicting patterns in the behavior of optimization processes to make appropriate and timely scaling decisions [11]. Among the different ML algorithms used, the Random Forest (RF) model was found to be the most effective to predict the time required to complete each evolutionary task. K-fold cross-validation was employed to ensure the robustness and accuracy of the models. The auto-scaler component uses these predictions to decide the proper time for scaling, to adjust the number of container pods according to the speed at which generations evolve.

5   VM Consolidation and VM Placement Solutions

Optimizing the mapping of VMs to PMs is guided by maintaining a balance between conflicting objectives, such as reducing power consumption while simultaneously avoiding SLA violations. VM consolidation and placement aim to identify and avoid potential under loaded or overloaded hosts. In VM consolidation if overloaded host is expected, a specific algorithm selects the VMs to migrate. The final step chooses the most suitable host for relocating the migrated VMs, as shown in Fig. 2.

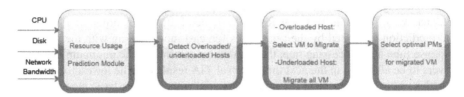

Fig. 2. VM Consolidation diagram

Although the CPU is known to have the greatest influence on power consumption, evaluating all types of resources is necessary to optimally handle overloaded or under loaded host states. Awad.M, Leivadeas, and Awad.A considered various resources (CPU, memory, bandwidth received and bandwidth transmitted) but did not address resource interdependencies [5]. Their workload consolidation mechanism, compares the predicted resource usage against a specific threshold, and in case of overloaded host, selects the VM that requires the minimal migration time. The Power Aware Best Fit Decreasing strategy selects the appropriate host to relocate VM by considering the host capacity to fulfill the VM's resource requirements, preventing the new host from becoming overloaded after the VM allocation, and choosing the server with the lowest power consumption increase. Lastly, this algorithm generates a map outlining the placement decisions for migrated VMs on selected hosts, initiating the final phase of pre-copy live migration. This approach implemented in CloudSim outperformed other approaches in terms of energy consumption (achieved 23.22% reduction), SLA violations and number of migrations. In the case of under loaded hosts, all VMs are migrated to shut down the PM.

An alternative approach is to use the under loaded hosts for consolidating additional workloads from overloaded hosts, acting as a load balancing strategy. Paul & Adhikari employed a deep learning model to maintain load balance by categorizing servers based on their load levels [16]. They allocate the task to the best fit VM based on the resource requirements and find the optimal server to maintain load balance while minimizing execution time.

Khan, Tian, Ilager, & Buyya exploited workload prediction to conduct energy state prediction in the VM level, by considering the workload metrics that affect power consumption like resource usage & provisioning metrics, network and memory throughput. This prediction is valuable for optimal decision-taking in resource provisioning and VM consolidation [9]. Semi-supervised affinity propagation based on transfer learning (TSSAP) achieved the highest accuracy in clustering.

The study of Perennou and Chiky provides insights into the use of a multi-class classification approach for predicting VM runtimes, highlighting the potential for improved allocation of physical machines [17]. The model utilizes a variety of features available at the launch of a VM like the request timing, the requested amount of resources. The research contributes to the field by demonstrating the value of incorporating descriptive tags into the prediction model, which enhanced the model performance. Tags are freely typed text strings, used to distinguish VMs.

RL is well-suited for addressing the issue of VM consolidation in dynamic cloud environments due to its ability to operate online and adaptively learn from ongoing interactions, even in the absence of a complete environmental model, unlike other machine learning techniques such as neural networks, SVM, or ARIMA, which require offline training and periodic updates to incorporate new data.

Shaw, Howley, and Barrett proposed a decision-making framework for VM consolidation, which employs Temporal Difference (TD) learning algorithms, a subcategory of RL [18]. These methods have shown to offer more accurate results and faster convergence speeds than traditional solutions. TD learning updates estimates based on other learned estimates, without the need to wait for a final outcome. Predictions are incrementally updated after each step within an episode, utilizing the "temporal difference" between consecutive predictions to refine the value of previous predictions. The study compares Q-Learning and SARSA, that differ in their approach to updating value estimates and choosing actions. Q-Learning is an off-policy algorithm that aims to learn the optimal policy regardless of the agent's actions, while SARSA is an on-policy algorithm that updates action value estimates based on the agent's experiences following a specific policy. To address the slow convergence rate of RL, the authors integrate the potential-based reward shaping technique (PBRS), which enhances the learning process by integrating domain knowledge into the reward structure, thereby providing better directional guidance. They also employ softmax and ε-greedy techniques to optimize the trade-off between exploration and exploitation, with softmax providing a more strategic approach to exploration, by prioritizing actions with potentially higher rewards. State is represented as a percentage of the number of active servers or PMs relative to the total number of hosts. The action space is defined by a variable that combines the resource utilization level at the host level with the size of the VM to be migrated. SARSA with softmax showed its effectiveness in maintaining low energy consumption and fewer SLA violations, as well as its ability to quickly adapt to the optimal policy. The introduction of PBRS with SARSA further improved its performance by enhancing its ability to quickly converge to an optimal solution, improved energy efficiency by 25%, reduces SLA violations by 63% and migrations by 49.17% compared to PowerAware benchmark.

Caviglione, Gaggero, Paolucci and Ronco [19], proposed Deep Q-Networks, a deep RL method, for optimal VM placement. The algorithm takes as input CPU, Disk, Network demand, the class of VMs and a snapshot of the previous system's placement state. Based on these inputs, the agent at each step determines the most suitable heuristic method (among six selected heuristics) for each newly requested VM. The algorithm's objectives are to minimize the impact of churning related to the reliability of the PM, minimize co-location interference among VMs, and minimize power consumption. These objectives are inherently conflicting. The authors have developed a comprehensive function by combining these three objectives, each with a corresponding coefficient that represents their priority. This method outperforms traditional heuristics, by reducing power consumption and achieving better QoE (Quality of Experience-metric that quantifies the adherence of IaaS to SLA).

5.1 Live Migration

The main concept of live migration in the context of VM consolidation involves the transfer of VMs from one PM to another without significant downtime or service interruption. This process is crucial for cloud computing as it enables better resource utilization, load balancing, and energy management, while maintaining service availability [20].

Recent research has proposed various mechanisms to improve live migration and VM consolidation. For instance, an improved genetic algorithm has been suggested to address the multi objective optimization problem of VM consolidation, considering factors such as power consumption, load balancing, and migration cost [21]. Another study introduced a queue-based migration model to efficiently migrate VM memory pages [22].

We observe a broad focus on developing techniques in the realm of green computing. Seddiki, Galan, Exposito, Ibanez, Marciniak, and Prado, proposed a meta-scheduler for multiple geographically dispersed cloud data centers (CDCs) [23]. It dynamically moves VMs across CDCs based on the availability of renewable energy and the capacity of the CDC to avoid overloaded hosts. While migration techniques are numerous, they are not the focus of our research.

Live migration of VMs introduces overhead, as it involves transferring the state of a VM from one physical server to another. This includes the VM's memory, storage, and network state, which can lead to significant consumption of CPU, memory, and network bandwidth. It is essential to evaluate metrics such as the number of migrations, migration time, and SLA violations before deciding to proceed with VM migration. D. Minarolli, A. Mazrekaj, B. Freisleben [24] proposed a utility function that evaluates whether the potential SLA penalties from not migrating outweigh the costs of migration overhead. This helps decide on migration actions that balance performance against operational overhead effectively.

6   Conclusions

In this paper, we explore the support provided by ML for optimizing decision-making in cloud resource management. This process is essential for addressing today's critical issue of reducing carbon footprint through decreased power consumption. Hence, the primary objectives of Cloud Providers are the reduction of power consumption without compromising QoS. Therefore, every solution must consider QoS as a fundamental constraint. A range of ML techniques are employed, from supervised and unsupervised learning to Reinforcement Learning.

Below, we summarize why ML is suitable and crucial for cloud environments:

- ML's predictive capabilities enable timely and efficient resource provisioning, matching the fluctuating demands of cloud workloads. We highlight data-driven ML algorithms that train on historical monitored metrics.
- ML's proficiency in solving complex optimization problems, such as mapping VMs to PMs, taking into account the variety of conflicting objectives in cloud. We discuss objective-driven ML algorithms, like RL category, in which the primary issue is the convergence rate. To reduce it, a well-managed tradeoff between exploration and

exploitation is crucial. We highlight the use of advanced exploitation techniques, or reward shaping. In high complex environments, combining RL with Deep Learning can be beneficial.

- ML's classification/clustering abilities that are used for categorizing workloads or VMs based on power consumption to aid in decisions regarding scaling, load balancing, or VM migration.

Characteristics that a ML model must fulfill for optimal efficiency in cloud include:

- Capturing non-linear behaviors of workload trends over time.
- Incorporation of constraints, overheads, and prioritized objectives.
- Minimal training time for data-driven solutions or a high convergence rate for objective-driven solutions.
- Low risk of local optima and overfitting.
- Ease of fine-tuning the ML algorithm.

For evaluating the proposed ML-based solution we use metrics related to prediction quality. To enhance the prediction accuracy of ML-based solution, we should:

- Pre-process the training dataset to eliminate outliers and noise.
- Specifically handle emergency situations in system workload.

7   Open Challenges

- *Generic Algorithm & Concept Drift:* When using ML for workload forecasting, the ML model needs to be generic. Studies indicate that using a single model for all types of workloads compromises forecast quality. It's critical to address concept drift to prevent degradation in forecasting accuracy. Ensemble learning techniques, which combine multiple forecasting models, are proposed to develop a more resilient model to workload fluctuations. The application of genetic algorithms aims to identify optimal model weights or priorities, improving forecast quality by adapting to new data online. The use of k-fold cross-validation is also recommended for model robustness and accuracy.
- *VM Affinity:* The necessity for VMs to interact should be considered for optimizing VM mapping to PMs. The literature review shows a lack of consideration for this factor during the consolidation/placement process.
- *Resources type:* When studying workload behavior, it is essential to analyze all types of resources, their interdependencies, and each one's impact on power consumption, which are often overlooked with a focus on CPU usage. These analyses are vital to avoid resource bottlenecks, minimize resource contention from VM co-location, etc.

Disclosure of Interests.   The authors have no competing interests to declare that are relevant to the content of this article.

References

1. St-Onge, C., Kara, N., Wahab, O.A., Edstrom, C., Lemieux, Y.: Detection of time series patterns and periodicity of cloud computing workloads. Futur. Gener. Comput. Syst. **109**, 249–261 (2020)

2. Bi, J., Yuan, H., Zhang, L., Zhang, J.: SGW-SCN: An integrated machine learning approach for workload forecasting in geo-distributed cloud data centers. Inf. Sci. **481**, 57–68 (2019)
3. Nawrocki, P., Osypanka, P.: Cloud resource demand prediction using machine learning in the context of QoS parameters. J. Grid Comput. **19**(2), 20 (2021)
4. Zhang, H., Guo, T., Tian, W., Ma, H.: Learning-driven hybrid scaling for multi-type services in cloud. J. Parallel Distrib. Comput. **189**, 104880 (2024)
5. Awad, M., Leivadeas, A., Awad, A.: Multi-resource predictive workload consolidation approach in virtualized environments. Comput. Netw. **237**, 110088 (2023)
6. Chouliaras, S., Sotiriadis, S.: An adaptive auto-scaling framework for cloud resource provisioning. Futur. Gener. Comput. Syst. **148**, 173–183 (2023)
7. Lanciano, G., Galli, F., Cucinotta, T., Bacciu, D., Passarella, A.: Predictive auto-scaling with OpenStack Monasca. In: Proceedings of the 14th IEEE/ACM International Conference on Utility and Cloud Computing, pp. 1–10. Leicester, United Kingdom (2021)
8. Moreno-Vozmediano, R., Montero, R.S., Huedo, E., Llorente, I.M.: Efficient resource provisioning for elastic cloud services based on machine learning techniques. J. Cloud Comput. **8**(1), 1–18 (2019)
9. Khan, T., Tian, W., Ilager, S., Buyya, R.: Workload forecasting and energy state estimation in cloud data centres: ML-centric approach. Futur. Gener. Comput. Syst. **128**, 320–332 (2022)
10. Messias, V.R., Estrella, J.C., Ehlers, R., Santana, M.J., Santana, R.C., Reiff-Marganiec, S.: Combining time series prediction models using genetic algorithm to autoscaling web applications hosted in the cloud infrastructure. Neural Comput. Appl. **27**, 2383–2406 (2022)
11. Ivanovic, M., Simic, V.: Efficient evolutionary optimization using predictive auto-scaling in containerized environment. Appl. Soft Comput. **129**, 109610 (2022)
12. Lin, L., Pan, L., Liu, S.: Learning to make auto-scaling decisions with heterogeneous spot and on-demand instances via reinforcement learning. Inf. Sci. **614**, 480–496 (2022)
13. Panwar, R., Supriya, M.: Dynamic resource provisioning for service-based cloud applications: a Bayesian learning approach. J. Parallel Distrib. Comput. **168**, 90–107 (2022)
14. Xu, L., et al.: A reinforcement learning based approach to identify resource bottlenecks for multiple services interactions in cloud computing environments. In: Proceedings of the 16th International Conference on Collaborative Computing: Networking, Applications and Worksharing (CollaborateCom), Part II, pp. 58–74. Springer LNICST, vol. 350, Shanghai, China (2020)
15. Chouliaras, S., Sotiriadis, S.: Auto-scaling containerized cloud applications: a workload-driven approach. Simul. Model. Pract. Theory **121**, 102654 (2022)
16. Paul, S., Adhikari, M.: Dynamic load balancing strategy based on resource classification technique in IaaS cloud. In: Proceedings of the 2018 International Conference on Advances in Computing, Communications and Informatics (ICACCI), pp. 2059–2065. Bangalore, India (2018)
17. Perennou, L., Chiky, R.: Applying supervised machine learning to predict virtual machine runtime for a non-hyperscale cloud provider. In: Proceedings of the 11th International Conference on Computational Collective Intelligence (ICCCI), Part II, pp. 676–687, Springer LNCS vol. 11684, Hendaye, France (2019)
18. Shaw, R., Howley, E., Barrett, E.: Applying reinforcement learning towards automating energy efficient virtual machine consolidation in cloud data centers. Inf. Syst. **107**, 101722 (2022)
19. Caviglione, L., Gaggero, M., Paolucci, M., Ronco, R.: Deep reinforcement learning for multi-objective placement of virtual machines in cloud datacenters. Soft. Comput. **25**(19), 12569–12588 (2021)
20. Singh, S., Singh, D: Live virtual machine migration techniques in cloud computing. In: Data Security in Internet of Things Based RFID and WSN Systems Applications, pp. 99–106, 1st edn. CRC Press (2020)

21. Qiu, W., Qian, Z., Lu, S.: Multi-objective virtual machine consolidation. In: Proceedings of the 10th IEEE International Conference on Cloud Computing (CLOUD), pp. 270–277. Honololu, USA (2017)
22. Liaqat, M., Ninoriya, S., Shuja, J., Ahmad, R.W., Gani, A.: Virtual machine migration enabled cloud resource management: a challenging task. arXiv preprint (2016)
23. Seddiki, D., et al.: Sustainable expert virtual machine migration in dynamic clouds. Comput. Electr. Eng. **102**, 108257 (2017)
24. Minarolli, D., Mazrekaj, A., Freisleben, B.: Tackling uncertainty in long-term predictions for host overload and underload detection in cloud computing. J. Cloud Comput. **6**, 1–18 (2017)
25. Jin, H., Ibrahim, S., Bell, T., Gao, W., Huang, D., Wu, S.: Cloud types and services. In: Handbook of Cloud Computing, pp. 335–355. Springer (2010)

Blockchain-Based Decentralised Marketplace for Secure Trading of Intellectual Property

Vijon Baraku[1](✉)(ID), Simeon Veloudis[2,3](ID), Iraklis Paraskakis[2,3](ID),
and Poonam Yadav[1](ID)

[1] Department of Computer Science, University of York, York, UK
vibaraku@seerc.org, poonam.yadav@york.ac.uk
[2] SEERC - South East European Research Centre, Thessaloniki, Greece
{sveloudis,iparaskakis}@seerc.org
[3] CITY College, University of York Europe Campus, Thessaloniki, Greece

Abstract. This paper presents the development and implementation of a secure, web-based decentralised marketplace for trading intellectual property (IP). By leveraging blockchain technology, this marketplace eliminates the need for intermediaries, fostering a transparent, cost-effective, and unbiased trading environment. The proposed system ensures transaction integrity and confidentiality of the traded artefacts. The key contributions include the design of a robust security protocol, the implementation of smart contracts, and the application of multiple encryption schemes to enhance security. The research underscores the potential of blockchain to revolutionise the trading of intangible creations by providing a secure and efficient platform.

Keywords: Blockchain technology · Smart contracts · IPFS · Microstocks

1 Introduction

The evolution of the World Wide Web can be categorised into three phases: Web 1.0, Web 2.0, and Web 3.0. Each phase reflects a dramatic shift in how users engage with the digital environment, affecting both the digital economy and the mechanisms for exchanging data.

Web 1.0, the initial generation of the web, was characterised by static web pages and decentralised, open protocols. Users primarily consumed content rather than interacted with it, and individual websites functioned independently without the intricate interconnectedness observed today. This era laid the groundwork for digital communication and content sharing, albeit in a limited and unidirectional manner [1,2].

The emergence of Web 2.0 marked a turning point, transforming the web into a platform for user-generated content, interaction, and social collaboration. This period saw the rise of social media, blogs, wikis, and other platforms that enabled user participation and collective knowledge creation [3]. Web 2.0 democratised content creation, allowing anyone to contribute and distribute knowledge widely. However, this was achieved through the centralisation of services by dominant platforms like Amazon, Google, and Meta, which held large amounts of user data and directed online interactions [3,4]. While these platforms provided unparalleled convenience and connectivity, they also raised issues about data privacy, market monopolisation, and biases in transaction processing [5].

As the limitations of Web 2.0 became more evident, the concept of Web 3.0 emerged, promising a more decentralised and user-centric web. Web 3.0 is not only based on blockchain technology, but also incorporates emerging technologies such as artificial intelligence (AI) and augmented reality (AR). This phase of the internet is often described by the tagline "less trust, more truth," emphasizing openness, security, and user empowerment [5]. In Web 3.0, users gain ownership stakes by contributing to develop and maintain applications, resulting in a more equitable digital economy [6].

The transition from Web 1.0 to Web 3.0 has enabled a significant digital transformation, culminating in a vibrant data economy. This economy involves the exchange of various types of data, such as personal, financial, and intellectual property. For example, personal data stored in personal data stores, and intellectual property like microstock pictures, and music are all critical components of this economy. Current platforms, while offering essential services, often exhibit biases (such as seller bias and buyer bias), collect user data for profit, and impose fees on both buyers and sellers. These drawbacks highlight the need for a decentralised approach to data trading, where intermediaries are eliminated and users have more control and transparency [7].

In response to these challenges, this paper proposes the development of a decentralised marketplace specialised in trading intellectual property in the form of microstock pictures. This marketplace, leveraging blockchain technology, aims to eliminate the need for intermediaries, resulting in a transparent, cost-effective, and unbiased platform for transactions. The proposed solution will ensure that the entire operation is decentralised, with no single server directing data flow. This decentralisation guarantees transaction integrity and confidentiality, as all data is encrypted and only authorised users, namely the microstock purchasers, have access [8,9].

The decentralised microstock marketplace will benefit both buyers and sellers. Clients will pay less for artefacts due to the removal of intermediaries and associated costs. Merchants, on the other hand, will receive the full value of each transaction, enhancing their revenue potential. By addressing the constraints of current centralised marketplaces and demonstrating the promise of blockchain technology, this paper aims to contribute to the ongoing discussion about digital transformation and the future of the data economy. The paper will describe the protocol for trading electronic intellectual property, using the microstock marketplace as a specific example to show how decentralisation can enable the secure, efficient, and equitable exchange of data in the digital economy.

2   System Description

The system being developed is a web application that allows users to trade microstock (in the form of pictures) securely and in a decentralized manner.

Conventional web applications typically have a frontend and a backend. While the frontend of decentralized applications (dApps) and web applications use similar technologies, the backend of dApps interacts with blockchain networks via wallets. These wallets store blockchain addresses and cryptographic keys to identify and validate users. They also invoke smart contracts for blockchain transactions. Unlike web applications, dApps exclude backend servers and possible censorship.

To use the system, new users must connect their blockchain wallets. Once linked, users can make requests through the frontend. These requests are either handled by smart contracts on the blockchain, the InterPlanetary File System (IPFS), or processed on the frontend. IPFS handles file uploads and retrievals as a decentralized database. Requests related to business logic are managed by blockchain smart contracts. Files or keys are encrypted and decrypted on the frontend, ensuring no unnecessary data storage.

Figure 1 provides an overview of the activities that each actor (seller or buyer) can perform with the system.

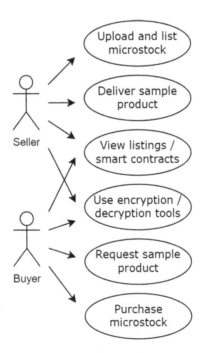

Fig. 1. Activities of buyers/sellers with the system

Sellers provide the necessary information for the smart contract, including the seller's address, the price of the microstock, and the IPFS address of the encrypted microstock. This information is sent to the blockchain, which deploys a new smart contract.

Buyers can request a sample and, if satisfied, submit a purchase request. The smart contract confirms the terms and completes the transaction, transferring funds to the seller and the microstock to the buyer. Section 3 explains these interactions in detail.

3   Security Protocol Design

Since the system handles intellectual property, each procedure must be secure. Given the public nature of blockchain transactions, a system is needed to protect file confidentiality from unauthorized access.

1. **Files to sell** - Handling the files that are to be sold is the first stage in the security protocol. The files will be sold in bulk, and the seller must ensure that the product can only be viewed by authorised users (buyers once purchased). The seller achieves this confidentiality by encrypting each file with symmetric encryption, thus generating a set of keys. This set of keys remains with the seller for the time being.

2. **Sampling** - Buyers must ensure that the product they are acquiring meets their expectations and is appropriate. They accomplish this by supplying their public key and requesting a sample product. This sample must not have been picked by the seller, since they may have chosen a sample that is of greater quality than the rest of the files on purpose. As a result, this selection must be a random file that will be selected by the smart contract deployed in the blockchain. Through blockchain, transparency on the selection is also achieved.

3. **Delivering sample** - Once a potential buyer has been identified and their public key has been received, the seller encrypts the set of keys using the buyer's public key and hashes the results. These hashed results are uploaded and stored on the blockchain for the smart contract to pick one at random. The seller must then provide the non-hashed version of the randomly selected sample in order for the potential buyer to decrypt the file and view the sample. This asymmetric encryption assures that only the buyer, using their private key, can decrypt the sample. Additionally, the stored hashes are utilised to verify that the key sampled and the set of keys to be delivered match and have not been altered.

4. **Delivery of products** - If the buyer is satisfied with the product, they can proceed to purchase the full product. As a result, the remaining keys are provided by the seller, encrypted with the buyer's public key. The smart contract rehashes these keys and compares them to the hashed keys that were initially uploaded. If everything is correct, the buyer receives the set of keys and the seller receives the Ether. The buyer has now acquired the keys to the IPFS files, and they must do a final decryption to view the product.

This protocol ensures that the seller maintains confidentiality of their product, even from the system itself. Because a malicious system administrator would not have access to the keys at any moment, the seller's obligation to trust the system itself is eliminated. Buyers, on the other hand, are informed that the product they are about to purchase meets the criteria and is not fraudulent (since the sample is chosen at random), and they are assured that the sample key comes from the set of keys they are about to purchase (through the hash comparison).

To visualize the security protocol, two sequence diagrams have been designed. The sequence diagram 2 depicts the actions taken in requesting a sample, whereas the diagram 3 represents the steps taken in purchasing the product. After each diagram, a step by step explanation is provided (Fig. 2).

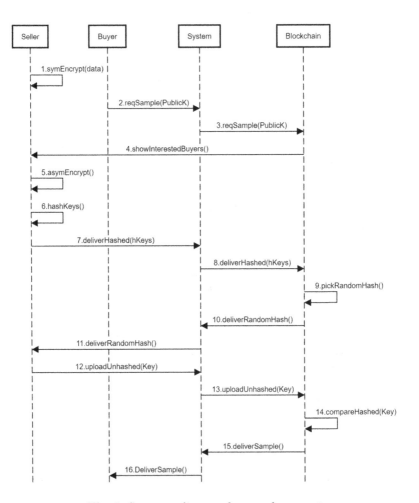

Fig. 2. Sequence diagram for sample request

1. Seller encrypts their data symmetrically, generating a set of keys.

2-3. A potential buyer sends a sample request and provides their public key which is stored on the blockchain.

4-6. The seller is informed that there is a new potential buyer. They encrypt the set of keys from step 1 with the potential buyer's public key. The seller then hashes the results.

7-13. The hashed keys are stored on the blockchain, and the smart contract selects a random hash that corresponds to one key. The seller is presented this random hash, and they must then deliver the original key representing the chosen hash.

14-16. The smart contract validates the provided key (by hashing it and comparing the hash to the randomly picked hash) and then provides the key to the potential buyer (Fig. 3).

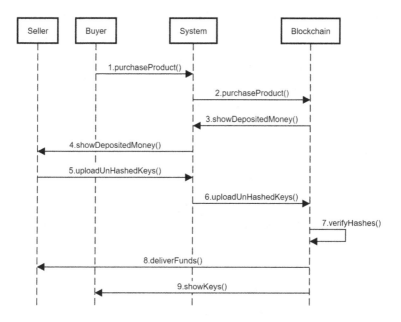

Fig. 3. Sequence diagram for purchasing request

1-2. If the buyer is satisfied with the sample, they submit a purchase request. This request is delegated to the blockchain, which holds the funds until the seller delivers the keys.

3-6. The blockchain informs the seller that the buyer has submitted a purchase request and deposited funds. To claim these funds, the seller must upload the non-hashed keys.

7-9. The submitted keys are compared to the previously uploaded hashes (in the sampling step), and if they match, the transaction is valid. The blockchain delivers the funds to the seller and provides the buyer with the keys.

3.1 Converting a Public Address into a Public Key

The second step in the security protocol is requesting a sample. To request a sample the potential buyer must provide their public key. The issue is that users do not have direct access to their public key; instead, they can only see their public address, which is a hashed form of the public key. To recover the public key from the hashed version, a user (Alice) must sign a transaction. This signing provides the signature values r, s which are needed alongside the message m (transaction) to perform the following public key recovery algorithm [10].

1. Validate that r and s are integers in $[1, n-1]$. If otherwise, the signature is incorrect.
2. Compute a curve point $R = (x_1, y_1)$, where x_1 is one of r, $r + n$, $r + 2n$, (given x_1 is not too large for a field element) and y_1 is a value that satisfies the curve equation.
3. Compute $e = HASH(m)$, where HASH is the same algorithm that was used to generate the signature.
4. Let z represent the L_n leftmost elements of e.
5. Compute $u_1 = -zr^{-1} \bmod n$ and $u_2 = -sr^{-1} \bmod n$
6. Compute the curve point $Q_A = (x_A, y_A) = u_1 \times G + u_2 \times R$
7. If Q_A matches Alice's public address, the signature is valid and Q_A represents Alice's public key.

4 Implementation

4.1 Public Key Recovery Implementation

The algorithm behind recovering the public key was described under Sect. 3.1, and listing 1.1 shows this implementation.

Listing 1.1. Recovering the public key from the public address

```
async function recoverPublicKey() {
const ethAddress = await signer
.getAddress();
const hash = await ethers.utils
.keccak256(ethAddress);
const sig = await signer.signMessage
(ethers.utils.arrayify(hash));
const pk = ethers.utils.recoverPublicKey(
ethers.utils.arrayify(
ethers.utils.hashMessage(ethers.utils
.arrayify(hash))),sig);
try { const transaction =
await contract.requestSample(pk)}}
```

2-3. The `ethAddress` represents the Ethereum address of the user. This address is then hashed with the `keccak256` hashing algorithm and stored under the constant `hash`. Now that the address and its hash are both given, the user generates the signature by signing a message of the hash.

4-11. To calculate the public key, first the message needs to be converted to binary: `ethers. utils. arrayify (hash)`. Next, the prefixed-message hash needs to be computed: `ethers. util. hashMessage (hashBytes)`. The result needs to be converted to binary: `ethers. utils. arrayify (messageHash)`. These steps provide the digest, which together with the signature (4.) are utilized to recover the public key: `ethers. utils. recoverPublicKey (digest , signature)`.

12-13. With the public key recovered, the frontend delivers a sample request with the pk as the parameter.

4.2 Smart Contract Security System Implementation

The sample request is the initial security protocol step. The function for this request is shown in listings 1.2 and 1.3.

Listing 1.2. Sample request implementation 1

```
contract  Purchase{
string [ ]  public  interestedBuyers ;
...
function  requestSample(string  memory
pkOfBuyer)  public  {interestedBuyers
. push ( pkOfBuyer ) ; }

function  getInterestedBuyers ()
public  view  returns  (string [ ]  memory)
{ return  interestedBuyers ; }
... }
```

2. String array variable to hold all the public keys of the interested buyers.

4-10. Function for adding the public key (calculated in the frontend) to the array of interested buyers, and a return function to get this variable.

After encrypting the keys to the files with the buyer's public key and hashing them (explained under 3), the seller uploads these hashes to the blockchain. Listing 1.3 shows this function.

Listing 1.3. Sample request implementation 2

```
contract  Purchase{
...
string [ ]  public  hashedSamples ;
string  public  randomHashPicked ;
string  public  unHashedSample ;
...
```

```
function pickHashedSample( string []
memory hashedKeys) public OnlyOwner {
hashedSamples = hashedKeys ;
uint256 randomIndex = uint256(
keccak256( abi . encodePacked ( block . timestamp ,
msg . sender ))) % hashedKeys . length ;
randomSampleId = randomIndex ;
randomHashPicked = hashedKeys [ randomIndex ] ;
}

function returnRandomHashPicked ()
public view returns ( string memory
randHash , uint256 hashId ){
return ( randomHashPicked , randomSampleId );}

function putUnhashedSample( string memory
unHashedS) public OnlyOwner {
string memory hashingToCompare =
Strings . toHexString ( uint256 ( keccak256
( abi . encodePacked ( unHashedS ))) ,32 );
require (
keccak256( abi . encodePacked
( hashingToCompare )) == keccak256( abi .
encodePacked ( randomHashPicked )) ,
" hashes do not match" );
unHashedSample = unHashedS ;}
...}
```

3-5. Variable declaration for the hashed samples, the random hash picked, and the non-hashed sample.

7. When the user has encrypted the keys and hashed them, they upload them to the blockchain with this function.

8-15. The provided hashes are first stored in the blockchain (**8.**), then a random sample is picked by the smart contract. Solidity contracts are deterministic, thus it is difficult to obtain a truly random number; however, a pseudo-random number is sufficient for this system. To generate the pseudo-random index, the timestamp of the block is combined with the msg.sender and hashed. To get an index within the range of the array, result modulo the length of the array is calculated. Lastly, the random sample id (index) and the random hash picked are stored on the blockchain.

17-20. The randomly selected hash is returned, along with the hash's id. This is done since the number of hashes is large and the user can get lost attempting to locate the randomly selected hash.

22. Once the randomly selected hash has been returned to the seller, they must provide the unhashed version. The function in line 20 is responsible for this operation.

23-32. The provided sample key (unHashedS) must be hashed and compared to the hash uploaded in the previous step. To hash the input, the keccak256 function (part of SHA-3) is called. Solidity provides the hashing function directly, however, it expects bytes as input, therefore to hash a string, the function encodePacked() is used. This function returns a bytes32 hash of the unhashed key. To convert from bytes32 to hex string (which is what the randomHashPicked is stored as), the Strings.toHexString() function is utilized. The final step is comparing randomHashPicked (the original hashed sample chosen) with the variable hashingToCompare. In Solidity the ''=='' operator is not compatible for string types, but it is for bytes32, therefore the two hex strings are hashed again to produce bytes32 outputs which are comparable.

30. If the hashes match, the unhashed sample is stored on the blockchain for the interested buyer to view.

Listing 1.4. Purchase request function

```
contract Purchase{
...
address payable public buyerAddress;
uint256 public depositTime;
...
function purchaseProducts() public payable
SellerCantBuy { require (requestedAmount
== msg.value, "invalid amount");
buyerAddress = payable(msg.sender);
depositTime = block.timestamp;}

function returnDeposit() public {
require (msg.sender == buyerAddress,
"You have nothing deposited"); require (
block.timestamp - depositTime > 86400,
"24 hours have not passed yet,
please wait"); buyerAddress.transfer
(address(this).balance);}
...
}
```

3-6. If the buyer is satisfied with the sample, they send a purchase request. This request is handled by the purchaseProducts() function (line 5). The Ethereum address of the account purchasing the product is also stored in the variable buyerAddress (line 3).

7-9. The purchase function is a payable function, meaning the function accepts Ethers that are passed to it. This Ether will be deposited in the smart contract and must match the requested amount (specified when the contract is constructed) by the seller. If this is the case, the address is updated to hold the msg.sender address, which corresponds to the buyer calling the function. Lastly, the deposit time is recorded on the blockchain.

`12-19`. After the funds have been deposited, the seller has 24 h to provide the rest of the keys. If they fail to do so, the buyer can take back their deposit. The function in line `12.` is responsible for determining whether the `msg.sender` (function caller) matches the address of the user that deposited the Ether and whether the required amount of time has passed. In this case, the funds will be transferred back to the buyer's account.

5   Conclusion and Future Works

This paper presents the culmination of a comprehensive exploration into the development of a decentralised application leveraging blockchain technology and encryption methodologies. Presently, the developed application enables users to securely transact microstock on a transparent and decentralised platform. By combining encryption techniques with smart contracts deployed on the blockchain, users can engage in transactions with heightened security and efficiency. Notably, the system supports the upload and retrieval of files via the InterPlanetary File System (IPFS), ensuring data integrity and accessibility. The security protocol in place protects both buyers and sellers and provides a safe environment where transactions can take place without the need for trust on either side.

Some of the improvements and additions to the system are presented as the following:

Facilitate all Intellectual Property - The current system enables users to securely trade microstock in the form of pictures. Music compositions and videos can also be intellectual property and support to include them in the system could be easily provided. To integrate this functionality, the security system would not need to be changed; instead, while uploading files, the appropriate check would be performed to discern between the different types of files.

Search & Categorise - Currently, all products are displayed in a single screen, ordered from newest to oldest. A system enhancement to categorise products and provide a search tool to quickly locate what the user is looking for might be a beneficial addition to the system, further improving the user experience.

References

1. Jacksi, K., Abass, S.M.: Development history of the world wide web. Int. J. Sci. Technol. Res. **8**(9), 75–79 (2019)
2. Hiremath, B.K., Kenchakkanavar, A.Y.: An alteration of the web 1.0, web 2.0 and web 3.0: a comparative study. Imperial J. Interdiscip. Res. **2**(4), 705–710 (2016)
3. Kollmann, T., Lomberg, C., Peschl, A.: Web 1.0, Web 2.0, and Web 3.0: the development of e-business. In: E-Commerce Platforms, pp. 167–184. IGI Global (2016)
4. Adeyoyin, S.O., Ezeudu, B.O., Adegun, A.I., Tomomowo-Ayodele, S.O.: The metamorphosis of world wide web: an overview of Web 1.0, 2.0, Semantic Web 3.0 and their application in library and information services delivery. University of Ibadan Institutional Repository (2013). http://repository.ui.edu.ng/handle/123456789/5721

5. Barassi, V., Treré, E.: Does Web 3.0 come after Web 2.0? Deconstructing theoretical assumptions through practice. New Media Soc. **14**(8), 1269–1285 (2012)
6. Chi, D.M., Salanță, I. I.: Web 3.0 and the evolution of the world wide web. Rev. Manag. Econ. Eng. **13**(3), 375–381 (2014)
7. Pattal, M.M.I., Li, Y., Zeng, J.: Web 3.0: a real personal Web! More opportunities and more threats. In: Proceedings of the 3rd International Conference on Next Generation Web Services Practices (NGMAST), pp. 125–128, Cardiff UK (2009)
8. Singh, H.A.: Evolution of Web 1.0 to Web 3.0. Int. Res. J. Modernization Eng. Technol. Sci. **4**(9), 915–920 (2022)
9. Dwivedi, Y.K., Williams, M.D., Mitra, A., Niranjan, S.: Understanding advances in Web technologies: Evolution from Web 2.0 to Web 3.0. In: Proceedings of the 19th European Conference on Information Systems (ECIS), pp. 257 (2011)
10. Johnson, D., Menezes, A., Vanstone, S.: The elliptic curve digital signature algorithm (ECDSA). Int. J. Inf. Secur. **1**, 36–63 (2001)

Medical and Health Issues

An Intelligent Agent-Based Approach to Enhancing Urban Health and Resilience under Climate Change

Kalliopi Kravari[1,2](✉) ⓘ and Anastasia Pentagioti[1]

[1] UNESCO Chair for the Conservation and Ecotourism of Riparian and Deltaic Ecosystems, Democritus University of Thrace, Mikrochori, 66100 Drama, Greece
kkravari@csd.auth.gr
[2] RESHUB LTD, 157A G.S. Rakovski Sofia, 1000 Sofia, Bulgaria

Abstract. More than half of the world's population lives in urban areas and it is expected to reach 70% in 25 years. At the same time, rising temperatures and extreme weather events lead to concerns in the climate change era. In this context, climate resilience, health, and equity are among the priorities for urban residents and city leaders. Even more interesting is that reports on urban threats pose these priorities higher than other health outcomes like food-borne diseases or chronic stress. This reveals an increasing concern on how climate change can negatively impact the overall quality of urban life given the lack of green spaces and the more frequent extreme heat events. Hence, this article provides a discussion on the climate-health vulnerabilities and their current state in urban areas. Following that, it discusses intelligent agents (IAs), an Artificial Intelligence technology, that can act autonomously and learn, providing a promising solution for urban resilience challenges. The proposed methodology uses a multi-agent approach to improve climate action strategies. It mainly focuses on health equity, air pollution, extreme heat, and floods, since they are increasingly frequent in urban areas. To this end, predictive analytics, real-time monitoring, personalized health interventions, resource allocation, and disaster response are some of the concepts that are studied. Finally, the article concludes by outlining factors that should be considered when IAs are deployed in urban applications and studies.

Keywords: Artificial Intelligence · Intelligent Agents · Climate Resilience

1 Introduction

Climate change, with its rising temperatures and increasingly extreme weather events, poses a significant threat to urban health and well-being. Cities, home to over half the world's population, face the complex challenge of ensuring the health and well-being of residents in the face of a changing climate. Taking into account that the world's urban population is rapidly growing, with projections suggesting that by 2050, 68% of the global population will reside in cities [1], makes the challenge even greater. This urbanization trend coincides additionally with a worsening climate crisis, posing an

C. Bădică et al. (Eds.): BCI 2024, CCIS 2391, pp. 223–240, 2025.
https://doi.org/10.1007/978-3-031-84093-7_16

even more significant challenge to urban health and well-being. As a result, cities are particularly vulnerable to climate-related threats like extreme heat events, flooding, air pollution, and disruptions to food and water security [2]. In this context, the Resilient Cities Network and Yale University report [3] on resilient cities at the intersection of climate and health reveals the critical need for collaboration and innovative solutions to address climate and health challenges in cities.

This paper aims to identify the aforementioned critical issues, especially in terms of quality of life/built environment and extreme heat events, and the challenges they present. It envisions the development of a novel technological solution based on intelligent agents (IAs), AI-powered systems capable of autonomous learning and action. To this end, intelligent agents equipped with a rule-based methodology will integrate and promote climate action strategies, aiming to address air pollution, extreme heat, and health equity concerns. The subsequent sections of this paper delve into the details of the proposed rule-based methodology, exploring their capabilities for predictive analytics, real-time monitoring, personalized health interventions and resource allocation without requiring human intervention.

The rest of the paper is organized as follows: In Sect. 2 we review the main issues on urban health and resilience. In Sect. 3 we briefly discuss intelligent agents while in Sect. 4 we discuss rule-based systems and defeasible logic. The methodology of our approach, including the rule-based decision-making approach is discussed in Sect. 5. Ultimately, we summarize our conclusions on Sect. 6.

2 Climate Resilience and Urban Health

Climate change effects and public health are two connected concepts and have become more relevant than ever. Climate change will have unavoidable impacts on urban systems and populations and climate adaptation will be essential. Planning for adaptation should include enhancing infrastructure resilience, promoting conservation measures, strengthening public health systems, and fostering innovation and research.

2.1 Urban Health and Climate Change

With the increase in extreme heat events caused by climate change, policymakers, urban planners, and public health officials must act to protect the health of urban citizens, for example, by implementing climate adaptation measures, preparing for emergency response, and establishing heat warning systems. Hence, there is a growing need for detailed climate information for urban areas.

At the same time, cities must plan and implement climate mitigation measures because they are responsible for over 70% of global CO_2 emissions. The conflicts and synergies between climate mitigation and adaptation measures still need to be fully understood because such an effort requires a very high-resolution representation of future urban climate conditions [12].

2.2   Urban Health and Sustainable Development Goals

The 2030 Agenda for Sustainable Development has prominently spotlighted urban areas, positioning Sustainable Development Goal 11 (SDG 11) at the forefront, to foster inclusive, safe, resilient, and sustainable cities and human settlements. The interplay of SDG 11 with other SDGs underscores a fundamental principle of the 2030 Agenda: the challenges of sustainable development are intertwined, and thus the solutions must be as well (Fig. 1).

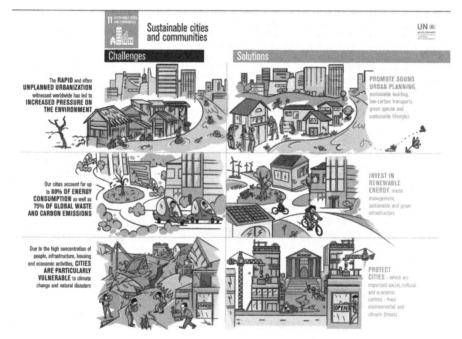

Fig. 1. Sustainable Development Goal 11 - Sustainable Cities and Communities United Nations Environmental Programme

If we combine the targets of SDG 11 (Sustainable Cities and Communities) with the targets of SDG 3 (Good Health and well-being) and SDG 13 (Climate Action) we can create strategies that integrate health, urban sustainability, and climate resilience. To achieve although, cities need to understand the features and processes that make them vulnerable to crises and environmental emergencies – and their associated health impacts – and to recognize the most effective policies and actions to reduce risk, be better prepared, and become more resilient. The solution is given with the combination of SDG9 (Industry - Innovation, and Infrastructure) and SDG 17 (Partnership for the Goals) which suggest developing systems to monitor health outcomes, environmental quality, and climate resilience, enabling data-driven policy decisions, and support research on the intersections of health, urban development, and climate change to inform best practices and innovative solutions.

2.3 Sustainable Development and Resilience

According to the Organization for Economic Co-operation and Development (OECD) building "climate resilience involves all actors (governments, communities and businesses) having the capacity to anticipate climate risks and hazards, absorb shocks and stresses, and reshape and transform development pathways in the longer term". The organization proposes six steps that actors need to take in developing climate resilience:

1. Awareness-raising and advocacy – Be clear that the future will not resemble the past; base this on science and examine different scenarios (e.g. 1.5-degrees and higher) and their impacts.
2. Carry out climate risk assessments at national, local (city/region), sectoral or organizational level and use a systems approach.
3. Develop and implement appropriate actions and interventions.
4. Mobilize resources – Build capacity and scale up actions.
5. Monitor and track progress.
6. Share knowledge, experiences and solutions (Fig. 2).

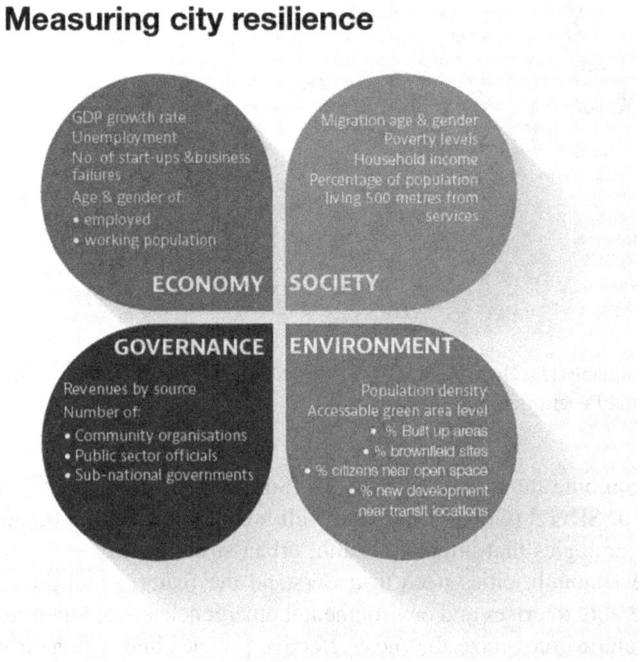

Measuring city resilience

Fig. 2. Measuring City Resilience - OECD

Climate Resilience involves the capacity of social, economic, and environmental systems to cope with hazardous events, trends, or disturbances related to climate change, thereby reducing the impacts of these events. This resilience is built upon five pillars:

threshold capacity, coping capacity, recovery capacity, adaptive capacity, and transformative capacity [13]. Sustainable development principles underpin these efforts by promoting inclusive, equitable, and long-term strategies that protect both human and environmental health.

3 Intelligent Agents

Intelligent agents (IAs), also known as autonomous intelligent systems, are an established domain of Artificial Intelligence (AI), studied already for some decades. These software agents are entities that can operate autonomously without human intervention, being able to sense their environment, take actions, and achieve goals. Autonomy, reactivity, proactivity and communication ability are some of their properties (Table 1). The most interesting is their ability to reason, learn from past experiences, and communicate with other agents and entities. As a result, they are capable of acting as humans, namely the virtual alter ego of a human [4]. More specifically, a multi-agent system is a system where a number of intelligent agents act representing human or virtual entities, services or even devices. IAs can be rational, rule-based and/or with internal state, allowing them to learn and adapt their behavior over time.

Table 1. Intelligent agents' properties.

Autonomy	Migration
Adaptability	Learning
Social ability (Collaboration/ Coordination/Interaction)	Reactivity
Persistence (execution)	Proactivity
Communication ability	Mobility

3.1 Intelligent Agents for Urban Climate Action

The question that arises is if and how intelligent agents can be involved in urban climate action. Although the answer is not simple, there are some key areas in which IAs can make a difference in improving urban health and resilience (Fig. 3) [7–11].

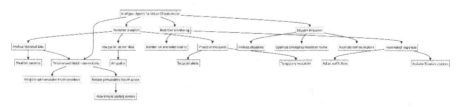

Fig. 3. Intelligent Agents for Urban Climate Action

Predictive Analytics. IAs are able to handle large amounts of data, such as historical weather data, medical records, and real-time sensor data from IoT (Internet of Things) sensors (e.g., air quality, traffic). Through analysis, it is possible to predict climate-related incidents such as heatwaves, flooding, or the risk of disease outbreak. For example, an IA might identify a heatwave in the process of developing and, based on historical precedence and vulnerability mapping, project where heat stress risk would be highest. This enables anticipatory measures such as targeted alerts to susceptible groups, pre-positioning of cooling centers, or even modifying urban planning for long-term resilience.

Real-Time Monitoring. IAs can be constantly tracking key urban metrics such as air and water quality, traffic density, and energy consumption. Upon detecting anomalies or exceeding predefined thresholds, they can trigger automatic responses. For example, an IA tracking air quality may detect a sudden spike in pollutants. The system could then adjust traffic patterns in the area affected, turn on air filtration systems in public buildings, and issue health alerts to the public. For instance, consider an intelligent agent that is monitoring water quality sensors; upon detection of a contamination event, it would promptly alert the responsible authorities, start water treatment procedures, and alert the public of potential hazards.

Personalized Health Interventions. Integrating IAs with wearable health monitors provides the possibility of personalized health advice and intervention. An IA could analyze an individual's physiological data (e.g., heart rate, body temperature) and environmental data (e.g., heat index) to provide personalized advice during heat waves. This may involve advising the best times to be outdoors, recommending particular methods of cooling off, or even notifying medical professionals if the person's health is in danger. For instance, an intelligent assistant may take a diabetic patient's blood glucose levels and activity patterns into consideration, along with meteorological predictions, in order to prescribe customized exercise regimes and dietary adjustments.

Disaster Response. During climatic catastrophes, IAs may play a pivotal role in directing emergency response activities. They may examine current information from numerous sources (e.g., weather predictions, social networks, emergency departments) to improve evacuation paths, distribute resources, and support communication with the residents affected. Take an example of flooding. An IA can process real-time water level data, traffic, and crowd density to calculate evacuation routes that are most safe and quickest to travel. It can then warn citizens via mobile alerts and coordinate the dispatch of emergency responders. IAs also can learn from past disaster events in an effort to improve response strategies and create more durable infrastructure.

4   Rule-Based Systems and Defeasible Logic

A common approach when using IAs to integrate policies of real-world stakeholders is to use rule-based systems. The reason behind this is that rules are usually explicit and easy to understand. As a result, stakeholders can easily find out how their policies are being adjusted into the agent's decision-making process, fostering trust. Furthermore, rules can be added, modified, or removed relatively easily. Hence, the system remains adaptable to changing policies or new stakeholder requirements. Additionally, rule-based systems usually are computationally efficient since they can be applied in well-defined cases with a limited set of rules. This is important for IAs that need to make real-time decisions.

Yet, using just rule-based approaches with IAs has some serious limitations. For instance, in real-world cases, like urban health and resilience optimization, the complexity increases when the number of rules and policies increases [19, 20]. Moreover, the real world can be unpredictable in the sense that may arise situations that are not explicitly covered by the rules. In this context, traditional rule-based systems are unable to learn and adapt their behavior as fast as it is demanded by such dynamic environments where policies and situations might change over time.

Hence, to overcome these limitations, this paper reports on the use of defeasible logic, although there is a number of logics, and subsequently reasoning, that can be used. Defeasible logic (DL), also known as non-monotonic logic, was introduced by [5] and it is a logic that allows IAs to reason even if the information is incomplete or inconsistent. DL is a simple and efficient rule based no-monotonic formalism that utilizes defeasible rules which are rules that can be defeated by stronger or more specific rules. Hence, it derives plausible conclusions from partial and sometimes conflicting information, allowing more realistic representation of real-world situations where exceptions and conflicts may arise. These conclusions, despite being supported by the currently available information, could nonetheless be rejected in the light of new, or more refined, information. Additionally, DL enables assigning priorities to rules, ensuring that more important stakeholder policies are followed when conflicts arise. DL can even support trust building in multi-agent systems since it allows the tracing of the reasoning process behind an agent's decision. Furthermore, compared to more mainstream non-monotonic approaches, the main advantages of defeasible reasoning are enhanced representational capabilities and low computational complexity [6, 14]. In this context, defeasible logic can be used to enhance the capabilities of rule-based systems for integrating stakeholder policies with IAs. It is able to equip intelligent agents with the necessary capabilities to deal with the real-world complexities, adapting to changing circumstances and resolving conflicts effectively.

4.1 Defeasible Theory

This paper represents the knowledge base of each intelligent agent as a defeasible theory (D) consisting of three basic parts; namely a set of facts (F), a set of rules (R) and a superiority relationship ($>$). Hence, D can be represented by the triple (F, R, $>$). In other words, each agent maintain its own defeasible theory, representing its beliefs, goals, and reasoning rules.

The set of rules R consists of three distinct types of rules; namely strict rules, defeasible rules and defeaters. Strict rules are denoted by A $\rightarrow$ p and are interpreted in the typical sense that whenever the premises are indisputable, so is the conclusion. An example of a strict rule could be "Extreme heat is climate-related shock" which written formally is r1: extremeHeat (X) $\rightarrow$ climateRelatedShock (X).

Defeasible rules are rules that can be defeated by contrary evidence and are represented as A ⇒ p. An example of a defeasible rule could be "Population displacement is considered to be climate-related shock" which written formally is r2: populationDisplacement (X) ⇒ climateRelatedShock(X).

Defeaters are rules that do not actively support conclusions, but can only prevent some of them. They are represented as A ∈ p. These rules can be used to defeat defeasible rules by producing evidence to the contrary. An example of such a rule could be "If a Population displacement occurs, but its scale is under a threshold, then it might not be climate-related shock" which written formally is r3: populationDisplacement(X), scale(X,Y), Y > threshold ∈ ¬ climateRelatedShock (X). Hence, this defeater can defeat, for instance, rule r2: populationDisplacement (X) ⇒ climateRelatedShock(X).

Finally, there is a superiority relationship among the rule set R that it is an acyclic relation > on R. An example of such a relationship could be the following: given the defeasible rules r2 and r4 (populationDisplacement (X) ⇒ ¬climateRelatedShock(X)), no conclusive decision can be made about whether the population displacement is climate-related shock or not since rules r2 and r4 contradict each other. Yet, if superiority relation > with r2 > r4 exists then r2 overrides r4 and the conclusion that the population displacement is climate-related shock can be derived. In this case rule r2 is called superior to r4 and r4 inferior to r2.

Another important element of defeasible reasoning is the notion of conflicting literals, where literals are considered to be conflicting and at most one of a certain set should be derived. An example of such a case is a negotiation about classifying population displacement as a climate-related shock. The proposal can be determined by several rules, whose conditions may or may not be mutually exclusive. All rules have proposal(X) in their head, since a proposal is usually a positive literal. However, only one offer should be made. Therefore, only one of the rules should prevail, based on superiority relations among them. In this case, the conflict set is: $C(proposal(x, y)) = \neg proposal(x, y) \cup proposal(x, z)|z \neq y$.

A defeasible theory example for the above case could be:

r1: recentNaturalDisaster(L) → potentialClimateRelatedShock(L), which is a strict rule indicating that recent natural disasters are potential climate-related shocks.

r2: populationDisplacement(L, high) ⇒ climateRelatedShock(L), which is a defeasible rule indicating that large-scale population displacement suggests climate-related shock.

r3: conflictResolution(L), humanitarianAid(L, high) ∈ ¬climateRelatedShock(L), which is a defeater indicating that if a conflict is resolved and high levels of humanitarian aid are provided, it might not be climate-related.

The superiority relationship (>) of the example is r2 > r1, indicating that population displacement carries more weight than a potential link from a natural disaster.

Finally, the conflict set (C) is $C(climateRelatedShock(L1)) = \{\neg climateRelatedShock(L1)\}$, indicating that climate-related shock for L1 can either be true or false, but not both.

5   An Intelligent Agent Approach with Defeasible Logic

Our approach, as already discussed is based on a multi-agent system that utilizes defeasible logic to optimize urban health and resilience in the era of climate challenges. In this context, we model three main types of entities (Fig. 4):

- Agents: These are virtual or human agents, i.e., citizens, governmental organizations, utility companies, and community organizations. Every agent contains a unique set of attributes (C), i.e., age, health, income, and access to resources, and preferences (P) according to their goals and priorities for urban health and resilience. For example, a citizen agent would appreciate the availability of green spaces and clean air, whereas a government agent would appreciate the minimization of heat-related illnesses and the preservation of critical infrastructure integrity.
- Services: They consist of fundamental city services like public transport, healthcare, energy supply, and emergency services. There are attendant properties for each service, i.e., capacity, availability, and response time, that are being tracked by the IAs. For instance, an agent for a healthcare service can track hospital bed availability and emergency room waiting times, and an agent for a transport service can track traffic density and public transport schedules.
- Environmental Sensors: These sensors collect real-time information about various environmental parameters, including temperature, air quality, water levels, and energy consumption. This data provides critical input to the IAs to assess the present state of the urban environment and predict future states. Temperature sensors, for example, provide data for heatwave prediction, while air quality sensors monitor pollution levels and inform public health warnings.

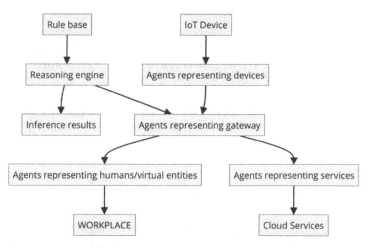

Fig. 4. Approach abstract architecture

Each entity has a set of characteristics (C) and preferences (P) relevant to urban health and resilience (C_x^k & P_x^m | k,m ∈ [1, N], x ≡ entity). Characteristics (C) include information like population density, green space availability, and infrastructure capacity. Preferences (P) represent societal goals and priorities like minimizing heat-related illnesses, ensuring access to clean water, and minimizing disruptions to critical services. These characteristics and preferences have weight values (ranging from 0 to 1) reflecting their relative importance; namely W_c^k & W_p^m | k,m ∈ [1, N], c ≡ characteristic, p ≡ preference.

5.1 Defeasible Rules for Decision-Making

Defeasible rules guide the intelligent agent's decision-making process. These rules have antecedents (conditions) and consequents (conclusions) and can be strict or defeasible. Part of the rule set is depicted below:

- R1: extreme_heat(L) → increase_cooling_center_hours(L), which means that extreme heat demands extending cooling center hours
- R2: air_pollution(L) ∧ high_asthma_rates(L) ⇒ advise_mask_usage(L), which means that air pollution and high asthma rates suggest recommending mask usage
- R3: air_pollution(L) ∧ high_asthma_rates(L) ∧ low_outdoor_activity(L) ∈ ¬ advise_mask_usage(L), which means that if air pollution and high asthma rates coincide with low outdoor activity, mask usage advice might not be necessary

In cases of conflicting rules, a superiority relationship (>) determines which rule prevails. This ensures the agent prioritizes the most relevant actions. For instance, R2 > R1. This superiority relationship indicates that addressing air quality and health concerns might take precedence over extending cooling center hours during peak pollution.

5.2 Assessing Urban Health and Resilience

The intelligent agents continuously evaluate characteristics and preferences based on the defined rules. Each agent taking into account weights and superiority relationships can identify potential threats to urban health and resilience, such as extreme heat waves or air pollution spikes, as well as recommend actions based on the identified risks and priorities. These recommendation could include public health advisories, infrastructure adjustments, or resource allocation strategies. In this context, an example rule for resource allocation is the following: R4: heat_wave(L) ∧ low_income_population(L, high) ⇒ allocate_cooling_resources(L). This defeasible rule indicates that if heat waves are combined with a high concentration of low-income residents that might mean a cooling resource allocation. Furthermore, in case of conflicts, defeater rules and the superiority relationship, enable the agent to handle them and prioritize its actions. The proposed approach can adjust recommendations based on the specific context and real-time data. An example is the following: Suppose R4 suggests allocating cooling resources, but another rule with higher priority identifies a critical infrastructure failure requiring immediate attention. The defeasible logic system would prioritize resolving the infrastructure issue before allocating cooling resources.

5.3 A Defeasible Logic Approach - Heatwave Scenario

In a major metropolitan city experiences a prolonged heatwave with temperatures exceeding 38 °C (100°F) for several days. This scenario (Fig. 5) puts a strain on urban infrastructure and increases the risk of heat-related illnesses, especially for vulnerable populations. The involved entities are the following:

- Agent: City Resilience Intelligent Agent
- Services: Public health department, emergency response services
- Sensors: Environmental sensors monitoring temperature, air quality

The defeasible theory of this example includes:

Characteristics (C)

- C1: temperature(L, 38), stating that the current temperature in the city is 38 °C
- C2: high_density_housing(L), stating that the city has a significant portion of high-density housing
- C3: elderly_population(L, high), stating that the city has a high proportion of elderly residents
- C4: air_quality(L, moderate), stating that the current air quality is moderate

Preferences (P)

- P1: minimize_heat_related_illness(L) [weight(P1) = 1 (Highest importance)]
- P2: ensure_access_to_cool_spaces(L), stating that the system should ensure access to cool spaces for vulnerable populations [weight(P2) = 0.8 (High importance)]
- P3: minimize_strain_on_infrastructure(L), stating that the system should minimize strain on electricity grid [weight(P3) = 0.5 (Moderate importance)]

Rules. Part of the rule set is presented below.

- R1: extreme_heat(L) → increase_cooling_center_hours(L), meaning if extreme heat, extend cooling center hours
- R2: high_density_housing(L) ∧ elderly_population(L, high) ⇒ advise_stay_indoors(L), meaning for high-density housing and high elderly population, recommend staying indoors
- R3: high_density_housing(L) ∧ elderly_population(L, high) ∧ air_quality(L, poor) ∈ ¬ advise_stay_indoors(L), meaning if poor air quality coincides with high-density housing and high elderly population, staying indoors might not be advisable
- R4: elderly_population(L, high) ∨ low_income_population(L, high) ⇒ prioritize_outreach_to_vulnerable(L), meaning that for high elderly or low-income populations, prioritize outreach
- R5: extreme_heat(L) ∧ increased_cooling_center_usage(L, high) ∧ capacity_cooling_centers(L, low) ⇒ request_emergency_cooling_resources(L), meaning that if extreme heat leads to high cooling center usage and low capacity, request additional resources

- R6:   extreme_heat(L)   ∧   predicted_duration(heatwave,   long) ⇒ advise_energy_conservation(L), meaning that for long heatwaves, recommend energy conservation measures
- R7: extreme_heat(L) ∧ predicted_duration(heatwave, long) ∧ high_risk_population(L) ∈ ¬ advise_energy_conservation(L), meaning that the agent should not recommend conservation if it compromises health of high-risk populations
- R8:   air_quality(L,   poor) ∧ ozone_levels(L, high) ⇒ advise_limited_outdoor_activity(L), meaning that for poor air quality and high ozone levels, recommend limited outdoor activity
- R9: air_quality(L, poor) ∧ ozone_levels(L, high) ∧ high_unemployment_rates(L) ∈ ¬ advise_limited_outdoor_activity(L), meaning that if high unemployment coincides with poor air quality, limited activity might not be feasible
- R10:   water_pressure_low(L) ∧ heatwave(L) ⇒ request_emergency_water_distribution(L), meaning that if low water pressure coincides with a heatwave, request emergency water distribution

Social Equity:

- R11: low_income_population(L, high) ∧ lack_of_air_conditioning(L, high) ⇒ prioritize_cooling_center_access(L)
- R12: elderly_population(L,   high)   ∧   social_isolation(L,   high)   ⇒ proactive_health_checks(L)

Infrastructure Resilience:

- R13: extreme_heat(L) ∧ electricity_demand(L, high) ⇒ alert_energy_provider(L)
- R14: extreme_heat(L) ∧ water_consumption(L, high) ⇒ alert_water_utility(L)

Dynamic Adaptation:

- R15: heatwave_duration(L,   long)   ∧   cooling_center_capacity(L,   low)   ⇒ request_additional_resources(L)
- R16: air_quality(L,   deteriorating)   ∧   wind_direction(L,   changing)   ⇒ revise_air_quality_alerts(L)

Superiority Relationship. R1 > R2, which indicates that addressing health risks takes precedence over general stay-indoors advice.

Discussing the Example. The agent perceives the high temperature (C1) through sensor data. As a result, it concludes extreme heat exists (strict rule), based on a pre-defined threshold. Hence, R1 is triggered, recommending increased cooling center hours (fulfilling P2). Simultaneously, it considers social equity (R11 and R12). Recognizing the

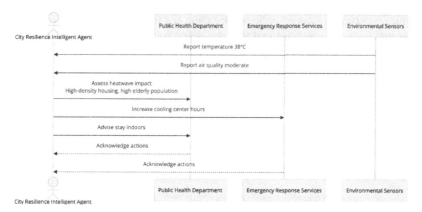

Fig. 5. Sequence diagram of the heatwave scenario

high proportion of low-income residents without air conditioning, it prioritizes cooling center access for these individuals. Furthermore, it identifies elderly individuals living in social isolation and recommends proactive health checks to ensure their well-being. R2 is also triggered due to high-density housing (C2) and high elderly population (C3). However, since air quality is moderate (C4), defeater rule R3 is not applicable. Furthermore, due to the superiority relationship (R1 > R2) that prioritizes health risks (P1), the agent recommends both increased cooling center hours and advises residents, especially the elderly in high-density housing, to stay indoors (fulfilling P2).

Of course, depending on available information the agent might also consider additional actions. For instance, it might recommend increased electricity grid capacity or alternative cooling solutions (fulfilling P3) if the heatwave is anticipated to last and strain the infrastructure. In this example, the agent also monitors infrastructure strain (R13 and R14). Sensing high electricity and water demand due to the heatwave, it alerts the respective utility providers to prepare for potential strain on their systems. As the heatwave persists (R15), the agent observes that cooling center capacity is becoming strained. It proactively requests additional resources, such as mobile cooling units or extended operating hours for existing centers. Finally, if air quality deteriorates and wind direction changes (R16), the agent revises its air quality alerts to reflect the updated situation, ensuring that public health advisories are accurate and timely. In this context, the system will collaborate with public health services to distribute heat advisories and outreach programs to vulnerable populations.

Finally, it is worth mentioning that there are rules in the rule set dealing with specific issues, such social and financial challenges. For instance, R4 highlights the importance of considering factors like income and age when allocating resources, R5 demonstrates how the agent can adapt its recommendations based on real-time data on cooling center usage and capacity while R6 and R7 showcase the need to balance competing priorities, health risks vs. infrastructure strain, using defeater rules. On the other hand, R8 and R9 illustrate how the agent can tailor public health messages based on air quality and socio-economic factors while R10 emphasizes the agent's ability to interact with external services, such as water distribution, to address emerging issues.

Figure 6 depicts a sample performance chart for the scenario where we found out that the system is able to learn and perform better in terms of recommendations. It is our intention to proceed with more simulation and evaluations by domain experts to calibrate the rule set.

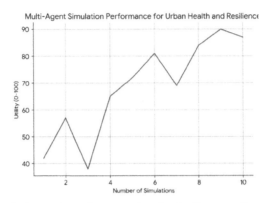

Fig. 6. A sample performance chart for the Heatwave Scenario.

Another scenario that illustrates even better the proposed approach is one focused on urban flood resilience as discussed below.

A coastal urban area is experiencing a heightened threat of flooding from rising sea levels and a heightened frequency of extreme precipitation events. The municipal government is taking an integrated strategy to flood management, comprising the building of seawalls, the upgrading of drainage systems, and community-based preparedness initiatives.

The involved entities are the following:

Agent: Coastal Resilience Intelligent Agent
Services: Flood warning system, emergency response services, infrastructure management
Sensors: Sea level sensors, rainfall gauges, river flow monitors, soil moisture sensors

Characteristics (C):

C1: sea_level(L, rising) – Sea level is rising in location L
C2: rainfall(L, heavy) – Heavy rainfall is occurring in location L
C3: soil_moisture(L, high) – Soil moisture is high in location L
C4: drainage_capacity(L, low) – Drainage capacity is low in location L
C5: seawall_integrity(L, compromised) – Seawall integrity is compromised in location L
C6: vulnerable_population(L, high) – A high concentration of vulnerable population (e.g., elderly, low-income) resides in location L

Preferences (P):

P1: minimize_flood_damage(L) [weight(P1) = 1] – Minimize flood damage in location L (highest importance)

P2: ensure_public_safety(L) [weight(P2) = 0.9] – Ensure public safety in location L

P3: maintain_critical_infrastructure(L) [weight(P3) = 0.8] – Maintain critical infrastructure in location L

P4: maximize_resource_efficiency(L) [weight(P4) = 0.7] – Maximize resource efficiency in flood response

Rules (R):

R1: sea_level(L, rising) ∧ rainfall(L, heavy) ∧ soil_moisture(L, high) → flood_risk(L, high) – Rising sea level, heavy rainfall, and high soil moisture indicate high flood risk.

R2: flood_risk(L, high) ∧ drainage_capacity(L, low) Þ issue_flood_warning(L) – High flood risk and low drainage capacity suggest issuing a flood warning.

R3: flood_risk(L, high) ∧ seawall_integrity(L, compromised) Þ evacuate_area(L) – High flood risk and compromised seawall integrity necessitate evacuation.

R4: flood_risk(L, high) ∧ vulnerable_population(L, high) Þ prioritize_evacuation(L) – High flood risk and a high concentration of vulnerable population prioritize evacuation.

R5: flood_risk(L, high) ∧ rainfall_forecast(L, heavy, future) Þ prepare_emergency_resources(L) – High flood risk and forecasted heavy rainfall suggest preparing emergency resources.

R6: flood_risk(L, high) ∧ river_flow(L, critical) ∈ ¬evacuate_area(L) – If the river flow is at a critical level, then evacuation might not be the best solution because evacuation itself can cause casualties.

R7: seawall_integrity(L, compromised) ∧ repair_resources(L, available) Þ repair_seawall(L) – If seawall integrity is compromised and repair resources are available, repair the seawall.

R8: flood_risk(L, high) ∧ emergency_resources(L, deployed) Þ activate_emergency_plan(L) – If flood risk is high and emergency resources are deployed, activate the emergency plan.

R9: issue_flood_warning(L) ∧ public_awareness(L, low) Þ launch_public_awareness_campaign(L) – If a flood warning is issued and public awareness is low, launch a public awareness campaign.

Superiority Relationship (>):

R3 > R2 – Evacuating an area takes precedence over just issuing a flood warning.

R4 > R3 – Prioritizing evacuation of vulnerable populations takes precedence over general evacuation.

R7 > R5 – Repairing a compromised seawall takes precedence over preparing emergency resources.

The Coastal Resilience IA is constantly collecting information from a number of sources, such as sea level sensors, rainfall gauges, river flow gauges, and soil moisture sensors, and combines this real-time data with weather forecasting. This information drives the flood risk analysis of the IA, using rule R1. Specifically, if the IA perceives a rising sea level (C1), heavy rainfall (C2), and elevated soil moisture (C3), it concludes that there is a high flood risk (flood_risk(L, high)). Based on this high flood risk assessment, and considering drainage capacity (C4) and seawall integrity (C5), the IA applies rules R2 and R3. Poor drainage capacity initiates the issuance of a flood warning (R2), whereas weakened seawall strength causes evacuation recommendation (R3). We also see that the existence of many vulnerable individuals (C6) activates rule R4, wherein special attention is warranted in evacuating them. Lastly, with predicted heavy rainfall based on weather observations, the IA applies rule R5 to preposition emergency resources accordingly. But if the river flow is critical, then R6 beats R3 and thus evacuation may not be the optimal answer. If the seawall is damaged (C5) and repair materials are on hand, the IA prefers repairing the seawall (R7) to merely preparing for a flood.

6 Related Work

Artificial Intelligence (AI) has already been used in the growing field of climate action research. Leal Filho et al. (2022) provide an overview of the capabilities of AI in environmental monitoring and response [15]. The application of intelligent agents and multi-agent systems for irrigation scheduling was also studied in [16], indicating the capability of managing the non-deterministic nature of the agricultural fields. In [17] Climebot project highlights the key aspects of an AI tool based on ontologies for educating people about climate change. In [18] authors discuss resilient cities and propose the use of AI Intelligent Agents to predict, adapt and manage resources during disruptions. In this context, the proposed approach focuses on building resilient cities, complementing existing research on AI for environmental monitoring, education, and resource management. It goes beyond education/prediction to potentially manage climate issues by providing a generic rules based approach used by autonomous intelligent agents.

7 Conclusions and Recommendations

This paper proposes a novel approach for optimizing urban health and resilience in the face of climate challenges. The approach leverages multi-agent systems equipped with defeasible logic, a type of artificial intelligence that allows for reasoning with incomplete or conflicting information. Intelligent agents can address urban health and resilience challenges by integrating data from sensors, historical records, and stakeholder policies. Hence, they can provide real-time monitoring, predictive analytics, personalized health interventions, and disaster response support. Using defeasible rules allows the agents to prioritize actions, handle conflicting information, and adapt their recommendations to the specific context. This is crucial for real-world scenarios with complex and dynamic factors. The approach considers social determinants of health by designing a defeasible rule-based system that can incorporate factors like income and age when allocating resources, ensuring a more equitable response to climate threats. Overall, the paper argues that intelligent agents with defeasible logic have the potential to become valuable tools for enhancing urban health and resilience in a changing climate.

The paper acknowledges the need for further research and development to fully realize the potential of this approach. More extensive simulations and real-world pilot projects are needed to evaluate the effectiveness of the approach in various urban contexts, although a sample performance chart is already presented. Another future direction is to involve domain experts in refining existing rules and developing new ones to address a wider range of climate-related challenges. Finally, the success of this approach relies on public trust. It is our intention to explore strategies for engaging citizens and stakeholders in the development and deployment of intelligent agents for urban health and resilience.

Acknowledgments. This study was funded by Project 101092458 — GROWTH, Strengthening resilience by offering targeted national and local scientific and practical training activities, for capacity building and awareness-raising of the risks and impacts of manmade disasters, ERASMUS-EDU-2022-CB-VET, European Education and Culture Executive Agency.

Disclosure of Interests. The authors have no competing interests to declare that are relevant to the content of this article.

References

1. United Nations, Department of Economic and Social Affairs, Population Division. World Urbanization Prospects: The 2018 Revision (ST/ESA/SER.A/420). United Nations, New York (2019)
2. Pörtner, H.-O., et al. (eds.): Climate Change 2022: impacts, adaptation and vulnerability. contribution of working group II to the sixth assessment report of the intergovernmental panel on climate change. Cambridge University Press (2022)
3. Resilient Cities Network & Yale University. Resilient Cities at the Intersection of Climate and Health. Resilient Cities Network & Yale University (2023)
4. Cervantes, J.A., Rosales, J.H., López, S., Ramos, F., Ramos, M.: Integrating a cognitive computational model of planning and decision-making considering affective information. Cogn. Syst. Res. **44**, 10–39 (2017)
5. Nute, D. Defeasible logic. In: Revised Papers of the 14th International Conference on Applications of Prolog (INAP), pp. 151–169 (2003)
6. Maher, M.J.: Propositional defeasible logic has linear complexity. Theory Pract. Logic Program. 1(6), 691–711 (2001)
7. Watts, N., et al.: The 2015 lancet planetary health commission report: COP21 climate change negotiations special issue. Lancet Planetary Health 1(1), e20–e22 (2015)
8. Kim, J.-Y., Kabir, E., Bae, S.-W.: A review of the vulnerability of urban health to climate change. J. Environ. Health Res. 16(2), 161–170 (2018)
9. McMichael, A.J., Woodruff, R.E., Hales, S.: Climate change and human health: risks and responses. Lancet **367**(9513), 859–869 (2006)
10. Bastarianto, F., Hancock, T., Choudhury, C., Manley, E.: Agent-based models in urban transportation: review, challenges, and opportunities. Eur. Transp. Res. Rev. **15**, 19 (2023)
11. Batty, M.: The new science of cities. The MIT Press (2018)
12. Hoffmann, P., Bouwer, L., Huang-Lachmann, J.-T.: Understanding the climate change impact on health. Open Access Government (2023)
13. de Graaf-van Dinther, R., Ovink, H.: The five pillars of climate resilience. In: de Graaf-van Dinther, R. (eds.) Climate Resilient Urban Areas. Palgrave Studies in Climate Resilient Societies. Palgrave Macmillan (2021)

14. Yao, X., Liu, Z., Li, G., Jin, L., Deng, X., Leung, K.S.: Examining the impact of COVID-19 lockdowns on air quality in Beijing using machine learning. Environ. Sci. Eng. **54**(10), 7424–7431 (2020)
15. Leal Filho, W., et al.: Deploying artificial intelligence for climate change adaptation. Technol. Forecast. Soc. Chang. **180**, 121662 (2022)
16. Jimenez, A., Cardenas, P., Canales, A., Jimenez, F., Portacio, A.: A survey on intelligent agents and multi-agents for irrigation scheduling. Comput. Electron. Agric. **176**, 105474 (2020)
17. Toniuc, D., Groza, A.: Climebot: an argumentative agent for climate change. In: Proceedings of the 13th IEEE International Conference on Intelligent Computer Communication and Processing (ICCP), pp. 63–70, (2017)
18. Kozhevnikov, S., Svitek, M., Skobelev, P.: Multi-agent approach for smart resilient city. In: Proceedings of the International Workshop on Service Orientation in Holonic and Multi-Agent Manufacturing (SOHOMA), pp. 215–227 (2020)
19. Chen, L., Chen, Z., Zhang, Y., et al.: Artificial intelligence-based solutions for climate change: a review. Environ. Chem. Lett. **21**, 2525–2557 (2023)
20. Konya, A., Nematzadeh, P.: Recent applications of AI to environmental disciplines: a review. Sci. Total Environ. **906**, 167705 (2024)

MAS-PatientCare: Medical Diagnosis and Patient Management System Based on a Multi-agent Architecture

Kristijan Cincar[1], Todor Ivascu[1(✉)], and Viorel Negru[1,2]

[1] Computer Sciences Department, West University of Timisoara, Timisoara, Romania
{kristijan.cincar,todor.ivascu,viorel.negru}@e-uvt.ro
[2] E-Austria Institute, Timisoara, Romania
https://info.uvt.ro/en/

Abstract. This paper presents a multi-agent system MAS-PatientCare, specifically designed to manage patient scheduling, resource allocation and diagnostic processes in hospitals. The system architecture integ-rates specialized agents, each with different responsibilities, including patient management, hospital resource allocation, scheduling, medical special-ization, data preprocessing, machine learning, and decision support, to improve operational efficiency and quality of patient care across mul-tiple hospital departments, including colonoscopy and emergency, with the flexibility to add more departments as needed. We explore the inter-connectivity and collaboration between these agents, detailing how they interact to ensure seamless operations. To evaluate the effectiveness and practical applicability of the MAS-PatientCare system, it has been tested in two different situations: in emergency situations in hospitals and in the screening process for patients undergoing a colonoscopy. The impact of the MAS-PatientCare system on patient outcomes, particularly in terms of reducing waiting times, improving diagnostic accuracy and improving resource utilisation is analysed.

Keywords: Multi-agent system · Hospital Scheduling and management · Recommendation system · Colonoscopy

1 Introduction

Modern solutions are needed to manage patient care effectively since hospi-tal operations are becoming increasingly complicated. Hospitals must coordi-nate activities across many departments to address several difficulties, including scheduling patients, allocating resources, and making clinical judgments. Because traditional approaches cannot constantly adjust to shifting situations and needs, they frequently fail to handle this complexity. We suggest the MAS-PatientCare architecture, a multi-agent system made to improve hospital operations by providing precise diagnostic assistance and effective scheduling, to solve these problems.

C. Bădică et al. (Eds.): BCI 2024, CCIS 2391, pp. 241–255, 2025.
https://doi.org/10.1007/978-3-031-84093-7_17

Multi-agent systems (MASs) have gained recognition for their capacity to manage intricate, dispersed assignments by utilizing a group of independent agents who cooperate to accomplish shared objectives. MAS may help healthcare by promoting improved resource usage, greater coordination, and support in clinical decision making. The MAS-PatientCare system leverages MAS's capabilities to streamline hospital workflows, reduce patient wait times, and enhance the overall quality of care. To evaluate the effectiveness and practical applicability of the MAS-PatientCare, it was tested in two distinct cases: emergency response in hospitals and the screening process for colonoscopy. However, it should be noted that the system is designed to be flexible, allowing for the addition of different hospital departments. In the emergency response scenario, the system was evaluated based on its ability to manage unplanned, high priority cases efficiently. The MAS-PatientCare agents demonstrated their capability to quickly assess the situation, allocate resources, and coordinate medical personnel. The analyzed case revealed the system's robustness in handling urgent situations, reducing wait times, and improving patient outcomes. In the colonoscopy scenario, the system was tested on its ability to streamline the scheduling and management of routine medical procedures.

This paper details the architecture of MAS-PatientCare, the roles of its constituent agents, and how these agents interact to achieve the system's objectives. We also examine related work in the field, demonstrating the advancements and potential of MAS in healthcare settings. Finally, we discuss the impact of MAS-PatientCare on patient outcomes and propose future research directions to enhance the system's capabilities further.

The paper is organised as follows: Section 2 presents the existing literature on this topic, Sect. 3 outlines the architecture of MAS-PatientCare, Sect. 4 describes the interaction of the agents and the operation of the system, Sect. 5 presents the conclusion and future work.

2   Related Work

The application of multi-agent systems (MAS) in healthcare has attracted considerable attention in recent years due to its potential to increase operational efficiency and improve patient care. Numerous studies have investigated different aspects of MAS in this context, demonstrating their versatility and effectiveness in addressing complex challenges.

Paper [1] focuses on the development of a multi-agent architecture for an automated medical diagnosis system. On the one hand, it enables the implementation of standard functions for data collection, processing and storage. On the other hand, it introduces specialised diagnostic functions based on a unique technique developed by the authors.

In paper [7], a MAS has been created to bridge the gap between patient and doctor. The proposed system uses intelligent agent services to assist patients at home and has been validated through a prototype. The results show that the developed agents can select appropriate care plans and communicate with physicians for validation and approval.

Another study presents a novel medical system called Medical Multi-Agent System (MMAS) [6]. This system integrates MAS into healthcare to improve efficiency by facilitating collaboration between hospital departments, improving medical diagnosis, coordinating between medical facilities, and collecting patient information.

In paper [9], MAS applications are explored through a comprehensive literature review covering system architecture, consensus algorithms, multi-agent platforms, frameworks and simulators. In addition, a distributed underfrequency load shedding scheme using MAS is proposed.

To improve health monitoring, a MAS-based system is presented in [5]. This system consists of a set of intelligent agents that collect patient data, engage in reasoning processes, and recommend actions to patients and healthcare professionals in a mobile environment. The MAS framework is evaluated through a case study, showing that it provides an efficient health monitoring solution for chronic, elderly and remote patients.

In paper [8], an Interrelated Decision Model (IDM) is proposed for an Intelligent Decision Support System (IDSS) in healthcare. This model, referred to as IDM-IDSS-healthcare, uses MAS to make informed decisions by utilising knowledge from previous and subsequent stages of treatment.

Study [2] develops and implements an architecture that integrates MAS with microservices, combining the strengths of both methodologies to harness artificial intelligence in healthcare. The paper evaluates the advantages and limitations of the proposed architecture, its applicability to different healthcare use cases, and its impact on the scalability, adaptability and maintainability of the system.

3   Architecture of MAS-PatientCare

3.1   Overview

The proposed system, MAS-PatientCare (Integrated System for Hospital Scheduling, Colonoscopy, and Recommendation), represents a platform for managing medical procedures and patient care within hospital settings. The architecture of MAS-PatientCare has been designed to facilitate collaboration and interaction between the various components and agents involved in the process of managing medical procedures. The agents are responsible for different aspects of the system, including patient scheduling, resource management, data analysis, and providing medical recommendation. The interconnectivity and communication between these agents allow the proposed system to improve processes and workflows within a hospital, thereby enhancing the quality of patient care and the efficiency of medical services. A significant aspect of the MAS-PatientCare system is its capacity to furnish patient care solutions by examining medical data. The generation of these solutions is facilitated by data analytics and machine learning agents, which employ algorithms to identify pertinent patterns and trends in patient data.

Furthermore, the MAS-PatientCare architectural framework enables more efficient scheduling of medical procedures, thereby reducing wait times and optimizing the utilization of available hospital resources. Agents engaged in the administration of patient scheduling collaborate to allocate resources and schedule procedures in accordance with the availability of physicians and rooms. This coordinated approach enables MAS-PatientCare to facilitate the reduction of congestion and the improvement of operational efficiency within hospitals.

The MAS-PatientCare system is designed as a modular and scalable architecture that incorporates various specialized agents to manage different aspects of hospital operations. The core components of the architecture include the following departments: *Colonoscopy Department*: Focuses on scheduling and managing colonoscopy procedures. *Emergency Department*: Handles urgent care cases, ensuring rapid response and resource allocation. Additional departments can be integrated into the MAS-PatientCare system as needed, making it a flexible solution for comprehensive hospital management.

3.2   Type of Agents

The MAS-PatientCare architecture comprises the following types of agents:

Patient Agent (PA). This agent serves as the gateway into the system for patients. It collects essential information about patients, such as the department to which they are scheduled, priority, arrival time, age, and gender. It also provides estimates of the costs of medical treatment. To illustrate, a patient who arrives at the hospital for a colonoscopy is considered. The PA gathers scheduling and preference data, which informs the patient's allocation to the most appropriate department and the scheduling of the necessary medical procedure. Agents are divided so that for each patient one agent is allocated.

Hospital Resource Agent (RA). When a patient arrives for surgery, the RA ensures that an appropriate specialist physician is assigned and that the necessary resources, such as the operating room and medical equipment, are available for the procedure. To illustrate this, when a patient is scheduled for colonoscopy surgery, the SA is responsible for ensuring the availability of the appropriate specialist physician and preparing all necessary resources for the medical intervention. Each subtype of specialist medical agent, such as an endocrinology MPA or a diabetology MPA, possesses distinctive expertise and engages in interactions.

Hospital Scheduling Agent (SA). The SA bears responsibility for coordinating activities and scheduling within the hospital. Agent SA assigns each specialist physician to the available resources, makes lists of patients scheduled for surgery, and proposes the next terminals. For example, when a patient is scheduled for colonoscopy surgery, the SA ensures that the appropriate specialist physician is available and that all necessary resources are prepared for the medical intervention.

Medical Specialist Agent (MPA). This agent is responsible for evaluating and treating patients within the scope of their specialization. Each subtype of specialist medical agent, such as an endocrinology MPA or a diabetology MPA, possesses unique expertise and interacts with the other agents to ensure patient care following best medical practice. For instance, a colonoscopy MPA will be involved in the diagnostic and treatment procedures associated with bowel disorders and will collaborate closely with the PA and RA to schedule and perform colonoscopies following the patient's requirements and preferences.

Hospital Section Agent (SCA). This agent oversees the activities and resources within a specific hospital section, such as the surgical or intensive care unit. The SCA works with the other agents to ensure resource availability and efficient utilization within that department. For example, when a patient is scheduled for surgery, the SCA coordinates activities in the operating room and ensures all necessary resources are available.

Colonoscopy Monitoring Agent (CMA). This agent is responsible for collecting and analyzing data associated with colonoscopy procedures. It monitors procedure performance and identifies potential areas for improvement in medical processes. For instance, the CMA may discern trends or patterns in the duration or efficacy of colonoscopies and propose adjustments to diagnostic and treatment procedures with the objective of optimizing outcomes.

Association Rule Extraction Agent (ARA). The ARA is responsible for identifying and extracting patterns and rules from the collected medical data. The patterns and rules are then used to improve medical processes and outcomes. For instance, the ARA is capable of identifying associations between specific conditions and treatments and suggesting personalized treatment protocols that are tailored to each patient's individual characteristics.

Decision Support and Referral Agent (DSRA). This agent employs a data analysis process to generate personalized patient care recommendations. It utilizes data obtained from other agents to generate recommendations that are pertinent and efficacious. For instance, the DSRA is capable of analyzing a patient's diagnostic data and medical history and subsequently formulating a customised treatment plan to the patient's individual needs and preferences.

Data Preprocessing Agent (DPA). This agent is responsible for processing raw data to prepare it for analysis. It cleans the data, eliminates errors, and removes redundant information to ensure the quality and accuracy of the data being analyzed. For example, the DPA can remove missing or incomplete data from datasets and standardize the data format to facilitate further analysis by other agents.

Machine Learning Agent (MLA). The ML agent uses machine learning algorithms to generate recommendations and solutions based on the collected medical data. It analyzes patterns and trends in the data and trains algorithms to identify and predict future behaviors. For example, MLA can use machine learning to detect anomalies in medical data and identify potential patient risks.

Database Agent (DBA). The DB agent manages the storage and access of data in the database. It ensures data integrity and security and facilitates fast and efficient access to health information. For example, the DBA may use storage and indexing technologies to optimize database performance and ensure the availability and confidentiality of medical data.

Notification Agent (NA). The NA agent is responsible for sending notifications to users and medical staff. It ensures efficient communication of important and urgent information and facilitates stakeholder interaction. For example, the NA can send notifications to patients to inform them of appointments or medical test results, and alert medical staff of emergencies or patient conditions changes.

4   Agent Interaction and System Operation

Collaboration between agents is fundamental to efficiently operating the healthcare system in the MAS-PatientCare architecture presented in Fig. 1.

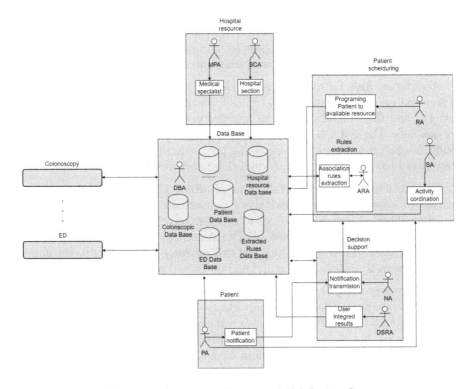

Fig. 1. Multi-agent architecture MAS-PatientCare

Interaction and collaboration begin with the exchange of information between agents. For example, the PA agent provides patient information such as appointments, priorities, and personal details. RA and SA agents use this information to organise and schedule medical procedures.

Data Analysis and Processing component contains agents responsible for analyzing data, such as the DPA, who represents the agent in charge of processing the raw data to prepare it for analysis, are closely linked with the CMA and

MLA, which likewise collaborate to process incoming information and extract relevant knowledge. For example, the CMA collects data about colonoscopy procedures, and the MLA uses machine learning algorithms to identify patterns and trends in the collected data.

For *Resource and Program Management* component, the RA and SA work closely together to manage available resources and schedule medical procedures efficiently. The RA agent assesses patient priorities and needs, while the SA agent coordinates resource allocation and schedules activities based on this information. Agent ARA analyzes data to detect patterns and associations between medical services. The DSRA agent uses the analyzed data and patient information to generate personalized recommendations for patient care. DSRA collaborates with data collection and processing agents to ensure recommendations are based on accurate and relevant data. The agent NA is also responsible for sending and receiving notifications between users and health care professionals.

Hospital Resource Component is represented by MPA agent, who is responsible for evaluating and treating patients in their area of specialization. For example, a colonoscopy MPA will be involved in the diagnostic and treatment procedures associated with bowel conditions and will work closely with the PA and RA to schedule and perform colonoscopies according to the patient's requirements and preferences, the SCA agent manages the activities and resources within a specific section of the hospital, such as the surgical or intensive care department.

In *Database Management and Communication* component, the DBA agent manages medical data storage and access in the system database. It collaborates with all other agents to ensure the integrity and confidentiality of the information.

Interconnectivity between medical specialist agents MPA and other agents within the MAS-PatientCare architectures is essential to ensure quality healthcare and efficient patient management. Each type of MPA agent: endocrinologist, internist, diabetologist, and colonoscopy specialist has its own competencies and responsibilities, and its interaction with the other agents contributes to the delivery of comprehensive and personalized medical care.

Here is how these agents are interconnected within the MAS-PatientCare system: MPA specialist medical agents communicate with the SA agent to receive appointments and lists of patients scheduled for surgery. For example, an endocrinologist MPA may receive the list of patients with endocrinologic conditions scheduled for specific consultations or procedures and coordinate the scheduling and resources needed for these cases. The MPA interacts with the PA to obtain patient information such as medical history, presenting symptoms, and test results. This information is essential to providing personalized and appropriate medical care for each patient. The MPA agent specialized in colonoscopy may collaborate with the CMA agent to monitor and evaluate colonoscopy procedures performed in the hospital. This may include scheduling patients for procedures, monitoring results, and interpreting data for diagnosis and treatment. The MPA agent may interact with the DSRA agent to receive up-to-date recommendations and guidelines in their area of expertise. For example, an endocrinologist

MPA agent may receive recommendations on current treatments and protocols for managing diabetes or other endocrinologic conditions. The MPA agent may collaborate with the RA agent to secure medical consultations and procedures resources. This may include scheduling patients according to the availability of physicians and equipment needed and managing time and resources efficiently.

4.1   Interconnectivity of Colonoscopy Agents

The interconnectivity between the CMA agent and the other agents in the MAS-PatientCare architecture shown in Fig. 2 represents the fundamental link for managing and optimizing colonoscopy procedures in a hospital environment.

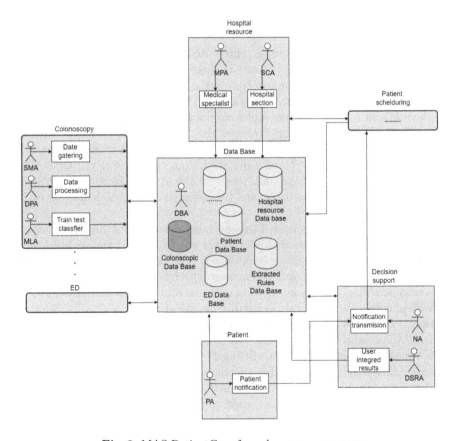

Fig. 2. MAS-PatientCare for colonoscopy use case

The CMA requests and receives data on colonoscopy procedures from the DPA. This data includes detailed patient information such as medical history, results of previous investigations and any relevant risk factors. Once it receives the processed data from the DPA, the CMA forwards it to the MLA for in-depth analysis, the MLA uses machine learning algorithms to identify significant patterns, trends, and correlations in the data related to colonoscopy procedures. This may include identifying risk factors associated with specific procedure outcomes or developing predictive models for early detection of certain conditions. The next step is for the CMA agent to provide the results of its analysis to the DSRA agent for the interpretation and generation of recommendations. The DSRA analyzes the data and identifies solutions and strategies for optimizing colonoscopy procedures and improving the quality of patient care. This may include recommendations on screening protocols, time and resource management, or identification of high risk patients requiring additional follow-up. Next CMA agent, utilizes the aggregated and processed data to continuously monitor the performance of colonoscopy procedures and evaluate the effectiveness of measures implemented due to recommendations generated by the DSRA. Storing and accessing data related to colonoscopy procedures is managed by the DBA agent, facilitating retrospective performance analysis and the identification of trends over time. The CMA can communicate the data and monitoring results to the NA, which can then generate notifications and warnings for patients or medical staff.

4.2   Interconnectivity of Emergency Department Agents

Interconnectivity between emergency receiving agents in the MAS-PatientCare architecture shown in Fig. 3 represents the fundamental link for managing and optimizing emergency receiving procedures in a hospital environment.

Interconnectivity and collaboration between PA, SMA, RA, and SA agents are essential for effective response to unplanned medical emergencies. Each agent plays a specific role in ensuring that patients receive the necessary care in a coordinated and efficient manner. The PA agent collects essential patient information such as medical status, priorities, and arrival time and forwards it to the RA and SA for resource needs assessment and scheduling.

Example: the PA identifies a patient with severe symptoms of acute abdominal pain, categorizing it as a high priority emergency and notifying the RA and SA. The RA assesses the information received from the PA and categorizes patients based on medical priority. The RA ensures that patients are assigned to available physicians and that the necessary resources are prepared.

Example: the RA assigns the urgent patient to an available general surgery specialist and prepares the necessary resources for an emergency evaluation. The SA agent adjusts the hospital schedule to accommodate the urgent patient, reassigning the necessary resources, and informs the SMA of the schedule changes and the resources allocated. The SA rearranges the surgery room schedule to allow an emergency surgery and notifies the SMA about the availability of the room and equipment. The SMA quickly mobilizes the medical team, prepares the procedure room for the urgent patient, monitors the procedure's progress, and adjusts resources if necessary. The SMA coordinates the surgical team and prepares the operating room for the urgent patient, ensuring everything is ready

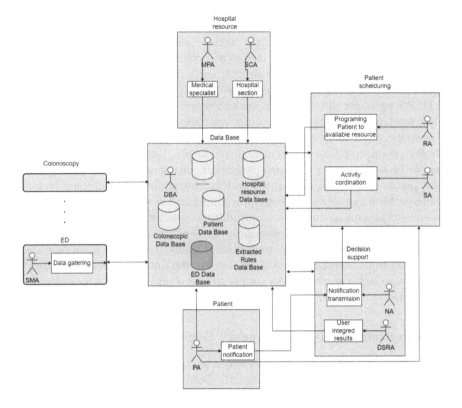

Fig. 3. MAS-PatientCare for emergency department use case

for the procedure. The DBA provides fast and secure access to patient data, facilitating informed decisions.

Example: the SMA accesses the database to check the patient's complete medical history, ensuring an informed and accurate intervention. NA sends immediate notifications to all involved parties to coordinate emergency response. NA notifies medical staff and administration about the urgent patient, ensuring rapid coordination and mobilization.

Interconnectivity and collaboration among the agents PA, SMA, RA, and SA are essential for effective response to unplanned medical emergencies within the MAS-PatientCare architecture. This system ensures appropriate and timely patient care through rapid and accurate information distribution and optimal resource coordination, demonstrating the power of a well integrated multi-agent system in the modern hospital environment. Interaction with other agents, such as DPA, DBA and NA, improves responsiveness and workflow, contributing to high quality healthcare.

5   Evaluation

In managing patient scheduling in the hospital context, another approach is to apply a customized solution to meet the specific requirements of scheduling management. Adopting a simulation based approach and using MAS, we intend to provide a flexible and dynamic solution capable of adjusting schedules according to unpredictable changes that may occur in the medical context. This system aims to facilitate efficient resource management and provide the adaptability required to respond quickly to the fluctuating needs of a hospital environment. The patient scheduling use case was previously published in [3] and the colonoscopy component, which is extended to a multi-agent architecture in this work, was published in [4].

Detailed simulations also allow the identification and assessment of potential blockages and the optimization of workflows. Utilizing historical data and variables specific to each section of the hospital allows for the creation of accurate predictive models that can improve both the patient experience and overall hospital efficiency. The system's effectiveness was evaluated through two cases, demonstrating its practical applicability and benefits in real world scenarios.

5.1   Use Case for Colonoscopy

Machine learning algorithms have become fundamental in modern medicine, especially in medical imaging. These algorithms are essential for analyzing the images and videos produced in colonoscopy. Their primary function is to detect abnormalities such as polyps or lesions and provide a preliminary assessment.

Integrating these algorithms into a multi-agent system involves the continuous transfer of colonoscopy data to the algorithm for analysis. The agent assisting the patient can communicate directly with the algorithm and receive its results. If a suspicious abnormality is detected, alerts can be sent to medical staff for immediate intervention. This real time interaction between the algorithm and the agents allows efficient and timely patient condition monitoring. Applying this multi-agent system in medical practice brings significant benefits. Early detection of abnormalities increases the chances of effective treatment and may reduce the risk of complications. In addition, the incorporation of machine learning algorithms helps to increase the accuracy of diagnoses, thereby improving health-care quality.

The Fig. 4 illustrates the flow of interactions between the different agents involved in scheduling and performing a colonoscopy, as well as collecting, preprocessing, and analyzing data to improve performance. Agents and Steps Involved:

1. Patient (PA) requests colonoscopy scheduling: The patient initiates the process by requesting a colonoscopy scheduling and providing information about their medical history and scheduling preferences.
2. SA receives requests and improves scheduling: The SA receives the patient's request and uses optimization algorithms to determine the most appropriate date and section for the colonoscopy.

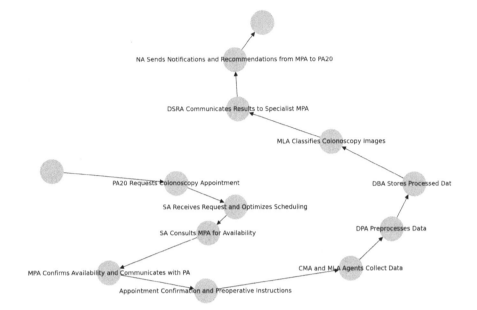

NA Sends Notifications and Recommendations from MPA to PA20

DSRA Communicates Results to Specialist MPA

MLA Classifies Colonoscopy Images

PA20 Requests Colonoscopy Appointment

DBA Stores Processed Dat

SA Receives Request and Optimizes Scheduling

DPA Preprocesses Data

SA Consults MPA for Availability

MPA Confirms Availability and Communicates with PA

CMA and MLA Agents Collect Data

Appointment Confirmation and Preoperative Instructions

Fig. 4. Patient flow for colonoscopy

3. SA agent consults MPA agent for availability: The SA consults with the MPA to verify the availability of a physician specializing in colonoscopies and to allocate resources for the procedure.

4. MPA confirms availability and communicates with PA: The MPA receives the appointment request, confirms availability, and communicates with the patient to confirm the appointment and provide necessary preoperative instructions.

5. Appointment confirmation and preoperative instructions: PA receives appointment confirmation and preoperative instructions from MPA.

6. CMA and MLA agents collect data: The CMA and MLA collate data pertaining to the duration and efficacy of medical procedures.

7. DPA preprocess data: DPA clean, format, and prepare the collected data for further analysis.

8. DBA stores the processed data: DBA stores the processed data ensuring that it is accessible and secure for further analysis.

9. MLA analyzes data and classifies colonoscopic images': Using machine learning techniques, MLA analyzes data to identify patterns and classifies colonoscopic images.

10. DSRA communicates the results to the MPA: DSRAs receive the results of the analysis and communicate the results to the MPA.

11. NA sends notifications and recommendations from the MPA to the PA20: NA sends appropriate notifications and recommendations to the patient.

12. Colonoscopy is performed: The actual medical procedure is performed as scheduled and confirmed.

The process is finalized, and all activities and agent interactions are completed.

5.2   Use Case for Hospital Emergency

Let us assume the following usage scenario to illustrate the functionality of the proposed component of multi-agent system presented in Fig. 5. At the county hospital, we have the following available resources: SurgeryRoom1 (RA1), SurgeryRoom2 (RA2), and SurgeryRoom3 (RA3), three specialist physicians (MPA1, MPA2, and MPA3), and the scheduling agent (SA), which coordinates hospital activity and patient arrival time. The SA agent assigns each specialist physician to the available resources (surgical rooms), draws up a list of patients scheduled for surgery and proposes the following terminals.

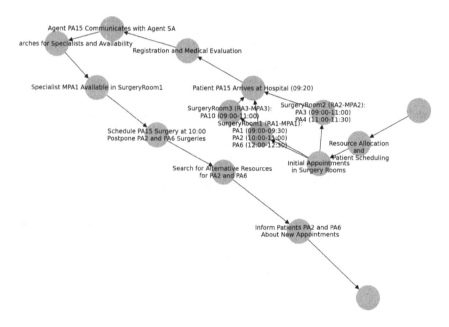

Fig. 5. Patient flow in the emergency department

SurgeryRoom1(RA1-MPA1): PA1 with medium priority medical condition is scheduled for surgery from 9:00 to 09:30, PA2 with medium priority level is scheduled for surgery from 10:00 to 11:00 and PA6 with medium level condition is scheduled for surgery from 12:00 to 12:30. SurgeryRoom2- (RA2-MPA2) has the following scheduling: PA3 is scheduled for surgery between 9:00 and 11:00, the patient's priority status level is high, and PA4 with medium priority level is expected from 11:00 to 11:30. SurgeryRoom3-(RA3-MPA3) has one patient (PA10), with a high priority level, scheduled for surgery from 9:00 to 11:00. The new patient in need of medical emergency arrives at the hospital at 09:20, after registration and medical assessment, a patient agent (PA15) representing that patient is created and communicates with the SA, informing him about the patient's health status. The SA first searches for specialists in the field and their availability. Let assume that specialist physician (MPA1) is in SurgicalRoom1. The SA informs the specialist physician (MPA1) about the subsequent scheduled surgery for the patient (PA15) at 10:00 a.m. and postpones other surgeries with lower priority levels, which affects PA2 and PA6 in this example. To reduce the waiting time, the SA component searches for other available resources for these two patients and automatically informs them about the new scheduling for the available sections.

6 Conclusions and Future Work

The MAS-PatientCare system represents a advancement in the application of MAS in healthcare, addressing critical needs in hospital management. The integration of various specialised agents within the system facilitates hospital operations, management of resource utilisation, and clinical decision making across multiple hospital departments, including Colonoscopy and Emergency.

The adoption of more effective, coordinated, and patient-centered methods to healthcare delivery is made possible by this integration. The modular and scalable architecture ensures its adaptability to different hospital settings and evolving healthcare demands, rendering it a versatile solution for a wide range of medical institutions. MAS-PatientCare's adaptability to the specific needs of different hospital departments and its potential for integration with additional units underlines its value as a suitable solution for a range of healthcare institutions.

In the future, we intend to conduct comprehensive real world testing of the MAS-PatientCare system to evaluate its performance and impact on patient outcomes in diverse hospital environments. This will entail the deployment of the system in various medical institutions, including small community hospitals and large academic medical centres, and an assessment of its capacity to enhance scheduling efficiency, resource utilisation, and clinical decision making. Another crucial area for future work is the integration of MAS-PatientCare with other healthcare technologies and systems. For instance, integrating the system with electronic health records (EHR) and health information exchange (HIE) platforms can facilitate data sharing and interoperability, thereby providing a more compre-hensive view of patient health and enabling more effective decision masking.

Acknowledgment. This research was partially supported by MOISE grant number 240/2020, ID 911 POC/398/1/1, and by AI4EUROPE+ grant number 24PHE, PN-IV-P8-8.1-PRE-HE-ORG-2023-0072, financed by the Romanian government. The views expressed in this paper do not necessarily reflect those of the corresponding project's partners.

References

1. Buldakova, T.I., Lantsberg, A.V., Suyatinov, S.I.: Multi-agent architecture for medical diagnostic systems. In: Proceedings of the 1st International Conference on Control Systems, Mathematical Modelling, Automation & Energy Efficiency (SUMMA), pp. 344–348 (2019)
2. Chaves, A., Montenegro, L., Peixoto, H., Abelha, A., Gomes, L., Machado, J.: Intelligent systems in healthcare: an architecture proposal. In: Proceedings of the 14th International Symposium on Ambient Intelligence (ISAmI), pp. 230–238 (2023). https://doi.org/10.1007/978-3-031-43461-7_23
3. Cincar, K., Ivascu, T.: Agent-based hospital scheduling system. In: Proceedings of the 21st International Symposium on Symbolic & Numeric Algorithms for Scientific Computing (SYNASC), pp. 337–338 (2019)
4. Cincar, K., Ivaşcu, T., Negru, V.: Comparative study of machine learning methods to classify bowel polyps. In: Proceedings of the 25th International Symposium on Symbolic & Numeric Algorithms for Scientific Computing (SYNASC), pp. 279–286 (2023)
5. Humayun, M., Jhanjhi, N.Z., Almotilag, A., Almufareh, M.F.: Agent-based medical health monitoring system. Sensors 22(8), 2820 (2022)
6. Jemal, H., Kechaou, Z., Ayed, M.B., Alimi, A.M.: A multi agent system for hospital organization. Int. J. Mach. Learn. Comput. 5(1), 51–56 (2015)
7. Lanza, F., Seidita, V., Chella, A.: Agents and robots for collaborating and supporting physicians in healthcare scenarios. J. Biomed. Inform. 108, 103483 (2020)
8. Mahiddin, N.B., Othman, Z.A., Bakar, A.A., Rahim, N.A.A.: An interrelated decision-making model for an intelligent decision support system in healthcare. IEEE Access 10, 31660–31676 (2022)
9. Xie, J., Liu, C.-C.: Multi-agent systems and their applications. J. Int. Council Electr. Eng. 7(1), 188–197 (2017)

Microsoft Copilot, Google Gemini, Openai Chatgpt and Anthropic Claude: Assisting in Cardiology Diagnosing - A Case Study

Maria-Ecaterina Olariu[1]([⊠]), Diana Vuza[2], and Adrian Iftene[1]

[1] Faculty of Computer Science, Alexandru Ioan Cuza University, Strada General Henri Mathias Berthelot Nr. 16, 700259 Iași, Romania
mariaecaterina.olariu@gmail.com
[2] Cardiocenter, Strada Lascăr Catargi 43, 700107 Iași, Romania

Abstract. The development of generative AI technology has brought new prospects in several industries, including healthcare. This paper presents a case study assessing how well Microsoft Copilot, Google Gemini, OpenAI ChatGPT, and Anthropic Claude, four most popular AI systems, help with cardiology diagnosis. Analyzing Holter monitor imaging data from six patient cases, we explore the accuracy and practicality of these AI models. Our approach emphasizes the need of crafting prompts, while following ethical principles and European privacy regulations, for the production of precise and thorough AI responses. All four AI systems are shown to perform well in the study, with Google Gemini being correct most of the time. Microsoft Copilot delivers reliable results, however Claude and GPT-4o tend to overestimate patient conditions even when they identify critical parameters like drug adherence and dosage efficacy. For a three-month patient assessment, GPT-4o showed competence. This work demonstrates how generative AI might improve diagnostic procedures and seeks to add to the conversation on AI's application in patient care.

Keywords: Artificial Intelligence · Generative AI · Healthcare · Cardiology · Holter monitoring · Prompt engineering · AI in healthcare

1 Introduction

The rapid advancement of generative artificial intelligence (Gen AI) has led to the development of powerful large language models that may aid in various tasks, such as medical diagnosing. Nevertheless, as these tools become more accessible to the public, there are concerns regarding the potential for misuse or misinterpretation, especially in areas such as healthcare. This paper focuses on the field of cardiology diagnoses produced by four generative AI tools. They were chosen because they were developed by top technology companies: Microsoft Copilot, Google Gemini, OpenAI ChatGPT, and Anthropic Claude. The objective of our work is to provide insight into the efficacy of these AI assistants when confronted with actual patient cases including some of the most prevalent cardiovascular conditions. To carry out this research, we have partnered with an

© The Author(s), under exclusive license to Springer Nature Switzerland AG 2025
C. Bădică et al. (Eds.): BCI 2024, CCIS 2391, pp. 256–271, 2025.
https://doi.org/10.1007/978-3-031-84093-7_18

experienced cardiologist who has supplied us with a range of patient cases and medical data, guaranteeing the accuracy and authenticity of the information. This collaboration allows us to thoroughly assess the diagnostic capabilities of the AI technologies and compare their results with expert medical analysis.

Our study seeks to address the concerns raised by patients who are becoming more skeptical about medical expertise, due, in part, to the rise of AI-powered applications. We will thoroughly examine the negative and positive aspects of generative AI in the field of cardiology diagnosis. Through the examination of varied patient cases and careful analysis of the AI assistants' responses, our objective is to pinpoint any potential inaccuracies or areas that may need improvement in these tools.

Our investigation was conducted using the free versions or free trials of the aforementioned AI technologies, since these options are more likely to be utilized by the patients. In addition, we have opted to employ ABPM Holter and Holter EKG/24h graphs due to their ability to provide patient data in a precise and succinct manner, facilitating the identification of potential sources of misunderstanding or inaccuracy in the AI models. Because these technologies provide the most crucial information in an understandable manner, the patient may decide to use Generative AI for self-diagnosis, verify the medical advice provided, or look for other options, if the evolution under current treatment proves unsatisfactory. We wish to provide insights that can guide the development of best practices, identify possible risks, and ultimately improve the responsible integration of these powerful technologies into medical diagnostics.

2 Motivation

Another goal of this study is finding the best artificial intelligence technology that can help medical professionals with diagnosis and is available to the public. This investigation is motivated by the growing dependence on AI by people who lack medical expertise. As of late, these people use AI for two main reasons: first, to confirm the diagnoses made by doctors and second, to self-diagnose. The motivation for this work comes from the AI's growing influence in medicine. As AI tools become more widely used, particularly by non-experts, there is the need to assess their usefulness and dependability. In the next chapters we will discuss separately about each tool, the data, the prompts and the results.

3 About Generative AI Tools

Generative AI, also known as gen AI, refers to artificial intelligence (AI) that has the ability to produce unique content, including text, photos, video, audio, or software code, in direct response to a user's input or inquiry [1]. Generative AI utilizes advanced machine learning models known as deep learning models, which are algorithms that replicate the cognitive and decision-making abilities of the human brain [2]. Every Generative AI tool is based on a certain model. Although Transformers are utilized by all of them as the underlying architecture [3, 4], the specific implementations and capabilities may differ depending on the design and training data of each model. For instance, Claude Sonnet is trained with data up to August 2023, GPT-4 Turbo up to April 2023 and Gemini Pro up to February 2023 [5]. It is important to mention that Microsoft Copilot is utilizing

OpenAI's GPT-4 and GPT-4 Turbo in Precise mode. In the following subsections, we will provide information about each tool and what it offers.

3.1 Microsoft Copilot

Microsoft Copilot offers three conversation styles. The first mode is Creative, which offers responses that are more descriptive and detailed. Next, there is Precise, providing concise and search-focused responses. The Balanced setting is an intermediate option [6]. The most suitable option in the framework of this academic evaluation was found to be the Precise conversation tone. Especially, this specific conversational style has been driven by the GPT-4 Turbo model since March 2024, which improves its accuracy and efficiency. The intuitive interface of Microsoft Copilot is one of its main advantages, making interaction and navigation easier. Furthermore, it provides the convenience of saving responses directly as text files, PDFs, or documents. This allows for seamless communication and documentation of research findings among collaborators.

3.2 Google Gemini

Google's DeepMind division presented in December 2023 Gemini, a multimodal language model that stands out for its scalability and flexibility. The three different Gemini versions are Ultra, Pro, and Nano. The most comprehensive model is Gemini Ultra, suited for very complex jobs. Whereas Gemini Nano is designed for efficiency and is best suited for jobs carried out on smartphones, Gemini Pro provides the best balance for a wide range of applications [7]. The default model in the web app is Gemini Pro; the Advanced version allows access to Gemini Ultra. Gemini Advanced is available for free trial for two months to users. Using both Gemini Pro and Gemini Ultra, we empirically evaluated their effectiveness in assisting medical diagnosis and recorded the results in this research. Finding that Gemini Ultra does not respond to medical questions was unexpected. An attempt to get around this restriction by asking for image processing without a diagnostic component produced a similar result; the model started to respond, then stopped, retracting its output and turning down more help on the grounds that it is an artificial intelligence. On the other hand, Gemini Pro, which is available for free and doesn't need an account or subscription, opened and ended its response with a little disclaimer. All the same, it answered the question put out in full.

3.3 OpenAI ChatGPT

Introduced by OpenAI in 2022, ChatGPT functions as both a chatbot and a virtual assistant. Users are given the choice to select the model that will produce responses. The default model provided is GPT-3.5, however, users have the option to upgrade to the more sophisticated GPT-4 and GPT-4 Turbo versions by subscribing to a premium plan [8]. As of the 13th of May 2024, the GPT-4o model was released for public use, with limitations on its daily usage. This iteration boasts superior performance in tasks related to image processing and text generation. For this reason, we chose to work with GPT-4o. Considering that the new model is limited to a currently unknown exact number of characters per day, and accounting for the image included in the prompt, the number of prompts per 24 h that we were able to ask was 3. After reaching the limit, we were not able to add images, but were able to continue conversing with model GPT 3.5, which was not the intention of this study.

3.4 Anthropic Claude

Anthropic created Claude, a family of large language models. Claude does exceptionally well at a wide range of language, reasoning, analytics, coding, and other tasks. The latest Claude models are Haiku, Sonnet, and Opus. These are cutting-edge text and vision models that, given both text and image inputs, can produce text outputs that resemble a human's answer. Strong visual capabilities present fascinating opportunities for applications related to computer vision and picture interpretation [9]. Users must register a free account to access the application. This grants them access to the Sonnet version, but with restrictions that reset every five hours. The most powerful version, Claude Opus, is not available to users in Europe via app or behind a paywall, but only via API, which undermines the purpose of this research. The feature of uploading several photos and having Claude analyze them all for any changes or evolution set it apart from the other generative AI tools.

4 Data

In this study, we attempted to evaluate the performance of different generative artificial intelligence technologies in visual interpretation, given a textual context about the patient. To this end, we concentrated our analysis on Holter monitor images. Six instances were deliberately selected to reflect the most common diseases that can be detected using Holter monitoring methods. Holter monitor images are the result of the data collected throughout 24 h by an electronic device. Every 10 to 60 min the device measures the arterial pressure and saves the values. The next day, the patient comes back to the clinic, the information is then downloaded and processed by the machine, which returns a graph and some highlights for further interpretation [10]. For the ABPM monitoring the protocol set for the device differentiated between day, set from 06 to 22, and night, from 22 to 6. During the day it measured the arterial pressure every 30 min, while during the night it measured every hour. The Holter EGK/24h continuously registers the electrocardiogram of the pulse and cardiac frequency on three channels, which is the most frequently used set-up. [11] The group included people of the adult age range, from 30 to 70 years old. Within these cases, there were four females and two males. We will mention each case and its particularities in the next subsections.

4.1 White Coat Hypertension

This diagnosis pertains to a 60-year-old female patient. Data collected throughout the day reveals an initial spike in blood pressure (see Holter 1) without a consistent pattern, suggesting a diagnosis of White Coat Hypertension (hypertension induced by the medical setting).

260   M.-E. Olariu et al.

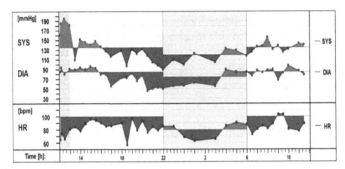

Holter 1. Image of the graph resulting from 24-h ambulatory blood pressure monitor (ABPM) and Heart Rate (HR) in a White Coat Hypertension case.

4.2 Hypertension

This 46-year-old female patient was diagnosed with Hypertension. Unlike the previous case, there is a pattern of high blood pressure throughout the 24 h of monitoring (see Holter 2).

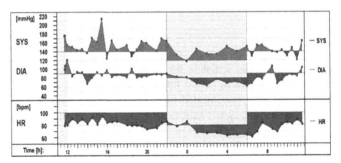

Holter 2. Image of the graph resulting from 24-h ambulatory blood pressure monitor (ABPM) and Heart Rate (HR) in a classic Hypertension case.

4.3 Borderline Profile

Male patient, 30 years of age, presenting a borderline profile (see Holter 3). This case also had data from a stress test on a cycloergometer separately analyzed by the tools.

4.4 Atrial Extrasystole Arrhythmia

The diagnosis belongs to a 70-year-old female. (see Holter 4).

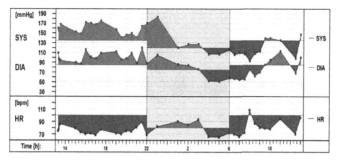

Holter 3. Image of the graph resulting from 24-h ambulatory blood pressure monitor (ABPM) and Heart Rate (HR) showing a borderline profile case.

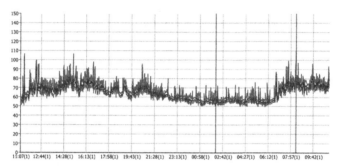

Holter 4. Image of the graph resulting from Holter EKG/24h in an Atrial extrasystole arrhythmia case.

4.5   Ventricular Extrasystole Arrhythmia

This case belongs to a 46-year-old male patient. The patient was seen for 3 consecutive months, each month undergoing the same investigation. For this diagnosis, it is imperative to see the evolution through time. If a Holter result from one month shows a minimal number of Ventricular Extrasystoles, and in another month there are some, but they account for less than 5% of the total registered heart beats, it is highly likely that the condition is benign. This implies that it is important to continue monitoring the patient. On the other hand, if in a subsequent month 20% of the total heart beats were found to be Ventricular Extrasystoles, the patient should be referred to a Rhythmologist and would be deemed eligible for an ablation procedure. Ablation is a minimally invasive surgery that eradicates the focal point responsible for initiating the irregular beats. The results from each month have been analyzed either separately or in perspective by the tools. In the Holter 5 we can see the graph belonging to one of the three months.

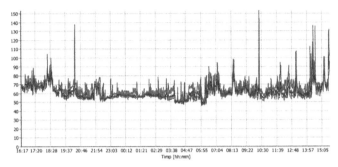

Holter 5. Image of the graph resulting from Holter EKG/24h in a Ventricular extrasystole arrhythmia case.

4.6 Repetitive Paroxysmal Atrial Fibrillation

At 46 years old this woman presents with paroxysmal atrial fibrillation (see Holter 6).

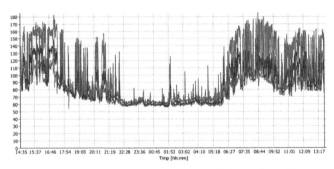

Holter 6. Image of the graph resulting from Holter EKG/24h in a Repetitive paroxysmal atrial fibrillation case.

5   Prompts

Prompts are the fundamental questions asked of chatbots in the field of conversational AI, which produce answers catered to the requirements of the user. The prompts used are carefully designed in compliance with prompt engineering concepts [12]. Contextual data incorporation is a key factor in the construction since it improves the accuracy and relevance of the AI's answer. Besides, the suggestions must be expressed clearly and also ask for thorough explanations. The opaque response mechanisms of the models raise an ethical issue that is also addressed by this technique. Through the organization of the question to require a detailed explanation, we obtain understanding of the fundamental logic of the AI's operation. Furthermore, especially in the medical field, the idea of privacy is paramount. In keeping with this norm, we protect sensitive information by including only relevant patient information, such age, gender, and prescribed medication. To create a brief but inclusive prompt, we used Microsoft Copilot to assess how well it adhered to the previously described prompt engineering concepts. Refinements to the original formulation were done in accordance with the comments received. When the question for the first patient was used, we found that the order of diagnoses was not clearly explained. As so, a directive was included to arrange the diagnoses according to likelihood. Given that the aforementioned AI technologies were developed by corporations based in the United States and the need to adhere to local medical norms, the model is instructed to follow the European Health Society recommendations. This specification guarantees that the diagnostic recommendations made by the AI are not only developed rationally but also suitable for the local context. Our design process resulted in a flexible template that was carefully adjusted to fit the subtleties of each scenario (see Fig. 1). As described in the part before this one, two distinct kinds of devices were used for Holter investigations in the cases selected. The devices provided different charts. The textual part of the prompt was the same in all cases. However, the approach for the visual input that went along with it differed. For the second kind, it showed the EKG graphically (see Fig. 2) or a composite of the graph and a brief tabular summary of important information (see Fig. 3). Remarkably, no changes to the order of diagnostic probability were caused by this change in visual information. Still, the later style, which combines a table and a graph, was used consistently for the rest of the study. The choice was made after a thorough analysis of how well each image kind compares in improving the diagnostic performance of the AI.

Based on the provided picture ABPM Holter image, knowing that this is a 60 year old woman, what might be potential diagnoses? Please detail your reasoning, the underlying medical principles, the typical diagnostic process a doctor adhering to EHS would follow, and detail the order of potential diagnoses.

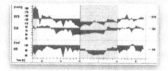

Fig. 1. Example of the final form of the prompt, including the image and text. Caption taken from Microsoft Copilot.

Based on the provided picture Cardiac Frequency Holter Graph 24h measurement, knowing that this is a 46 year old female, not taking medications, what might be potential diagnoses? Please detail your reasoning, the underlying medical principles, the typical diagnostic process a doctor adhering to EHS would follow, and detail the order of potential diagnoses.

Fig. 2. Example of the prompt for Holter EKG/24h, including the image with the text and the graph only. Caption taken from Microsoft Copilot.

Based on the provided picture Cardiac Frequency Holter Graph 24h measurement, knowing that this is a 46 year old female, not taking medications, what might be potential diagnoses? Please detail your reasoning, the underlying medical principles, the typical diagnostic process a doctor adhering to EHS would follow, and detail the order of potential diagnoses.

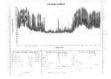

Fig. 3. Example of the same prompt for Holter EKG/24h seen in Fig. 2, including the image with the text, the graph and table. Caption taken from Microsoft Copilot.

6 Experiments

The interdisciplinary nature of our research team allows us to examine two critical features of AI-assisted diagnostics. The first part focuses on the way questions are posed to the AI system. This includes both the language accuracy and the context-related phrasing of the queries. The second one assesses the precision and consistency of the AI-generated answers with the known medical diagnoses. By analyzing these two dimensions, our research hopes to offer insight into the potential and limitations of publicly available AI tools in the medical field. In this section we will discuss for each case, the differences between the answers given by all four AI tools. We put emphasis on the fact that for each case, the same prompt was used across all tools.

6.1 White Coat Hypertension

The results of Copilot's analysis are promising, as it illustrates a comprehensive array of potential diagnoses, albeit not as expansively presented as those offered by Claude and ChatGPT. On the other hand, Gemini's report did not take into account the possibility of Masked Hypertension even if it included the right diagnosis. Although the result of Chat GPT-4o was more complex than that of its predecessors, Secondary Hypertension was not mentioned. Like Chat GPT-4o, Claude overlooked this specific diagnosis as well, but it did go into further depth about the remaining conditions (Table 1).

As the table above shows, Copilot deserves recognition for its comprehensive list of diagnostic options when assessing overall performance. For its detailed contributions, Claude deserves an honorable mention even though a diagnostic option was left out.

6.2 Hypertension

Due in large part to the lack of important factors like White Coat Hypertension and Non-Compliance to Treatment, the results from Copilot are noticeably brief. On the opposite side, Gemini performed admirably with the only significant flaw being the omission of the non-compliance treatment. In general, ChatGPT-4o makes a good impression, but its first diagnostic recommendation is vague, additionally the diagnoses must be reordered, with the fourth diagnosis receiving the most attention. Though Claude produced a competent output, it has to be rearranged to prioritize the final diagnosis. Inadequate drug dosage should also be given top priority in the current third diagnostic before non-compliance to treatment is addressed (Table 2).

Although Claude and GPT-4o list the diagnoses in more depth, their overall effectiveness is lower than that of Gemini. Gemini gives the diagnosis in the right order, admits that medicine might be unsuccessful, but ignores the part about non-compliance.

6.3   Borderline Profile

While precisely pointing up irregularities in the data patterns, Copilot's analytical output is neither very thorough nor arranged sequentially. Particularly, it ignores the possibility that the diagnosis of sleep apnea is directly related to the fourth. Moreover, the diagnostic process is out of order since the first diagnosis is wrongly placed as White Coat Hypertension. In contrast, while accurate, Gemini's diagnostic compilation has to be slightly reordered, more precisely, the second and third positions need to be swapped. Claude and Chat GPT-4o have both failed to notice the Non-dipping Profile of the ABPM. The most frequent cause for this is Sleep Apnea (Table 3).

In this diagnostic assessment, Gemini comes out on top, with the only criticism being that the second and third diagnosis should have been switched. Copilot comes next, and it needs to improve both the sequential presentation and the depth of its diagnostic output.

6.4   Atrial Extrasystole Arrhythmia

Copilot's tertiary diagnostic proposition contains a vast range of possibilities, but it lacks a clear direction. Though it is a good diagnosis, the second one does not identify the most likely arrhythmia. Conversely, Arrhythmias is wisely placed in the terminal position by Gemini, which clearly defines the best diagnostic candidates. Still, there must be a little recalibrating, more precisely, the 1st and 2nd should be switched (Table 4).

Based only on the patient's septuagenarian status, ChatGPT-4o hastily diagnoses the illness as an Ageing Heart, which does not capture the whole clinical image. In fact, not everyone who ages experiences these extra beats, clinically referred to as extrasystoles, nor arrhythmias. In this instance the first diagnosis should be removed from the list and the fourth one should be considered as the most important. About Claude, the dominant diagnosis is placed appropriately. But the next diagnosis, which is of a similar arrhythmic nature, should be removed from the list, since they have different therapeutic sanctions and is misleading.

In this situation, Gemini shows itself to be the pinnacle of diagnostic precision, with just a slight modification to the order of the first two diagnoses.

6.5   Repetitive Paroxysmal Atrial Fibrillation

It is clear from examining Copilot's diagnostic sequence that the third diagnosis should be given priority as the primary cause. Due to its misleadingness, the second diagnosis must be removed from the list since it is also subject to ambiguity. For this scenario, the ultimate diagnosis is neither clear nor relevant. Though it is accurate, Gemini's initial diagnosis is not very specific; considering that atrial fibrillation is classified under supraventricular tachycardias, it would have been appropriate to point it out. The fourth diagnosis deserves first placement; the second and fifth diagnostic proposals of Chat GPT-4o are not feasible, which results in the need for reorganization. The first diagnostic made by Claude is incorrect since it ignores the physiological heart rhythm associated with breathing patterns. Claude makes a third diagnosis that is misleading entirely from the actual issue which results in an exaggerated clinical picture (Table 5).

Gemini is shown to be the most precise in estimating the actual diagnosis. It is not without flaws, though, as the first diagnostic needs more accuracy to improve its clinical value and the second is unnecessary.

6.6 Ventricular Extrasystole Arrhythmia

This case can be examined from the perspective of three distinct Holter EKG/24-h investigations. Given that Claude and Chat GPT-4o possess the unique capability to process more than one image, their results will be analyzed independently from the other two entities. Initially, the findings from Copilot and Gemini will be addressed (see Table 6). Despite being presented with identical text for each month, with the sole variation being the accompanying image, it was noted that neither entity altered the sequence nor the diagnoses themselves. In both instances, the diagnoses pertaining to Atrial fibrillation or flutter were found to be inaccurate and, therefore, warrant complete omission. Ventricular tachycardia should be categorized as either the second or third diagnosis, whereas premature ventricular contractions (PVC) must be considered as the primary diagnosis.

Table 1. The diagnoses presented by each Gen AI tool in order of their likelihood.

Diagnoses order	Copilot	Gemini	Chat GPT-4o	Claude
1	Essential Hypertension	Hypertension	Hypertension (stage 2 or WCH)	Hypertension (primary or essential)
2	White Coat Hypertension	White Coat Hypertension	Isolated Systolic Hypertension	Non-dipping pattern or absence of nocturnal blood pressure dip
3	Masked Hypertension	Secondary Hypertension	Nocturnal Hypertension	Potential sleep disorders (sleep apnea)
4	Secondary Hypertension			White-coat effect (less likely as sole explanation)

Table 2. The diagnoses presented by each Gen AI tool in order of their likelihood.

Diagnoses order	Copilot	Gemini	Chat GPT-4o	Claude
1	Uncontrolled Hypertension	Uncontrolled Essential Hypertension (likely due to non-effective medication)	Hypertension	Uncontrolled or resistant hypertension with a non-dipping pattern
2	Secondary Hypertension	Masked Hypertension	White Coat Hypertension	Possible Secondary Hypertension
3		White Coat Hypertension and orthostatic hypotension	Masked Hypertension	Medication non-compliance or inadequate dosing
4			Poor medication adherence or ineffective regimen	

Table 3. The diagnoses presented by each Gen AI tool in order of their likelihood.

Diagnoses order	Copilot	Gemini	Chat GPT-4o	Claude
1	White-coat Hypertension	Primary Hypertension	Primary Hypertension	Hypertension (Primary or Essential)
2	Masked Hypertension	Secondary Hypertension	White Coat Hypertension	White Coat or Masked Hypertension
3	Sustained Hypertension	Sleep Apnea	Masked Hypertension	Labile Hypertension
4	Non-dipping or reverse dipping patterns		Secondary Hypertension	

Claude's analysis encompassed three images from February, March, and April. However, its performance was suboptimal. The initial diagnosis of Atrial Fibrillation or Atrial Flutter was wrongfully attributed to this patient. Similarly, the subsequent diagnosis of Paroxysmal Supraventricular Tachycardia (PSVT) is incorrect. The third diagnosis, encompassing Ventricular Tachycardia or Ventricular Fibrillation, presents a significant risk of misinterpretation, as the patient's clinical presentation does not suggest anything related to this high mortality risk condition. Chat GPT-4o delivered a comprehensive and

Table 4. The diagnoses presented by each Gen AI tool in order of their likelihood.

Diagnoses order	Copilot	Gemini	Chat GPT-4o	Claude
1	Sustained ventricular Tachycardia	Sinus Tachycardia	Normal Aging Heart	Atrial Fibrillation
2	Supraventricular Arrhythmias: Atrial fibrillation or flutter	Sinus Bradycardia	Supraventricular Tachycardia (SVT)	Atrial Flutter
3	Bradycardia: Sinus node dysfunction or atrioventricular block	Arrhythmias (supraventricular or ventricular, but at low percentages)	Premature Ventricular Contractions	Sick sinus syndrome
4			Atrial Fibrillation (AFib)	Ventricular arrhythmias (less likely)
5			Sinus Bradycardia	

Table 5. The diagnoses presented by each Gen AI tool in order of their likelihood.

Diagnoses order	Copilot	Gemini	Chat GPT-4o	Claude
1	Sinus Tachycardia (if activity-related)	SVT (supraventricular tachycardia)	Sinus Tachycardia	Sinus Arrhythmia (most likely, based on the significant heart rate variation)
2	PSVT (if abrupt bursts observed)	Ventricular tachycardia	Paroxysmal Supraventricular Tachycardia (PSVT)	Supraventricular Tachycardia (SVT)
3	Atrial Fibrillation (if irregular rhythms persist)		Premature Atrial Contractions (PACs)	Ventricular Tachycardia (VT)

(*continued*)

Table 5. (*continued*)

Diagnoses order	Copilot	Gemini	Chat GPT-4o	Claude
4	Other Arrhythmias (based on specific patterns)		Atrial Fibrillation (AFib) or Atrial Flutter	Underlying Structural Heart Disease (e.g., coronary artery disease, cardiomyopathy, valvular heart disease)
5			Ventricular Premature Contractions (VPCs)	

Table 6. The diagnoses presented by Copilot and Gemini in order of their likelihood.

Diagnoses order	Copilot	Gemini
1	Atrial Fibrillation or Flutter	Atrial fibrillation
2	Supraventricular Tachycardia (SVT)	Atrial flutter
3	Ventricular Tachycardia	Ventricular tachycardia
4		Premature ventricular contractions (PVCs)

nuanced response. It provided general observations followed by a quartet of potential diagnoses (see Table 7). Subsequently, it offered a concise overview of the patient's progression over the three months, coupled with a series of recommendations.

Although the diagnoses were accurate, their sequence was misaligned. The correct order should be 3rd, 1st, 2nd and 4th diagnoses. Regarding the recommendations, the sequence should be the first, fifth, third, second, and fourth. The foremost recommendation is commendable; however, the rationale provided is flawed, as it attributes the changes from March to adverse effects. In contrast, the primary incentive for re-evaluation should be the treatment's efficacy for this particular patient. Among all the responses evaluated, ChatGPT-4o's contained the most precise information and diagnoses. A notable attribute of this entity is its capacity to analyze multiple images, thereby facilitating a multi-perspective analysis.

Table 7. The diagnoses and recommendations presented in order from Chat GPT-4o.

Order	Diagnosis	Recommendation
1	Ventricular Ectopy	Re-evaluate Flecainide Use
2	Arrhythmia Induced by Medication	Monitor Electrolytes and Renal Function
3	Benign Ectopic Activity	Holter Monitoring Continuation
4	Monitoring for Structural Heart Disease	Cardiac Imaging
5		Lifestyle and Risk Factor Management

7 Conclusions

In this investigation, we concentrated on two important elements of interaction with generative AI within the healthcare domain: the formulation of the questions and the accuracy of the responses provided. Concerning the prompt creation process, our approach was to encapsulate the most important of the required information to facilitate an accurate diagnosis. Ethical considerations were also taken into perspective by meticulously avoiding the inclusion of personal patient data. The prompts were crafted to request insights into the AI's reasoning processes while ensuring the adherence to European standards. This methodology was instrumental in mitigating the possibility for fabricated responses and ensuring regional appropriateness. Upon reviewing, for each the medical case, the responses rendered by each AI system, it is evident that all four show good performance, with each system demonstrating some consideration in certain diagnostic aspects or delivering brief and precise responses. While we were not able to definitively ascertain which tool is superior, it is noteworthy that Gemini consistently outperformed across various cases. Copilot yielded satisfactory results overall. Claude and GPT-4o distinguished themselves by acknowledging factors such as medication non-adherence or suboptimal drug dosing, albeit with a tendency towards overstatement of patient conditions. When considering the examination of a patient over a 3-month period, GPT-4o demonstrated superior performance in terms of the data obtained and its capacity to analyze several images simultaneously. It is our aspiration that the findings of this study will further the ongoing conversation regarding AI's role in healthcare and inform the development of best practices for its integration into patient diagnosis.

References

1. Stryker, C., Scapicchio, M.: What is generative AI? IBM (2024). https://www.ibm.com/topics/generative-ai
2. NVIDIA: What is Generative AI? (2024). https://www.nvidia.com/en-us/glossary/generative-ai/
3. Wagh, A.: What's new in GPT-4: an overview of the GPT-4 architecture and capabilities of next-generation AI, Medium (2023). https://medium.com/@amol-wagh/whats-new-in-gpt-4-an-overview-of-the-gpt-4-architecture-and-capabilities-of-next-generation-ai-900c445d5ffe

4. Protégé IGDTUW: Exploring the depths of gemini AI: a comprehensive journey from introduction to architecture — part 1, Medium (2023). https://medium.com/@protegeig dtuw/exploring-the-depths-of-gemini-ai-a-comprehensive-journey-from-introduction-to-arc hitecture-3467797bd597

5. Anthropic Support: How up-to-date is Claude's training data? (2023). https://support.anthro pic.com/en/articles/8114494-how-up-to-date-is-claude-s-training-data

6. Microsoft Support: Welcome to Copilot in Windows (2024). https://support.microsoft.com/ en-us/windows/welcome-to-copilot-in-windows-675708af-8c16-4675-afeb-85a5a476ccb0

7. Google Deepmind: Gemeni Models (2024). https://deepmind.google/technologies/gemini/

8. Wikipedia: ChatGPT (2024). https://en.wikipedia.org/wiki/ChatGPT

9. Anthropic: Welcome to Claude (2024). https://docs.anthropic.com/en/docs/intro-to-claude

10. Cardiocenter: Monitorizarea Ambulatorie a Tensiunii Arteriale (2024). https://www.cardio center.ro/service/abpm-monitorizare-ambulatorie-a-tensiunii-arteriale/

11. Cardiocenter: Monitorizare Holter EKG (2024). https://cardiologie-iasi.ro/monitorizare-hol ter-ekg/

12. PluralSight: Getting Started on Prompt Engineering (2024). https://app.pluralsight.com/lib rary/courses/getting-started-prompt-engineering-generative-ai

Web Issues and Tools

Enhancing Web Accessibility Through a Customizable Browser Extension for Users with Visual Impairments

Bianca-Stefana Popa, Stefan-Vladimir Sbarcea, Ciprian Amaritei, and Adrian Iftene(✉)

Faculty of Computer Science "Alexandru Ioan Cuza" University Iasi, Iasi, Romania
adiftene@gmail.com

Abstract. We live in a time when we want applications to be accessible to as many users as possible, regardless of their age, their health problems, or the diseases they suffer from. This paper introduces an approach to address the accessibility challenges faced by individuals with myopia, dyslexia, and color blindness through the development of a specialized browser plugin. The plugin empowers users to tailor their browsing experience at the browser level, enabling them to customize the presentation of information on desired web pages. By offering customizable features directed to specific visual impairments, such as font size and color contrast adjustments, the plugin enhances usability and promotes a better browsing experience for users with diverse needs. This initiative underscores the significance of measures in addressing digital inclusivity and underscores the potential of tailored technological solutions in advancing accessibility standards across web platforms.

Keywords: adapted interfaces · browser plugin · myopia · dyslexia · color blindness

1 Introduction

Tailoring a system to adapt to user needs could imply different techniques and strategies. *Personalization* and *customization* represent two of the most used strategies in persuading users undertaking a specific action [1].

Customization allows users to tailor a system's content and features to suit their individual needs and preferences. We've opted for this approach because it enhances the system's relevance, boosts user confidence, adds a personal touch, instills a sense of autonomy, and fosters a deeper connection with the system [2].

As opposed to customization, *personalization* is mostly concerned with the way system responds and adapts to user and contextual characteristics. Adaptation as a technique has been captured in the seven tailoring concepts by op den Akker [3]. In our work, adaptation aims to tailor messages based on individuals' levels of outcome expectations related to the browsing experience.

Interface personalization has been described as one of the four categories of personalization strategies that could drive an appropriate output [4]. In our application, a set of contextual and behavioral characteristics, together with psychological variables as described by Kankanhalli [4] will determine through interface personalization a comfortable browsing experience.

2   State-of-the-Art

The Internet is inherently designed to be inclusive, regardless of the hardware, software, language, location, or abilities of its users. When it lives up to this ideal, it becomes a platform accessible to a wide spectrum of people, irrespective of their hearing, mobility, vision, or cognitive capabilities. This transformative power of the web lies in its ability to remove the communication and interaction barriers that persist in the physical world. However, when websites, applications, technologies, or tools are poorly designed, they inadvertently create digital barriers, excluding individuals from the vast expanse of the Internet.

Web accessibility is a must for developers and organizations. It's about making websites and web tools that everyone, including people with disabilities, can use. Our goal is to create a web extension project that helps websites meet the Web Content Accessibility Guidelines (WCAG) [5] and ensures the extension itself adheres to the User Agent Accessibility Guidelines (UAAG) [6]. We aim to make the web more accessible and user-friendly for everyone, regardless of their abilities.

2.1   Similar Applications

Pixie: Web Accessibility and Productivity Tools. Pixie: Web Accessibility & Productivity Tools is a versatile browser extension designed to enhance the digital reading experience. It offers features such as Text-to-Speech (TTS), Screen Shader, Reading Ruler, OpenDyslexic Font, ePub Reader, and more. Users can customize their reading environment, modify text configurations for optimal readability, adapt color schemes to reduce eye strain, and care for their eyes with Screen Shader. Additionally, Pixie provides tools to enhance vocabulary, hide unnecessary images, mute unwanted noises, and more. With a focus on flexibility and control, Pixie Reader is ideal for those seeking a tailored digital reading experience [7].

Helperbird: Accessibility and Productivity App. Helperbird is an all-in-one browser extension designed to enhance reading, writing, and accessibility on the web. Packed with features like Text-to-Speech, dyslexia support, reading mode, and more, Helperbird provides personalized support to make web pages, apps, and PDFs more accessible. It includes powerful tools for reading, writing, and accessibility customization, making it a comprehensive solution for users with various needs and preferences [8].

CFR Calatori: Accessibility Extension for Web Services. CFR Calatori offers a robust accessibility extension directly incorporated into their website to ensure an inclusive online experience. Committed to adhering to the Web Content Accessibility Guidelines 2.1 (WCAG 2.1) at the AA level, CFR Calatori employs various technologies to make their site accessible to users with diverse abilities. The extension includes features like screen-reader optimization, keyboard navigation adjustments, and AI-based enhancements, aiming to accommodate individuals with visual impairments, motor impairments, cognitive disabilities, and more [9].

3 Proposed Solution

Our Visual Impairments Extension currently supports three default profiles: (1) Myopia, (2) Dyslexia, and (3) Color Blindness. These profiles are carefully crafted to address common visual challenges, providing tailored adjustments for each condition. Additionally, users have the flexibility to create custom profiles based on their specific requirements. The default profiles are fully customizable, allowing users to fine-tune the settings to match their preferences.

3.1 Key Features

The extension offers users a wide range of customizable settings to personalize their browsing experience. Some of the key functionalities include:

- Highlight links and titles,
- Enhance contrast,
- Set minimum font size,
- Change font family,
- Enlarge font by a percentage,
- Change image contrast,
- Adjust page saturation,
- Hide images,
- Set line height,
- Set letter spacing,
- Change font weight,
- Change font color,
- Set text alignment.

These features empower users to tailor the online content to their specific visual needs, ensuring a more accessible and comfortable browsing experience. The extension comprises two main components: (1) the popup and (2) the options page.

Popup. The popup, conveniently located in the corner of the web page you are browsing, provides quick access to essential settings. Here, users can:

- Choose from available profiles,
- Activate powerups, such as the ADHD powerup that creates a highlighted zone around the cursor,
- Select modes,
- Customize settings,
- Save profiles customization,
- Delete custom profiles.

The popup serves as a convenient tool for on-the-fly adjustments, ensuring a seamless and user-friendly experience (see Fig. 1).

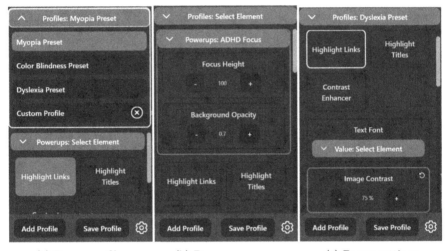

(a) Popup profiles   (b) Popup powerups   (c) Popup settings

Fig. 1. Popups

Options Page. On the other hand, the options page offers a more detailed interface for fine-tuning settings. This comprehensive dashboard allows users to visualize how each setting affects a small area of text or an image. Users can:

- Edit additional settings for modes and powerups.
- Modify profile names.

The extension automatically saves user customizations and the currently selected profile in the local storage, ensuring that preferences persist across browser sessions. It also lets the user revert the settings and the preset profiles to their default configurations. Whether using the popup for quick changes or delving into the options page for detailed adjustments, our extension offers a versatile solution for web accessibility (see Fig. 2).

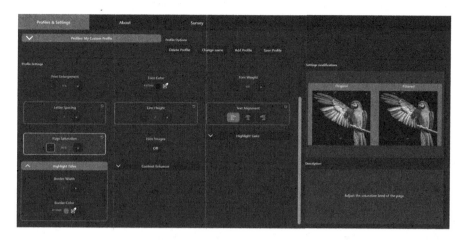

Fig. 2. Options Page

3.2   Technologies

For the web extension aimed at enhancing web accessibility, particularly for individuals with visual impairments, we have chosen a mix of robust technologies. These choices are essential in driving the development of an extension that is not only functional and user-friendly but also reliable and innovative. Below, we outline the essential technologies that have been used in crafting the web extension.

Chrome Extension APIs. Utilizing Chrome's extension APIs allows our application to deeply integrate with the browser and web pages, enabling significant modifications and enhancements to the content and style of web pages, ensuring seamless applicability of our accessibility features.

ReactJS. ReactJS forms the cornerstone of our web extension's development. This JavaScript library facilitates the building of dynamic user interfaces, enabling us to craft a responsive and user-friendly popup where users can effortlessly customize and select their accessibility settings.

4   Comparison with Similar Solutions

When comparing our Visual Impairments Extension with similar applications like Pixie, Helperbird, and CFR Calatori, it becomes evident that each addresses web accessibility with unique approaches. Here, we highlight key distinctions and advantages of our solution:

Default and Customizable Profiles. Our extension stands out by offering default profiles catering to Myopia, Dyslexia, and Color Blindness. Users can also create custom profiles, providing a highly adaptable solution. In contrast, Pixie and Helperbird, while comprehensive, don't offer the same level of profile customization. CFR Calatori, on the other hand, focuses on website-specific accessibility, offering a tailored solution for its platform.

Rich Set of Features. Our extension provides a diverse range of features, including the ability to highlight links and titles, adjust font settings, manipulate image visibility, and more. Pixie and Helperbird also offer robust features, but our emphasis on customizable profiles and a wide array of adjustments sets us apart. Additionally, Helperbird's advanced features, which set it apart from our app, are part of a paid subscription, while our Visual Impairments Extension is committed to providing a comprehensive set of features for free. CFR Calatori, with its website-specific extension, focuses on key accessibility enhancements tailored for its users.

In conclusion, our Visual Impairments Extension offers a unique combination of customizable profiles, rich features, and a robust technological foundation, setting it apart in the landscape of web accessibility solutions. Each application brings its own strengths, addressing specific needs in the realm of web accessibility.

5   Future Work

While our Visual Impairments Extension has made significant strides in providing web accessibility, we acknowledge that there are areas where additional features can further enhance the user experience. The following outlines our vision for future development:

5.1   User Feedback and AI Integration

One of our primary goals is to implement a robust system for collecting user feedback and seamlessly integrating artificial intelligence (AI) into our extension. User feedback is invaluable for improving our extension, and the AI will play a pivotal role in analyzing this feedback, identifying trends, and suggesting enhancements. By understanding user experiences and preferences, we aim to refine our extension continuously.

5.2   Customizable Profiles Through User Surveys

To further enhance user customization, we plan to introduce a user survey system. This system will enable users to provide specific information about their visual impairments and preferences. The data collected through these surveys will be subjected to advanced analysis by our artificial intelligence (AI) system.

The AI will identify patterns and insights from user feedback, allowing us to create customizable profiles tailored to users' unique requirements. This approach ensures that our extension evolves in response to the diverse needs of our user base, with AI playing a key role in interpreting and implementing the gathered insights.

5.3 Text-to-Speech with Image Analysis

In our future iterations, we aspire to integrate advanced features such as Text-to-Speech (TTS) with image analysis. This enhancement aims to provide users with a more comprehensive understanding of the content presented on web pages, particularly in images. By leveraging image analysis alongside TTS, we strive to offer a richer browsing experience for users with visual impairments, enabling them to grasp the visual elements present on websites.

5.4 Continuous Feature Expansion

We are committed to an ongoing process of feature expansion, taking inspiration from the successes of other applications in the field. Our goal is to bridge the gap between our current capabilities and the advanced features offered by similar applications. This includes exploring options for additional font adjustments, color schemes, and innovative tools that contribute to a more inclusive online environment.

6 Conclusions

During the early stages of testing, we welcomed and valued the feedback received from a small group of users, for the purpose of understanding only how users interact with the design of the application. Their input has been instrumental in further shaping the direction of the application. The positive aspects encountered so far are related to the way the extension simplifies web navigation for people with visual and cognitive challenges, by adjusting text size, contrast, and spacing. However, users have reported difficulty in understanding certain features. For instance, the options page doesn't indicate in any way that by pressing a setting, users will see the description and what it does. In the future, we will try to eliminate the negative elements reported by them and to complete the application with new functionalities that will be useful to them.

References

1. Orji, R., Vassileva, J., Mandryk, R.L.: Modeling the efficacy of persuasive strategies for different gamer types in serious games for health. User Model. User-Adap. Inter. **24**, 453–498 (2014)
2. Orji, R., Nacke, L., Di Marco, C.: Towards personality-driven persuasive health games and gamified systems. In: Proceedings of the CHI Conference on Human Factors in Computing Systems (CHI), pp. 1015–1027 (2017)

3. op den Akker, H.: Smart tailoring of real-time physical activity coaching systems, PhD Thesis, University of Twente (2014). https://www.rrd.nl/wp-content/uploads/2021/08/34-thesis_h_op_den_akker-1.pdf
4. Kankanhalli, A., Xia, Q., Ai, P., Zhao, X.: Understanding personalization for health behavior change applications: a review and future directions. AIS Trans. Hum. Comput. Interact. **13**(3), 316–349 (2021)
5. World Wide Web Consortium (W3C): Web content accessibility guidelines (WCAG) 2.1, W3C (2018). https://www.w3.org/WAI/WCAG21/quickref/
6. World Wide Web Consortium (W3C): User agent accessibility guidelines (UAAG) 2.0, W3C (2002). https://www.w3.org/TR/UAAG20/
7. Oziku Technologies. (n.d.), Pixie: web accessibility and productivity tools (2024). https://chromewebstore.google.com/detail/pixie-accesibilidad-web-y/oihhpemnlfdlkdhbiajjjkbbojdojchj
8. Helperbird. (n.d.), Helperbird: accessibility and productivity app (2024). https://www.helperbird.com/
9. CFR Călători - Romanian Railways (2024). https://www.cfrcalatori.ro/

Time Traveller - A RotSafeLinker Tool

Daniela Petrea, Cosmin Irimia(✉), and Adrian Iftene

Faculty of Computer Science, "Alexandru Ioan-Cuza" University,
700259 Iasi, Romania
irimia.cosmin@gmail.com

Abstract. In the digital era, the increasing reliance on web-based resources has introduced a critical yet often overlooked challenge: link rot, where hyperlinks deteriorate over time, posing a threat to the credibility and reliability of online information. To combat this challenge, we present Time Traveller, a user-friendly web tool that allows users to explore historical web snapshots. Drawing inspiration from the Wayback Machine, Time Traveller enables users to easily track the chronological changes of web pages. Through the capture and storage of web content snapshots, Time Traveller offers users the ability to revisit specific moments in internet history, ensuring the preservation of digital data. With its user-friendly interface and efficient retrieval methods, Time Traveller enhances the user experience, offering a seamless journey through the evolution of the internet, accessible to users of all technical backgrounds.

Keywords: Link rot · Flutter App · Cross-platform

1 Introduction

cLink rot is the term used to describe the phenomenon where hyperlinks on the internet become obsolete or broken. This occurs when content is relocated, deleted, or reorganized on servers, causing the URLs that previously directed users to specific web pages or resources to no longer function. Consequently, individuals navigating the digital realm often encounter a *"404 Not Found"* error message like the one shown in Fig. 1 [1].

The implications of link rot extend far beyond mere inconvenience. In academic research, legal documents, and journalistic work, broken links can lead to a loss of critical evidence or references, undermining the credibility and thoroughness of the work. In a world that increasingly relies on digital archives, the permanence and reliability of these links are crucial for maintaining the integrity of historical records and academic research [2,3]. Addressing link rot is a complex task. The decentralized nature of the internet, combined with the absence of universal standards for digital preservation, complicates efforts to maintain link integrity. While various solutions exist, such as web archives and permanent hosting services, these approaches have limitations and are not universally adopted.

C. Bădică et al. (Eds.): BCI 2024, CCIS 2391, pp. 283–295, 2025.
https://doi.org/10.1007/978-3-031-84093-7_20

404. That's an error.

The requested URL / was not found on this server. That's
all we know.

Fig. 1. Example of 404 Error

Archiving the entirety of the web is a resource-intensive task. It requires significant storage capacity, sophisticated technology, and ongoing maintenance. Organizations like the Internet Archive's Wayback Machine[1] undertake this monumental task, but even they cannot capture and preserve every change on every webpage [4]. Additionally, some content is dynamically generated or protected by privacy settings, making it inherently difficult to archive.

2   Academic Literature

This paper aims to introduce the concept of link rotting and present the academic literature on this subject. The initial report will be examined, "The Decay and Failures of Web References" authored by Diomidis Spinellis from the Department of Management Science and Technology at Athens University of Economics and Business in 2003 [5]. This publication serves as a valuable resource for comprehending and addressing the issue of broken links. The year of publication, 2003, holds particular significance as it coincided with the DotCom bubble, a period when web pages emerged as the primary means of information sharing. Within their research, Spinellis and colleagues delve into the technologies associated with web references and retrieval, outline their methodology, present the findings they obtained, and discuss the implications of their study.

Upon conducting their investigation, the researchers discovered that the most prevalent status code for unavailable URLs was 404, indicating that the requested resource no longer exists on the server. The second most common cause of unavailability (see Figs. 2 and 3) stemmed from server-related issues, resulting in the generation of error code 500. These errors occur when the server encounters unforeseen circumstances that prevent it from fulfilling the request. Error codes 404 and 500 collectively accounted for approximately 95% of the observed failures.

In rare instances, the researchers encountered several other types of failures. These included error code 400, which signifies a bad request and indicates

---

[1] https://wayback-api.archive.org/.

issues with the request itself, and error code 503, indicating a temporary service unavailability. The table below provides an average of each status code for unavailable URLs.

HTTP Code	Meaning	2004-09-09	2005-02-27
404	Not found	62.40 %	60.20 %
500	Internal sever error	32.51%	35.09 %
403	Forbidden	3.94 %	3.86 %
401	Unauthorized	0.74 %	0.62 %
200	OK but 0 length content	0.25 %	0.23 %
410	Gone	0.08 %	0.00 %
502	Bad gateway	0.08 %	0.00 %

Fig. 2. The Availability and Persistence of Web References in D-Lib Magazine, Frank McCown, Sheffan Chan, 2005 [6]

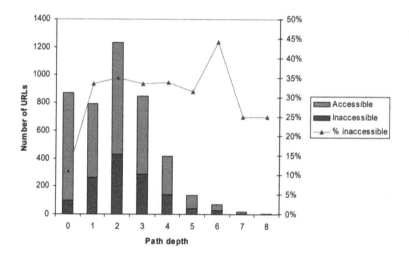

Fig. 3. The Availability and Persistence of Web References in D-Lib Magazine, Frank McCown, Sheffan Chan, 2005 [6]

The depth of paths plays a crucial role in evaluating the quality of decayed or inaccessible links. This metric allows us to gain an understanding of the complexity of the URL structure. To determine the path depth, we assigned a value of 1 for every directory or file encountered after the domain name. For instance, if we consider "http://foo.com/," the path depth would be 0. On the other hand, "http://foo.com/bar.html" would be assigned a depth of 1. Similarly, "http://foo.com/dir/bar.html" would have a depth of 2, and so on.

Additionally, we took into consideration any query strings present in a URL by adding 1 to the path depth for each query parameter. For example, if we analyze "http://foo.org/cgi?bar=2", the path depth would be 2. By analyzing the path depth, we can gain insights into how the length and complexity of URLs may impact their decay rates. This information is valuable in understanding web resource accessibility and link integrity.

The above figure illustrates a distinct pattern: there is a 22% rise in the number of URLs that cannot be accessed when transitioning from a path depth of 0 to 1. This indicates a significant change in the accessibility of URLs. Typically, an inaccessible URL with a path depth of 0 signifies a noteworthy event, such as a business undergoing a name change or closing down. On the other hand, when the path depth exceeds 0, the inaccessibility of URLs is more likely to be attributed to internal structural modifications, such as reorganization. This observation offers valuable insights into the factors contributing to URL inaccessibility and the influence of path depth on such instances.

Historically, scholarly works have relied on primary sources and academic literature to establish factual foundations, incorporate previous research, and bolster their arguments. A well-crafted citation serves as a link between an inquisitive reader and the author's sources, streamlining the process of locating, verifying, and delving deeper into the referenced materials.

In theory, when the referenced sources are available online, it should be more convenient for readers. Instead of necessitating a visit to the library to find the sources mentioned by an author, readers should be able to instantly access the cited material with a single click. Furthermore, the author of the cited source may have second thoughts about their argument and remove the material.

As we extracted from the research paperwork "Perma: Scoping and Addressing the Problem of Link and Reference Rot in Legal Citations" by Zittrain, Jonathan; Albert, Kendra; Lessig, Lawrence [7], a significant portion of earlier investigations into link decay took place during the early 2000s. In 2002, Professor Mary Rumsey analyzed references within legal documents and determined that as the utilization of URLs in citations grew, the issue of link decay also increased. Her 2002 study unveiled a consistent decline in the functionality of hyperlinks. Specifically, it revealed that 61% of links from articles published in the prior year were operational, while only 30% of links from articles published five years earlier remained functional.

The solution proposed in the research paper involves Perma.cc, a tool developed by the Harvard Library Innovation Lab. This tool enables authors and editors to preserve web content for long-term access. By capturing and storing web page data, Perma.cc provides a permanent link that can be used in citations. This ensures that even if the source changes or becomes unavailable, the preserved content remains accessible to users.

3   Similar Solutions

3.1   Web Archives (e.g. Wayback Machine)

Web archives, like the Wayback Machine (see Fig. 4), act as digital time capsules that save versions of websites over intervals, as can be seen in the above image.

These archives frequently record the appearance of websites, allowing users to view prior versions even if a site undergoes changes or becomes unavailable. This periodic capture of web content provides a historical record of the Internet.

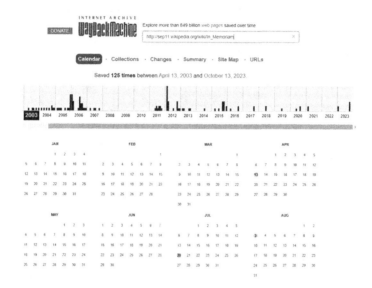

Fig. 4. Wayback Machine

For those concerned about obsolete links, web archives offer a robust mechanism to access earlier versions of content. Incorporating such archives within your system can serve as a reliable backup source.

3.2   Decentralized Systems (e.g. IPFS)

Systems such as IPFS (Interplanetary File System) offer a forward-thinking strategy for transforming the way online content is stored and accessed. In contrast to conventional techniques that fetch content according to its location, IPFS distinguishes content through a distinct ID. Consequently, the content stays available as long as it is present somewhere in the network. Through the decentralization of content storage, these systems diminish dependence on singular points of weakness. IPFS-like systems are in harmony to combat link decay, owing to their content-addressing method that guarantees robust, rot-resistant links.

3.3   Permanent Web Hosting (e.g. Perma.cc)

Platforms such as Perma.cc (see Fig. 5) offer permanent storage for digital content, which is particularly useful for academics and legal professionals who need stable citation sources. When users submit a web address to platforms like Perma.cc, the content gets stored, and they receive a link to the archived version. These platforms guarantee the continuous existence of digital content, essential for critical documents. By safeguarding crucial content, these platforms ensure that even if the primary source disappears, the information remains accessible.

Fig. 5. Perma.cc

3.4 WebCite

WebCite [8] stands out with its on-demand archiving feature, allowing users to choose which content they want saved. This tailored approach helps users guarantee the future availability of particular content. Collaborating with platforms like WebCite can provide users the freedom to decide what content they prioritize for preservation.

4 Proposed Solution

Time Traveller is a practical online tool developed to facilitate the exploration of historical web snapshots. Drawing inspiration from the user-friendly concept of the Wayback Machine, Time Traveller empowers users to effortlessly navigate through the chronological progression of web pages.

This web application captures and securely stores snapshots of web pages, allowing users to revisit specific moments in the history of the internet. Emphasizing efficiency, Time Traveller ensures swift retrieval and storage of snapshots without burdening the user's device.

With a user-friendly interface, Time Traveller offers a straightforward design that promotes ease of use. Users can seamlessly move back and forth in time, observing the evolution of web page content across different periods. The application's intuitive design caters to users of all technical backgrounds, making it accessible to a wide range of individuals.

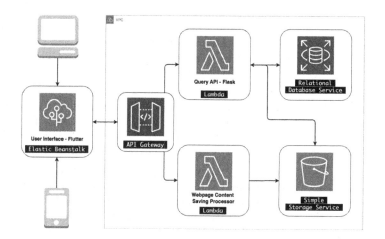

Fig. 6. Application Architecture

We used Amazon Web Services (AWS) (as seen in Fig. 6) in our application with the sole scope of ensuring scalability, reliability, and efficient management of web page snapshots, addressing the critical issue of link rot. The key components of our cloud-based architecture include AWS Elastic Beanstalk, S3, Lambda, and RDS, each playing a specific role in the overall system.

4.1 Query API (Flask)

At the core of the application is the Query API, built with Flask. This feature empowers users to effortlessly search for and retrieve archived snapshots. By sending requests through the API, users can seamlessly engage with the system and access valuable information about archived web pages.

4.2 Database (PostgreSQL)

The PostgreSQL database serves as the backbone of the system, storing crucial metadata and indices related to the archived web pages. Each captured snapshot is represented as a WebPage object in the database, containing information such as content, creation date, and URL. PostgreSQL's reliability and performance capabilities ensure efficient data management, enabling quick and precise retrieval of archived content.

4.3   Webpage Content Saving Process

When a new snapshot creation is triggered by a user, the Flask endpoint coordinates the entire process. Initially, the application retrieves the content of the specified webpage using the `get_webpage_content` function. Following this, a WebPage object is instantiated, containing the content, URL, and a timestamp denoting the creation time.

Subsequently, the WebPage object is inserted into the PostgreSQL database via the SQLAlchemy ORM. To streamline future content comparisons, the content is hashed using the Hashlib library before being stored. The system is equipped with error-handling mechanisms to manage potential issues, ensuring a seamless and dependable content-saving procedure.

Our web page history exploration application, Time Traveller, integrates a critical verification function to guarantee users always have access to the most recent snapshots of archived pages. At 10:00 every day, the application automatically checks for alterations in webpage content. This verification involves comparing the hashes of the current and previous content of the pages. Upon identifying variances that indicate modifications, the application generates a new entry in the database, capturing the updated snapshot of the page. This method guarantees that the web page history remains up-to-date, reflecting any notable changes in content.

4.4   User Interface (Flutter)

The user interface, developed using Flutter, provides an intuitive platform for users to interact with the application. Users can easily navigate through the system, search for specific web pages, and retrieve archived snapshots. Flutter's cross-platform capabilities ensure a consistent and visually appealing user experience across various devices, making the application accessible to a broad audience. Figures 7 and 10 depict visual snapshots of our application in the case of available and unavailable pages (Figs. 8 and 9).

In our study, we undertook a comparison between our solution and an existing one. To accomplish this, we employed the Wayback Machine to archive a randomly selected webpage from the internet. Additionally, we utilized our application to save the same webpage. However, it is important to note that our application currently does not support all the diverse frameworks utilized in webpage creation. As a result, there are discrepancies in the appearance of the webpage saved by our application compared to the version displayed by the Wayback Machine.

For instance, upon examining the snapshot captured by our product, it is evident that the icon above the 'Text Extractor Tool' text is absent, despite successfully preserving the menu from the webpage, unlike the Wayback Machine.

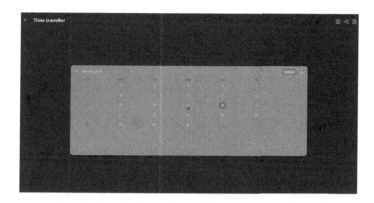

Fig. 7. Available snapshots of a page

Fig. 8. Unavailable page

Fig. 9. WayBack Machine

Time traveler seamlessly integrates Flask, PostgreSQL, and Flutter to provide users with a powerful and efficient solution for capturing, storing, and retrieving snapshots of web pages. The application's architecture is designed to prioritize performance, scalability, and a user-friendly experience.

Fig. 10. Time Traveller

5   Results and Evaluation

Effective evaluation of a web application's performance relies heavily on the availability of reliable metrics. The Locust.io dashboard plays a crucial role in this aspect by providing a comprehensive set of numerical data that indicates the application's efficiency under heavy user traffic. In the above section, we will delve deeper into these metrics and we'll also be presenting the code coverage to get a full picture of our application's performance and reliability.

The Locust.io dashboard (see Fig. 11) provides valuable performance metrics that indicate the current load on our application. According to the data, we are currently sustaining a load of 100 concurrent users. During the load test, the server can handle approximately 48 requests per second (RPS), as shown by the consistent trend in the 'Total Requests per Second' graph.

Analyzing the 'Response Times (ms)' graph, we can observe that the median response time remains stable, indicating consistent performance under the given load. Additionally, the graph includes a 95th percentile line, which helps us understand the response time for the majority of requests. It is noteworthy that this line remains below 1 s, suggesting that 95% of the requests are served within this time frame.

The 'Number of Users' graph confirms that the load test was conducted with a constant number of 100 users throughout this particular test snapshot. The graph shows a flat line at the 100 users mark, providing further evidence of this consistency. An important aspect to highlight is the absence of any reported failures, as indicated by the 'Failures' metric showing 0%. This is an excellent indication that our application can handle the specified load without any requests failing.

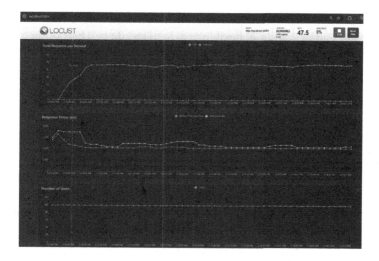

Fig. 11. Performance metrics using Locust.io

In terms of code coverage (see Fig. 12), the project has achieved 88% line coverage, which signifies that a significant majority of our code base is covered by automated tests. However, it is worth noting that this metric only includes 40% of the files. This suggests that there may be auxiliary or configuration files that are not subjected to testing, or that there is potential to expand our test suite to encompass more areas of the application.

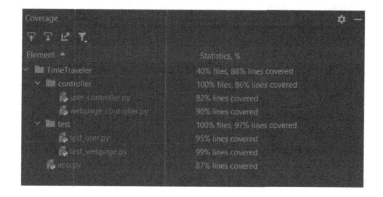

Fig. 12. Code coverage from unit tests

6   Future Work

Our current platform offers a comprehensive exploration of web page history, but several key concepts could enhance both functionality and user experience.

- *Customizable Scheduling* - Allowing users to customize when the system checks for updates adds a flexible touch. Users have the option to choose specific timeframes or intervals that suit their preferences and how they typically use the system. This means they can adjust the content verification process to match their schedules and habits, making the experience more personalized and convenient.
- *Visualizing Content Evolution* - Integrating visual elements to demonstrate how web page content evolves enhances the user experience. By incorporating graphical representations and interactive timelines, users can easily understand and analyze changes over time in a more user-friendly manner.
- *Advanced Search Filters* - Implement a set of advanced search filters that enable users to specify their search results based on specific criteria. These filters could include options such as date ranges, content types, or even specific domains. This provides users with the ability to pinpoint the information they are seeking more precisely.

7   Conclusion

In the modern digital landscape, the persistent issue of link rot poses a threat to the reliability of online information, underscoring the necessity for robust solutions that can preserve and provide access to historical web content. Our research introduces Time Traveller, an advanced application for exploring the history of web pages, which aims to tackle this pressing concern. Drawing inspiration from the widely acclaimed simplicity of the Wayback Machine, Time Traveller places a strong emphasis on efficiency and user-friendliness, enabling seamless navigation through the chronological progression of web pages.

By harnessing innovative technologies such as Flask for its Query API and PostgreSQL for efficient data management, Time Traveller ensures swift retrieval and storage of archived snapshots, all while upholding the integrity of crucial metadata. Furthermore, the integration of Flutter for cross-platform user interface development enhances accessibility and usability, catering to users with varying levels of technical proficiency. Looking ahead, Time Traveller holds great potential for further enhancement. Including customizable scheduling features and advanced search filters could enrich the user experience, while graphical representations of content evolution would provide valuable insights into historical web trends. Ultimately, Time Traveller emerges as a powerful and efficient tool, embodying a steadfast commitment to performance, scalability, and user-centric design.

In conclusion, Time Traveller is a testament to our unwavering dedication to addressing the challenges posed by link rot and preserving the intricate tapestry of digital history. Through its innovative architecture and user-centered approach, Time Traveller empowers users to delve into the past and paves the way for a more resilient and accessible digital future.

Disclosure of Interests. Data processing and analysis in this paper were supported by the Research center with integrated techniques for the investigation of atmospheric aerosols in Romania, under project SMIS 127324 - RECENT AIR (RA).

References

1. Link Rot: what it is and how to deal with it. https://prettylinks.com/blog/what-is-link-rot/. Accessed October 2024
2. Kille, L.W.: The growing problem of internet "Link Rot" and best practices for media and online publishers, The Journalist's Resource (2015)
3. Król, K., Zdonek, D.: The peculiarity of the bit rot and link rot phenomena. Glob. Knowl. Memory Commun. **69**(1/2), 20–37 (2020)
4. Zahner, T., Villiger, B.J.: Link management tool with internet archive integration. Doctoral dissertation, OST Ostschweizer Fachhochschule (2023)
5. Spinellis, D.: The decay and failures of web references. Commun. ACM **46**(1), 71–77 (2003)
6. McCown, F., Chan, S., Nelson, M., Bollen, J.: The availability and persistence of web references in D-Lib Magazine. arXiv:cs/0511077 (2005)
7. Zittrain, J., Albert, K., Lessig, L.: Perma: Scoping and addressing the problem of link and reference rot in legal citations. *Harward Law Review* **127**(4), (2014)
8. Eysenbach, G., Trudel, M.: Going, going, still there: using the WebCite service to permanently archive cited web pages. In: AMIA Annual Symposium Proceedings, pp. 919 (2006)

ShareFactory - Efficient and Accessible Content-Sharing Platform

Madalina Carausu, Isabela Haiura, Daniela Petrea, Cosmin Irimia$^{(\boxtimes)}$, and Adrian Iftene

Faculty of Computer Science, "Alexandru Ioan-Cuza" University, 700259 Iasi, Romania
irimia.cosmin@gmail.com

Abstract. In an increasingly digital world, the need for efficient and accessible content-sharing platforms has become of greatest importance. This paper introduces Share Factory, a platform that eliminates the complexities of traditional content-sharing methods by offering an array of features accessible without registration or payment. With its user-friendly interface and efficient technology stack, Share Factory platform allows users to generate custom short URLs, barcodes, and QR codes and convert colors from RGB to hex effortlessly. As the landscape of content sharing continues to evolve, such a solution plays a crucial role in shaping a more accessible, efficient, and user-centric sharing ecosystem.

Keywords: URL · Shortner · Barcode · QR (Quick Response) Code

1 Introduction

Link sharing is the process of sending a secure digital file to another person via a simple URL link [1]. People typically use link sharing to send files too large to send as email attachments securely. A URL (uniform resource locator) it's a type of uniform resource identifier (URI) that provides a way to access information from remote computers, like a web server and cloud storage [2]. This method is often found on computers, but a faster means of communication has been created that can only be done by scanning. A traditional, one-dimensional barcode (see Fig. 1) is scanned by a narrow beam of light [3]. That beam of light comes from a specialized scanner. The vertical bars in a one-dimensional barcode are where the information is encoded. Specifically, in their widths and their distances from each other. That's why it's called a one-dimensional barcode; scanners access the information in one dimension, horizontally.

But QR (Quick Response) codes contain information accessible along two dimensions: horizontal and vertical [4]. A QR code is a square made up of patterns of smaller squares. Information in a QR code is encoded by the arrangement of these smaller squares [5]. And, once scanned, it delivers information just like other barcodes.

C. Bădică et al. (Eds.): BCI 2024, CCIS 2391, pp. 296–308, 2025.
https://doi.org/10.1007/978-3-031-84093-7_21

640509 040147

Fig. 1. QR Code and Barcode Illustration for Content Sharing

Since Smartphones hit the market, QR Codes have multiplied exponentially as a vital component of every self-respecting advertisement, product or company and have recently even begun to appear on most people's business cards. QR Codes are easily scannable codes that redirect the scanner to a destination of the creator's choice, they are an incredibly useful tool for making your product, company or site, accessible and engaging in a creative manner [6].

The application we build is accessible without users registering or paying for the functionalities offered. We offer custom URL, barcodes, QR codes and color converter from RGB (Red Green Blue) to hex, all in the same place for faster accessibility according to the user's needs. The final goal of the application is to offer a quick way of content sharing free and available for anyone.

2   Similar Solutions

This section will present a couple of existing solutions in the industry that deals with the problem of URL shortening, QR and barcode creation. However, each system has a couple of disadvantages that will be presented. Those disadvantages will then serve as reference points for the development of our platform.

2.1   Free URL Shortener

Free URL Shortener is a site for transforming long, ugly links into nice, memorable and trackable short URLs [7]. Users will use it to shorten links for any social media platforms, blogs, SMS, emails, ads, or pretty much anywhere else they want to share them: *Twitter, Facebook, YouTube, Instagram, WhatsApp, emails, SMS, videos,* etc.

This site is also able to generate customized QR codes for different applications and in different formats. The only problem is that it asks you to log in to access certain facilities.

Free URL Shortener is generating the short url https://rb.gy/29w7qa, whilst our solution generates the short url http://16.170.208.217/ad23. If we were able to buy a domain with a length of maximum 5 characters our url would have been shorter, for example, it would have looked like http://domain/ad23. Moreover, we offer the functionalities to set an expiration date and number of accesses for the short url, while the given website doesn't have these options. When it comes to QR codes, our solution also offers the option to upload a mask photo, which is the photo that will be used to color the QR code.

2.2 Free Barcode Generator

Free Barcode Generator is a site for creating unique print-ready barcodes (UPC, EAN, and more) for product labeling, inventory control, shipping, and more. Since one barcode can be used for inventory and pricing information, it is possible to quickly obtain data on both [3]. Furthermore, barcodes can be customized to contain other relevant information as needed. They provide fast, reliable data for a wide variety of applications. This site also has the option of generating QR codes. Also, these applications do not have the possibility to set a minimum number of accesses or an expiration date for QR code, barcode or shortened URL.

3 Proposed Solution

The application we build is accessible without users registering or paying for the functionalities offered. We offer custom URL, barcodes [9] and QR codes [10], all in the same place for faster accessibility according to the user's needs. The final goal of the application is to offer a quick way of content sharing free and available for anyone.

3.1 Frontend Framework

The user interface is implemented using the Angular[1] framework, known for its robustness in creating dynamic and responsive single-page applications. Angular facilitates a smooth and interactive user experience, aligning with modern web development standards.

The QR code generation page features a form where users can input a mandatory link and optional parameters (see Fig. 2). Users have the flexibility to specify the number of accesses and expiration date for the generated QR code. Additionally, they can customize the fill color, defaulting to black, and background color, defaulting to white. Furthermore, users have the option to enhance customization by adding a mask and logo to the QR code.

The barcode generation interface presents users with a mandatory link field, ensuring essential information is included (see Fig. 2). Alongside this, users are provided with optional settings, such as the number of accesses and expiration date, allowing for controlled access and temporal restrictions. Furthermore, users have the option to customize the barcode's appearance with fill and background colors, set by default to black and white respectively.

---

[1] https://angular.io/.

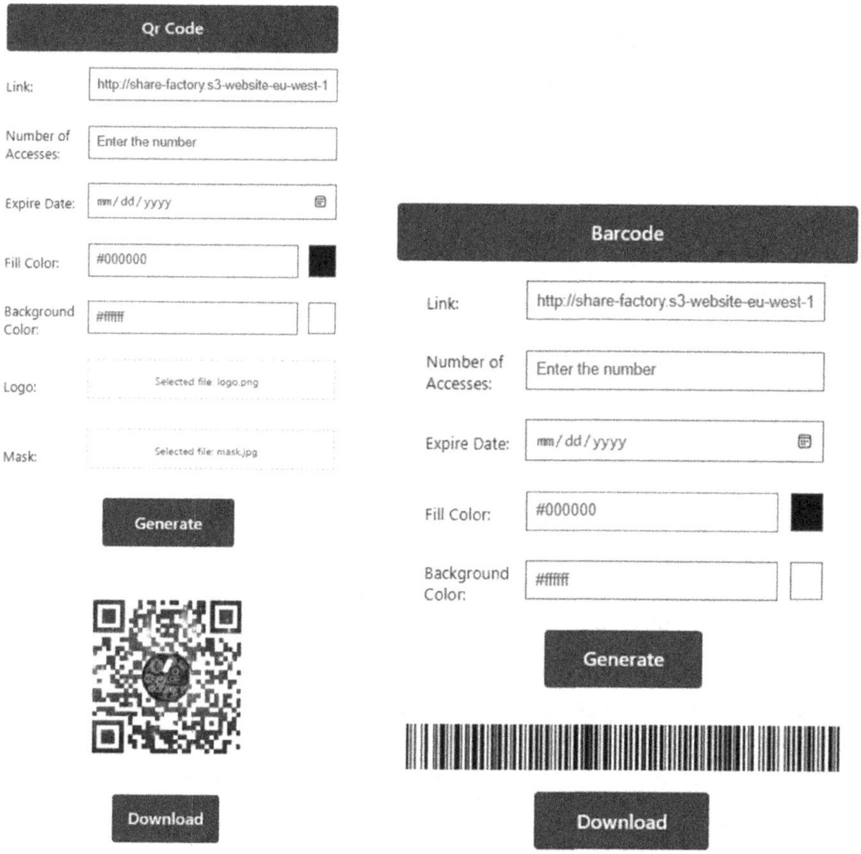

Fig. 2. App Frontend Display

The URL Shortener generation page necessitates the inclusion of a mandatory link (see Fig. 3). Users can also specify an expiration date and define the number of accesses allowed for the generated URL.

After successful completion of the generation process on each page (QR code, barcode, and URL), users are promptly notified through a color-coded pop-up system. A green pop-up signifies successful generation, providing users with immediate confirmation of completion. A red pop-up indicates generation failure, alerting users to potential issues that need attention. Additionally, during the generation process, users are informed of ongoing progress through a blue pop-up, ensuring transparency and visibility into the status of their request.

Fig. 3. App Frontend Display - URL Shortener Page

3.2 Backend Database

DynamoDB[2], a NoSQL database service, is employed as the backend storage solution. Its scalability and low-latency characteristics make it well-suited for managing the diverse data types associated with custom URLs, barcodes, and QR codes.

3.3 Content Generation

AWS Lambda functions [11] play a crucial role in dynamically generating barcodes, QR codes, and shortened URLs on-demand. This serverless architecture ensures optimal resource utilization and cost efficiency, allowing for scalable and parallelized processing during content generation.

The above diagram (see Fig. 4) shows the flow in the QR and Barcode generator lambda functions. There is only one diagram because both functions behave the same way, the only difference being that the generate QR code/barcode will return the corresponding image. When the client (frontend side) will call the function, the following steps will be followed:

1. *It will validate all fields*: the resource link should be a valid one, the expiration date should be from the future, the number of accesses should be a positive number and the colors should be contrasting enough. For the colors check we chose to do an euclidean difference on the hex representation of them and if this difference is greater than 50 then the colors are contrasting enough, therefore valid, otherwise the colors are not valid and the QR code will not be scannable.

---

[2] https://aws.amazon.com/dynamodb/.

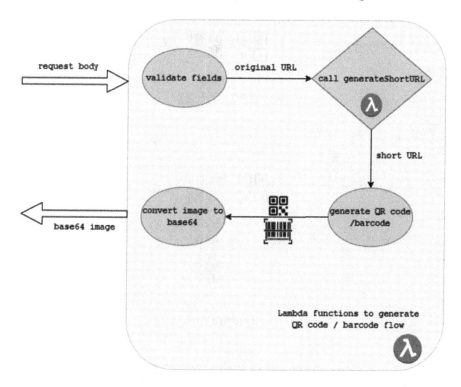

Fig. 4. QR and Barcode Generator Lambda Functions

2. *If the request body is valid*, it will call the lambda function that generates short urls for given links [12]. This function will generate the short url and will insert it in the database together with the original url, number of accesses and expiration date.
3. *After the short URL is returned from above*, the QR code or barcode will be generated having as the data this short URL.
4. *The image with the QR code/barcode* will be encoded to base64 to use it in the response body. The client(frontend) will receive this response and will decode the base64 text back into an image.

3.4   Backend Processing

The backend processing logic, responsible for reading and handling the generated content, is implemented using Python.

Figure 5 represents the overview image of the application flows and the technologies we are using. The frontend side uses Angular for its implementation and it is deployed to an Amazon S3 Bucket[3]. When the user presses the button

---

[3] https://aws.amazon.com/s3/.

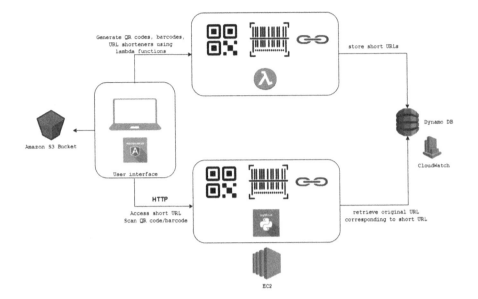

Fig. 5. The System's Architecture

to generate a qr code/barcode/short URL the client will call a lambda function which will insert the resource in the DB and will return the image/short URL.

When a user scans a QR code/barcode or accesses a short URL, the request will be handled by the python code which is deployed on an AWS EC2 [11] instance. The handling method checks the expiration date corresponding to the short URL in the database, then checks the number of accesses and if it is greater than 0 it will decrease it by one.

4   Functional and Non-functional Testing

We thoroughly tested our Share Factory platform to make sure it works smoothly. In functional testing (see Fig. 6), all 24 unit tests successfully passed, affirming the accuracy and reliability of the application's core functionalities. Furthermore, the achieved test coverage of 83% reflects a thorough examination of the codebase, ensuring a solid foundation for future development.

Non-functional testing, specifically load testing for custom QR codes, was conducted with different scenarios to assess system characteristics such as performance, latency, and reliability.

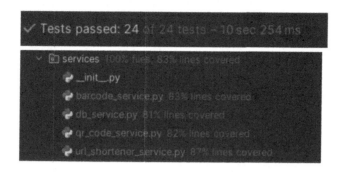

Fig. 6. Functional Testing

4.1 Latency

For testing the latency of our application, we did a request using the most complex functionality: generating QR code using mask and logo. This request was done in Postman [13] and it took: 20.38s (see Fig. 7).

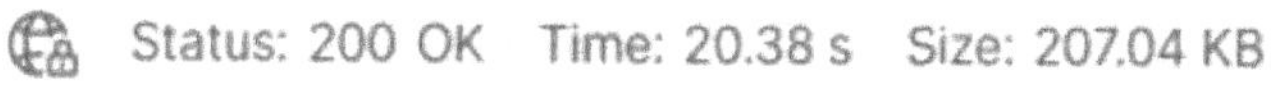

Status: 200 OK   Time: 20.38 s   Size: 207.04 KB

Fig. 7. Latency Testing Result

4.2 Performance

For 5 VU (Virtual Users) in 3 min with *Fixed mode*, which means that the number of virtual users are constant (see Fig. 8):

4.3 Reliability

We tested our application with a large number of virtual users in *Peak mode*. This mode is used for:

- *Concurrency*: Handling a large number of simultaneous requests can strain system resources.
- *Response Time*: Maintaining low response times under heavy load is crucial.
- *Failover*: Systems must gracefully handle failures and switch to backup resources if needed.

The test was done using 10 VU in 3 min (see Fig. 9). As it can be seen a huge amount of data was sent to our application that managed to handle them. One single request failed with a 429 error code, but after that call, the system was able to recover (see Fig. 9).

1. Summary

Total requests sent	Throughput	Average response time	Error rate
39	0.21 requests/second	20,646 ms	0.00 %

1.1 Response time

Response time trends during the test duration.

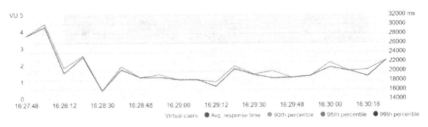

1.2 Throughput

Rate of requests sent per second during the test duration.

2. Metrics for each request

The requests are shown in the order they were sent by virtual users.

Request	Total requests	Requests/s	Min (ms)	Avg (ms)	90th (ms)	Max (ms)	Error %
POST qr-code https://e6nlatmycp65jdvpdq5ga23g7i0yghji.lambda-url.eu-north-1.on.aws/	39	0.21	15,767	20,646	28,767	30,063	0

Fig. 8. Performance Testing for 5 VU in 3 min with *Fixed mode*

For testing the *Failure Transparency* of our app we made a call and then interrupted the network. In this way, we could see how it reacts in case of network failure. After some time, the user received a pop up message in which is displayed the error message (see Figs. 10 and 11).

After the connection was established, the server resumed his activity and the user could generate the desired QR code (see Fig. 12).

1. Summary

Total requests sent	Throughput	Average response time	Error rate
56	0.30 requests/second	18,399 ms	1.79 %

1.1 Response time

Response time trends during the test duration.

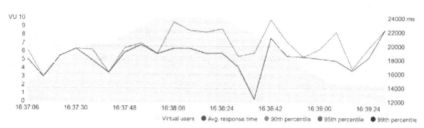

1.2 Throughput

Rate of requests sent per second during the test duration.

1.4 Requests with most errors

Top 5 requests with the most errors, along with the most frequently occurring errors for each request.

Request	Total error count	Error 1	Error 2	Other errors
POST qr-code ht(ps://e6nlatmycp65jdvpdq5ga23g7i0yghji.lambda-url.eu-north-1.on.aws/	1	429 Too Many Requests (1)	-	0

Fig. 9. Reliability Testing for 10 VU in 3 min

2. Metrics for each request

The requests are shown in the order they were sent by virtual users.

Request	Total requests	Requests/s	Min (ms)	Avg (ms)	90th (ms)	Max (ms)	Error %
POST qr-code https://e6nlatmycp65jdvpdo5ga23g7i0yghji.lambda-url.eu-north-1.on.aws/	56	0.30	2,527	18,399	22,046	23,820	1.79

3. Errors

3.1 Error distribution over time

Top 5 error classes observed during the test duration.

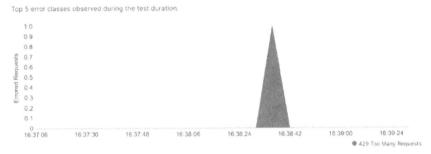

3.2 Error distribution for requests

Errored requests grouped by error class, along with the error count for each class.

Error class	Total counts
429 Too Many Requests	1
POST qr-code	1

Fig. 10. Reliability Testing - Error Case

5   Future Work

In future iterations, the Share Factory can be further enhanced to meet emerging technological trends and user expectations:

- *Augmented Reality (AR) Integration* - Explore the integration of AR features, allowing users to scan QR codes to reveal augmented reality content.
- *Social Media Integration* - Allow users to easily share their generated QR codes on social media platforms directly from the application.
- *Localization* - Support multiple languages and regional preferences to make our application accessible to a global audience.
- *Cross-Platform Compatibility* - Develop versions of our application for different platforms (iOS, Android, web) to reach a wider audience.

Fig. 11. Reliability Testing in Case of Network Error

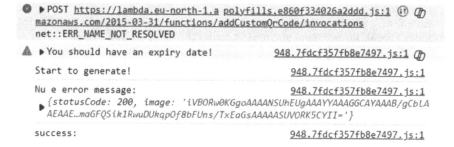

Fig. 12. Reliability Testing in Case of Network Error

6   Conclusion

In conclusion, Share Factory stands out not only for its user-friendly design and efficient technology stack but also for its forward-thinking features. A notable aspect of this application is its flexibility in content sharing - users can set expiration dates or limit the number of accesses to their shared content. Another key highlight is the application's user-centric approach, as users can customize their QR codes with logos and masks, and barcodes with colors, without incurring any costs. The objective of the app was successfully achieved by enabling effortless, cost-free, and personalized content sharing for a diverse user base.

Acknowledgements. Data processing and analysis in this paper were supported by the Research center with integrated techniques for the investigation of atmospheric aerosols in Romania, under project SMIS 127324 - RECENT AIR (RA).

References

1. Antoniades, D., et al.: we.b: The web of short URLs. In: Proceedings of the 20th International Conference on World Wide Web (WWW), pp. 715–724 (2011)
2. Sankhala, R., Kharbanda, M., Yadav, A., Suthar, P., Kaur, P.: Sukshma - A URL shortening service project. Int. J. Creative Res. Thoughts **10**(4), 347–351 (2022)
3. Cox, A.: What is code 128 barcode?, Triton Store, (2023). https://tritonstore.com. au/what-is-code-128-barcode/
4. Mandal, K.B., Aher, R.S., Deore, S.J., Mali, B.S.: QR code generator using Python. Int. J. Adv. Res. Innov. Ideas Educ. **8**(5), 1676–1682 (2022)
5. Raju, B.N., Venkatesh, N., Lakshmi, G.D., Chand, N.S., Haritha, D.: QR code generator and detector using Python. Compliance Eng. J. **13**(1), 345–353 (2022)
6. Jadhav, P.P., Patil, V.D., Shah, S.P., Mane, A.A., Barphe, S.S.: ScanIn: QR code based attendance system using Python. In: Proceedings of the International Conference on Sustainable Communication Networks and Application (ICSCNA), pp. 1491–1496 (2023)
7. Free URL Shortener. https://free-url-shortener.rb.gy/
8. OnlineLabels: barcode generator. https://www.onlinelabels.com/tools/barcode-generator
9. Knopf, F.: code128: a simple library to create Code-128 barcodes, Python Package Index (2015). https://pypi.org/project/code128/
10. Qrcode: A pure Python QR code generator. PyPI. https://pypi.org/project/qrcode/
11. Amazon Web Services: Free Tier. https://aws.amazon.com/free
12. Python. Documentation. hashlib - Secure hash and message digest algorithms. Python 3 Documentation. https://docs.python.org/3/library/hashlib.html
13. Postman. https://www.postman.com/

Security and Privacy

Steganalysis: A Study on Compression Attack, Methods and Transit Resilience

Cristiana Constantinescu[✉]

Faculty of Automatics, Computers, and Electronics, University of Craiova,
Craiova, Romania
constantinescu.cmaria@gmail.com

Abstract. Attacks have always been conducted upon systems to bypass security layers and access sensitive data. Attacks can be intentional - performed with the explicit intention and awareness - or unintentional - performed as a result of improper data manipulation. In steganography, an important *unintentional* attack is represented by compression. Within this paper, we analyze steganalysis methods and image compression algorithms alongside their means of affecting input images to study challenges and dilemmas for image steganography in context of data compression. This study represents yet another fundamental step to develop a feasible and robust steganographic scheme with application in insecure network communication.

Keywords: steganography · steganalysis · data protection · data hiding · information security · privacy protection · image steganography · image compression algorithms · lossy compression · lossless compression · near-lossless compression · compression attack

1 Introduction

Communication between two intended end points, in nowadays technological context, is never actually reduced to the sender and the recipient. Each and every communication channel humanity has access to today represents a hostile environment [14]. Certain maintainers, reviewers, authorized personnel of commercial communication environments might have access to our exchanged messages, in their plain representation, even in the case of those channels that claim to be protected by encryption. Data confidentiality is, therefore, at risk. An important tool to address this issue, that surpasses the limitation of cryptography is represented by steganography [16,17].

The analysis for steganography that addresses metrics of security in terms of confidentiality and data integrity, algorithm ranking and comparison, message detection with the ultimate goal to extract and recompose the secret is steganalysis. Steganalysis is considered the art of science of detecting secret data inside embedding environment [17,18,39]. It has relevance for various domains, from research ins steganography to cyber warfare, cyber forensics, tracking of criminal

© The Author(s), under exclusive license to Springer Nature Switzerland AG 2025
C. Bădică et al. (Eds.): BCI 2024, CCIS 2391, pp. 311–326, 2025.
https://doi.org/10.1007/978-3-031-84093-7_22

activities over the Internet, evidence gathering for cyber criminal and anti-social activities [14,15,19–22].

As steganography represents a method of protection, it falls subject to attacks. Intentional attacks implied by steganalysis, aim to decode the message. However, when steganography is properly implemented and intelligence upon the stego-system is low or absent, this is a task very difficult, if not impossible, to achieve. For that reason, steganalysis is not subject to failure if its ultimate goal is not achieved. Other reliable and usefully information can be exposed after steganalysis, such as estimations regarding the presence of absence of the message, its length, locations in which the message is embedded, techniques used etc. [15,20,21].

Conversely, there are unintentional attacks carried on without a direct link to the specific of steganography or with intentions to target the embedded data. Such attacks happen as a result of improper data manipulation. The characteristics of being *improper* applied to data handling and management in the case of steganography do not necessarily imply an incorrect or unaccepted management and processes for data manipulation. They denote by those activities that make steganography fragile and have the ability to affect the embedded data, such as compression, data format shifting, encoding etc.

As we mainly address in our study the embedding of steganography over insecure network channels and having in attention that data compression represent a useful and used concept for data storage and latency optimization, we will further address compression attacks carried to image steganography.

Many aim their steganography to be imperceptible but not transit resistant. To design and develop steganographic schemes resistant to a type of attack, it is important to understand the attack's work flow, methodology, concepts and goals. Therefore, within this paper, we will make discussion on the three types of image compression algorithms and analyze them in the context of image steganography.

2   Related Work

Steganography has emerged during the last three decades into the digital world as a manner of security and data protection via hiding techniques. Figure 1 illustrates the search results, expressed in number of publications by year (2000–2023) that contain 'steganography' in title, abstract or keywords, on an interrogation via scopus.com.

There is an abrupt advancement of the interest and research of the domain during the last two and a half decades in what regards the steganography domain. During these years, steganography has been implied in various domains, some with especially high levels of confidentiality and sensitive, such as military, biometric data, captcha security, QR-code voting systems, antivirus, forensics, medical, telecommunication [39–43].

More specifically military, communication and medical domains represent the hotspot for different types of attacks. The feature that quantifies the attack

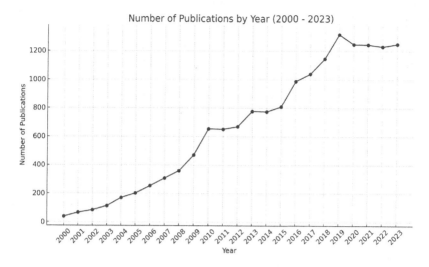

Fig. 1. Number of Publications on scopus.com, by Year

resistance of a steganographic scheme is robustness. However, when addressing the evaluation or protection of steganography itself, many researchers tend to treat robustnes as being imperceptibility or security [37, 38].

While it is true that perceptible steganography is subject to direct failure, in case of steganography in transit, the main aspects that protect and quantify the secret's integrity are security and robustness.

3   Steganalysis

Steganalysis represents the science and study of analyzing steganographic algorithms, outputs or systems to assert upon the presence of embedded data inside carrier data. The ultimate goal of steganalysis is to extract and reconstruct said embedded data.

3.1   Regular Singular Analysis

The Regular/Singular Analysis, or RS, is a specialized steganalysis procedure on LSB algorithm. Its intent is to denote whether a secret is present within an image and was firstly treated in [17]. The RS method operates on the principle that pixel values inside an image are not randomly distribute. Instead, color values of adjacent pixels are closer to facilitate a more gently visual transition of colors. However, in the presence of LSB steganography, in most cases, the cover object suffers a certain degree of artificial randomness (*a-rand*). RS makes use of this a-rand that it quantifies and interprets to assert the presence of steganography. Larger volumes of noise cause larger values of the discrimination function *f*, increasing the total number of the R groups inside the RS method, therefore indicating the presence of a stego-secret.

3.2 Subtractive Pixel Adjacency Matrix

The Subtractive Pixel Adjacency Matrix [36], also known as SPAM, is applicable to the Spatial Domain Steganography. It is applicable in LSB and DCT detection, thus being a universal steganalysis method. SPAM computes a matrix of differences between neighboring pixel's intensity values. It uses the said matrix to assert the presence of a secret inside the subject-image.

3.3 Textural Features Based Universal Steganalysis

In [23], TFUS was proposed as an approach to universal steganalysis, consisting on analyzing a cover's normalized histograms of the local linear transform coefficients. The Textural Features method applies to images in grayscale and also JPEG and JPEG2000 steganography.

3.4 Deep Learning Methods

DL methods bring valuable addition to the steganalysis field for having the ability to learn discriminative features from extensive data sets. A non-exhaustive list of algorithms implied in DL steganalysis methods are represented by MixNet [24], XuNet [25], YeNet [26], ZhuNet [27].

4 Assessing Methods for Robustness

Bit Error Ratio (BER) and Error Rate Extraction (R_e) are used to quantify data integrity upon extraction. The two methods are essentially treating the same features based on the total number of incorrectly decoded bits reported to the overall length in bits of the contained data. Despite R_e, BER has a percentile representation. Given their approach and data measured, this methods are useful in asserting the robustness of a stego-system. Few of the papers and studies that address these methods are [28–30, 32–35].

5 Image Compression

Image compression aims to reduce the physical size of image files while preserving their visual characteristics. The size reduction contributes in storage optimization and in obtaining shorter time responses for accessing resources of a network. Image compression achieves the reduction of size by different approaches that affect the integrity of data it is applied to. It continues to be an active field of research and development, with ongoing efforts to improve compression rate efficiency and image quality across various domains and applicability scenarios [5–10]. Paper [1] addresses the effects of image compression in medical imaging, study [2] proposes an approach for lossy image compression method, whereas paper [4] proposes a lossless image compression technique. Papers like [3] treat the advancement of image compression techniques capturing how this domain has evolved and emerged its initial limitations.

5.1 Lossy Compression

Lossy compression techniques achieve ratios of higher compression by discarding or altering certain image data. The amount and type of data that gets affected during a lossy compression varies depending on the specifics of the algorithm and image data used. However, data that is typically affected by lossy compression are:

- high frequency information: such as textures, sharp edges, small details, and
- color information: number of colors or color space is reduced

In addition, lossy compression alters the data not by only subtracting it, but also by introducing certain errors or artifacts that eventually lead to data integrity alterations.

Quantization in lossy compression represents a process that discards data by reducing the number of possible values for each pixel of the image. Despite elevating the efficiency of compression process, quantization can lead to rounding errors. Essentially, quantization implies the division of the range for each possible pixel values to a finite number of intervals and the assigning the nearest representative value within the said interval for each pixel value. (e.g. an 8-bit grayscale image can have values from 0–255, namely 256 values that can be reduced to only 64 by dividing 246 into 4 intervals of equal ranges). This leads to alterations brought to the fidelity of the image, especially in areas with gradients, where deviations in pixel values have a higher impact.

The quantization process in lossy compression can be rendered by:

$$P_{\text{quant}} = \text{round}\left(\frac{P_{\text{org}}}{Q}\right) \cdot Q \qquad (1)$$

where P_{quant} represents the quantized pixel value, P_{org} represents the original pixel value, Q represents the size of each quantization interval and *round* represents the rounding function.

Next to the effects produced by the quantization process in lossy compression stand the anomalies that are introduced by the compression process, known as artifacts. Artifacts are visual distortions that unintentionally occur during the compression process due to the approximations and simplifications techniques that are applied to pixel values and image traits.

Artifacts manifest as blockiness, blurring, ringing and banding and are perceptible by the HVS in the form of visual anomalies and distortion.

Blockiness is an effect often times caused by the division into blocks that some lossy compression algorithms imply to sequentially process the image. It appears as grid-like patterns in affected regions of the image and is particularly noticeable in regions with smoothness and color continuity should normally be present.

Blurring is often times the result of averaging or smoothing neighboring pixel values that lossy compression has to perform. It appears like unnecessarily and overly smooth regions, with results in loss of sharpness, details and textures.

Ringing is the result of over and undershoot of pixel values in compression and decompression processes. It appears like halos around edges or transition rich in contrast inside the image and is particularly noticeable in images with abrupt transition between light and dark regions.

Banding is the result of band-width or precision reduction of pixel values that compression implies. Banding appears as visible stripes of various intensities particularly noticeable in smooth gradients.

While it might be difficult to reduce all the possible lossy compression artifacts to a single mathematical equation, their presence can be weighted using metrics such as PSNR or SSIM. By analyzing the metrics' results, one can assess the level of artifacts distortion introduced by the lossy compression process.

The above explanation intentionally contains references to the visual aspect of the compressed image, considering the fact that structural representation are even more affected when their result is able to be perceived by the human visual system. Lossy compression is still being evolved and further developed by researchers such as but not limited to those of the papers [5–8,10].

5.2   Lossless Compression

Adversely, there is lossless compression - a type of compression that reduces the file size without discarding structural information from the image. Lossless compression algorithms achieve shrinkage in file sizing by addressing solely that information carried by images that is not relevant for the visual representation, thus reducing the amount of data an accurate reconstruction needs.

Lossless compression achieves this by addressing the redundancy, pattern exploitation and lossless transformations.

Spatial Redundancy mainly refers to pixel values. It is addressed by lossless compression algorithms by reducing this redundancy. As pixels are not subject to randomness inside an image, but they intermingle each others, neighboring pixel's values have a correlation that can be predicted based on adjacent values. Therefore, it becomes redundant to store the values of each pixel, thus lossless compression stores only the difference between predicted and actual values. While it may appear that information is lost, lossless compression algorithms apply the same prediction model when reconstructing the image. Stored data in compressed representation is relevant enough to reproduce the original representation. The prediction values obtained at the decompression process, summed with the differences stored during the compression process achieve data reconstruction in its visual integrity. In this manner, the size can be reduced without losing information.

Spatial Redundancy in the context of lossless compression can be understood by the following mathematical statements:

$$I(x,y) = I'(x,y) + D(x,y) \qquad (2)$$

where:

- $I(x, y)$ represents the original pixel value at position (x, y) in the image I to be compressed,
- $I'(x, y)$ represents the predicted pixel value at position (x, y) obtained using a prediction mechanism in the lossless compression process, and
- $D(x, y)$ represents the difference between the predicted and actual pixel values, i.e., $D(x, y) = I(x, y) - I'(x, y)$.

During the compression process LC, only the $D(x, y)$ values are stored. Upon decompression, the original pixel values $I(x, y)$ can be reconstructed using the predicted values $I'(x, y)$ and the stored differences $D(x, y)$. Therefore, despite that lossless compression only stores differences, the representation remains lossless.

Temporal Redundancy is another type of information redundancy addressed by lossless compression algorithms, with application to video compression. Despite this paper treats image steganography and compression, a brief addition about video files is sometimes brought to the attention due to the fact that videos are essentially composed by frames - still images - accompanied by sound. This is exactly the fact exploited by Temporal Redundancy reduction, where lossless compression algorithms store only the difference between successive frames, rather than storing the image representation for each frame. Similar to 2, the frames are recomposed when undergoing decompression, assuring no data lost.

Pattern Exploitation involves identifying repeated structures (patterns) in image representation and optimizing the method in which they are stored to render it more storage space efficient.

Repeating patterns are often times addressed using **Dictionary-based Compression** (further referred to as DbC in this paper). DbC represent dictionaries algorithm specific that assign significantly shorter representations to the patterns identified to frequently occur in image representation. Instead of redundantly storing the patterns for a repeated number of times, the algorithms only store the shorter encoded representation. Some of algorithms that are dictionary-based are LZW, LZ77, Sequitur, DEFLATE.

With certain similarities in principles, there are the **Entropy Encoding** pattern exploitation techniques, such as Huffman coding. Here, shorter codes are applied to frequently occurring symbols inside the data representation. This also results in a more compact storage and handling of the compressed image.

Research and advancements in lossless compression domain have often times conducted to the combination of Entropy Encoding and Dictionary Compression to provide even more efficient compression techniques [31].

Aside the aspects previously described, there are certain mathematical transformations that can be applied to images to rearrange the structural data to make images capable of being further compressed without loosing information. This is addressed to as **Lossless Transformations** and represents variants of Burrows-Wheeler Transform (BWT) or the Discrete Cosine Transform (DCT), where image representations are divided in such manner to become more addressable by compression to enhance the compression efficiency.

Although the lossless compression maintains the structural visual integrity of the compressed images, there are some types of steganography that are not resistant to it.

5.3 Near-Lossless Compression

Aside lossy and lossless compression, there stand the near-lossless compression [11–13], which aims to achieve significant compression ratios while providing a highly accurate representation of the compressed data.

Near-lossless process compression is typically used with applications in domains where preserving exact details is crucial, but compression is also required to reduce storage or transmission bandwidth. Examples of such domain application include but are not limited to medical imaging, satellite imagery, and archival storage of high-fidelity data.

One manner to approach near-lossless compression is to apply lossy compression techniques with a controlled degree of loss or error. For example, quantization may be performed with a larger step size or a more lenient threshold compared to traditional lossy compression methods, allowing for some loss of information while still maintaining a high level of fidelity between the two representations.

5.4 Features of Compression Algorithms that are Relevant to Steganography

Tables 1, 2 and Table 3, respectively, summarize a series of relevant aspects related to steganography of some of the compression algorithms mostly involved in image data formats. In addition, the Zstandard algorithm is included in discussion, despite not being specialized within a specific image type.

Lossy compression algorithms denote problems and challenges in steganography mostly due to their fundamentals. The manners in which lossy compression affects the visual integrity of image representation and the compaction of data are what dictates the challenges and limitations of steganography.

Lossless compression promise adaptability to image stegnaography. However, outputs of lossy compression can be susceptible to lossy compression accross transit and storage. Therefore, for steganography over networks, it is important to design solutions that are reliable on real life scenarios.

Some of the lossless algorithms have near-lossless variants that provide a certain level of data discarding.

As setgo-images can be shared over networks that are insecure in terms of compression attacks, a proper and robust steganographic scheme must take into consideration all the possible formats, lossy and lossless, the stego-image could be converted to across its transmission.

Theoretically, a universal steganographic scheme that would be resilient to potential compression and re-compression attacks should be based on the intersection of various compression algorithms' characteristics relevant to the domain.

Table 1. Near-Lossless Comp. Algorithms- Aspects Relevant to Steganography

Algorithm	Year	Types of Artefacts Introduced	Alters Number of Pixels	Alters Value of Pixels	Aspects Relevant to Steganography
JPEG-LS	1999	Minimal, mostly around sharp edges	No	Yes, within a small range	Good for steganography due to its prediction-based encoding.
FLIF (Free Lossless Image Format)	2015	None in lossless mode; minimal in near-lossless mode	No	Yes, controlled by quality parameter	Supports high degrees of compression with minimal visual change, beneficial for hiding data.
WebP	2010	Slight blurring and blocking artifacts in near-lossless	No	Yes, controlled by quality settings	The variable compression levels allow for data embedding with less detectable modifications.
JPEG XR	2009	Minimal; better handling of edges than JPEG	No	Yes, especially at lower compression ratios	Its tile structure can be advantageous for segment-based steganography.
BPG (Better Portable Graphics)	2014	Similar to WebP, with improved handling of textures	No	Yes, with adjustable compression levels	Offers better compression, which might be useful for embedding more data with less visibility.

Table 2. Lossy Comp. Algorithms - Aspects Relevant to Steganography

Compression Technique	Used In	Year	Affects Pixel Order	Color Depth Reduction	Modifies Pixel Number	Artifacts Introduced	Aspects Relevant to Steganography
DCT (Discrete Cosine Transform)	JPEG	1992	No	Yes	No	Blocking, blurring	DCT's quantization process may reduce the fidelity of embedded steganographic data, especially in high compression settings. Techniques need to be resilient to quantization noise.
Wavelet Compression	JPEG 2000	2000	No	Yes	No	Blurring, ringing	Wavelet-based methods offer a higher degree of robustness for steganography in transformed domains, allowing for efficient data hiding across different image resolutions.
VP8 or VP8L (WebP Lossy and Lossless)	WebP	2010	No	Yes	No	Similar to JPEG 2000	WebP's efficient compression can challenge steganography, requiring adaptive methods that can survive the lossy compression cycle without significant degradation of hidden information.
HEVC (High Efficiency Video Coding)	HEIF/ HEIC	2015	No	Yes	No	Improved over JPEG	HEVC's advanced compression techniques necessitate sophisticated steganography approaches, especially for maintaining hidden data integrity across extensive compression ratios.
HEVC (High Efficiency Video Coding)	BPG	2014	No	Yes	No	Similar to HEIF/HEIC	BPG, utilizing HEVC, presents similar challenges and opportunities for steganography as HEIF/HEIC; benefits from high-efficiency compression while demanding advanced hiding strategies.
Iterated Function Systems (IFS)	Fractal	1990s	No	Yes	Yes	Can vary	Fractal compression's unique properties of self-similarity and resolution independence offer novel vectors for data hiding, though practical implementation can be complex.
Wavelet Compression	Wavelet-based	Varies	No	Yes	No	Depends on implementation	Similar to JPEG 2000, wavelet compression techniques allow for data hiding that is less susceptible to compression artifacts, enabling more robust steganographic methods.

However, practical approaches illustrate that it is nearly impossible to develop such a universal system, thus researchers focus their work on certain compression algorithms and their particularities.

By understanding the ways in which information is manipulated and the exact manner in which images are altered at the pixel level and how they undergo changes, it becomes easier to create graphics that might highlight those parts of the images that are not affected.

Table 3. Lossless Comp. Algorithms - Aspects Relevant to Steganography

Algorithm	Used In	Year	Typical Use Case	Notable Features	Aspects Relevant to Steganography
DEFLATE	PNG	1996	Web images, transparency support	Lossless compression, supports transparency	Ensures no degradation of hidden data, ideal for high-quality steganography. The chunk-based structure of PNG enables sophisticated embedding strategies without altering the visual or structural integrity of the image.
LZW	GIF	1987	Web animations	Limited to 256 colors, supports animation	Supports embedding data within the limited color palette and animation frames, making it possible to create steganographic messages that are difficult to detect without altering the perceived animation.
Various	TIFF	1986	Professional imaging, scanning	Supports multiple compression schemes	The flexibility of TIFF's compression options, including lossless methods, combined with its ability to store multiple images and metadata, makes it exceptionally versatile for embedding hidden information across different layers or components.
FLIF algorithm	FLIF	2015	Efficient image storage	High compression efficiency, supports progressive decoding	The FLIF algorithm's progressive decoding feature allows for multi-level steganography, where information can be hidden in various layers of image detail, enhancing the depth and robustness of the steganographic content.
VP8L (WebP Lossless)	WebP (Lossless)	2010	Web images, advanced web use	Supports both lossy and lossless compression	WebP lossless compression provides an excellent balance between efficiency and steganographic potential, allowing for the embedding of data with minimal impact on file size or image quality. The format's support for transparency and animation opens additional avenues for data hiding.
Zstandard	Zstandard	2015	General-purpose compression	Very high compression ratio and speed, dictionary compression	Zstandard's efficiency and the use of dictionary compression make it suitable for embedding data within a wide range of data types beyond images, offering new steganography applications in file and data streams with rapid access to hidden information.

Nonetheless, given the diversity of images, characteristics and representations, the same algorithm applied to images of similar sizes and formats does not affect the samples uniformly to the reference image. As seen previously in this section, compression algorithms take into consideration pixel values that inside a specific scene (as banding is more visible in images with smooth gradients, such as sky and water scenes).

Steganography is an alterative process in itself, as it affects certain information in the image. When met with compression, it is important that the stego-alterations to be made in areas not affected by compression, if possible. It is also crucial that these regions to be universally found in images considered similar at some level, based on a set of characteristics and specifications shared by all or most elements of the collection.

6 Steganography Risks

6.1 Attacks

Any intentional or unintentional effort to breach the security measures in steganography represent an attack. An attack that is carried out with preparation, discernment, and purpose is an intentional attack. On the other hand, an attack resulting from incorrect or inadequate handling of data is an unintentional attack.

Passive Attack

In a passive attack, E attempts to learn information from $T(m)$ without altering the message. Mathematically, this can be represented as:

$$E(T(m)) \to m' \qquad (3)$$

where $m' \approx m$. The goal of E is to approximate m as closely as possible to m' without detection, implying that E does not modify $T(m)$.

Active Attack

Conversely, in an active attack, E not only intercepts $T(m)$ but also attempts to alter the message before it reaches B. This can be expressed as:

$$E(T(m)) \to T'(m) \qquad (4)$$

where $T'(m) \neq T(m)$. Here, $T'(m)$ represents the altered message that is forwarded to B. The intention behind $T'(m) \neq T(m)$ is for E to inject, modify, or in some way influence the communication to achieve a malicious goal.

Active attacks are different than on-going attacks. On-going attacks are those attacks that are taking place at a certain moment in the present. An active attack is either a past, future or on-going attack that alters the ciphered data.

Detection and Mitigation

To mitigate these attacks, additional encryption of the embedded message and integrity checking mechanisms can be implemented:

$$T(m) = Stg_{K_{AB}}(m) \qquad (5)$$

$$V(m, T(m)) = \begin{cases} 1, & \text{if integrity and authenticity are verified} \\ 0, & \text{otherwise} \end{cases} \qquad (6)$$

Here, $Stg_{K_{AB}}(m)$ denotes the encryption of m with a key K_{AB} shared between A and B. The verification function $V(m, T(m))$ checks the integrity and authenticity of the message, returning 1 if the message is verified to be authentic and intact, and 0 otherwise.

6.2   Placing Compression on Attack's Chart

Attacks in steganography imply:

- **Detection Attacks (Steganalysis)**: has as a primary and achievable goal to assert and detect the presence of hidden information (**passive**).
- **Extraction Attacks**: has the goal of recovering or extracting the secret message. Is achievable mainly with additional information about the steganosystem/persons involved (**passive**).
- **Destruction Attacks**: even for the cases in which the extraction of the hidden message is not possible, an attacker might attempt to corrupt the embedded message to prevent its intended recipient from successfully retrieving the message (**active**).

Compression Attacks as Opposed to Classical Attacks. Mainly, compression attacks can be unintentional, as classical attacks have a defined purpose. Alterations that are brought by different compression techniques alongside the channel are the result of an unintentional compression attack.

A compression attack in digital steganography aims to disrupt the hidden information within a file by applying a compression algorithm that reduces the file size, discards or alters structural data potentially degrading or completely removing the embedded content. This type of attack does not necessarily destroy the cover's visible quality.

Given an original image I, let m represent a secret message, and $S(I, m)$ be the function that embeds m into I to produce a steganographic image I_s. The compression attack can be represented by a compression function C that takes I_s and produces a compressed version of the image $I_c = C(I_s)$. The compression aims to reduce the size of I_s while potentially disrupting the embedded message m. After compression, the extraction function E attempts to retrieve the message m' from I_c, where m' may not equal m due to the loss of information:

$$I_s = S(I, m), \quad I_c = C(I_s), \quad m' = E(I_c) \tag{7}$$

Ideally, in the absence of attacks, $m' = m$. However, due to the compression attack, there's a high probability that $m' \neq m$ or that m' is irretrievably corrupted. A compression attack is an active attack, regardless of the direct intentions it relies on. It implies a high-risk potential of alteration of the embedded data, thus endangering the stego-system's integrity and confidentiality.

7   Summary of Findings

Compression attacks in image steganography represent a significant challenge for the field, as they aim to disrupt the hidden information without necessarily degrading the visible quality of the image. The dangers of data compression put image steganography at risk from its early development stages. Compression techniques involved in formatting and encoding the images are the first to attack a steganographic system. Despite an imperceptible, secure embedding of the secret data, with a satisfactory payload-capacity at the bit level, if the formatting of the binary file to the shape of an image fails, all the efforts were in vain.

The compression attack lurks image steganography for both data at rest and in transit. For at rest data, particular functionalities of the hosting system that involve storage optimization might unwittingly subject the stego-images to incompatible compression. For in transit data, compression is handled by the software that gets, at some point and level, to manipulate the stego-image. As particular specifications of these systems is not widely known, the steganographic scheme must attempt to achieve resistance to as many compression techniques at once. This represents an incredibly difficult achievement, giving the vast number of compression algorithms, their variants and combinations. Therefore, it might become usefull to specialize certain stego-systems for certain integration with particular and widely used software, protocols and applications.

Compression attacks are especially important due to the fact that they can be conducted without direct malicious intentions. Paradoxically, compression attacks can be performed accidentally, during beneficial efforts. Storage optimization, latency reduction for backup or transfer represent only a few of non-malicious actions that involve compression attacks.

There is presumably no direct risk of compression attacks associated with the bare implementation of transport layer protocols, due to the lack of default compression of the protocols. However, segmentation can indirectly suppress the embedding data's viability, when there are incidents in the network. To address the dangers of compression attacks, the following guidelines can be traced:

Comprehending Lossy Compression: implies the understanding of how lossy compression techniques work, of how they assess and affect data is crucial for compression attack mitigation.

Aim for Robust Steganography: addresses the importance of the robustness aspect in steganography is often times reduced and subject to almost complete trade-off mainly for imperceptibility. Despite imperceptibility being the first naked eye steganalysis method, with embedding that fail to provide resilience to their carried secrets, steganography yet again fails at its early principle evaluation

Aim for Adaptive Steganography: despite being a particularly difficult achievement, a steagnographic scheme resistant to more than one compression algorithm or to more than one compression session is a desiderate. As treated in Sect. 5, same algorithm does not necessarily discard the same sections of data inside similar size or type images. For this reason, a steganographic scheme able to address the content of the mask to anticipate the affected areas to designated safer locations for embedding is an important achievement.

Balance the Trade-Off: a general trade-off tendency is observed in the domain of steganography research and development. Mainly, imperceptibility and payload capacity is preferred over security or robustness. It is difficult to assert whether this is beneficial or not, as the specifications of each use case dictate the specifications of the stegosystem to be integrated. Nonetheless, it is important to properly address the trade-off between payload capacity and resilience. Compression attacks in image steganography highlight the dynamic nature of the field, where advancements in steganographic methods and compression/detection technologies are constantly evolving. Addressing these challenges requires a deep understanding of both image processing and information security, underlining the interdisciplinary nature of research and development in image steganography.

The present study serves as yet another important comprehension and learning phase in the work of research and developing a viable, feasible, robust and reliable steganographic scheme for usage over insecure networks.

References

1. Alkinani, M.H.: Effects of lossy image compression on medical image registration accuracy. In: Proceedings of the IEEE International Conference on Consumer Electronics (ICCE), Las Vegas, NV, 2021, pp. 1–4 (2021)
2. Akhtar, N., et al.: A novel lossy image compression method. In: Proceedings of the 4th International Conference on Communication Systems & Network Technologies, Bhopal, India, 2014, pp. 866–870 (2014)
3. Sandeep, P., et al.: Advancements in image compression techniques: a comprehensive review. In: Proceedings of the 2nd International Conference on Edge Computing & Applications (ICECAA), Namakkal, India, 2023, pp. 821–826 (2023)
4. Sikka, N., et al.: Lossless image compression technique using HAAR wavelet and vector transform. In: Proceedings of the International Conference on Research Advances in Integrated Navigation Systems (RAINS), Bangalore, India, 2016, pp. 1–5 (2016)
5. Krivenko, S., et al.: Lossy compression of images corrupted by spatially correlated noise. In: Proceedings of the 13th International Conference on Modern Problems of Radio Engineering, Telecommunications & Computer Science (TCSET), Lviv, Ukraine, 2016, pp. 698–702 (2016)
6. Nassef, M., Alkinani, M.H.: A novel multilevel lossy compression algorithm for grayscale images inspired by the synthesization of biological protein sequences. IEEE Access **9**, 149657–149680 (2021)
7. Sadchenko, A., et al.: Fast lossy compression algorithm for medical images. In: Proceedings of the International Conference on Electronics & Information Technology (EIT), Odessa, Ukraine, 2016, pp. 1–4 (2016)
8. Hu, R., et al.: A new lossy compression scheme for encrypted gray-scale images. In: Proceedings of the IEEE International Conference on Acoustics, Speech & Signal Processing (ICASSP), Florence, Italy, 2014, pp. 7387–7390 (2014)
9. Kamatar, V.S., et al.: Two phase image compression algorithm Using diagonal pixels of image blocks. In: Proceedings of the 2nd International Conference for Emerging Technology (INCET), Belagavi, India, 2021, pp. 1–6 (2021)
10. Qin, C., et al.: Flexible lossy compression for selective encrypted image with image inpainting. IEEE Trans. Circ. Syst. Video Technol. **29**(11), 3341–3355 (2019)
11. Koc, B., et al.: Near-lossless image compression with parity reduction. In: Proceedingfs of the 24th IEEE International Conference on Intelligent Engineering Systems (INES), Reykjavík, Iceland, 2020, pp. 225–230 (2020)

12. Schiopu, I., Tabus, I.: Lossy and near-lossless compression of depth images using segmentation into constrained regions. In: Proceedings of the 20th European Signal Processing Conference (EUSIPCO), Bucharest, Romania, 2012, pp. 1099–1103 (2012)

13. Tai, S.C., et al.: A near-lossless compression method based on CCSDS for satellite images. In: Proceedings of the International Symposium on Computer, Consumer & Control (IS3C), Taichung, Taiwan, 2012, pp. 706–709 (2012)

14. Nissar, A., Mir, A.H.: Classification of steganalysis techniques: a study. Digit. Sig. Process. **20**(6), 1758–1770 (2010)

15. Chanu, Y.J., et al.: Image steganography and steganalysis: a survey. Int. J. Comput. Appl. **52**(2), 1–11 (2012)

16. Fridrich, J.: Applications of data hiding in digital images (tutorial). In: Proceedings of the 5th International Symposium on Signal Processing & its Applications (ISPACS), vol. 1, Melbourne, Australia (1999)

17. Fridrich, J., et al.: Detecting LSB steganography in color and gray-scale images. IEEE Multimedia **8**(4), 22–28 (2001)

18. Johnson, N.F., Jajodia, S.: Steganalysis of images created using current steganography software. In: Aucsmith, D. (ed.) IH 1998. LNCS, vol. 1525, pp. 273–289. Springer, Heidelberg (1998). https://doi.org/10.1007/3-540-49380-8_19

19. Johnson, N.F., Jajodia, S.: Exploring steganography: seeing the unseen. IEEE Comput. **31**(2), 26–34 (1998)

20. Wang, H., Wang, S.: Cyber warfare steganography vs. steganalysis. Commun. ACM **47**(10), 76–82 (2004)

21. Bender, W., et al.: Applications for data hiding. IBM Syst. J. **39**(3–4), 547–568 (2000)

22. Miaou, S., et al.: A secure data hiding technique with heterogeneous data-combining capability for electronic patient records. In: Proceedings of the 22nd Annual International Conference of the IEEE Engineering in Medicine & Biology Society (EMBC), vol. 1, Chicago, IL, 2000, pp. 280–283 (2000)

23. Li, B., et al.: Textural features based universal steganalysis. In: Proceedings of SPIE 6819, Security, Forensics, Steganography, & Watermarking of Multimedia Contents X, vol. 681912 (2008)

24. Amrutha, E., et al.: MixNet: a robust mixture of convolutional neural networks as feature extractors to detect stego images created by content-adaptive steganography. Neural Process. Lett. **54**, 853–870 (2022)

25. Xu, G., et al.: Structural design of convolutional neural networks for steganalysis. IEEE Sig. Process. Lett. **23**, 708–712 (2016)

26. Ye, J., et al.: Deep learning hierarchical representations for image steganalysis. IEEE Trans. Inf. Forensics Secur. **12**(11), 2545–2557 (2017)

27. Zhang, R., et al.: Efficient feature learning and multi-size image steganalysis based on CNN. arXiv:1807.11428 (2018)

28. Kadhim, I.J., et al.: High capacity adaptive image steganography with cover region selection using dual-tree complex wavelet transform. Cogn. Syst. Res. **60**, 20–32 (2020)

29. Sukumar, A., et al.: Robust image steganography approach based on RIWT-Laplacian pyramid and histogram shifting using deep learning. Multimedia Syst. **27**, 651–666 (2021)

30. Kadhim, I.J., et al.: Improved image steganography based on super-pixel and coefficient-plane-selection. Signal Process. **171**, 107481 (2020)

31. Shrividhiya, G., et al.: Robust data compression algorithm utilizing LZW framework based on huffman technique. In: Proceedings of the International Conference on Emerging Smart Computing & Informatics (ESCI), Pune, India, 2021, pp. 234–237 (2021)
32. Tao, J., et al.: Towards robust image steganography. IEEE Trans. Circ. Syst. Video Technol. **29**(2), 594–600 (2019)
33. Zhu, Z., et al.: Robust steganography by modifying sign of DCT coefficients. IEEE Access **7**, 168613–168628 (2019)
34. Lu, W., et al.: Secure robust JPEG steganography based on autoencoder with adaptive BCH encoding. IEEE Trans. Circ. Syst. Video Technol. **31**(7), 2909–2922 (2021)
35. Zhang, Y., et al.: On the fault-tolerant performance for a class of robust image steganography. Signal Process. **146**, 99–111 (2018)
36. Gu, X., Guo, J.: A study on subtractive pixel adjacency matrix features. Multimedia Tools Appl. **78**, 19681–19695 (2019)
37. Perumal, K., et al.: Robust multitier spatial domain secured color image steganography in server environment. Clust. Comput. **22**, 11285–11293 (2019)
38. Khan, A., Sarfaraz, A.: Novel high-capacity robust and imperceptible image steganography scheme using multi-flipped permutations and frequency entropy matching method. Soft. Comput. **23**, 8045–8056 (2019)
39. Setiadi, D.R.I.M., et al.: Digital image steganography survey and investigation (goal, assessment, method, development, and dataset). Sig. Process. **206**, 108908 (2023)
40. Mohsin, A.H., et al.: Real-time medical systems based on human biometric steganography: a systematic review. J. Med. Syst. **42**(12), 1–20 (2018). https://doi.org/10.1007/s10916-018-1103-6
41. Douglas, M., et al.: An overview of steganography techniques applied to the protection of biometric data. Multimedia Tools Appl. **77**, 17333–17373 (2018)
42. Dalal, M., Juneja, M.: Steganography and steganalysis (in digital forensics): a cybersecurity guide. Multimedia Tools Appl. **80**, 5723–5771 (2021)
43. Cucurull, J., et al.: QR steganography: a threat to new generation electronic voting systems. In: Proceedings of the 11th International Conference on Security & Cryptography (SECRYPT), Vienna, Austria, 2014, pp. 1–8 (2014)

A Practical Guide for Application Security Baselines in the Software Development Process

Mariya Harseva[(⊠)] [iD] and Milen Petrov[(⊠)] [iD]

Sofia University St. Kliment Ohridski, Sofia, Bulgaria
{mharseva,milenp}@fmi.uni-sofia.bg

Abstract. Through a systematic review of scientific literature, we summarize the most practical approaches for security in the application design phase. Incorporating threat modeling and secure design principles from the outset is critical to mitigating risks. Implementing secure coding guidelines helps avoid common software vulnerabilities, which means that software development teams should receive comprehensive training on secure coding techniques and integrate these practices into their workflows. In our paper we investigate practices, existing tools and literature and extract methodology to be adopted by the teams. One direction is by using IDE plugins - those can increase awareness by providing real-time feedback. Utilizing scores from tools such as Static Application Security Testing (SAST) and Software Composition Analysis (SCA) improves quality process and gives quantitative approach in decision-making during deployment, ensuring vulnerabilities are addressed early. Another direction of the research is embedding secure coding techniques in early software development lifecycle phases which helps to maintain agility in the process without affecting the release lifecycle. The third direction of research is applying the principles of separation of environments which ensure that development, testing, and production stages are isolated, reducing cross-environment contamination risks. On fourth place, we propose using the segregation of duties to further strengthen security by dividing responsibilities to prevent unauthorized access or changes. Security testing during the QA phase should include best and worst-case scenario automation, authorization matrix tests, and Dynamic Application Security Testing (DAST) to uncover potential weaknesses. Finally, assessing infrastructure vulnerability status, whether on a server or serverless level, ensures comprehensive security coverage. It is furthermore proposed to use regular external vulnerability scanning exercises which provide an additional layer of security by identifying potential threats that may have been overlooked internally. By integrating these practices, organizations can maintain a robust security posture while preserving the agility and efficiency of their development processes.

Keywords: Application security · DevSecOps · Static Application Security Testing (SAST) · Software Composition Analysis (SCA) · Dynamic Application Security Testing (DAST) · Code review · Threat Modelling · Agile development · secure coding guidelines · secure design principles

C. Bădică et al. (Eds.): BCI 2024, CCIS 2391, pp. 327–340, 2025.
https://doi.org/10.1007/978-3-031-84093-7_23

1 Introduction

We all live in modern times, where technology has become an integral part of our lives. There is a wave of technology-intensive innovations that seek to improve our lives and our interactions with the world. In this set of changes in our way of life, thinking, and living, which are constantly changing and adapting to the environment, we do not realize how the technologies we rely on and trust our lives upon can show weaknesses or unexpected actions can compromise our personality in the cyberspace and have an enormous adverse impact on our lives.

At the time of this strident growth and technology development, we have evidence of services that provide an insufficient level of security and have led to security incidents that they have exposed to the public and for misuse of financial, personal, medical, sensitive data to their users. Here is a prioritization of the emerging threats in the cybersecurity space as per Enisa's Foresight for Cybersecurity threats 2030 report [21].

The threat prioritization based on [impact * likelihood] assessment is presented in the table below, starting with the most prioritized (Table 1).

Separately, over the years, various vulnerabilities have emerged for all well-known and wide-spread technologies, and the insufficiently resilient security strategies of some organizations have led to the malicious use of these vulnerabilities to compromise the organizations in question or their customers [13].

The vulnerability ecosystem has matured considerably in the last few years. A significant amount of effort has been invested to systematically capture, curate, taxonomize and communicate the vulnerabilities in terms of severity, impact and complexity of the associated exploit or attack.

That's why all these conditions and happenings set the key to good and effective security management strategies in an organization.

The motivation of this paper to address the issue of how writing and securing programming code is related to the root cause of system and technology weaknesses that are rooted in the underperforming and insufficiently resilient software development process in terms of secure development practices. We try to discover consequences if from the very beginning of creating a software application, however trivial and unimportant, it is appropriate to define security requirements to be incorporated into the design, architecture, and programming code process.

Basic principles, good practices, and security recommendations should be an integral part of the software development and development process because they are not trivial and should be given special attention at all phases of the development process to achieve optimal effectiveness of the security controls of an organization.

This paper is structured in the following way:

In the section Goals and Objectives of the Article we outline the paper's objective to provide a sustainable process for creating secure code. It aims to ensure that security principles are integrated into the software development process, enhancing the overall security posture of applications. The paper also seeks to raise awareness among developers about secure coding practices. In the next section, Security in the Application Design Phase, we outline that the importance of incorporating security architecture during the product design phase must be emphasized. Best practices for security in design, such as least-privilege access, user-friendly security controls, and secure defaults, are

Table 1. Prioritization of threats

	THREATS	IMPACT * LIKELIHOOD	IMPACT	LIKELIHOOD
1	Supply Chain Compromise of Software Dependencies	17,71	4,21	4,21
2	Skill Shortage	17,20	4,10	4,20
3	Human Error and Exploited Legacy Systems within Cyber-Physical Ecosystems	16,69	3,96	4,22
4	Exploitation of Unpatched and Out-of-date Systems within the Overwhelmed Cross-sector Tech Ecosystem [Optional]	16,21	4,05	4,00
5	Rise of Digital Surveillance Authoritarianism/Loss of Privacy	15,34	3,96	3,88
6	Cross-border ICT Service Providers as Single Point of Failure	15,12	4,14	3,65
7	Advanced Disinformation/Influence Operations (IO) Campaigns	14,38	3,42	4,21
8	Rise of Advanced Hybrid Threats	14,03	3,68	3,81
9	Abuse of AI	13,22	3,43	3,86
10	Physical Impact of Natural/Environmental Disruptions on Critical Digital Infrastructure [Optional]	12,99	3,68	3,53
11	Lack of Analysis and Control of Space-based Infrastructure and Objects	12,52	3,63	3,45
12	Targeted Attacks (e.g. Ransomware) Enhanced by Smart Device Data	12,29	3,39	3,63
13	Increased Digital Currency-enabled Cybercrime [Optional]	10,25	3,06	3,35
14	Manipulation of Systems Necessary for Emergency Response [Optional]	10,02	3,27	3,07

(*continued*)

Table 1. (*continued*)

	THREATS	IMPACT * LIKELIHOOD	IMPACT	LIKELIHOOD
15	Tampering with Deepfake Verification Software Supply Chain [Optional]	9,83	3,00	3,28
16	AI Disrupting/Enhancing Cyber Attacks [Optional]	9,78	3,07	3,19
17	Malware Insertion to Disrupt Food Production Supply Chain [Optional]	9,33	3,11	3,00
18	Exploitation of E-health (and Genetic) Data [Optional]	9,32	3,11	3,00
19	Attacks Using Quantum Computing [Optional]	7,32	2,76	2,65
20	Disruptions in Public Blockchains [Optional]	5,96	2,47	2,41
21	Technological Incompatibility of Blockchain Technologies [Optional]	5,91	2,25	2,63

outlined. The section also introduces the concept of a secure software development life-cycle (SDLC), which integrates security activities throughout the development process. In the following section, Secure Design Principles we provide detailed principles for secure design, including minimizing attack surface area, establishing secure defaults, enforcing least privilege, applying defense in depth, ensuring secure failure modes, and avoiding security by obscurity. These principles are intended to guide developers in creating secure applications from the outset. The next few sections discussing various security testing methods, such as SAST, SCA, and DAST, which are essential for iden-tifying and mitigating vulnerabilities early in the development process will be further outlined in follow-up papers. However, those are equally important as they emphasize the need for continuous security assessments and the use of automated tools to enhance the effectiveness of security testing. Furthermore, those sections highlight the importance of assessing infrastructure vulnerabilities, including server and serverless environments. Regular external vulnerability scanning exercises are recommended to identify potential threats that may have been overlooked internally.

2 Goals and Objectives of the Article

Through the realized concept of a sustainable process of creating secure code, guaranteed at different phases by multiple and different checks on the effectiveness of the security controls that are embedded in the design of an application, we will have indisputable evidence that all good practices, information security principles and recommendations are followed, which guarantees an optimal launch of new versions of software technologies. This concept will allow security rules to be followed in the future, as well as serve as a compass for finding the right and secure direction of development with a view to protecting the principles of confidentiality, integrity, and availability of information throughout the life cycle of a technology.

Another motivation for the article, as well as a corresponding benefit from this implementation, is the need to raise awareness among programmers and other software professionals that it is extremely important to know and follow good practices for writing code, as well as to use additional sanity checks already in the code development environment during its compilation.

We expect that applying security guidelines will significantly enhance our system's protection against potential threats, reduce vulnerabilities, and ensure compliance with industry standards, thereby safeguarding sensitive data and maintaining user trust. Defining the goals of this paper leads us to formulating the following research questions:

If we have easy to follow and practical guidelines for developers, would this make them more educated and prone to following industry recommendations for secure development.

Which factors/guidelines are available for consideration?

From the performed literature review which practices can be selected as the most effective, practical and easy to follow?

During the preparation of this article, it was noted that there are many different sources of information on the topic, but none of them offer thoroughness and comprehension or a practical, useful and easy to follow combination of executable steps in the right order to be considered an educational material and practices guide for software development professionals. Our literature review showed that the application security topic, as well as the secure development, secure coding and secure design topics are hot and show a growing trend in papers we have reviewed mostly in the years after 2010. The review aims to be integrative to summarize past research based on overall conclusions. We have found hundreds of thousands of articles appearing with those key words on Scopus and Google Scholar, which are considered reputable sources for scientific literature and out of those based on filters for recency (after 2010 with short review performed over the years before, as those have quite rudimental coverage for the topic) we have selected and shortlisted appr. 200 papers which have important information on this topic, but none of them had the level of completeness and practicality which we are seeking to summarize in this paper. We have decided to quote only the most significant of those articles and scientific studies in our paper, however we are proposing a combination of all reviewed approaches and guidelines.

There are many such different techniques that can be instated and used in the development environment, but only the good combination with the right order is supposed to be giving the expected results.

Separation of roles and responsibilities among participants in the development process is well adopted in the community of practice, but it is also critical to ensure that ultimate control and access is not concentrated in any one role, which could compromise the process of creating secure code. In the process of developing secure code, it is good to have quality managers as well as system administrators to ensure the migration of code between different environments without having to give extended access to the programmers themselves, as this is considered bad practice.

The greatest benefit from raising awareness of how important security principles is in the development process will be society and future generations, whose daily lives will likely be entirely in the digital world. It is right for all of us to know that it is extremely important to invest as much effort as is necessary to ensure the security and sustainability of the technologies to which we entrust our lives and existence. All of them should serve us only and only with their usefulness, and not become weapons to our personality and existence in cyberspace.

Creating software technology and ensuring its sustainability, availability, confidentiality, integrity, etc. is not an easy task that is done by default. It is a way of thinking and a purposeful multi-step process to ensure compliance with the principles of information security throughout the entire life cycle of the relevant technology. Without the maturity in any and all organizations creating software products to realize the need for this process and way of thinking, recognize it and implement it in its processes, it could not exist successfully and long in the future cyber world.

3   Security in the Application Design Phase

The security architecture is an inevitable component of the overall product architecture and is developed to provide guidance during product design in terms of functional and non-functional requirements to act as system security controls. This architecture aims to outline the required level of security and the potential impacts that this level of security is expected to provide during the development stages and the product as a whole. Security should be considered a systemic requirement, similar to performance, capacity, cost, etc. To create a global concept and create a strategy for the security of our system, it is appropriate to follow the following best practices [3]:

- To implement the concept of security in the initial design and prototyping phase of your system or application
- To allow for the implementation of future security improvements that may become necessary over time
- Reduce as much as possible and isolate security controls
- Always use least-privilege access principles
- To structure security-related functions well
- Make security controls user-friendly, not overly complicated and complex
- Do not rely only on confidentiality for security, but also use other methods and techniques to ensure the principles of availability, integrity and confidentiality.

Our concepts of a secure architecture and default security for a given project can be implemented both for newly developed products and services, and for services and products that have had some life cycle after their initial release for consumer use [10].

There are different types of testing and analysis that are performed during the life cycle of a system or service and depending on its scope and requirements, so security-related testing, analysis and evaluation are an integral part of the entire project life cycle [5].

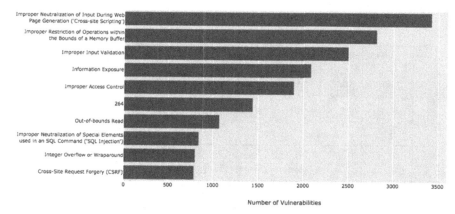

Fig. 1. Top 10 Weaknesses (CWEs)

The diagram in Fig. 1 describes the industry standard for the secure software development life cycle, which follows the US Department of Defense methodology. The primary purpose of the Department of Defense is to provide military forces to prevent war and protect the security of the United States of America. It has addressed security issues through guidance and requirements consolidated into a framework and issued by the Office of Management and Budget (OMB) version A-130. The IT security focus was further drawn from State Department Directive 8500.2.

Integrating software assurance into the software development lifecycle (see Fig. 1.) while complying with the US Department of Defense standards for secure software development is the best option to ensure that security requirements are met, and the system is given optimal start for existence and operation.

The security activities involved must seamlessly connect with the existing activities found in the software development life cycle of an organization that strives to provide secure and competitive services to its users. To achieve such a unified process, we must first consider all the activities that are required within the secure software development life cycle.

The International Information Systems Security Consortium (ISC2), a world leader in creating security certification standards, also publishes good practices for integrating security into the system development lifecycle. The security activities proposed by ISC2 should be further mapped into the secure software development life cycle using the already existing software life cycle phase definitions.

Security aspects should be minded and taken into consideration during the development phase, as they cannot be left to happen by coincidence. Security controls should be designed and put in the right place when taking into consideration the functional and non-functional requirements of the application we are developing. A very important principle to remember here – security cannot and does not appear out of thin air; it must be designed before implementation. For the purpose, design phase should involve a security architect or a security expert who will guide the solution architect at the right direction. One example of a SDLC containing all significant phases of a lifecycle following industry best practices [7]:

334   M. Harseva and M. Petrov

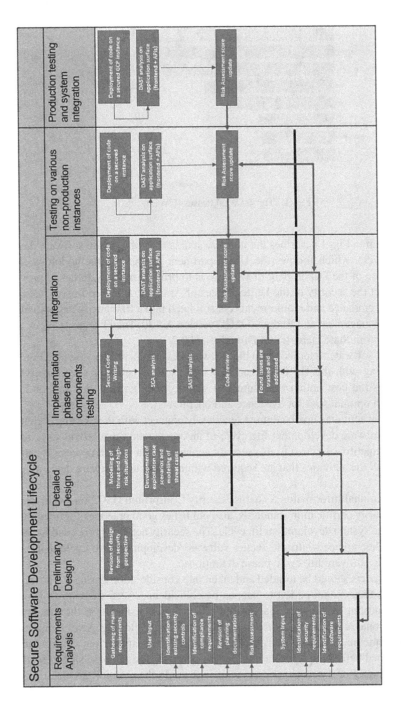

Fig. 2. Secure Software Development Lifecycle

Security aspects should be minded and taken into consideration during the development phase, as they cannot be left to happen by coincidence. Security controls should be designed and put in the right place when taking into consideration the functional and non-functional requirements of the application we are developing. A very important principle to remember here – security cannot and does not appear out of thin air; it must be designed before implementation. For the purpose, design phase should involve a security architect or a security expert who will guide the solution architect at the right direction. One example of a SDLC containing all significant phases of a lifecycle following industry best practices [7]:

The International Information Systems Security Certification Consortium (ISC2), a global leader in the creation of security certification standards, has published best practices for integrating security into the system development life cycle. The security activities suggested by ISC2 should be further derived into the secure SDLC using existing SDLC phase definitions. We propose, based on well-known software engineering architecture and the proposal of ISC2 the following lifecycle representation (see Fig. 2). The individual contribution to the below figure involves reshaping the SDLC phases by following the most used ones in the corporate world, which are mostly a combination of all industry-recognized development methodologies Like Waterfall, Agile, Spiral etc. [20]. Further changes to the original figure involve renaming the steps in the different phases to sound more generic and be valid for all types of deployments – e.g. replacing VM with instance to integrate cloud deployments.

4 Secure Design Principles

Furthermore, as follows few basic principles to take into consideration during the solution design phase which will guarantee security at a decent level [7, 18]:

1. Minimize attack surface area [24]. A larger surface area indicates increased exposure to threats and a higher risk of compromise. Ad-hoc addition of dynamic proactive defenses to distributed systems may inadvertently increase the attack surface. The principle of minimizing the attack surface area involves limiting the functions that users can access to reduce potential vulnerabilities.
2. Establish secure defaults [22]. Most computer systems that interface with the internet today presume that users will adopt additional security measures to protect themselves against phishing and malware attacks and can configure software to obtain optimal security. This assumption is worrying, as prior work has repeatedly shown that not all computer users face similar levels of risk, and at-risk users may not have the resources or know-how to adopt to obtain optimal levels of security. Establishing secure defaults involves setting strong security standards for user registration processes, password complexity, password update frequency, and other related practices.
3. Principle of Least Privilege [12, 19]. Adhering to the least privilege principle involves ensuring that only legitimate subjects have access rights to objects. Sometimes, this is hard because of permission irrevocability, changing security requirements, infeasibility of access control mechanisms, and permission creeps. The Principle of Least Privilege (POLP) dictates that a user should have only the minimum level of access necessary to perform a specific task.

4. Principle of Defense in Depth [11]. This measurement capability lets developers choose security countermeasures in such a way that not only the security risks decrease but also the number of defense-in-depth increases. Although the software security community acknowledges the importance of such a principle in developing secure systems, it has not been investigated enough to be the basis of security analysis of software systems. The principle of defense in depth advocates for using multiple layers of security controls that address risks in different ways to effectively secure an application.

5. Fail securely [17]. A secure system must provide a framework for defining its mandatory security policy and translating it to a form interpretable by the underlying mandatory security mechanisms of the operating system. Without such a framework, there can be no real confidence that the mandatory security mechanisms will provide the desired security properties. This principle emphasizes that applications should fail in a secure manner, ensuring that failure does not grant additional privileges to the user or expose sensitive information, such as database queries or logs.

6. Don't trust services [1, 15]. Commodity operating systems are considered vulnerable. Therefore, when an application handles security-sensitive data, it is highly recommended to run the application in a trusted execution environment. The proposed architecture should consider privacy of every stakeholder: final users, service providers and infrastructure providers. This principle means that an application should always validate data received from third-party services and should not grant those services high-level permissions within the app.

7. Separation of duties [6]. Separation of duty, as a security principle, has as its primary objective the prevention of fraud and error. This objective is achieved by disseminating the tasks and associated privileges for a specific business process among multiple users. Separation of duties is a practice to prevent fraudulent activities by ensuring that a user on an eCommerce website, for instance, is not given administrative privileges, which could allow them to manipulate orders or self-assign products. Similarly, an administrator should not have the ability to perform customer-level actions, like placing orders from the front end.

8. Avoid security by obscurity [23]. In the open versus closed source debate, the source of the "security by obscurity" aspersion refers to the programming practice of hiding secrets in source code, releasing only the executable code, and the belief that code secrecy in general can make a system more secure. Although hiding source code does provide some trivial protection from attack if secrets are stored in it, the underlying assumption, that binary encoding secures either the source which created it, or the secrets inside it, turns out to be proven false. This principle asserts that relying on security through obscurity is inadequate. If an application depends on hiding its administration URL to remain secure, then it is not truly secure. Proper security controls should be in place to protect the application without relying on concealing core functionality or source code.

9. Keep security simple [14]. Security is an increasingly fundamental requirement in any system nowadays. However, the pace of adoption of secure mechanisms has been slow, which we estimate to be a consequence of the performance overhead of traditional solutions and of the complexity of the support infrastructure required. Developers should avoid overly complex architectures when designing security controls for their applications, as complexity can increase the risk of errors.
10. Fix security issues correctly [16, 25]. Secure software development is a challenging task requiring consideration of many possible threats and mitigations. Given how the "patching treadmill" plays a central role for enabling sites to counter emergent security concerns, it behooves the security community to understand the patch development process and characteristics of the resulting fixes. Illumination of the nature of security patch development can inform us of shortcomings in existing remediation processes and provide insights for improving current practices. When addressing security issues, it is essential to resolve them properly and effectively to ensure that vulnerabilities are fully mitigated. If a security issue has been identified in an application, developers should determine the root cause of the problem. They should then repair it and test the repairs thoroughly. If the application uses design patterns, it is likely that the error may be present in multiple systems. Programmers should be careful to identify all affected systems.(Andress 2011)

5 Secure Coding Techniques to Development Teams

Embedding security into the development phase starts with educating all participants in the development process what are the fundamental principles of writing secure code. Few very easily comprehensive and practical rules that should be defined and established as coding guidelines for each member of the development teams (Bagnara et al. 2022). People must understand what it means to write secure code and secure coding techniques should not be left only to common sense. Here are few practical rules that should be communicated to the development teams (Gasiba et al. 2023):

- The code works
- The code is easy to understand
- Follows coding conventions
- Names are simple and if possible short
- Names are spelt correctly
- Names contain units where applicable
- There are no usages of magic numbers
- No hard coded constants that could possibly change in the future
- All variables are in the smallest scope possible
- There is no commented out code
- There is no dead code (inaccessible at Runtime)
- No code that can be replaced with library functions
- Variables are not accidentally used with null values
- Variables are immutable where possible
- Code is not repeated or duplicated
- There is an else block for every if clause even if it is empty

- No complex/long boolean expressions
- No negatively named boolean variables
- No empty blocks of code
- Ideal data structures are used
- Constructors do not accept null/none values
- Catch clauses are fine grained and catch specific exceptions
- Exceptions are not eaten if caught, unless explicitly documented otherwise
- Files/Sockets and other resources are properly closed even when an exception occurs in using them
- null is not returned from any method
- == operator and === (and its inverse ! ==) are not mixed up
- Floating point numbers are not compared for equality
- Loops have a set length and correct termination conditions
- Blocks of code inside loops are as small as possible
- No methods with boolean parameters
- No object exists longer than necessary
- No memory leaks
- Code is unit testable
- Test cases are written wherever possible
- Methods return early without compromising code readability
- Performance is considered
- Loop iteration and off by one are taken care of
- All data inputs are checked (for the correct type, length/size, format, and range)
- Invalid parameter values handled such that exceptions are not thrown
- No sensitive information is logged or visible in a stacktrace, event log lines etc.

Those fundamental principles for secure coding should be taken into consideration during the core review process. Furthermore, a scoring mechanism could be defined for code review phase to be completed based on measurable results and not only on gut feeling. Measurements that could be taken into consideration are various results from IDE plugins for code optimization, Static Analysis (SAST) tools which can give information about vulnerabilities on static code level, smelly code, bugs etc., as well Software composition analysis (SCA) tools which can deliver information about vulnerabilities in embedded external components like libraries, plugins etc. (Harer et al. 2018).

6   Conclusions

In conclusion, integrating security baselines into the software development process is essential for creating robust and secure applications. This guide has outlined the importance of embedding security principles from the initial design phase through to completing the development phase. The rest of the phases of the Software Development Lifecycle will be further looked at in a follow-up paper. By adopting best practices such as least-privilege access and secure coding guidelines, development teams can significantly reduce vulnerabilities and enhance the overall security posture of their applications.

This study on the topic will continue in the sense that we will further follow-up with a questionnaire among software development professionals to assess their acquaintance with the good practices. Furthermore, we will follow up on the improvements of the security posture on a few software projects those participants are working to see how the security posture has improved after raising their awareness for more practical implementations of the secure design and secure coding principles. Furthermore, there is motivation for further explorational activities on the topic and how practical guides and educational materials can improve the security aspects of software products over time.

Acknowledgments. Special thanks to Prof. Milen Petrov, vice-dean of Faculty for Mathematics and Informatics of Sofia University St. Kliment Ohridski, for his enormous help and continuous support during my academic road trip and all faced adventures, past and future. Big thank you also to all students and volunteers who further support our studies and are willing to improve their secure coding skills to achieve operational excellence in their career path onwards. This study was funded by the project "Research and Application of Machine Learning Algorithms in the Analysis and Development of Highly Secure Software", funded with contract grant number: KP-06- N57/4 from 16.11.2021 by Bulgarian National Science.

Disclosure of Interest Statement. Mariya Harseva and Prof. Milen Petrov declare that there are no conflicts of interest regarding the publication of this article. Mariya Harseva and Prof. Milen Petrov have ensured that all aspects of this research have been conducted with the utmost integrity and objectivity, adhering to the ethical guidelines of Sofia University St. Kliment Ohridski.

References

1. Alonso-Lupez, J.A., et al.: Level of trust and privacy management in 6G intent-based networks for vertical scenarios. In: Proceedings of the 1st International Conference on 6G Networking (6GNet), pp. 1–4 (2022)
2. Andress, J.: The basics of information security: understanding the fundamentals of InfoSec in theory and practice, 2nd edn. Syngress, Waltham, MA (2014)
3. Anto Ajisha Shriny, M., Srinivasan, C.: Design and implementation of the protocol for secure software-based remote attestation in IoT devices. In: Proceedings of the 2nd International Conference on Soft Computing and Signal Processing (ICSCSP), pp. 189–197 (2020)
4. Bagnara, R., Bagnara, A., Hill, P.M.: Coding guidelines and undecidability, arXiv:2212.13933 (2022)
5. Barabanov, A., Markov, A., Fadin, A., Tsirlov, V., Shakhalov, I.: Synthesis of secure software development controls. In: Proceedings of the 8th International Conference on Security of Information and Networks (SIN), pp. 93–97 (2015)
6. Botha, R.A., Eloff, J.H.P.: Separation of duties for access control enforcement in workflow environments. IBM Syst. J. **40**(3), 666–682 (2001)
7. Dawson, M., et al.: Integrating software assurance into the software development life cycle (SDLC). J. Inform. Syst. Technol. Plan. **3**(6), 49–53 (2010)
8. Gasiba, T.E., Oguzhan, K., Kessba, I., Lechner, U., Pinto-Albuquerque, M.: I'm sorry Dave, I'm afraid I can't fix your code: On ChatGPT, cybersecurity, and secure coding. In: Proceedings of the 4th International Computer Programming Education Conference (ICPEC), pp. 2:1–2:12 (2023)
9. Harer, J.A., et al.: Automated software vulnerability detection with machine learning, arXiv: 1803.04497 (2018)
10. Heiner, A.P., Asokan, N.: Secure software installation in a mobile environment. In: Proceedings of the 3rd Symposium on Usable Privacy and Security, pp. 155–156 (2007)

11. Jalali, A., Hadavi, M.A.: Software security analysis based on the principle of defense-in-depth. In: Proceedings of the 15th International ISC Conference on Information Security and Cryptology (ISCISC), pp. 1–6 (2018)

12. Jero, S., et al.: Practical principle of least privilege for secure embedded systems. In: Proceedings of the 27th IEEE Real-Time and Embedded Technology and Applications Symposium (RTAS), pp. 1–13 (2021)

13. Katos, V., et al.: State of vulnerabilities 2018/2019, European Union Agency for Cybersecurity (2019)

14. Kreutz, D., Yu, J., Esteves-Verissimo, P., Magalhães, C., Ramos, F.M.V.: The KISS principle in software-defined networking: an architecture for keeping it simple and secure, arXiv:1702.04294 (2017)

15. Lee, U., Park, C.: SofTEE: software-based trusted execution environment for user applications. IEEE Access **8**, 121874–121888 (2020)

16. Li, F., Paxson, V.: A large-scale empirical study of security patches. In: Proceedings of the ACM Conference on Computer and Communications Security (CCS), pp. 2201–2215 (2017)

17. Loscocco, P.A., Smalley, S.D., Muckelbauer, P.A., Taylor, R.C., Turner, S.J., Farrell, J.F.: The inevitability of failure: the flawed assumption of security in modern computing environments. In: Proceedings of the 21st National Information Systems Security Conference (NISSC) (1998)

18. Mead, N.R., Laird, L.M., Shoemaker, D.: Getting secure software assurance knowledge into conventional practice: three educational initiatives. Proceedings of the 35th IEEE Annual Computer Software and Applications Conference (COMPSAC), pp. 193–198 (2011)

19. Ng, B.H.: Towards least privilege principle: limiting unintended accesses in software systems, Ph.D. dissertation, University of Michigan (2013)

20. Ragunath, P.K., Velmourougan, S., Davachelvan, P., Kayalvizhi, S., Ravimohan, R.: Evolving a new model (SDLC Model-2010) for software development life cycle (SDLC). Int. J. Comput. Sci. Network Secur. **10**(1), 112–119 (2010)

21. Mattioli, R., Malatras, A.: Foresight cybersecurity threats for 2030 – Update – Extended report. European Union Agency for Cybersecurity (2024)

22. Simoiu, C.: Secure by Default: A Behavioral Approach to Cyber Security, Ph.D. thesis, Stanford University (2020)

23. Smith, J.C.: Effective Security by Obscurity, arXiv:2205.01547 (2011)

24. Soule, N., et al.: Quantifying and minimizing attack surfaces containing moving target defenses. In: Proceedings of the Resilience Week (RSW), pp. 220–225 (2015)

25. Votipka, D., Fulton, K.R., Parker, J., Hou, M., Mazurek, M.L., Hicks, M.: Understanding security mistakes developers make: qualitative analysis from build it, break it, fix it. In: Proceeding of the 29th USENIX Security Symposium (USENIX Security), pp. 109–126 (2020)

Author Index

C. Bădică et al. (Eds.): BCI 2024, CCIS 2391, pp. 341–342, 2025.
https://doi.org/10.1007/978-3-031-84093-7

Printed in the United States
by Baker & Taylor Publisher Services